Public Feminism in
Times of Crisis

Public Feminism in Times of Crisis

From Sappho's Fragments to Viral Hashtags

Leila Easa and Jennifer Stager

LEXINGTON BOOKS
Lanham • Boulder • New York • London

Published by Lexington Books
An imprint of The Rowman & Littlefield Publishing Group, Inc.
4501 Forbes Boulevard, Suite 200, Lanham, Maryland 20706
www.rowman.com

86-90 Paul Street, London EC2A 4NE

Cover image *of extreme lyric I*, a dance theater collaboration between Maxe Crandall and Hope Mohr, featuring Anne Carson's translations of Sappho and projection design by Ian Winters. Dancers pictured: (L to R) Tara McArthur, Suzette Sagisi, Jane Selna. Not pictured: Karla Quintero. Photo by: Robbie Sweeny.

A version of chapter six first appeared as "Overwriting the monument tradition: Lists, loss, and scale" in *Res: Anthropology and aesthetics*, volume 75/76, 2021, President and Fellows of Harvard College. Published by The University of Chicago Press for the Peabody Museum of Archaeology and Ethnology, Harvard University. https://doi.org/10.1086/717461, reprinted with permission.

"128 [here now]," "60 [having encountered]," "147 [someone will remember us]," "74 A, B, C [goatherd/roses/longing/sweat]," "118 [yes! radiant lyre speak to me]," "176 [lyre lyre lyre]," "25 [quit]," "114 [virginity]," "184 [danger]," "185 [honeyvoiced]," "186 [Medeia]," "187 [of the Muses]," "188 [mythweaver]," "92 [robe]," "94 [I simply want to bedead]," "191 [celery]," and "189 [soda]" from IF NOT, WINTER: FRAGMENTS OF SAPPHO by Sappho, translated by Anne Carson, copyright © 2002 by Anne Carson. Used by permission of Alfred A. Knopf, an imprint of the Knopf Doubleday Publishing Group, a division of Penguin Random House LLC, and Little Brown Book Group. All rights reserved.

Danez Smith, excerpts from "not an elegy" from Don't Call Us Dead. Copyright © 2017 by Danez Smith. Reprinted with the permission of The Permissions Company, LLC on behalf of Graywolf Press, Minneapolis, Minnesota, graywolfpress.org

Credit: Maggie Smith, excerpts from "Good Bones" from Good Bones: Poems. Copyright © 2017 by Maggie Smith. Reprinted with the permission of The Permissions Company, LLC, on behalf of Tupelo Press, tupelopress.org.

British Library Cataloguing in Publication Information Available

Library of Congress Cataloging-in-Publication Data

Names: Easa, Leila, author. | Stager, Jennifer, author.
Title: Public feminism in times of crisis : from Sappho's fragments to viral hashtags / Leila Easa
 and Jennifer Stager.
Description: Lanham : Lexington Books, [2022] | Includes bibliographical references and index.
Identifiers: LCCN 2022023551 (print) | LCCN 2022023552 (ebook) |
 ISBN 9781793648105 (cloth ; alk. paper) | ISBN 9781793648129 (paper ; alk. paper) |
 ISBN 9781793648112 (ebook)
Subjects: LCSH: Feminism--History. | Feminism and mass media. | Feminism
 and art. | Feminism and literature.
Classification: LCC HQ1150 .E27 2022 (print) | LCC HQ1150 (ebook) |
 DDC 305.4209—dc23/eng/20220519
LC record available at https://lccn.loc.gov/2022023551
LC ebook record available at https://lccn.loc.gov/2022023552

For our children, Soren, Felix, Astrid, Carter, Juniper, Clementine, and Hazel

Contents

Acknowledgments

A book that focuses on structural and material restrictions and support for women and nonbinary people seems to necessitate a comprehensive acknowledgments section, yet we fear we could never fully capture each person whose support enriched this project and our lives. Above all, we have benefited from the everyday conversations we are lucky enough to be immersed within, at home, at school, and in the world. We have learned from our mentors and our students, our friends and our neighbors, our colleagues and our children, and, through the writing of this book and the close to two decades of intellectually curious friendship that enabled it, from each other. We are both mothers who have lost our mothers but who remain inspired by the women they were and grateful to have this time to work when they did not. We have drawn on our decades of familiarity with and trust in each other's thinking and writing in the conception and writing of this book, truly a product of abiding friendship, and we are grateful for our varied strengths and the tight weave of personal and professional intersections that have shaped our respective lives.

Additionally, certain individuals helped this project in specific ways. Judith Lakamper, our editor at Lexington Books, reached out after a conference presentation to suggest a book and gave us space to explore that possibility in a variety of ways over the course of a year. We are so grateful that she believed in the project before we knew entirely what shape it would take. Lisa Regan and Amyrose McCue Gill helped us improve and refine this project immeasurably. Collaborating with two partners on a project that engages the politics of feminist collaboration added an additional layer of "rightness" to our collective practice. Specifically, Lisa Regan offered a birds-eye view of the whole manuscript and a rich and strategic engagement that allowed us to pull the book's threads tighter. Amyrose McCue Gill's graceful editorial hand and generosity shepherded the project across the finish line while also keeping us focused on our beliefs and politics. Thanks also to Rachel Lefkowitz, whose eye for detail facilitated the mammoth task of pulling together the bibliography. Lael Ensor-Bennet, curator of the Visual Resources Collection at Johns Hopkins, patiently fielded endless questions about images from permissions to production. Librarians Dr. Mack Zalin and Don Juedes supported our research from all directions, solving bibliographic mysteries in many different languages and types of sources across a vast time frame. Ashley Costello supported the administration of our permissions and editing processes with astonishing efficiency. Hope Mohr and Maxe Crandall inspired us with their collaborative work and generously shared the cover image for this book as well as responded to our project with a buoying enthusiasm. Athena Kirk not only read and commented on multiple chapters but also shared her own work and pointed us to fruitful sources for exploration. Verity Platt provided brilliant feedback and support and continues to model important merging of academic and public practices. Deirdre O'Dwyer offered a deep read early in our process that set an important direction for our final chapter. Ella Gonzalez and Cynthia Colburn assisted some of our earliest efforts, and their constructive comments motivated us to keep working. Marian Feldman, Karen ní Mheallaigh, Andres Reyes, and Katie Couch each offered feedback on individual chapters at critical junctures in the writing process, improving the work with their attention and critique. Karen Cox and Elizabeth Smith read a version of one of our earliest chapters, and their insights and suggestions not only improved that chapter immeasurably but also modeled lines of thinking we continued to be inspired by in crafting and editing later sections. Rachel Brahinsky, one of our oldest mutual friends, supported us in multiple ways, reading a chapter, brainstorming with us more generally, and helping us think through our title. Nandini Pandey offered a sounding board in the crucial final stretch of this project. Sanchita Balachandran's incisive questions deepened our thinking about ancient collectives. Sonal Khullar continues to model and share feminist modes of writing and practice. Beatrice Sasha Kobow enriched our thinking through her own engagement with a philosophy of the *oikos* (household) and feminist thinkers in philosophy. Meilani Clay, Paula D'Oyen, and Joni Spigler shared their unpublished writing with us generously. Academics including Jacquelyn Ardam, Shadi Bartsch, Allison Caplan, Judith Peller Hallett, Athena Kirk, Amy Lather, Michael Leong, and Caroline Costin Wright provided early versions of their work, often prior to its publication, to accommodate our publication timeline or access issues. Their generosity greatly enriched our thinking and writing on related topics. Aaron Hyman pointed us to work on mapping and cartography that grounded our thinking in historical precedents. Marden Nichols discussed many different aspects of this project and shared incisive thoughts on translation. Stephen J. Campbell talked us through the deep scholarship surrounding Artemisia.

Alice Mandell shared important work in Judith Studies. Katherine Blouin, Sarah Bond, Roberta Mazza, and Judith Peller Hallett collectively improved our archival knowledge of Medea Norsa. Michele Asuni supported the image permissions with a keen eye for detail and has been a wonderful interlocutor for many different ancient Greek and Latin texts. Yayoi Kambara connected us to scholars in the dance world and to resources on devised choreography and other frameworks within which to theorize dance. The Mroz-Snodgrass family helped us with photography on a particularly frantic day. Our children gave us space for this endeavor, often by caring for each other, and their teachers and care providers also helped make this work possible. And critically, our departments and institutions also supported the writing of this book; Jennifer benefited from a research leave at Johns Hopkins, research support from the Deans of KSAS and the office of the Provost, and a fellowship from the Center for Hellenic Studies, while Leila was able to reduce her teaching load to focus on its completion. Finally, we are grateful to the Alexander Grass Humanities Center and the Ivy Bookshop's Humanities in the Village program for hosting our first public book talk and for modeling public humanities in the community.

Additionally, Jennifer would like to thank my mentors from UC Berkeley, Andrew Stewart, Whitney Davis, Chris Hallett, and Leslie Kurke, who provided both the underlying intellectual bedrock on which this work builds and enduring support for my own nonlinear path. Alexa Sekyra at the Getty Research Institute offered incisive words of encouragement at a crucial moment. Additionally, structural support for writing made this book possible. Lute Lu, thank you for your loving and creative engagement with the children while I worked and your enthusiasm for this book—we could not have made it through without you. Charlie Lehodey, your own fierce feminism and care for the children during that first intense transition to Baltimore are both such gifts. In addition, the children's tireless and dedicated teachers, especially during these pandemic years that demanded too much from teachers, supported their well-being and thus increased mine. Pia Hargrove, our decades of friendship, daily conversation, and your belief in me and in this work continue to lift me up; watching your star summit is among my great joys. Kristen Vagliardo, your friendship from the days of me alphabetizing offprints under your supervision to the years following my father's funeral have been so important. Samantha Kamras, our conversations offer the comfort of being known and seen as well as fresh perspectives. Jenny Salomon Omabegho, you showed me the rich possibilities of collaborative practice. Anita Walker, Allicia Wertheim, Irene Winter, and Shelby White, you have each nurtured and advised me at critical moments when my own mother was no longer able to do so. To the staff at my mother's care facility, your capacity to care with such empathy continues to be such an incredible gift and never more so than through this pandemic when you have done so much to keep vulnerable elders safe. Peter Radavich, you have always greeted each new project and direction with love and support and modeled a resilience that inspires me. Kelsey Stager, our conversations are so meaningful and have contributed directly to this book. David Stager, talking with you always leaves me thinking differently and I am grateful that we have walked through so much of life together. I love you both. To my late father Lawrence Stager and my mother Susan Simmons, I am grateful for the intellectual rigor that you each brought to daily life and the community of creative friends that you brought into our world. To my father, you could light up a room with your charisma, and I'm sorry that you lived in a time when the choice to be fully yourself felt incompatible with the success you sought. To my mother, I'm so grateful for the calm, loving support that you offered throughout my childhood, and, as our caregiver roles have long reversed, I lament that you did not get enough of a chance to focus on your own dreams. I love and miss you both.

Leila would also like to thank Professor Sarita Cannon at San Francisco State University, who taught the class for which the conference presentation that initiated this book was originally written and whose mentorship genuinely changed my life. Professor Sara Hackenberg, also at SFSU, taught me how to give a conference presentation in the first place while also modeling deep intellectual engagement with theoretical texts; readings from her classes guided this project in many ways. Professors Julie Paulson, Jennifer Mylander, Summer Star, and Loretta Stec and colleagues Angela Chang, Zoe Dumas, and many others from the SFSU English department supported me in my renewed exploration of literary research well into my forties. In Creative Writing at SFSU, Professor Andrew Joron introduced me to *Zong!* and to the work of Michael Leong, both of which have become important to my thinking about this project, and Professor Nona Caspers continues to model brilliant and productive ways to tilt my perspective. My University of Pennsylvania; University College, London; and Duke University professors inspired me with their lives in scholarship and made this work exciting on campus and beyond. Jen Sullivan Brych, Cullen Bailey Burns, Karen Cox, Chante McCormick, Michelle Simotas, Elizabeth Smith, Saramanda Swigart, Julie Young, and many other colleagues at CCSF along with those at other institutions including Andrew DuBois, Eisa Gray, Ben Jahn, and Teresa Savin challenged me with their brilliance, inspired me with their ideas, and supported me with their friendship for years and even decades before this book was written. Alisa Messer taught me about feminist citation, not to mention so many other insightful and delightful things over the course of two decades. My brilliantly fun and talented friends Rachel Brahinsky, Erica Goldman, Ian Greeb, Amy Loflin, Jeff Snodgrass, Sean Thomas, and so many more have blessed me with the gift of their company and insight. My "big brothers"

Rob Clough, Brian Dietrick, Jack Friedman, and Lee Hachadoorian modeled living a life of quiet (and sometimes quite loud!) brilliance. My Punahou, Epworth/Duke, UCL, and UPenn crews in wide-ranging (often 3:00 a.m.) conversations sowed the seeds for a love of sustained engagement with ideas and are to this day some of the most dazzling and wonderful humans I have ever known. My critique group members Paisley Schade, Beth Graubart, Christie Anderson, Korrie Leer, and Jackie Friedman Mighdoll supported me on and off the page—and looked the other way when this book took over my creative pursuits. My mom friends and dance friends made life fun and forced me to take breaks to move my body or even watch bad movies. Debra Ruben modeled intellectual engagement with all areas of life and reminded me that rest and renewal are important too. Jillian Wasick was my weekly partner in crime for dancing, creativity, and intellectual exploration. Chante McCormick and I had many adventures and supported each other through life transitions. Jesse Lawrence Brown, pulvis et umbra, but the writing remains. Each week for many years, Jen Kollmer and I wrote together into the night; her memory inspires me. Krista Cole, my sister in ways more powerful than blood, makes everything possible and I love her infinitely. Susan Hopkins took over the job of mom when my own mom could no longer be there to do it, and I'm not sure I'll ever have the words to explain what that has meant. Linda Burnett was one of my earliest feminist models, and I treasure all she has taught me throughout my life. Phillip and Miriam Hellreich will always be family. My incredible aunts, Frances Kirven, Leila Hanna, Suad Zeibeq, and Widad George, remain some of the most powerful women role models in my life. Gavin Murphy gave me the time and space to do this work and so much more—really, this life—and I am forever grateful. My brother, David J. Easa, was one of my earliest debate partners, and I appreciate his modeling. My family spans the globe, and I treasure the weird mix of Arab and Southern traditions by which I was raised and love all my relatives, present and departed. In particular and to conclude this section, I appreciate and remember my mother Scherer James Easa and my father David Easa. Mom, the inspiration you embodied in both academic and domestic realms—not to mention your unconditional love—has fueled almost five decades of my life, despite only having you here for two. Dad, you are an unstoppable force, and I am in awe of the lives you have saved and the difference you have made in the experience of so many. Thank you both for believing in me, teaching me to ask questions and give my ideas space, and supporting an education that has been the great privilege of my life.

Finally, we are humbled by and grateful to the many women and nonbinary people who have amplified their voices individually and collectively in acts of public feminism that have taught us, over and over again, that change is possible.

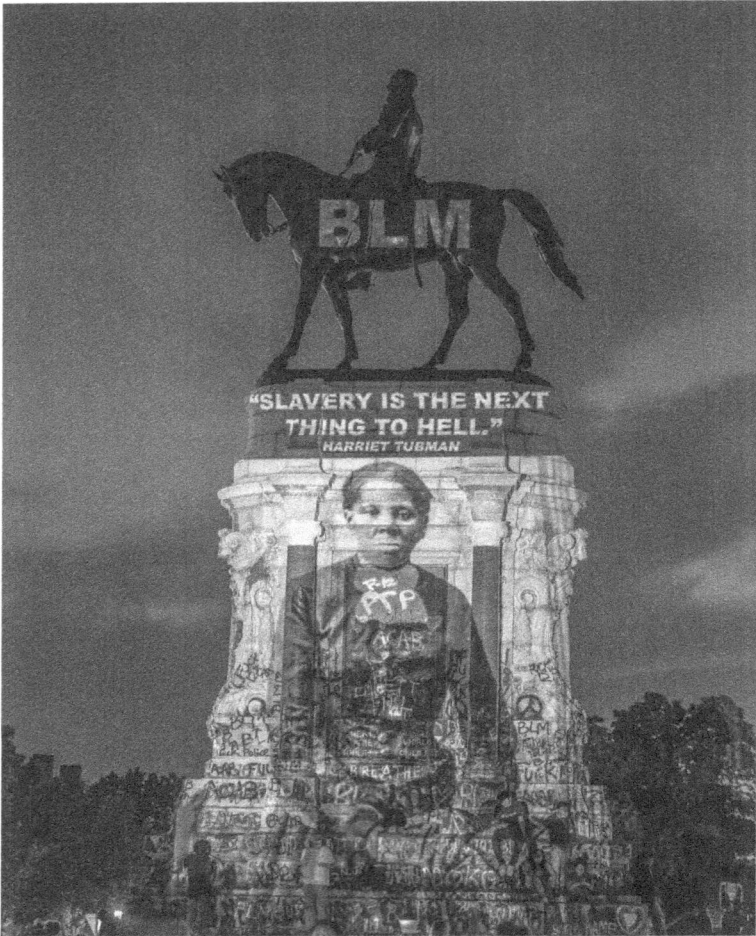

Figure 0.1 **David Parrish Photography and Dustin Klein Projection.** Portrait and quotation of Harriet Tubman "Slavery is the next thing to hell" and "BLM" projected onto the marble plinth and bronze equestrian statue of a confederate general, Richmond, VA. Color digital photograph. 2020.

Introduction

On the morning of October 22, 2018—about halfway, as it turned out, through the Trump presidency—law student Laurel Raymond encountered something that had not been there the evening before. Someone had used large stencils to paint a quotation in white capital letters across the flagstone entrance to Sterling Hall at Yale Law School. Raymond snapped a picture of the scene and posted it to Twitter.[1] The white paint read: "Indelible in the hippocampus is the laughter . . ."[2] Flecks of spray can paint had settled around the edges of the stenciled letters to frame the quotation that appeared before the heavy wooden door of the building like a welcome mat.[3] Christine Blasey Ford had spoken these words the previous month during the confirmation hearings for Brett Kavanaugh, a man who—along with a friend—had sexually assaulted Ford at a party when the three of them were teenagers and whom Trump had appointed to the Supreme Court to fill the vacancy left by Anthony Kennedy. To give her wrenching testimony of the assault and its impact on her life, Ford had to relive this trauma on live television, under hostile questioning from senators, and in the court of public opinion.[4] Despite Ford's sacrifice, Kavanaugh was confirmed to the bench to serve a lifetime appointment. In contrast, Ford and her family were forced into hiding.

When Ford described the way that Kavanaugh and his friend's laughter had inscribed itself in her brain the night that they assaulted her, she also offered her listeners words for the ways in which trauma endures. In painting Ford's words onto the steps of Yale Law School—from which Kavanaugh had graduated and from where many students sought prestigious clerkships with the Supreme Court—the painter overwrote the unchecked prestige and power the school (and institutions like it) afforded its graduates through high-level placements in government and the private sector with evidence of the collateral damage such power all too often demands. Although her bravery cost her greatly and did not derail the machine of white male privilege, speaking these words in and to the public etched what had been indelible in her own hippocampus into the public sphere. While the painter's choice to close the quotation with ellipses might have intended to signal that Ford's testimony continued beyond the words quoted, it also marks the truth that the work to which she contributed remains unfinished. The ellipses hold space for words, acts, and histories to follow. Within the framework of this book, each engagement with these words—Ford's testimony, the anonymous spray can artist's nighttime intervention, and Laurel Raymond's photograph and subsequent social media post—are acts of public feminism.

Public Feminism in Times of Crisis examines the public practice of feminism in the age of social media and analyzes the deep histories threaded through this new(er) enactment. Although many feminist acts take place in private, public feminism refers to feminist interventions carried out in some form of public sphere. As the internet has moved conversations that were previously shared in closed spaces or as private interactions between individuals into the public, the pre-internet contours of what counts as "public" have changed. We now understand contemporary public space to constitute both virtual and physical spaces.

In this book, we explore the dynamics of this feminism committed in public through the lens of history, and we use history as a framework from which to understand its current and potential future dynamics. We do this to illuminate the ways in which contemporary public feminism acquires its shape and associations. History also, in some manner, teaches us how to perform public feminism. Additionally, our contemporary moment's access to the tools of global communication—provided in part by social media—radically expands historic possibilities, giving a platform to a wide range of voices while increasing access to information about the historic past beyond the traditional boundaries of academic institutions. This, in turn, changes what we see and value from the past in the present, as well as the ways in which virtual spaces now also circulate and mobilize historical examples in the service of contemporary arguments, whether to advance feminism or to undercut it.

In the face of these phenomena, our book seeks to connect deep history with the contemporary moment using cultural, historical, and academic lenses to analyze the opportunities that virtual spaces have opened for feminism in recent years while also tracking the long history of regulating women's bodies and voices. We assert that exploring this lineage is critical in combatting erasures of the history of feminist activism. Such erasures are often mobilized to render activism illegitimate in the present and to claim history for self-described victors. Contemporary resistance often faces a process of being "made new" in order to be dismissed, but if we can discern its antecedents we can, in certain ways, bolster its staying power and dismantle facile critiques against it.[5] Ultimately, the present volume seeks to outline the shape of public feminism today by tracing its flare-ups and refractions through time.

Along with these issues, we are also concerned with the possibility of feminism as a force during crises in particular, whether global or local, momentary or perpetual. With other recent texts that investigate this current moment, we attempt to understand the tension exerted on intersectional feminism by contemporary politics and pressures.[6] In our book, we focus in particular on the years of the global COVID-19 pandemic and the Trump years that preceded them, yet while Trump's election can be framed as an inflection point of crisis, we also understand that what makes something a "crisis" may be less a change in circumstance and more an unveiling of what was there all along but became newly visible. For example, many theorists endeavor to remind us that Trump is a symptom of some of the most oppressive structures of the United States. Duchess Harris notes the "hereness" of such structures, explaining that, in the aftermath of Trump's election, "the answer to the question—'How did we get here?'—was all too easy to identify and articulate. There was no shocked bewilderment, for there was no transition to 'here'. The 'here' had always been there, at least for Black Americans."[7] Similarly, Bonnie Honig frames Trump's reign semiotically: "Like many things Trump, Trumpism is just a name slapped onto things that were already out there."[8] Honig goes on to say that "Trumpism will have other names in the future" and that it "names a kind of male entitlement for which it feels like freedom to just be able to say what you think and grab what you want."[9] In this context, we see these years as exposing the multilayered crises underlying them: toxic masculinity, profound inequality, racial reckoning, and the stratified experience of women in both the household and the workforce, among others.

At the same time, there is no doubt that Trump himself and the particular historical moment that elevated him to the highest office in the United States do deserve consideration. Ta-Nehisi Coates contextualizes Trump's election as a violent opposition to the Obama presidency: "Trump truly is something new—the first president whose entire political existence hinges on the fact of a black president. . . . He must be called by his rightful honorific—America's first white president."[10] Harris also situates Trump in this opposition:

> For the majority of Black Americans—and, it must be said, for plenty of other Americans of color and for many white Americans, too—the transition of presidential power that occurred on January 20, 2017, was a devastating sociopolitical, cultural, and historic moment. . . . President Obama was leaving the Oval Office, handing over its literal and metaphorical keys to a man who would come to be nicknamed—and not unfairly—by many individuals, organizations, political analysts, and even media outlets as the white-supremacist-in-chief.[11]

The disparities embodied in this presidential transition deserve further investigation, especially in light of their ties to the public feminism that emerged in response.

Public feminism during and beyond the years of Trump must have been shaped, then, by the conditions that were there all along but that became legible—and even semiotically named—by the phenomenon of Trump's rise to power and the daily reminders of his despotism, evidenced even by his tweets.[12] We also note material shifts in the lives of women as Trump's aforementioned ideology threatened the safety of some women even as others were used as spokespeople and tools of Trump's regressive policies.[13] Additionally, we observe the tragic process by which the pandemic—like Trump's oppression—widened existing inequalities along all fault lines, with differential burdens born by Black, Brown, and Indigenous people, working-class people, and women across lines of race and class, following what Honig names the "asymmetrical vulnerability to the virus."[14] What we understand to be contemporary public feminism was shaped by all of these stressors and thereby responds within their contexts and often directly to them. Thus, while we situate these responses in historical terms, we also examine them through the specifics of the current moment.

Finally, we trace a shift in feminist movements partially evoked by the changing access to platforms provided by social media and other internet-based discursive tools. Trump's manipulation of Twitter itself highlighted the paradox that the same platforms that support some aspects of public feminism also enable misinformation as well as facilitate some of the worst abuses found online. Such online abuses parallel real-life abuse. Christine Blasey Ford was driven into hiding in the real world; public feminists have been driven into hiding from social media and even doxed, blurring the lines between virtual and real life and demonstrating the impact both systems have on women's lives.

Yet while social media tools were radically abused by Trump, they were also powerfully engaged by public feminism. When feminists take up the same tools, they do so in the context of a battle over the fate of public dissemination of information, as seen in the work of public historian Heather Cox Richardson, whose "Letters from an American" were initiated on September 15, 2019, to help readers understand the historical context of US politics as they unfolded.[15] Additionally, actions like the #MeToo movement, #BlackLivesMatter, and #SayHerName as well as other forms of activism organized by hashtags continue to demonstrate the empowering potential of having a public voice.[16]

With Roxane Gay, who argues in "When Twitter Does What Journalism Can't" that the power of social media lies in making more voices heard, we have watched transformation happen through these public channels. As the conversation broadens, more people express arguments and amplify issues that were previously strictly regulated by traditional media.[17] And yet, we have also seen how social media can silence and deflect. For example, the #MeToo movement, started by Black feminist Tarana Burke, was co-opted by a range of mostly white celebrities who amplified the message with the hashtag #MeToo and became the movement's public face. However, outcry over Burke's erasure on the very social media channels that had perpetrated it eventually reestablished her role as a founder. Therefore, while the benefits of open access platforms are nuanced and complex, the overall flow of dialogue into a more public forum and into the hands of everyday people—often through the tools of social media—clearly marks an important change.

Most of all, our hope in this book is to bridge academic feminist theory and the everyday feminisms of the public and, through this process, to consider what the future might mean for feminism. How might public feminism evolve, leveraging its networks in a world that, while clearly divided, can also be seen as connected? In the words of Gay:

> Social networks are more than just infinite repositories of the trivial, snap judgments or convenient outlets for mindless joy and outrage. They are more than the common ground and the solace we may find during culturally significant moments. Social networks also provide us with something of a flawed but necessary conscience, a constant reminder that commitment, compassion and advocacy neither can nor ever should be finite.[18]

In light of these words, we suggest that feminism might find some sort of infinite, recursive purchase moving between real and virtual public spaces so that its ideas and debates can lift an array of voices and produce communities of care.

WRITING HISTORY COLLABORATIVELY

Although the two authors of this book live far apart, when quarantine began and most of our social and professional interaction moved to Zoom, we found ourselves just as close to each other as each of us was to her local community. And, like many, we both found ourselves teaching and presenting virtually with children learning at home, upsetting many routines—occasionally in productive ways. In the midst of this syncopation, the awkward three-hour time difference that had posed such a challenge to regular conversation now seemed less significant.

The truth is, we had been working toward this book for a while before the shutdown, but the project really didn't begin to take shape until restrictions began in earnest. The shutdown produced two conditions that made this book possible: it brought us together on regular Zoom discussions during which we brainstormed broadly about a range of topics that excited us, and it demonstrated the disproportionate impact of the pandemic on less privileged populations and those traditionally bearing the brunt of US labor within and outside of the home.[19] As we watched that impact unfold to devastating effect, we began to ask questions not just about the pandemic but also about the years that came before. Specifically, we wondered how the Trump years created conditions that necessitated the evolution of public feminism into its pandemic form—and we began a journey through historical time looking for connections through the centuries. Like many of the public feminists whose work we explore in this book, we see the possibilities of renewed attention to women's voices from the past in connection with amplifying women's voices in the present.[20]

Our working collaboration also emerges out of decades of engaging with each other's writing, rotating through formal roles of editor and writer for journals and more informal critique. Although we work in different disciplines in the humanities (English and History of Art) and focus on different historical moments (relatively contemporary Anglophone literature and ancient Mediterranean art), we share feminist commitments that traverse disciplinary boundaries. We had both analyzed and taught Roxane Gay's *Hunger* but from different vantage points; our conversations around that shared engagement became the basis for the first chapter of this book.

With each topic that we explored, we also confronted unquestioned language of and patterns from our different disciplines that demanded explanation and analysis in the context of collaborative writing. We also encountered different labor conditions within academia. When we both taught at City College of San Francisco, we were contingent instructors without job security. When Jen later moved across the country for a tenure-track role (and health insurance) at Johns Hopkins, Leila moved into a full-time tenure-track role at City College. Thereafter, Leila carried a heavy teaching load with a focus on pedagogy while Jen transitioned to an institution for which research and published writing are the primary evaluative metrics. While both institutions value research and teaching, the terms on which junior faculty are evaluated for tenure and promotion in situations where tenure exists—or for renewal of contracts where it does not—necessarily determine how each researcher allocates their time. To collaborate, we had to be transparent with ourselves and each other about the different conditions under which we work and how to carve out time for this project while also fulfilling the other parts of our respective professional roles. In this way, our collaboration not only traverses disciplinary boundaries but also working conditions within the academy that are too often held apart.

Academic disciplines create frameworks and tools with which we train and work—and around which languages build up—but they also shape silos that structure the academy and can obscure learning and progress.[21] Since the study of antiquity, in particular of the Graeco-Roman world, surveys some of the foundational material on which North American patriarchal disciplinary structures were built, reclaiming and revising these materials through a feminist lens is a critical step in reshaping disciplinary structures. Indeed, the barriers of disciplinarity pose a threat to feminism. And yet interdisciplinary work, of which this book is an example, need not situate itself entirely outside of the disciplinary formation of its authors but can depend on their collaboration and community.

The formalization of modern academic disciplines goes back to the late eighteenth century and the foundation of critical research universities; it emerges from a masculinist tradition of the single-author or single-artist male genius that has its roots in antiquity. This model's focus on the individual often erases collaboration and support structures from its stories. Collaboration, a necessity for much deep interdisciplinary work, does not fit easily into academic reward structures. Disciplinarity's rise alongside the construction of the modern nation-state—which is itself dependent on the violence of transatlantic enslavement, colonialism, imperialism, the enforcement of borders, and the subjugation of women and nonbinary people—demands that we engage with hard historiographies even as we push against enclosure. Dismantling these silos requires resources: time, access to libraries, quality health insurance, childcare, and a baseline income, or better yet a salary—precarity is an enemy of health and also of creativity. Interdisciplinary work also involves risk, for gatekeepers of traditional disciplinary enclosures whose power such work necessarily threatens often marginalize or minimize these contributions. Women and nonbinary people, who have traditionally been marginalized in the academy, have more to lose in resisting enclosure—and yet we believe that waiting quietly for change poses the greater risk.

DEFINING TERMS

A challenge for anyone writing about feminism is defining what is meant and understood by the word "woman." We stand against trans-exclusionary radical feminists (TERFs) and others wishing to exclude women-identified and nonbinary people who choose this powerful label. Instead, we follow Sara Ahmed's clear construction of the Butlerian idea that the word "woman" refers to "all those who travel under the sign women. . . . No one is born a woman; it as an assignment (not just a sign, but also a task or an imperative . . .) that can shape us; make us; and break us."[22] The notion of moving through the world under the sign of our gender identity (both as imposed upon us and as shaped and created by us) allows us to maintain an open categorical definition.

We also want to comment on our use of "us" and "we" in this book. We recognize that assuming a community, especially as two white-presenting women (one of whom is Palestinian American), can be problematic. When we imagine "we," we try to offer a subject position rather than an assumption of sameness—a we that recognizes differences within plurality. In other words, while we note its vexed construction, we imagine a place for women but invite all our readers to accept or decline this invitation as we also continue to reflect on and fight against our own biases. As Aruna D'Souza argues in the second act of her book *Whitewalling: Art, Race, and Protest in Three Acts*, white feminists in the 1970s often presented public solidarity with their colleagues in the art world who were not white while simultaneously mobilizing the back channels of patriarchal power made contingently available to them by race and class to advance their own interests.[23] One can trace a direct lineage from second-wave white feminism in the 1970s to Sheryl Sandberg's capitalist insistence in the twenty-first century that more women "lean in"—both are modes of feminism that trade in proximity to and emulation of patriarchal power. Problematic modes of acquiring such power, complete with dependence on the invisible labor of caregivers and lower-wage workers behind the scenes, make #GirlBossing possible for white women or women who have embraced whiteness—or its proximity—under capitalism.[24] And yet, as renewed attention to the work written in the 1970s, 1980s, and beyond by feminists of color and collectives like the Combahee River Collective makes visible, other modes of feminism and critiques of the existing power structures often employed by white feminists have long been possible.[25] As the Combahee River Collective writes in their statement, "Black, other Third World, and working women have been involved in the feminist movement from its start, but both outside reactionary forces and racism and elitism within the movement itself have served to obscure our participation."[26] We look in particular to such thinkers—who have imagined ways out from the enclosures of patriarchy and capitalism undergirded by white supremacy—and assert that elevating their ideas is critical for public feminism, as is attention to the layered positionalities that shape our subject positions.

Kimberlé Crenshaw highlighted this notion of layered identities when she introduced the theory of intersectionality in the context of her 1989 intervention in the field of law (though slightly earlier feminist work like that of Barbara Christian theorized similarly from a different field).[27] Crenshaw's essay aimed to expose the ways in which antiracist and feminist work erased the experiences of Black women by pursuing what Crenshaw names a "single-axis" understanding of race or sex-based discrimination organized around the experiences of privileged classes.[28] She writes, "For feminist theory and antiracist policy discourse to embrace the experiences and concerns of Black women, the entire framework that has been used as a basis for translating 'women's experience' or 'the Black experience' into concrete policy demands must be rethought and recast."[29] The thinking that has built up around Crenshaw's theory has expanded to encompass many disciplines. In a 2013 issue of the feminist journal *Signs*, Crenshaw and others captured this expanded thinking under the term "intersectionality studies," analyzing the ways in which an intersectional lens can be and has been applied to a range of fields, the debate surrounding its scope, and its use as both a term of academic analysis and applied public praxis.[30]

The evolution of Crenshaw's work also demonstrates an iteration of the circulation of ideas through social media that we wish to capture in this book. In 2013, mounting conversation around Crenshaw's term had inspired the special issue of *Signs*, but by 2021 the framework moved beyond academia and is now regularly invoked through social media channels in the context of public feminism.[31] Likewise, the editors' emphasis on a turn to praxis at end of their introduction to the *Signs* special issue demonstrates their belief, shared by the authors of this book, that such ideas are applicable to everyday lives and lived experiences. An essential characteristic of Crenshaw's framework is this practical applicability and, in it, a repudiation of conversations that remain only in rarified and theoretical academic contexts. Instead, Crenshaw engages with real-world legal experiences in the courtroom and returns their lessons to public space to be taken up by public feminism.

Finally, with many feminists before us, we work in this book on the idea of men—in particular, white men—as an institution under patriarchy. With theorists like Ijeoma Oluo, who argues in *Mediocre: The Dangerous Legacy of White Male America* that the continued elevation of mediocrity in the form of patriarchal systems of reward does harm, we look critically at the unearned rewards of patriarchy while also recognizing and appreciating that of course men can be feminists and allies.[32]

SOCIAL MEDIA AS PUBLIC FEMINIST TOOL

During the election period of 2016, people on the internet embraced and circulated Zoe Leonard's 1992 piece "I want a president," an essay that opens with the lines: "I want a dyke for president. I want a person with aids for president and I want a fag for vice president and I want someone with no health insurance."[33] Initially written during the 1992 election cycle and later circulated as a postcard by feminist genderqueer journal *LTTR* in 2006, Leonard's essay made waves that reverberated for decades, though its mode of distribution evolved through time. Prior to the postcard run, Leonard's essay had passed organically from hand to hand but had not been formally published as the journal for which she had originally composed it had folded prior to the text's planned publication, itself an indication of the way the collapse of independent journals limits the circulation of vital feminist ideas. In the wake of the essay's viral turn in 2016, Leonard's words moved back into real space. The arts institution The High Line in New York commissioned and displayed a blowup of her essay at Twelfth Street in New York less than a month before the election. The arc of Leonard's essay—moving from hands to postcards to internet vitality and then into (institutionalized) public space—tracks some of the ways digital tools have newly catalyzed public feminist practice.

Throughout the book, we pay careful attention to such stories, many of which highlight the possibilities of short-form social media—as well as essay-based social media platforms—as particularly fruitful tools for public feminism. We even, in chapter 4, narrate the way several scholars helped us fill in gaps in our access to historical archives in a thread on Twitter about papyrologist Medea Norsa. Despite such examples, we do not see social media as an unvexed good. Our goal is to recognize that public feminists can carve out spaces on social media and, through these platforms, shine a populist light. At the same time, there is always the danger that taking on the spotlight of a public feminist platform might also consolidate power, especially given the tendency of social media to create and shape star culture and other forms of elitism. Consider, as an example, the "blue check" of Twitter accounts. This badge, meant to verify the authenticity of the account holder, quickly shifted instead to convey status. In addition, there are potentially damaging aspects to the endless immediacy of public writing, not the least of which is the way the speed of conversation prevents deep reflection prior to response. We experienced this in writing this book: perceiving our work as time sensitive meant it had to be produced more quickly than some of our other modes of writing.[34] And significantly, as the 2016 election demonstrated, social media can quickly create echo chambers.[35] If nothing else, the move to social media presents the citational risk of forgetting meaningful voices from the past—or those from the present that are not as publicly accessible as, for example, the uneven gender distribution of Wikipedia entries makes visible.[36]

The anglocentricity of social media is also a risk. While such tools can be democratizing, most of those with the highest number of users worldwide emerge in some form from Silicon Valley and its outposts, representing a trajectory of linguistic colonization. And while social media may be more inclusive than traditional academia, clear inequities of power and access still exist. Even more nuanced questions arise in terms of the labor required to participate in social media at all. For example, using social media to educate others on issues of social justice requires precisely the form of free labor so often demanded of people with marginalized identities. One can't do everything, and the same people are consistently asked to balance a vast array of responsibilities, making the addition of yet more unpaid labor potentially unwelcome.

Within the broader category of social media as a feminist tool, we are particularly interested in the specific phenomenon of hashtags. Chris Messina, whose 2007 proposal for using the pound symbol to increase "contextualization, content filtering and exploratory serendipity" on social media became the modern hashtag, sought a tool to facilitate getting the right information into the hands of the people who needed it in order to create a "better eavesdropping experience" on the web.[37] The evolution of this information-filtering tool—in essence, a tool to promote more efficient searching—into what might be one of the most powerful weapons of public feminism today (as seen in tags like #BlackLivesMatter, #SayHerName, and #MeToo, among others) looked less significant until the Trump years. Then hashtags became tools of mapping, networking, relational citation, and activism in earnest. Of course, hashtags can also be co-opted—by corporations seeking to sell or brand, by hate groups hoping to silence, and sometimes, when we're very lucky, by activists taking back the narrative.[38] In the end, we believe that the positive impact of hashtags far outweighs their drawbacks; we see the hashtag as a kind of metaphor for the most powerful possibilities of contemporary feminist movements due to their interlocking connections as much as to their status as public speech.

HOW THIS WORK UNFOLDS: FEMINIST STRUCTURES, CITATION PRACTICES, AND SHARING

Writing in an academic context but through a feminist practice poses challenges as well as opportunities. Specifically, our book moves among feminist remakings of canonical objects and texts, opening out categories of evidence to embrace unfamiliar or nontraditional forms of citation and research. We assert that, as the personal is already such a significant focus of feminist theory and scholarship—and as public feminism draws from both conventionally academic work and public-facing essay writing and commentary—its exploration demands a style of inquiry that traverses multiple evidentiary categories under the umbrella of public feminism. Other modes of academic writing, from Audre Lorde's first person to Hélène Cixous's "women's writing," remade and rejected traditional structures.[39] These modes laid foundations for different voices and forms—and, most significantly, for surfacing rather than suppressing the author's subject position in a text. In this lineage and while reflecting on writing history in 2021, Robin Mitchell writes that she is primarily interested in "the networks of scholars who do work on 'unruly subjects' and who embrace new and unconventional ways of approaching them: ones who aren't completely dismissive of the 'I.'"[40] Mitchell tracks the significance of the first person as one means by which historians might acknowledge that they bring themselves to the stories they are telling. Given the historical and ongoing oversight of girls' and women's bodies, public writing, speaking, and simple public presence—along with overall acknowledgment of the individual self—are powerful and important aspects of the public feminist movement.

Our exploration also eschews linearity in favor of weaving and layering voices throughout the book. Some feminist theorists, including Roxane Gay, Emily Wilson, and Sara Ahmed, thread through multiple chapters, as do themes of counter monuments, performance, mapping, relational networks, (re)translation, and undervalued objects, subject positions, people, and ideas. These themes resist and remake the long-standing paradigm of the lone genius in favor of a more collective practice. Additionally, recognizing the Anglophone hegemony of social media (English being not exclusively but predominantly a lingua franca), our own situatedness on opposite coasts of the United States, and the limits of our own whiteness and white presentingness as we write amid a global pandemic that has restricted geographic mixing and against a backdrop of increased attention to much-delayed racial reckoning, we highlight both the limits and privileges of our subject positions. We also track the significant impact of Black feminists on our thinking and on public feminism more broadly. As we move among these and other theorists, weaving their ideas across multiple chapters and threading together historical epochs, we create what we believe to be a feminist structure even in the form of our book and our approach to its writing.

We have written our text in the dialectical model with a split down the middle. This form emerged naturally from an inquiry process that asked the question: Is there an outside? In shaping this book, we wondered, along with countless feminists over a period of many decades, whether it was possible to imagine a space beyond the structural systems of patriarchy, colonialism, and capitalism inside which we are caught—or whether we are too deep in their waters to be able to see a shore. To approach this question, we created three chapters that recognize the systems we work within and a second set of three chapters that imagine outside possibilities. In the process of writing, we noted that the first three chapters were easier to write than the second three.[41] Upon reflection, our own difficulty writing otherwise made a kind of sense. Perhaps the easier path is the more conventionally established one. It may be simpler to intervene from within a patriarchal frame than to imagine a way out.

Following the dynamic of breaking out of traditional restrictions we have also, due to the kindness and generosity of a "post-patriarchal mode" of scholarly sharing, benefited by looking at work we otherwise would not have had access to: scholars including Jacquelyn Ardam, Shadi Bartsch, Allison Caplan, Athena Kirk, Amy Lather, Michael Leong, and Caroline Costin Wright have sent us their (often pre-published) work to accommodate our publication timeline; we are so appreciative of their trust. Finally, the feedback of multiple anonymous peer reviewers, including exceptionally generous and helpful comments on the project as a whole, greatly improved our book. While academia may disincentivize collaboration more broadly, the practice of peer review, at its best, opens up deeply productive collaborative possibilities for which we are very grateful.

THE CHAPTERS

In this book, we theorize public feminism as historically situated in very recent times, but we search for its antecedents throughout history. While both the project and the concept of public feminism emerge from a moment of acute crisis (the Trump years and the COVID-19 pandemic as described above), to theorize this crisis, we locate the foundations for current public feminism in our observation that public feminists are often engaging across time to meet the current moment. As we examine the way that these years of crisis created conditions that necessitated the evolution of public feminism into its current form, we also begin a journey through broad swatches of historical time looking for connections across the centuries via art and literature and culture. With Bonnie Honig, who argues that "feminist criticism is oriented to the time of now while connecting to larger patterns, contexts, and timelines," we analyze particular details of public feminism across a deep history.[42] Each of the chapters that makes up this book is therefore an assemblage of past and present—often the very distant past of the ancient world, which we put in dialogue with contemporary examples—inspired by these crises as well as their layered historical frames. In short, while we are interested in the immediate public feminist response to these crises, we also seek to contextualize such responses into their historical lineages and direct parallels. We locate fruitful intersections between the practice of writing history and the current operations of public feminism that so often involve writing, overwriting, or otherwise recording statements and names. As we navigate this parallel, we strive to attend to the material conditions of writing histories in the past and to our own writing of this book in the present, along with those shaping a variety of public feminist acts and protests. Sculpting, painting, translating, performing, carving, and weaving all craft the public feminism that we write here, and we move among these pursuits and others in a series of chapters that analyze overlapping and interwoven themes in ways both discrete and continuous.

While each can be read separately as a stand-alone essay, our chapters also move along a linear path, building on the foundations of those that came before. And in each, we remain focused on what public feminists do. Public feminists gain control over an archive that otherwise contains or excludes them; they recover their own stories and their subjective experiences, sometimes for activist use; they investigate images and words that construct women in patriarchal texts; they situate the individual within a collective and the collective within an individual; they confront the limitations of that process due to the containment of patriarchy, reclaiming new systems of power in response; and they resurface a deep history for the alternative strategies of memorializing that they employ.

More specifically, in chapter 1, "Managing the Public Body: The Archive, Trauma, and Silence," we take inspiration from Roxane Gay's theorization of the "unruly" female body to analyze bodies in unruly manifestations from Paleolithic sculpture to contemporary photography. Discourse surrounding the process by which patriarchal structures present women subjects as objects has meant that stories of objects directly shape stories of women; therefore, in this chapter, we bring together narratives projected onto artistic representations of women and those crafted by and about living or historical women, asking how such stories shape what women can do and be as well as how they condition the archive around women's identity and work. Using the lineage of Venus as our through line, we begin with a very ancient prehistorical statuette of a naked woman from Willendorf to which the Venus label has been belatedly attached but of whom no textual archive exists. Moving forward in time, we navigate the concept of the archive created around or by women that narrates their bodies and their cultural value, examining, in particular, the work of public feminist and queer Black woman writer Roxane Gay. In contrast with the women and representations of women whose archival histories contribute to the Venus tradition, Gay shapes her own archive through memoir. Using repetition and strategic silence as literary tools, Gay conditions her audience and narrates her story, resisting and rewriting the Venus lineage through acts of public feminism.

In chapter 2, "Mapping Enclosure and Disclosure," we move from defining the body to exploring its boundaries. We begin with the life and work of seventeenth-century painter Artemisia Gentileschi, whose violent rape and the subsequent refraction of her work through a biographical frame have shaped her reception for centuries, both through the silence around and the misattribution of her work following her death and her rediscovery in the twentieth century. The feminist reception of Artemisia's work and life illuminates the complexities surrounding biography, self-fashioning, and disclosure. Later artists and writers addressed this problem directly through the practice of overlay, a process of placing a new filter over what was previously understood to be objective in order to claim one's own stories. This practice undergirds feminist mapping, which foregrounds artists' and writers' subjective experiences even as it implicitly critiques the imposition of biography. Surveying work that layers personal experience over delineations of space in forms of "mapping" helps us understand the #MeToo movement as a cartographic system of disclosure that illuminated one of public feminism's central challenges: how to protest violence and oppression while controlling which private details to reveal. Understanding, as Rebecca Solnit proposes, the map as a possible tool of connection and community across difference allows us to see feminist mapmaking as an instrument of liberation that frees public feminists to rethink the entanglement of the private with the public.

In chapter 3, "On the Gendered Politics of Translation," we move from physical boundaries of the body to intellectual boundaries of the canon by tracing the contemporary moment in translation. Over the Trump and pandemic years—in other words, during a very particular historical moment of crisis—women translators have taken on foundational male-authored texts to connect them to the events of the present as seen through a feminist lens. This strategy has always been one practice in the overall arsenal of feminist activism—instead of troubling, deconstructing, and replacing a patriarchal canon of texts, artifacts, and cultures, one can reexamine that canon in order to highlight other voices that have always been there. We argue that when women translate texts that have been both written and previously translated by men, they uncover parts of those texts that have historically been overlooked. Foundational texts play an outsized role in situating contemporary culture in terms of its imagined lineage, but misunderstandings pepper this vision. Translation itself is not a neutral act but one of interpretation, making the subject position of the translator critical to the translation they produce. To demonstrate this, we explore three recent translations by women of canonical epic texts—Emily Wilson's *The Odyssey* (2017), Maria Dahvana Headley's *Beowulf* (2020), and Shadi Bartsch's *Aeneid* (2021)—all of which foreground their translator's "I" and the related contingency of their new texts, a strategy that turned out to be particularly effective in the years during which it gained momentum.

In chapter 4, "The Collective Lyric I," we shift our focus. While our first three chapters situate public feminism in the context of patriarchy, starting in this chapter and continuing through the end of the book, we imagine other options and possibilities outside of oppressive systems. In chapter 4, we build on the questions of translation initiated in chapter 3 and move from epic to lyric, using the work of Sappho to theorize a framework for feminist translation. Specifically, we navigate possibilities inherent in our concept of the collective or "plural I," an idea that dates back to the "lyric I" of the Greek chorus. We argue that, through the embrace of a plural I, feminist translation as a practice takes what may be understood as singular (i.e., the rarified writing of a canonical author) and makes it more accessible and knowable by many, especially in its reworking of the "singular I" that has been a primary mode of patriarchal culture. This same tension exists in public feminism more broadly as each public voice, while often encountered as an individual I, always intersects, in some manner, with collective politics. Grounding our exploration in feminist citational practices that create an implied collective, we use this framework to examine Anne Carson's translation of Sappho into English as well as Hope Mohr and Maxe Crandall's metatranslation of Carson's translation into dance, tracking the accumulation of touches a body of work like Sappho's can receive through time—touches that turn its translation and reception into something like a collective project.

In chapter 5, "The Parabolic Curve," we move from collectivity into a set of intersecting examples of our interconnectedness, beginning with the (unsurprising yet also disquieting) material connectedness of bodies (re) revealed by the COVID-19 pandemic and its reverberations for an academic study of materialism and virality through a public feminist lens. As the virus spread across the globe through shared breath and spit, our world developed a renewed awareness of the way the air we share has both constrained our physical proximity to others as well as enhanced the attention we now pay to these quotidian markers of each body's imperfect boundaries. Yet throughout history, whether through wet-nursing or HIV or other fluid sharing examples, cultures have recognized that they cannot entirely escape interconnection through the ideological bunkers of behaviors and identities. In this chapter, we suggest that the operation of contamination is a fundamental aspect of patriarchal society—one of the threats its system is designed to neutralize.

While the containment of fluid in a pandemic expresses collective consciousness and care, the patriarchal containment of women's bodies is wholly different—a tool of regulation that produces power differentials that undergird oppression. The pandemic helps us see how women's bodies can themselves be constructed as viral contaminants that threaten others. In the face of this threat lies the dream of invulnerability, sometimes figured in a fantasy of immortality—or even vaccination—that might protect the body from contagion. Reclaiming virality in light of this fantasy thus becomes a public feminist project. To examine this operation, we trace the apparatus of decentralization in redistributing power and contend that virality can be used as an important practice of feminist activism. Specifically, Black feminists who founded the Black Lives Matter movement in deliberately decentered ways allowed others, as they did in summer 2020, to pick up their megaphones.

In chapter 6, "Scaling Loss, Listing Names," we consider the possibilities of a less patriarchal tradition of memorialization—the feminist list—to argue that listing individual names as a form of protest became a special focus of public feminism during the Trump and pandemic years. Memorializing loss by drawing attention to individual people rather than aggregating them into emblematic representations is an impactful tool in the arsenal of feminism, especially when the emphasis is on the general public (in contrast to the few, the famous, or the powerful). While engaged in modernity, this feminist tradition has a surprisingly deep, though often deemphasized, history. In this chapter, our intention is to capture that history, resurfacing it and tracing its ongoing place in the public conversation about loss and memorializing. The public feminist moment invites engagement with fallism—the practice of toppling monuments to symbols of oppressive power—but the parallel feminist tradition we trace, running from ancient Greece to contemporary times, also offers feminists new forms of possibility to engage and include a more diverse set of voices. We journey through from the ancient Greek casualty lists set up in Athens in the fifth century BCE to Maya Lin's Washington, DC, Vietnam memorial; the *New York Times* COVID-19 memorial cover; and contemporary poetry, protest, and performance, including #SayHerName, narrating the ways this lineage mobilizes naming and the poetic power of the list to elevate not singular hegemony but instead a plurality of raised voices.

As we move through time, connecting moments of broad history together, our focus remains on public feminism itself. For millennia, feminists have confronted oppressive structures and pushed back against them, seeking change. Like the activists who projected the words and portrait of Harriet Tubman over the Richmond, Virginia, confederate statue of Robert E. Lee in the summer of 2020 (Fig 0.1), contemporary public feminists find new—and often newly productive—ways to resist. From Artemisia to #MeToo, from Sarah Baartman to #BlackLivesMatter, from enslavement in the *Odyssey* to the memorial of *Zong!*, the projects of feminism continue to transform our world.

NOTES

1. Laurel Raymond (@RayOfLaurel), "Entrance to the Yale Law School this Morning," *Twitter*, October 22, 2018, 6:14 a.m., https://twitter.com/RayOfLaurel/status/1054360220971995137.

2. Jasmine Webber, "A Tribute to Christine Blasey Ford Appears at the Entrance to Yale Law School," *Hyperallergic*, October 22, 2018, https://hyperallergic.com/466934/a-tribute-to-christine-blasey-ford-appears-at-the-entrance-of-yale-law-school.

3. The spray can intervention paralleled Black Lives Matter protesters who spray-painted on top of confederate statues and empty plinths—and who left cans of spray paint for others to use. Our photo for this chapter (Fig 0.1) captures a related practice of projection onto these statues.

4. Bonnie Honig, *Shell Shocked: Feminist Criticism After Trump* (New York: Fordham University Press, 2021), 92–7.

5. Scientist Chanda Prescod-Weinstein identifies the weaponizing of dehistoricization in response to the 2021 suggestion that Black people have only recently begun paying attention to track with the success of Sha'Carri Richardson. Prescod-Weinstein traces in her rebuttal her own childhood as a track star; Florence Griffith Joyner's stellar career; Black Olympians Tommie Smith and John Carlos raising a fist on the podium in the 1968 Olympics; and Olympian Carl Lewis's success in the 1936 Olympic games in Munich under Hitler. Chanda Prescod-Weinstein (@ IBJIYONGI), "I'm a Second Generation Track Athlete, and I Medaled at the National Championships as a Kid and Also Ran in the Regional Junior Olympics.," *Twitter*, July 2, 2021, 5:12 a.m., https://twitter.com/IBJIYONGI/status/1410934459914932225.

6. See, for example, Duchess Harris, *Black Feminist Politics from Kennedy to Trump* (Cham, Switzerland: Springer International Publishing AG, 2018) and Honig, *Shell Shocked* (many thanks to a generous anonymous reviewer for bringing these publications to our attention) as well as Valerie Bryson, *The Futures of Feminism* (Manchester: Manchester University Press, 2021) and Jessalynn Keller, "A Politics of Snap: Teen Vogue's Public Feminism," *Signs* 45, no. 4 (2020): 817–43.

7. Harris, *Black Feminist Politics*, 185.

8. Honig, *Shell Shocked*, xiii.

9. Honig, *Shell Shocked*, xiii–xiv.

10. Ta-Nehisi Coates, "The First White President: The Foundation of Donald Trump's Presidency is the Negation of Barack Obama's Legacy," *The Atlantic*, October 2017, https://www.theatlantic.com/magazine/archive/2017/10/the-first-white -president-ta-nehisi-coates/537909.

11. Harris, *Black Feminist Politics*, 182. In contrast to Obama—who, as Zadie Smith has argued, could speak the diversity of American ("Obama can do young Jewish male, black old lady from the South Side, white woman from Kansas, Kenyan elders, white Harvard nerds, black Columbia nerds, activist women. . . . This new president doesn't just speak for his people. He can speak them.")—Trump employed one voice whose goal was to silence dissent. Zadie Smith, "Speaking in Tongues," *New York Review*, February 26, 2009, https://nybooks.com/articles/2009/02/26/ speaking-in-tongues-2.

12. As Harris narrates: "From the inauguration onward, the assaults on decency, diplomacy, and facts haven't just been daily. They have been ongoing, all day, every day. They start at the moment Trump wakes up and starts tweeting foreign policy blunders, conspiracy theories, and vacuous 'thoughts and prayers' about the latest school shooting, to the moment he goes to bed, still tweeting." Harris, *Black Feminist Politics*, 184–5.

13. For a tracing of the rise of hate crimes specifically on college campuses and a corresponding shift in pedagogy for classes focusing on gender, sexuality, and

race following the election, see Nathian Shae Rodriguez and Jennifer Huemmer, "Pedagogy of the Depressed: An Examination of Critical Pedagogy in Higher Ed's Diversity-Centered Classrooms Post-Trump," *Pedagogy, Culture, and Society* 27, no. 1 (March 2019): 133–49.

14. Honig, *Shell Shocked*, xiii.

15. For more on the past two years of her letters, see Heather Cox Richardson, "September 15, 2021," *Letters from an American*, September 15, 2021, https://heathercoxrichardson.substack.com/p/september-15-2021.

16. At the same time, we note that the benefits of online platforms are far from straightforward. As José van Dijck expertly summarizes, "Social scientists and journalists have argued that social media open up a new private sphere or are at least an exciting experiment in mixing private and public. For instance, communications scholar Zizi Papacharissi (2010) argues that social media platforms have introduced a space where boundaries between private and public space have become fuzzy, claiming that this imprecision opens up new possibilities for identity formation. Jeff Jarvis (2011) also cheers this ambiguity; he attributes its redeeming potential to Facebook's and other sites' ideal of openness and connectedness. On the other end of the spectrum, we find two types of detractors. Political economists assailed the incorporation of social media, labeling them as failed experiments in democratic participation or dismissing them as dependent on a naive belief in the possibility of developing a new or alternative public sphere alongside the existing public, private, and corporate spheres (Milberry and Anderson 2009; de Peuter and Dyer-Witheford 2005; Skageby 2009). The incorporation of platforms, some critics contend, hampered the development of Web 2.0's full potential as an instrument for participatory culture, self-regulation, and democracy. Instead, commercial platforms introduced new modes of surveillance, bartering privacy for the accumulation of social capital (Cohen 2008; Haythornthwaite and Kendall 2010). Other critics of platforms object to users' being doubly exploited, both as workers—deliverers of data to UGC and SNS platforms—and as consumers forced to buy back their own processed data by relinquishing privacy (Terranova 2004; Petersen 2008). More profoundly, some observe that the selling of privacy may be mistakenly viewed as the natural consequence of users' eagerness to connect and promote the self, rather than being understood as the corollary of a political economy deeply rooted in audience commoditization (Fuchs 2011a)." José van Dijck, *The Culture of Connectivity: A Critical History of Social Media* (Oxford: Oxford University Press, 2013), 17.

17. Though regulation by social media also persists: "Twitter's history revolves around a double paradox: first, the functions of following and trending presume a neutral technological infrastructure where all users are equal and all content is carried indiscriminately. In practice, Twitter's filtering mechanisms inscribe more weight to some twitterers and tweets, thus promoting the creation of big followings and popular trends. Second, Twitter presents its network as an online 'town hall' for networked communication, but the platform has manifested itself as a potent instrument for manipulating opinions. In light of this paradox, we need to interpret how Twitter changed its initial ambitions from wanting to be a 'utility' to becoming an 'information networking company.' Using instruments like predictive analytics, the

site increasingly aims at capitalizing the flow of tweets rushing though its veins." Van Dijck, *The Culture of Connectivity*, 68.

18. Roxane Gay, "When Twitter Does What Online Journalism Can't," *Salon*, June 27, 2013, https://www.salon.com/2013/06/26/when_twitter_does_what_journalism _cant.

19. We are aware of the multitude of ways in which writing this book has only been made possible because of white and white-presenting privileges that granted us access to supports allowing us to keep working against a lot of odds and in the midst of caregiving work. While the internet emerges as a (sometimes problematic) theme of this book, we also note that without the distractions the internet afforded our children while we worked and the connections it enabled through technologies of search, digitization, and videoconferencing, writing this book would not have been possible.

20. For example, one of the translators we explore in this book, Emily Wilson, captured this exact framework in the context of the #MeToo movement and #BlackLivesMatter in her 2020 *London Review of Books* essay: "In a time when we're thinking about the voices marginalized in modern democracies, and about whose histories we want to tell, it is worth turning back, with curious and critical eyes, to Aeschylus' great dramatic meditation on the politics of exclusion. Perhaps, after this huge gap of time, we can begin to hear what the gagged, murdered Iphigenia might have wanted to say." Emily Wilson, "Ah, How Miserable!" *London Review of Books* 42, no. 19 (October 8, 2020), https://www.lrb.co.uk/the-paper/v42/n19/emily-wilson/ ah-how-miserable.

21. For example, in a fascinating *Inside Higher Ed* piece, Laurel Smith-Doerr suggests that colleges might solve equity problems with the research of their own faculty, commenting that "this 'silo' problem is well-known in higher education and not unique to any one institution." Laurel Smith-Doerr, "Universities Should Look in the Mirror," *Inside Higher Ed*, September 15, 2021, https://www.insidehighered.com /views/2021/09/15/colleges-should-research-dei-their-own-campuses-opinion.

22. Sara Ahmed, *Living a Feminist Life* (Durham, NC: Duke University Press, 2017), 14–15. See also Judith Butler, *Gender Trouble* (New York: Routledge, 1990), which we discuss in more detail in chapter 5.

23. Aruna D'Souza, with artwork by Parker Bright and Pastiche Lumumba, *Whitewalling: Art, Race, and Protest in 3 Acts* (New York: Badlands Unlimited, 2018), 65–103. Harris addresses a similar point, explaining: "Feminism—that is to say, white feminism—has historically taken credit for Black women's ideas and achievements while at the same time writing them out of narratives, failing to welcome them at the metaphorical (and often literal) table." Harris, *Black Feminist Politics*, 2.

24. As early as 1984, Audre Lorde wrote: "If white american feminist theory need not deal with the differences between us, and the resulting differences in our oppressions, then how do you deal with the fact that the women who clean your houses and tend your children while you attend conferences on feminist theory are, for the most part, poor women and women of Color?" Roxane Gay, ed., *The Selected Works of Audre Lorde* (New York: Norton, 2021), 42.

25. Keeanga-Yamahtta Taylor, ed., *How We Get Free: Black Feminism and the Combahee River Collective* (Chicago, IL: Haymarket Books, 2017).

26. Taylor, *How We Get Free*, 15.

27. In her essay "The Race for Theory," Christian notes that "seldom do feminist theorists take into account the complexity of life—that women are of many races and ethnic backgrounds with different histories and cultures and that as a rule women belong to different classes that have different concerns. Seldom do they note these distinctions, because if they did they could not articulate a theory. Often as a way of clearing themselves they do acknowledge that women of color, for example, do exist, then go on to do what they were going to do anyway, which is to invent a theory that has little relevance for us." Christian's intervention ties the very process of producing academic work to flattening the notion of "women" that structures it. First published as Barbara Christian, "The Race for Theory." *Cultural Critique*, no. 6 (1987): 51–63 and republished with changes, including the above quotation, in Barbara Christian, "The Race for Theory," *Feminist Studies* 14, no. 1 (1988): 75.

28. Kimberlé Crenshaw, "Demarginalizing the Intersection of Race and Sex: A Black Feminist Critique of Antidiscrimination Doctrine, Feminist Theory, and Antiracist Politics," *University of Chicago Legal Forum* 1 (1989): Article 8, 139–67; expanded on in Kimberlé Crenshaw, "Mapping the Margins: Intersectionality, Identity Politics, and Violence against Women of Color," *Stanford Law Review* 43, no. 6 (1991): 1241–99.

29. Crenshaw, "Demarginalizing the Intersection of Race and Sex," 140.

30. Sumi Cho, Kimberlé Crenshaw, and Leslie McCall, "Toward a Field of Intersectionality Studies: Theory, Applications, and Praxis," *Signs* 38, no. 4 (2013): 785–6.

31. For an exploration of the use of the term "intersectionality" on the internet, see Safiya Umoja Noble and Brendesha M. Tynes's introduction to *The Intersectional Internet: Race, Sex, Class, and Culture Online*, ed. Safiya Umoja Noble and Brendesha M. Tynes (New York: Peter Lang, 2016), 2–9.

32. Ijeoma Oluo, *Mediocre: The Dangerous Legacy of White Male America* (New York: Seal Press, 2020).

33. Zoe Leonard, "I Want a President," *High Line*, October 11, 2016, https://www.thehighline.org/art/projects/zoeleonard.

34. And yet the slowness of academic publishing can hamper productive conversation. At the time of our printing, almost no scholarly work in the humanities has been published about Roxane Gay's 2017 memoir *Hunger*, a text we explore in depth in chapter 1. Multiple essays, however, look at Gay from a medicalized lens, presumably because scientific publications tend to publish more quickly than humanities work. At times, this slowness drives scholars to more immediate media like Twitter. We believe that the humanities must speed its pace of publication if it wants to continue being a vibrant site of academic exchange.

35. For a fascinating look at this phenomenon, see the infographic "Red Feed, Blue Feed," *Wall Street Journal*, archived 2019.

36. Francesca Tripodi, "Ms. Categorized: Gender, Notability, and Inequality on Wikipedia," *New Media and Society*, June 27, 2021, https://doi.org/10.1177/14614448211023772.

37. Chris Messina, "Groups for Twitter; or A Proposal for Twitter Tag Channels," *Factory Joe*, August 25, 2007, https://factoryjoe.com/2007/08/25/groups-for-twitter-or-a-proposal-for-twitter-tag-channels.

38. For a classic corporate hashtag fail, see Alexia Tsotsis, "Entenmann's Hashtag Surfing Fails Hard with #NotGuiltyTweet," *Tech Crunch*, July 5, 2011, https://techcrunch.com/2011/07/05/entenmanns-hashtag-surfing-fails-hard-with-notguilty-tweet. For hate groups using hashtags to silence, see Elizabeth Weise, "Trending Hashtags Co-Opted by Pro-Terrorist Accounts," *USA Today*, September 11, 2015, https://www.usatoday.com/story/tech/2015/09/11/pro-isis-twitter-commandeering-hijack-hashtags/72078270. For activists taking back the narrative, see Justin Curto, "K-Pop Stans Continue to Run the Internet, Flood Racist Twitter Hashtags," *Vulture*, June 3, 2020, https://www.vulture.com/2020/06/kpop-stans-fancams-racist-hashtags-twitter.html.

39. Notably both Lorde and Cixous wrote not only essays but also poetry and plays, respectively. Hélène Cixous, "The Laugh of the Medusa," *Signs* 1, no. 4 (1976): 875–93.

40. Robin Mitchell, "Bringing Ourselves Along with Us: The Realities of Historical Writing," *Women's History Network*, June 28, 2021, https://womenshistorynetwork.org/bringing-ourselves-along-with-us-the-realities-of-historical-writing.

41. Luise von Flotow's writing about the effects of feminine rewriting also highlights the challenge of such writing more broadly: "It is not easy . . . to read new utopias created and described in new language with new syntactic structures." This challenge does not mean we should not persist in experimenting with new forms but rather that at times such forms will present difficulties. Luise von Flotow, *Translation and Gender: Translating in the "Era of Feminism"* (Manchester: St. Jerome Publishing, 1997), 12.

42. Honig, *Shell Shocked*, 7.

Figure 1.1 Andreas Feininger, *Venus of Willendorf.* c. 1960. Gelatin silver print. 13 9/16 × 10 11/16 in. (34.5 × 27.1 cm). Paleolithic figurine of a woman. Oolitic limestone and red ochre. 4 3/8 in. (11.1 cm). Andreas Feininger Archive, Center for Creative Photography 81.27.100, via Getty Images.

Chapter 1

Managing the Public Body
The Archive, Trauma, and Silence

A foundational focus of this first chapter—indeed of our book—is examining the way stories are told about women, a term intended to include all who move through the world under the sign of woman.[1] Specifically, in this chapter and in the book as a whole, we analyze how stories are created about, around, and on the bodies of women as well as onto representations of women throughout history. Discourse surrounding the process by which patriarchal structures present women subjects as objects has meant that stories of objects directly shape stories of women. Therefore, in this chapter, we bring together narratives projected onto artistic representations of women and those crafted by and about living or historical women, asking how such stories shape what women can do and be and how they condition the archive around women's identity and work.

We find a starting point for this analysis in the work of public feminist and queer Black woman writer Roxane Gay, who highlights the idea of the "unruly" body in her memoir *Hunger* (2017), a text that deals, in part, with fat as a metaphor for unruliness. Gay's public feminism responds to a deep history of the regulation of women's bodies. In naming the unruly body, an idea and construct that predates Gay's memoir but to which she gives heightened visibility through naming, Gay also shows us its opposite: the controlled body, which has been operative for a long time.[2] Borrowing from Gay, we contend that the unruly body gains power in the twenty-first century to disrupt the controlled body that is always superimposed onto women in the form of gender norms, expectations around appearance, and the linkage of compliance to various forms of success. Audre Lorde captures this image of the controlled body in her term "the mythical norm" and describes it, in a section Gay includes in her role as editor for a recent volume of Lorde's selected works, as that

which each of us knows within our hearts is "not me." In this society, that norm
is usually defined as white, thin, male, young, heterosexual, Christian, and finan-
cially secure. It is within this mythical norm that the trappings of power reside.[3]

That power resides in a norm that is unreachable for most necessarily creates
a system of control—and the controlled body's rules of regulation become
more visible when held in contrast to the unruly body. This, in part, is why
constructing the unruly body becomes particularly important, especially in
the historical moment at which we begin our journey.[4]

Gay's memoir defies expectations of its genre in refusing the conventional
paradigm of successful control of the unruly body one might expect from a
memoir that focuses on fat. In contrast, Gay explains that her book "is not a
book that will offer motivation. I don't have any powerful insight into what it
takes to overcome an unruly body and unruly appetites. Mine is not a success
story. Mine is, simply, a true story."[5] *Hunger*'s contribution is therefore not
found in the regulation of the body but surfaces instead in the control Gay
seizes by writing the unruly body into the archive. If constructing an archive
in some sense always entails fighting against a tendency to slip back into
merely (re)recording patriarchy, Gay's choice to remove moral valence in her
investigation of fat and replace it with the concept of "truth" registers a small
sidestep against this tendency. Ultimately, Gay's text makes more knowable
possibilities of ownership by women over narratives imposed on their own
bodies, though in Gay's text such possibility is tied to trauma and its performance of ownership is linked to the freedom to choose silence. Through
writing her story, Gay chooses what does and does not enter her archive.

This term we use to explore Gay's narrative—"the archive"—has engaged
interdisciplinary work for decades, referring to the collected texts surrounding
a given subject, event, or material object. That archive expands beyond
these texts to include contemporaneous objects, materials, and contexts that
produce a material archive as well as relevant receptions of artistic ideas
and practices from different historical moments. In the largest sense, the
archive is the written and material record of ideas about and around what we
examine. Yet when categories collapse and bodies are treated as objects—
when, as Katherine McKittrick has demonstrated, the status of Black bodies
as commodities underwrites what the historical record does and does not
preserve—the archive itself can be predicated on violation:

> As noted, access to new-world blackness dwells on the archival display of
> the violated body, the corpse, the death sentences, the economic inventories
> of cargo, the whip as the tool that writes blackness into existence. How might
> we take this evidence and venture toward another mode of human being—so
> that when we encounter the lists, the ledgers, the commodities of slavery, we
> notice that our collective unbearable past, which is unrepresentable except

for the archival mechanics that usher in blackness vis-a-vis violence, is about something else altogether.[6]

McKittrick suggests a solution, arguing that "the racial economy of the archive begins a story that demands our betrayal of the archive itself."[7] Thus part of our work in this chapter is to explore how the archive is engaged, tamed, and betrayed in contemporary work. To better conceptualize its power, we will also explore its lack: What do objects or people look like when they lack an archive all together? Like the contrast between controlled and unruly bodies made more visible by Gay's naming, a pre-archival body can tell us about the power of having or building an archive—and about the kinds of control over stories and archives that have or have not been available to women throughout history.

A critical text for the theorization of the archive is Jacques Derrida's "Archive Fever," in which Derrida argues that control of the archive and democratic political power are related.[8] Derrida traces the etymology of the term "archive" to its ancient Greek precursors—*arkhē*, which means "beginning," and *arkheion*, which means "house"—and to the emergence of political leaders, *archons*, who housed files. In this way, the history of the archive is etymologically tied to ancient Athenian democracy of the fifth century BCE, but connecting the production and protection of archives and democratic freedoms also illuminates the patriarchal structures and colonial powers built into democratic societies and the occlusions in the archive that these structures produce.[9] These occlusions extend to nonelite class positions, including enslaved people, foreigners and guest workers, and women and nonbinary people who have historically been kept out of positions of power as well as excluded from the kind of intense research that might produce an archive or dehumanized by the lens through which they are viewed. Indeed, as Marlene Manoff argues: "One way of defining women's studies might be as a project to write women back into the historical record—to fill the gaps and correct the omissions in the archive."[10]

Recent calls to decolonize the archive foreground its role in upholding empire and power.[11] These calls also engage debates about whether the dilution of the term "decolonization" might overlook the precise settler–Indigenous relationships that decolonization is intended to disrupt. As Tuck and Yang argue:

When metaphor invades decolonization, it kills the very possibility of decolonization; it recenters whiteness, it resettles theory, it extends innocence to the settler, it entertains a settler future. Decolonize (a verb) and decolonization (a noun) cannot easily be grafted onto pre-existing discourses/frameworks, even if they are critical, even if they are anti-racist, even if they are justice frameworks.[12]

In contrast to an extension of an Enlightenment project grounded in Platonic philosophy to "think oneself free" (or decolonize our minds), Tuck and Yang invoke the turn to feeling (citing Audre Lorde) as an alternative practice grounded in a different set of priorities.[13]

If negotiation between political protection of and public access to the archive is a feature of democratic power and control, the concurrent democratization and monetization of knowledge with the development of the internet and digital technologies must particularly interest us. Digital space has been one important place in which women have worked to write themselves back into the archive. Our book's titular term, "public feminism," seeks, in part, to account for this radical practice of building a new, self-created archive by many individual women whose voices have enacted social critiques of the status of women in general.[14] Undergirding this practice is the process by which these women and their bodies have moved out of domestic spheres and into public discourse.[15] Of course, historians have noted the ways in which women have been "in the public" for centuries, but we find a shift at the start of the twenty-first century as ordinary (meaning not otherwise famous) women begin to have a public voice through new, internet-based content distribution channels, including blog posts, podcasts, and social media, among others. These forms of democratized (but sometimes capitalistic) content have evolved to supplement traditional media, though they have their own limitations—including the quickness of online conversation, which, as mentioned in our introduction, sometimes inhibits thoughtful debate. We also note that, at the same time and often through the same means, some academics whose voices had previously been either more rarely heard or even barred from the academic center have begun to reach the larger public as well.[16] These shifts have provided an unprecedented number of women with access to shape their own archives and to participate in a much broader and farther-reaching feminist-leaning public conversation about the experiences of women. Of course, as we will see, by making something public, one controls only the story's entry into the archive, not its reverberations. While stories can counteract violent silences in the archive, they may not always be the only viable strategy or even a safe choice. We therefore also consider the ways in which silence and refusal constitute their own power.[17]

The term "public body" as we use it in this text refers both to the spectacle of women's bodies in popular culture (a phenomenon that has been documented by academics for decades) and the (relatively contemporary) shift of the work of policing of that body in the public sphere—the now virtual "town square."[18] While for great swaths of time, cultural norms did this work more privately (or, at the very least, within communities), now "regular" people directly engage in such public policing—what Foucault calls ordinary people being "caught up in power situations of which they themselves are the bearers"—through, for example, internet comments.[19] We recognize that, in a culture buttressed by images, the public construction of women's bodies is of foundational importance to the creation and shaping of a variety of social norms and to social regulation more broadly. In light of this, we argue that contemporary culture depends on the construction, regulation, and fight over public bodies, and we ask, along with many feminist critics before us, how undermining the regulation of women's bodies can itself be a form of activism.[20]

In picking up the dichotomy that Roxane Gay foregrounds between unruly and controlled bodies, we turn now to fat to ask why the size of women's bodies threatens systemic control over them so profoundly—and how such characteristics shape the stories we tell and the stories we erase. We investigate the iconic Paleolithic statuette of the so-called Venus of Willendorf as an example of a body with no textual archive that therefore becomes, in some ways, a blank shape to be overwritten by a plethora of narratives (Fig 1.1). The absence of an archive surrounding this representation of a woman—an absence that results from deep time and the lack of historical documentation—is a particular kind of absence that we contrast to the absence that surrounds the archives of women and nonbinary people captured by the historical record. That absence, a consequence of the dynamic tension between visibility and invisibility that women face—one that is heightened for women of marginalized identities—is imposed rather than accidentally arrived at, yet both types of absences shape the way we encounter these works and, as we will argue, converge in their reception. We then trace the many Venuses that this figurine's name might invoke, establishing a history of the naked image of the powerful Graeco-Roman goddess Aphrodite/Venus and the application of the name Venus to models, sex workers, and enslaved girls and women whose given and chosen names escape the public record. We also consider the way the racialized Venus tradition allows for the possibility of unruly bodies within the category that exceeds the nude (if the nude Venus has been cast as the white female subject under patriarchy). Lastly, we return to Roxane Gay's selective archive of a body generated in response to trauma, in which Gay carefully curates a division between narratives to share and narratives to suppress.

WILLENDORF, THE "FIRST VENUS"

Thin forearms rest across the tops of her pendulous breasts; round hips and a full, soft belly tug at her deep belly button and vee toward her outer labia;

remnants of red pigment still mark her vulva and cling to its cleft (Fig 1.1).[21] Her curved thighs press together—no gap—and narrow to the knee and calves before breaking off above her feet and ankles. Hair fully and symmetrically covers her head and face; no features show through. For all the abundance of this faceless female body, the figurine, which was carved from oolitic limestone and painted with red ochre, is just over 4 inches in height and would fit into a pocket or a palm.[22]

Cross-hatched marks in her limestone flesh show that artists working over 27,000 years ago used stone tools to carve her body, producing a representation of soft flesh by modulating hard limestone with harder stone tools. The chronological period to which this figurine belongs is called the Paleolithic, a pre-textual period of human life named with two compound ancient Greek terms—*palaio* + *lithos* (ancient + stone). This particular ancient stone was excavated in 1908 from an archaeological site in what is now the modern nation-state of Austria near a village called Willendorf. Found on modern Austrian soil, her body now resides within a custom-made vitrine setup in a small gallery with red velvet walls in the Natural History Museum in Vienna, a museum that also exhibits meteorites, protozoa, the bones of an extinct cow, and other specimens of natural history.[23] The figurine's placement in the natural—rather than art—history museum likely draws on the time of her creation: she, like protozoa, was made before written language. With no archive to map to her body, we are left with only the actions her body implies—hands wielding stone tools carved limestone into curves, painted ground red ochre over her body (traces of this ancient ochre still cling to the tool marks and incisions), and enacted the decision to show no part of her face. Her findspot marks the end of her human use, after which she spent thousands of decades buried within the soil amid other archaeological markers of a Paleolithic settlement.[24] The figurine might have been made anywhere and carried around, passed from hand to hand, for years.

In the absence of texts, many stories have been told about her body.[25] As she claims no face and no name, those who first removed her from the soil drew on what they knew and saw and so they named her the Venus of Willendorf. We might accept the "Willendorf" designation as mapping the figurine's place of discovery, though the nation-state of Austria did not come into being until 1918 CE. What we understand, however, about Paleolithic culture and her palm-sized scale suggest that she would have moved across lands before her burial. In addition, similar naked female-presenting figurines have been found at Paleolithic sites across the globe, from Australia to Russia.[26] In the end, the "Venus" label absorbed this prehistorical object into historical narratives wherein what we know about an object develops not only from its own material evidence but also from modern archives of written texts (including inscriptions, histories, drama, poetry, novels, and medical texts), a process that anachronistically came to suggest that this much later Venus archive might apply to a Paleolithic limestone statuette. In other words, she was named Venus from a twentieth-century perspective.[27]

The connection to Venus, a Roman goddess active tens of thousands of years after a Paleolithic stone carver fashioned this body, however, is certainly based on the figurine's nakedness. The historical tradition of Venus's nakedness is associated with her Greek forerunner, Aphrodite, who was first depicted naked by Praxiteles, a sculptor. Praxiteles produced a statue in the fourth century BCE of the naked goddess in the act of bathing.[28] As ancient writers recount, the sculptor had initially created two versions of the Aphrodite, one with clothes and one without.[29] People from the island of Chios had commissioned their sculpture first, and they chose a conventional clothed version, leaving the people of Knidos with a naked Aphrodite in a second-place finish that put them on the map. The naked statue, widely copied or cited in antiquity, became known as the "Aphrodite of Knidos." Although by no means the first image of a woman or goddess naked in the history of image making, this naked Aphrodite and its reception propelled the artistic tradition of depicting women naked in sculpture, paintings, and other media.[30] While earlier images of the goddess Aphrodite depicted her clothed, after Praxiteles's statue, images of naked or partially naked Aphrodites, often termed Venuses, proliferated— including the topless (and armless) iconic Venus de Milo (Venus from Milos) now in the collection of the Louvre, an object that has achieved its own iconic status due in some part to the absence of its arms.[31]

The tradition of the female nude in art, for which living women have often modeled, is built on this ancient concentration of marble statues of the naked goddess.[32] And the influence of this tradition endures: in 2018, Beyoncé and her husband Shawn Carter (Jay-Z) filmed the music video for their song "Ape$hit" in the Louvre and mixed images of the statue of the Venus de Milo with Beyoncé and other performers' own evocations of it in dance. Yet over a period of centuries, these statues have been misunderstood as monochrome white marble despite the pigments and gilding known to have been a part of ancient Greek and Roman statues.[33] In the "Ape$hit" video, Beyoncé and her dancers respond to the costume of racialized whiteness that the statue— stripped of its surface pigments—now wears, sporting dancewear in a range of tones from pale peach to deep brown that slightly contrast with each of their own skin tones and emphasize their collective claim to the historically white and colonized space of the museum.[34] The afterlife of the Aphrodite of Knidos and depictions of the female nude in what has come to be called "Western art"—however constructed that term might be—have defaulted to the white female body as their subject, despite the fact that the modern construction of racialized whiteness does not apply to the cultures that produced either the Venus of Willendorf or the Aphrodite of Knidos.[35]

THE CULTURAL CONSTRUCTION OF "VENUS"

While the Venus label named only this specific palm-sized statuette from
Willendorf, its connection to the many other prehistoric naked female figurines found across the globe also brings them into this Venus narrative.[36] The
Venus label absorbed these prehistoric statuettes into a story of the female
nude in Western art that stretched from fourth-century BCE Greece to nineteenth-century France, from Praxiteles through Courbet's *The Origin of the
World* (*L'origine du monde*, 1866), and even into contemporary critiques of
this history from activist groups like Guerilla Girls (further discussed in chapter 2).[37] Stories from antiquity include the hypothesis that Praxiteles modeled
the Aphrodite of Knidos on the naked body of the renowned (and archived)
courtesan Phryne. These possibly apocryphal stories inaugurate a long association of artists' models with prostitution; the trope of the artist's model as a
prostitute persists into modernity as, for example, we identify in contentions
about the model for Manet's *Olympia*, Victorine Meurent.[38] Such constructions of both the naked Venus and the model as a prostitute are among the
many extractive uses of the female body throughout history.

By the eighteenth century, however, one finds Venus not only in stone
statues and on the painted canvases of public and private art collections but
also, according to Saidiya Hartman, in

> the baracoon, the hollow of the slave ship, the pest-house, the brothel, the cage,
> the surgeon's laboratory, the prison, the cane-field, the kitchen, the master's
> bedroom—[these] turn out to be the same place and in all of them she is called
> Venus.[39]

In "Venus in Two Acts" (2008), Hartman uses a rhetorical construction evoc-
ative of Ciceronian *praeteritio* (I will pass over . . .) to interrogate the ethics
of building out a story (fabula) of two enslaved Black girls whom archival
documents only barely register. Of the two girls whose stories Hartman tells,
only one, Venus, is named in the archive. That naming serves as label for a
category, not of the ancient goddess but of a modern girl or woman with limited agency over her own body due to class, race, or enslavement. Hartman
crafts what she terms "critical fabulation," an analytical tool by which one
might shape stories about a person for whom the formal archive is violent or
silent, to theorize the support two enslaved Black girls might have offered
each other in the face of the ship captain's violence. Hartman simultaneously
critiques her own fabulation's romanticizing potential with an analysis that
mirrors Gay's choice to both build her archive and maintain silences within
it. Having speculated on the possibility of imagining the two girls' whispered
encouragements to each other, Hartman cautions:

> My account replicates the very order of violence that it writes against by plac-
> ing yet another demand upon the girl, by requiring that her life be made useful
> or instructive, by finding in it a lesson for our future or a hope for history. We
> all know better.[40]

Here, Hartman both offers a critical fabulation—a story beyond what the formal textual archive records—and reminds us that imagining this story exacts
a cost. By the time we read Hartman's warning, however, she has already
told us her tale.

In Hartman's theorization, this paradox remains unresolved, leaving us to
justify the replicatory violence of critical fabulation as an antidote for archival silence's more obdurate violence. Hartman does suggest that this engagement with the archive is necessary. In the context of Hartman's ideas, Patricia
Saunders argues that "drawing these connections is another way of engaging
the archive differently, not necessarily to make meaning of slavery but to
engage the meaning of our present moment."[41] M. NourbeSe Philip, whose
work we explore in chapter 6, suggests that the limitations of the archive
themselves produce innovation:

> It's as if we're moving towards an understanding that there's a built-in limit to
> how much those tools, including the archive, have helped us to this point. And
> this limit requires new approaches to engage the task at hand, to tell the stories
> of our time.[42]

Some of those new approaches are tracked in this chapter, while others thread
throughout our book.

The abovementioned use of the name Venus to mark a woman or girl
whom those in power chose not to know or name contributes to our analysis
of the Willendorf figurine. Hartman's expansion, too, of the associations of
the Venus label beyond its ancient parameters informs the connections we
trace between the Venus of Willendorf and what we understand as its reverberations through time. These reverberations extend not only to objects but
also to people. With this complexity in mind, we turn to the story of Sarah
Baartman, a woman around whom an archive has built up without her consent
and whose name has even itself become subject to colonial violence to the
degree that multiple variants appear in the quoted material in this chapter.

In the early nineteenth century, two men trafficked a young Khoekhoe
woman from South Africa to Britain and France, where they exhibited her
naked to British and French audiences from 1810 until her death in 1815.
Sarah (Saartje) Baartman, as she came to be called, was born in 1789 to
the Khoekhoe, a nomadic Indigenous tribe of Southwestern Africa whose
language incorporates clicking sounds. Dutch colonizers as well as British
and French audiences applied their own transliterations and translations to

construct the anglicized name Sarah Baartman, to whom they also attached
the label "The Hottentot Venus," with "Hottentot" a colonizer's mistranslation
of Khoekhoe self-referentiality.[43]

The focus of the living exhibition of Sarah Baartman, first in London and
then Paris, was to establish an alternative version of Venus—one against
which to position the canonical Graeco-Roman marble version (and the
living, white women constructed as her descendants). To accomplish this,
Baartman's traffickers emphasized to an eager audience the display of her
near-nakedness and specifically of her buttocks (pathologized as steatopygia
and represented as a focal point of her body), though Sarah Derbew reframes
this hyperfocus through the lens of the Greek label "Callipygian" (beautiful
buttocks), used in antiquity for a type of Venus statue.[44] Through these displays, Baartman's body was constructed as unruly and, as a site of fascination
and desire, was forced into the archive by her captors' collusion with a complicit public.[45] Analyzing the archive of drawings, broadsheets, and essays
that rose up around Baartman's years in France and in the aftermath of the
Haitian Revolution, Robin Mitchell writes:

> Sarah Bartmann served as a foil, establishing and regulating normative French
> behaviors to reverse what was seen as the degeneration of white French male
> virility and increasingly inappropriate behavior of white Frenchwomen and to
> help white Frenchmen regain a sense of control.[46]

Postcolonial theory highlights this operation more generally: to shore up a
sense of self, a differentiation must be established between that self and the
"other."[47] In Baartman's case, markers her traffickers presented as indicating
an unruly sexuality (buttocks, near nudity) added overt titillation to this act
of differentiation.

That same ricochet between desire and repulsion has been wielded against
women within patriarchy for centuries. For Baartman, this exploitation did
not end with her death. Instead, the French surgeon general acquired her
body, had casts of it produced, and studied and dissected it, seeking in and
from her body evidence to advance scientific racism with a specific focus on
Black female sexuality.[48] And with the switch from her living body to medical specimens of her body, the focus of exhibition shifted from her buttocks
to her labia.[49] Curators displayed the plaster casts and her preserved genitalia
in the Musée de l'homme in Paris until the early 1990s, when her body parts
were finally removed from public display. Baartman's bones were repatriated
to South Africa in 2001.[50]

The label "Hottentot Venus" both absorbed Baartman's public nakedness
within a set of artistic conventions and also emphasized her otherness from that
same Venus standard. On the one hand, art history's many Venuses typically

deviate from the controlled norms applied to women's size, often appearing rounder and curvier than white European tastes demanded; on the other hand, Sarah Baartman's form was even rounder and curvier than the Venus norm itself and this difference was racialized, doubling her difference as both Black and woman.[51] Baartman and the category "Hottentot Venus" were understood as something potentially antithetical to the Roman Venus tradition, which is constructed as whiter, thinner, and more sexually restrained (in other words, a "nude"), despite mythological origins that emphasized the goddess' sexuality and an antiquity that predates modern racecraft, the construction of race as a biological and social category in modernity.[52]

As the Venus statuette from Willendorf was excavated nearly a century after Sarah Baartman's trafficking, this full Venus history plays out in how the Venus of Willendorf is labeled—in other words, the archive of Venuses remains active in the label "Venus."[53] Within that name are a range of associations—goddess of love and sexuality, artistic subject, thin body, fat body, sex worker, white woman, Black woman. Common to each of these remains the publicness of her naked body.

Although we know very little of this object's Paleolithic biography, many other disciplines have also appropriated the iconic statuette. Some have interpreted its lush curves as those of a fertility figure; others have focused on the modern aversion to its fat female body, invoking the Paleolithic object in medical articles about modern weight and cardiac health. Specifically, contemporary medicine has used the statuette as a frame for research related to fatness; a survey of peer-reviewed medical journals turns up the following titles "Obesity: A Lesson from the Venus of Willendorf" (2007); "Obesity, Hippocrates, and the Venus of Willendorf" (2006); and "Back When Big Was Beautiful" (1995). This constructed medicalization dovetails with that of Sarah Baartman's shape, including the pathologizing of the size of her buttocks as steatopygia and the claiming of the shape of her labia as non-normative. The same frame has extended to Gay's memoir as well; as of the printing of this book, little scholarly work has been published on the book as memoir, but several articles have emerged in journals that focus on the practice of medicine or psychology.[54]

The Venus of Willendorf has also entered pop culture. A quick search on the handmade lifestyle site Etsy produces soaps, candles, and jewelry charms in the shape of this figurine for sale, keeping the modern goddess movement—which has taken the figurine as an icon—supplied. Otherwild, a contemporary queer, feminist boutique (the creators of the widely adopted "The Future is Female" T-shirt), sells a candle in the form of the Venus of Willendorf alongside a T-shirt that reads "The Patriarchy is a Pyramid Scheme" and a gender-neutral swimsuit, "Hirsuit," remaking the Willendorf figurine into both a domestic accessory and a portable feminist icon.[55]

Ekphrastic poetry and modern photographs have also evoked her body.[56] Rita Dove's "The Venus of Willendorf," for example, narrates the experience of a Black American Anglophone woman studying abroad in German-speaking Austria who visits her professor's house to see a replica of the Venus. While there, she encounters an innkeeper who bemoans that the figurine, described with language that emphasizes excess ("sprawling buttocks and barbarous thighs / breasts heaped up in her arms / to keep from spilling"), wasn't kept on display near the local archaeological site where it was found.[57] Dove's ekphrasis blurs her subject's and the statuette's presumed subjectivity, triangulated through the conversation with the innkeeper. The displacement of the student parallels that of the Venus, whose miraculous discovery is framed in contrast to the simplicity of the village. The poem asks the statuette to do various forms of work—to stand in for the other (which also makes it a commodity that can be trafficked, traded, let go, or lost); to embody a "miracle" of serendipity; and to ally with those who are, in one way or another, uprooted.

Projections onto the Venus's body and confusion over the statuette's imagined personhood have even triggered algorithmic checks. For example, in February 2018, Facebook—which has refused to deplatform hate speech connected to violent white supremacist nationalism—censored an image of the Venus of Willendorf.[58] That Facebook, itself a contemporary archive, restricts a Venus that exceeds its narrow patriarchal construction of acceptable images of women while permitting various iterations of violence against women exemplifies the very management of public female bodies with which we began this chapter.

FASHIONING AN ARCHIVE: MEMOIR AS EXEMPLAR

Roxane Gay's 2017 memoir *Hunger*, though separated in time by thousands of years from some of the objects we survey in this chapter, must nevertheless contend with these histories of the female body. Although Venus does not figure explicitly in Gay's memoir, she writes against the backdrop of all that this tradition encompasses about being a girl or woman in public space. Marked by racial, sexual, and physical differences, Gay constructs herself into something of a liberated anti-Venus. In the face of the trauma of her rape, Gay narrates the process by which she worked to deepen that difference by building a protective fortress in the form of fat. The physical and textual bodies she makes free others, for the very act of creating a body that flaunts patriarchal restrictions makes room for more to do the same.

While the women whose histories we have explored thus far in this chapter have lacked control over the archives that built up around them, feminists like Gay have fought to regain ownership over their own archives. Gay employs a variety of strategies in this fight, performing acts of public feminism that combat the histories examined earlier in this chapter. One of these strategies is the foregrounding of subjective experience. Unlike the Willendorf figurine, which is all material object and no archive, Gay writes her memoir in the first person. Memoir as a genre is a particular version of history, and Gay's text emphasizes this concept in her opening lines: "Every body has a story and a history. Here I offer mine with a memoir of my body and my hunger."[59] As a story of an unruly body, Gay's memoir thereby arises from the trajectory of the Venus story yet plays a much different (and more active) role in shaping its archive, one with lessons for a study of public feminism more broadly.

Women who attempt to own their stories face significant challenges—challenges that paradoxically clarify the importance of such work.[60] In a recently published conversation between Roxane Gay and Monica Lewinsky, for example, Gay recounts how even journalists whom she had previously held in esteem—including popular radio show host Terry Gross—could not restrain themselves from asking about the highest number her weight reached. In this way, the reviews, fixated on weight data and not on the work of Gay's story, act as misreadings that expose the patriarchal structures within which women move and act.[61] A guiding question of our exploration, not only in this chapter but in the book as a whole, is whether public feminism can ever model a path out of this system entirely. How can the creation of an archive enact personal freedom from within a structure that continuously strips away agency?

Public feminism must, in part, entail a practice of reasserting control over the story of women's bodies and identifying the violence that results from the myriad forms of policing or erasure imposed upon them. This very process can be observed in Gay's text. Gay begins by accepting authorial control over the presumed subject of the book—the size of her body—while also identifying the shared responsibility borne by patriarchal violence. Writing about her body, Gay explains:

> This is what I did. This is the body I made. . . . I did this to myself. This is my fault and my responsibility. This is what I tell myself, though I should not bear the responsibility for this body alone.[62]

Gay's chain of assertions slips as it progresses, letting the notion of "responsibility" move from personal to communal. Gay's body was shaped by her choices but also by the violence of her rape and its aftermath—extending, perhaps, to implicate the reader of her text. Indeed, the book-long fight over control of her textual body that Gay stages with her rapist is woven into the (less significant) tension she constructs with her readership over the text's reception.[63]

As theorized at the very start of this chapter, Gay's assertion of control extends to questions of genre, as those who author their own stories must also fight against expectations of what these narratives must look like. In Gay's case, some of these expectations center on the idea of the "good" fat narrative. Gay resists the generic expectations of the "fat book" in providing *resolution* for her hunger—those victories that would sate it—and instead emphasizes the truth of her story in contrast to its "success." This distinction demonstrates the struggle against an imposed archive (in the form of the stories women are *meant* to tell) by the self-created narrative (what resonates as true for the individual speaker/writer). It also performs the fight in which public feminism must continually engage so as to counter the expectations in which every archival act is mired.[64]

Appropriate "fat" narratives in contemporary Western culture are typically limited to achieving thinness or accepting one's size. Gay chooses neither of these neat successes, instead contrasting them by announcing directly that she will not be participating in their directive. She will tell a "true story" rather than an acceptable one, building her archive by resisting patriarchal expectations of fat narratives, sometimes by raising and then dismissing them. For example, Gay asks:

> To tell you the story of my body, do I tell you how much I weighed at my heaviest? Do I tell you that number, the shameful truth of it always strangling me? . . . Or do I just tell you the truth while holding my breath and awaiting your judgment?[65]

This opposition between a number and a truth expands on the adages that weight is just a number or health is more than a number but also contrasts forms of veracity, numerical and narrative. And even this pattern of raising and dismissing is a powerful strategy that reminds readers of the oppressiveness of such expectations by framing them as if to suggest that readers must occupy the subject position of questioner, if only for a moment.[66]

The language that Gay uses to tell her true story always also leaves space for a body's pluralities, even when readers fail to recognize such nuance. Gay has emphasized that audiences assume intimacy and familiarity with her because she writes memoir and first-person creative nonfiction; these audiences, drawn to the truth of her stories, may fail to recognize that Gay has offered specific truths that amount to an archive while her "self" exceeds this archive. Knowing this truth is not the same as knowing her.[67] As genres, memoir and nonfiction have been plagued with questions of accuracy and fallacies of interpretation that force us to interrogate whether or not we can assume a persona to be the same as an actual person.[68] Yet Gay employs a strategy to resist these mechanisms: by recognizing the conventions her narrative might be expected to adhere to (announcing her number, being appropriately shamed) and by anticipating judgment, she manages to configure its delay—or, at the very least, to implicate her audience. The power to shape and tell her own story could therefore be called a success story—not of size reduction but of archive production.

VIOLENCE AND TRAUMA

Gay's text is multifaceted. Not simply a story about her body, it is also a story about violence and trauma, one that asks us to speculate about the ways that trauma underwrites female bodies generally and the shape their stories take more specifically.[69] Structurally, the book is split between the times before and after her rape, a split that parallels two types of archives examined in her text. Gay writes: "What you need to know is that my life is split in two, cleaved not so neatly. There is the before and the after. Before I gained weight. After I gained weight. Before I was raped. After I was raped."[70] Describing this "before," Gay writes about the photo archive her parents constructed of her as a child and contrasts its pictures to the invisibility she sought in the aftermath of her trauma, explaining that she has "photo albums taken from my parents' house [in which it] seems like every moment of my life was photographed, and then each picture was developed and meticulously archived."[71] The passive construction of this passage ("was photographed," "was developed") indicates Gay's vision of subject-less action, a sense that capturing and archiving were just "in the air" instead of being choices made by the specific people who photographed her. The "after" times involve personal control over her archive that also coincides with great trauma. In the wake of her rape, Gay avoids such documenting all together until she crafts a space for writing the unruly body and thereby secures the agency to produce a different kind of archive.

Gay's equivalency—that fat was a coping mechanism, a strategic response to rape, and that she ate herself into an unruly body that read as fortress and thereby offered protection—provides context for readers to understand her theory of the relationship between trauma and authorship.[72] Trauma is silencing. Often the aftermath of trauma cannot be expressed in language, so Gay instead expresses it through her physical form, making her body the document on which trauma is written. So while the unruly body can in itself enact activism, we must also realize, via Gay, the (often violent) forces that can shape its creation (while reminding ourselves that unruly bodies can exist outside of trauma). As Gay ties the unruliness of her body to the unruly afterlives of trauma acting on the self, her truth carves out space for other unruly bodies with different stories.

Gay narrates feeding her hunger in order to build a fortress that both protects and hides her, employing a notion of the body as something built up and constructed that inverts the terms of the Venus de Willendorf. That Venus invokes soft flesh from hard limestone while Gay seeks hard boundaries through the expansion of her soft flesh. The formulation of the body as a fortress also aligns with the early language of the archive—a space to house, protect, and order documents. Building, making, and constructing are all verbs that suggest control; it is precisely this control that Gay has sought in her fortress and her story. And yet, as Bessel van der Kolk has argued in *The Body Keeps the Score*, bodies house trauma much like an archive, though that trauma acts on and in the body at times without our knowledge or control.[73] In van der Kolk's model, trauma records itself indelibly and invisibly on the body, but Gay's rewriting of the paradigm leaves open the possibility of greater authorial ownership. Gay's vision shows, however, that trauma can also bring about a degree of dissociation from one's body.

This dissociation has a historical lineage. In writing about the role of ancient Greek myth in normalizing rape narratives in art and text, Helen Morales recounts the story of the nymph Daphne, who sought to escape rape by the god Apollo. She called out to her father and

Daphne asked him to destroy her beauty, which had "made her too pleasing." The myth of Daphne's attempted rape tells us that it is the woman's appearance that is to blame for inciting male sexual aggression: she was asking for it.[74]

In his attempt to save his daughter, Daphne's father turns her into a laurel tree, a transformation Morales, in the context of Tarana Burke's #MeToo campaign (further discussed in chapter 2), links to dissociation common after trauma (and perhaps the same dissociation Gay raises).[75] In Daphne's case, her transformation does not protect her from Apollo, who breaks off her branches, incorporating the laurel branch into his cult practice, including as a wreath to crown victorious athletes. Morales writes of how Ovid used this and other myths that showed Apollo as an abuser of women and power to critique the autocratic Roman emperor Augustus, who likened himself to Apollo.[76] Later, Morales takes us into Trump's New York penthouse, decorated with multiple images of Apollo, to suggest that Trump's "grab them by the pussy" art historical associations are more prescient than Trump might have intended or understood, reminding us not of his power but his abuse.

Contextualizing her engagement with ancient myths of sexual violence with her own assault as a teenager, Morales takes up another even more extreme rape story from antiquity—that of Philomela. Philomela's brother-in-law Tereus rapes her and then cuts out her tongue to prevent her from disclosing. Voiceless, she documents the rape by weaving an account of it for her sister, Procne, who believes her and helps to avenge her. Morales concludes:

> At its core, the myth of Procne and Philomela is a myth about the refusal of a rape survivor to be silenced and the ability of women to take down abusive and powerful men, when they work together to do so.[77]

Weaving or writing an archive might counter the violence to which these women have been subjected—not by enclosing it but by documenting and opening a self up and out of its story. In the end, each of these narratives moves from an archive into a public space and demonstrates how telling a story and building an archive might reanimate the petrified body. The archive of Tarana Burke's #MeToo campaign, for example, brings together experiences that illuminate and therefore resist patriarchal violence.

In some ways, Gay's construction of fat as a response to violence may be problematic, as it suggests that fat is a chosen response to the trauma of a repressive patriarchal society instead of just something that *is*—a characteristic of some bodies and not others. But both options might be equally possible: building oneself the shelter of a fat body or simply inhabiting one. Gay chooses to tell a particular story of her fat, mitigating the potential problem of this equivalence of fat and trauma by connecting her own work of healing to that of the larger community. Just as Philomela collaborated with her sister, so does Gay build a cooperative of writers and readers. Like many other trauma memoirs, *Hunger* shares its pain in part to heal collective hurt: "I all too often write around my story," Gay explains, "but still, I write. I share parts of my story, and this sharing becomes part of something bigger, a collective testimony of people who have painful stories too. I make that choice."[78] The process of sharing heals the silence of individual stories by adding each together through a connection to the larger community, creating a logic and an archive of unspeakable trauma that can yet be shared and healed by collective community support.[79] Once a community is involved, disclosure becomes testimony, reading becomes witnessing, and words have a political impact beyond the typical boundaries of published writing—enacting what may a central form of public feminism.

RESHAPING THE ARCHIVE

In the most extensive sense, Gay models a process by which women can write, claim, and reclaim their own archive by foregrounding her own silence, speaking, and revision. In her text, the narrating self looks back decades into the past to explore her rape. After a long paragraph detailing what she does and doesn't remember (she doesn't remember her attackers' names but she does remember their smells, their weight, their strength, and, like Ford as captured in our introduction, their laughter), Gay provides us with a short paragraph about omission:

> They did things I've never been able to talk about, and will never be able to talk about. I don't know how. I don't want to find those words. I have a history of violence, but the public record of it will always be incomplete.[80]

Gay's trauma thereby does something remarkable: it creates a new system of time, one within which the speaker can assure us not only of the events of the past but also of the uncertain events of the future ("will never be able"). Gay has stated that she will never name her primary attacker, the person most familiar to her of the group, in sharp contrast with other forms of public feminism like the #MeToo movement that advocate for public naming as a path through trauma. Gay claims her "history of violence" as something owned by the survivor—something she *possesses* that compensates for the incompleteness of the record of her experience. Gay does not have an articulation of all that happened to her, but she does have a history—a story that traps her but also names her.[81] Its record is incomplete in part because she wants it to be. This possession, something that belongs to her alone, demonstrates that the lacunae in her story are not failures, indicators of invisibility, or other forms of patriarchal disinterest or neglect but instead her own fabrication—in other words, a deliberate choice. Yet Gay highlights a tension between the creation of this record and the impossibility of articulating traumatic experiences—a tension that structures the entire memoir and that, we note, parallels the challenges women face generally as they attempt to reassert ownership over their archives. Despite their apparent differences, Gay's written archive and other women's public naming of their attackers share a similar potential to create and access community healing through public sharing and agency.

Ultimately, Gay's text demonstrates the fight at the heart of questions over who is permitted to tell our stories and truths and who is allowed to guard our silences. In Gay's case, the construction of truth is linked to the speaker's own agency. Truth must be shaped for and by ourselves through the process of claiming our own history. For example, when looking at the family albums discussed earlier in this chapter, Gay explains that "sometimes we try to convince ourselves of things that are not true, reframing the past to better explain the present."[82] This privileging of the current narrative voice (the "now" of the text) over previously held conceptions (the "history" of the text) might be read as an argument for control, even retroactively, over one's archive through revision—up to and including stories about the past.

SPEECH, SILENCE, AND CONTROLLING
THE NARRATIVE

The drive to share stories returns us to the public part of public feminism, which Gay both promotes and resists in her text in order to show her readership the difficulties of being in the public eye and under its continual judgments. Specifically, she considers her complicated relationship to the internet, which is both the place from which much judgment comes and a safe harbor from it. The internet is a space where Gay can become text more than body, but it is also where her body will always resurface.

Although we argue in this book as a whole that the internet is a significant part of the platform allowing for new forces of public feminism, it can also be a refuge from public existence. For example, Gay narrates spending the majority of her waking hours online, where she can shape the way she would like to be seen.[83] Unlike the Venus de Willendorf's archive-less anonymity that allows her body to become a touchstone for the narratives of others, the anonymity of the internet permits Gay to craft her own truths and archive as a self that is simultaneously materially invisible and meticulously crafted. As a safe space for self-creation, the internet provides the extra benefit of encouraging human connection, albeit virtual. Yet as we have discussed and as we further explore, the internet is also a place of judgment and misreading (for example, consider Gay's Twitter followers who think they know her or Gay's anxiety about training her readers, ideas we will examine at the end of this chapter) that may delay the very operation of "seeing" Gay hopes for. "Ultimately," she writes, "this is a book about disappearing and being lost and wanting so very much, wanting to be seen and understood."[84] This desire to emerging from hiding and reclaim a body whose authorship was contested is cast in almost utopian terms, yet it also captures a central question *our* book seeks to investigate: What does it mean and what does it cost for women to want to be visible, especially when they cannot control the reception of their archives, only (possibly) their creation?

Gay's text foregrounds her frustration with that very fact. She fights the limitations of reception by attempting to establish authorial control throughout her memoir. Gay's intentions are clear: "If I must share my story, I want to do so on my own terms."[85] Gay eschews attention, pity, appreciation, and advice, seeking instead simply the opportunity to speak. The strong need in the text to control the uncontrollable—the reader's response to the text, which is obviously out of Gay's hands—runs parallel to the need for agency, for the speaking voice to reclaim its subjecthood out of the objecthood to which it has been relegated. In this way, the drive to create an archive and the drive to shape its reception are significantly intertwined—and even emphasized as topics of Gay's text.

Further, once trauma is the immediate subject of the text, the link between the need to create and archive and the simultaneous drive to shape an archive's reception is even more clear. For instance, Gay connects her elision of the details of her rape to anxiety around the possible response to her writing, explaining that she "write[s] around what happened because I don't want to have to defend myself."[86] By making an explicit link between her plea for a certain type of reception and the trauma she endured, Gay seeks to train and convince her reader to respond according to her desired range of permitted interpretations. When she does describe her assault, she calls her readers into her story: "In my history of violence, there was a boy. I loved him. His name was Christopher. That's not really his name. *You know that*."[87] By acknowledging the reader's expectations for her narrative, Gay once again implicates the reader as a voyeur, complicit in the consumption of the story. Readerly complicity will thereby be used as a kind of debt that Gay will cash in to ensure an appropriate reception and balance the silence of the unspeakable acts she will not narrate.

Toward the end of the book, Gay recounts an inappropriate act of reception to teach readers the correct and incorrect way to approach her memoir. Specifically, she narrates the way that her Twitter followers read her posts about her physical training sessions incorrectly. Her followers wish to support her with their own suggestions, but she is "just sharing [her] suffering. I am looking for commiseration."[88] Here, Gay employs a double agenda. The first is to ensure that readers understand the right and wrong ways to respond to her life writings so that they will be better consumers of the book. The second—and one of the key motivations of the memoir itself—is to correct misperceptions Gay has faced in her public life, to respond to her critics with the validation of book form, and to have the "last word," even if that last word is silence.[89]

Of course, women's voices are always held at bay by the threat of silence and the threat of violence. In Gay's case, the trauma of the book is not only her rape but also the misunderstanding and unfair judgment of her story by the world at large. The potential healing or redemption of the book may reside in the platform it gives Gay to talk back when previously she had suffered in shame and silence. And indeed, by the end of the book, Gay asserts a newfound power over herself and her body: "My body is a cage, but this is my cage and there are moments when I take pride in it."[90] She reaches for power by confronting head-on the violence her primary attacker did to her body, calling him over and over, often hanging up but eventually holding the line, until one day they share something: they share a silence. Gay recounts that her rapist kept saying hello, almost as if he knew it was her, and "then after a long time he stopped saying hello and we sat there in silence and I kept waiting for him to hang up but he didn't and neither did I so we just listened to each other breathing."[91] While the two cannot share a conversation in words, while Gay cannot or does not wish to narrate more details about the rape or her attacker's name, they can share silence together, an interaction now performed on Gay's terms.

Escaping from the story her rapist constructed for her that she could not understand as a child, Gay wins agency, gaining ownership over information, narration, and contact. That this ownership is figured as silence suggests that, as women construct their archive and gain narrative power, they may also choose other forms of archival construction than we might have initially guessed. Silence—the refusal to speak, the refusal to name, the refusal to indulge every reader's curiosity—is its own form of power, perhaps a particularly feminist one. For as much as the book projects Gay's story out into the world, it also offers a platform for her silences and for what she chooses to occlude.[92]

In asserting her right to certain silences while also narrating her story, Gay establishes her authority over the levers of the archive itself. When archives record what patriarchy and power suggest they should (as they typically do), silences mark out those with less power. In Gay's hands, however, silence also marks her authorial and archival control (partially realized through agency and partially as an effect of trauma). By foregrounding her silence, Gay moves between intervening in what an archive can be and holding up a mirror to the very structures that produce silences—including but not limited to rape itself. In doing so, Gay offers implicit commentary on the status of an archive as a record that must constantly fight against merely recording patriarchy's broadest operations.

VENUS'S AFTERMATH

If Gay's text helps us establish something at the start of our own, perhaps it is the very nature of this struggle: we are fighting a battle with dominant narratives and with the violence and repressiveness of patriarchal structures that regulate our bodies and our voices, during which we reshape, little by little, the collective archive of the experience of women. Memoir can act as an exemplum of the larger process by which women may curate their own experiences as they choose, taking back ownership over various forms of their own images. But memoir also reminds us that we are forever inside larger systems of patriarchy and power. Electing silence can sometimes perform a powerful critique.

Another sculpture of Venus carved by a Roman artist fits, like the Willendorf, in the palm of one's hand.[93] This figurine, however, was carved from rock crystal. Like the Willendorf it has no specific textual archive, no known story, no truth—although unlike the Paleolithic statuette, it dates to the time of written Latin, the historical era of Venus. Due to its transparent rock crystal material, this figurine acts on the person or place that holds it. A person's palm colors the statuette, infusing it with the hue of the holder's flesh. One might misread this object's silent self-reflexivity as the cooperation of a willing Venus. Instead, the transparency of the rock crystal draws each beholder's body into the Venus, entwining each of us with her truth and forcing us to look at ourselves.

NOTES

1. See "Defining Terms" in our introduction for more on this.
2. Gay connects her framework to her reading of Hanne Blank's *Unruly Appetites: Erotic Stories* (New York: Seal Press, 2002). Terri Waters, "Roxane Gay's Latest Project Talks Unruly Bodies and Redefining Body Image," *The Unedit*, April 10, 2018, https://www.the-unedit.com/posts/2018/4/10/roxane-gays-latest-project -talks-unruly-bodies-and-redefining-body-image.
3. Audre Lorde, "Difference and Survival: An Address at Hunter College (Undated)," in *Selected Works of Audre Lorde*, 175.
4. *Hunger*, Gay's memoir, was published in 2017; Gay's edited volume, *Selected Works of Audre Lorde*, in 2020. Roxane Gay, *Hunger: A Memoir of (My) Body* (New York: Harper, 2017).
5. Gay, *Hunger*, 4.
6. Katherine McKittrick, "Mathematics Black Life," *Black Scholar* 44, no. 2 (2014): 22.
7. McKittrick, "Mathematics Black Life," 22.
8. Marlene Manoff, "Theories of the Archive from across the Disciplines," *Portal: Libraries and the Academy* 4, no. 1 (2004): 10; Jacques Derrida and Eric Prenowitz, "Archive Fever: A Freudian Impression," *Diacritics* 25, no. 2 (Summer, 1995): 9–10. On the complexity of the relationship between state and archive, see Achille Mbembe, "The Power of the Archive and its Limits," in *Refiguring the Archive*, ed. Carolyn Hamilton et al. (Boston, MA: Kluwer Academic Publishers, 2002), 19–27. In relation to Ancient Greek practice, see Athena Kirk, *Ancient Greek Lists: Catalogue and Inventory across Genres* (Cambridge: Cambridge University Press, 2021), 139–40.
9. Manoff, "Theories of the Archive," 7.
10. Manoff, "Theories of the Archive," 15.
11. "Unsettling Knowledge #9: Decolonizing the Archive; Sites of Memory or Manipulation?" *Utrecht University*, January 29, 2021, https://soundcloud.com/ utrechtuniversity/unsettling-knowledge-9-decolonising-the-archive-sites-of-memory -or-manipulation.
12. Eve Tuck and K. Wayne Yang, "Decolonization Is Not a Metaphor," *Decolonization: Indigeneity, Education & Society* 1, no. 1 (2012): 3.

13. "Freire's theories of liberation resoundingly echo the allegory of Plato's Cave, a continental philosophy of mental emancipation, whereby the thinking man individualistically emerges from the dark cave of ignorance into the light of critical consciousness. By contrast, black feminist thought roots freedom in the darkness of the cave, in that well of feeling and wisdom from which all knowledge is recreated." Tuck and Yang, "Decolonization Is Not a Metaphor," 20.

14. Sometimes merely gaining a voice is a radical action. Sometimes the work must be to amplify the voices of people whose voices have been silenced. For more on the term "public feminism," please see our introduction.

15. On the other hand, for a critique of an oversimplified "public/private" framework in the context of Victorian studies, see Caroline Levine's comment that "scholars have successfully unsettled the notion of a rigid divide between public and private, showing that Victorian women played significant roles outside of the home, while men struggled to find their proper places within the domestic sphere." Caroline Levine, "Strategic Formalism: Toward a New Method in Cultural Studies," *Victorian Studies* 48, no. 4 (2006): 267. We also note deep class differences here even in the concept of being confined to the home itself. For example, consider the long-standing trope of (elite) women confined to the home while nonelite women enjoyed a kind of greater bodily freedom because of their lack of class privilege. Ultimately, their wombs were perceived as less valuable, so their bodies required less policing, a trope we trace back to at least the ancient Greek context of Lysias (see, for example, the speech "On the Murder of Eratosthenes" by the canonical Attic orator).

16. By "rarely heard or even barred," we mean both academics who might normally be heard only within the academy, whether by choice or default, as well as those who are given a very limited volume and space more broadly. In terms of public access to scholarship, some academic platforms like JSTOR now provide online access to content without a login; see Orla Murnaghan, "Open-Access JSTOR Materials Accessible to the Public," *University Times*, March 19, 2020, https://universitytimes.ie/2020/03/jstor-makes-database-accessible-to-the-public. In the UK, an updated open access policy for publicly funded research was announced in August of 2021. The new policy requires that such scholarship be made open access within a minimal time frame. "UKRI Announces New Open Access Policy," *UK Research and Innovation*, August 6, 2021, https://www.ukri.org/news/ukri-announces-new-open-access-policy.

17. We recognize both the silence of the dominant narrative about women, especially women marginalized by race, class, immigration status, or other forms of outsidership *and* the individual silences that a woman might choose in constructing her own narrative. Distinguishing between these different forms of silence is critical.

18. See, for example, the collection Londa L. Schiebinger, *Feminism and the Body* (Oxford: Oxford University Press, 2000) or the documentary *Killing Us Softly*, directed by Jean Kilbourne, now in its fourth evolution shepherded by cultural theorist Sut Jhally.

19. Jeremy Bentham's conception of the panopticon conceptualizes this silent policing as the internalization of external pressures so that external enforcement is no longer needed—the subject takes on the job of policing their own self (or, in this

case, their neighbors). Here is this concept articulated by Foucault: "The major effect of the Panopticon [is] to induce in the inmate a state of conscious and permanent visibility that assures the automatic functioning of power. So to arrange things that the surveillance is permanent in its effects, even if it is discontinuous in its action; that the perfection of power should tend to render its actual exercise unnecessary . . . in short, that the inmates should be caught up in a power situation of which they are themselves the bearers." Michel Foucault, *Discipline and Punish: The Birth of the Prison* (New York: Vintage Books, 1979), 201.

20. For example, Sonya Renee Taylor connects radical self-acceptance to social justice more broadly in *The Body Is Not an Apology* (Oakland, CA: Berrett-Koehler Publishers, 2018).

21. We use this term "first" quite loosely. There are many other Paleolithic objects, some of which are also called Venuses, and their chronological range spans millennia, so from a purely historical perspective, it is impossible to tell which object from this time period is "first."

22. Ian Chilvers, ed., "Venus of Willendorf," in *The Oxford Dictionary of Art* (Oxford: Oxford University Press, 2004).

23. "Venus Cabinet," *Naturhistorisches Museum Wien*, September 12, 2020, https://www.nhm-wien.ac.at/en/exhibitions/permanent_exhibitions/mezzanine_level/hall_11-13_prehistory.

24. O. Soffer, J. M. Adovasio, and D. C. Hyland, "The 'Venus' Figurines: Textiles, Basketry, Gender, and Status in the Upper Paleolithic," *Current Anthropology* 41, no. 4 (2000): 511–37; Silvia Tomášková, "Nationalism, Local Histories, and the Making of Data in Archaeology," *Journal of the Royal Anthropological Institute* 9, no. 3 (2003): 485–507.

25. Bessel van der Kolk, *The Body Keeps the Score: Brain, Mind, and Body in the Healing of Trauma* (New York: Penguin Books, 2015).

26. See Jill Cook, *Ice Age Art: The Arrival of the Modern Mind* (London: British Museum Press, 2013).

27. More recent textbooks have substituted "Woman of Willendorf" for "Venus of Willendorf," but the legacy of the name persists—and even this substitution implies that "Venus" and "woman" are commensurate terms, despite the fact that the ancient Venus was a divinity whose true form could blind human beholders.

28. Andrew Stewart, *Greek Sculpture: An Exploration* (Cambridge: Cambridge University Press, 1990), 177–8.

29. Lucian, *Images*, 6; pseudo-Lucian, *Amores*, 13–14; Pliny, *Natural History*, 36.20–21.

30. Kris Seaman, "Retrieving the Original Aphrodite of Knidos," *Atti della Accademia Nazionale dei Lincei. Rendiconti: classe di scienze morali, storiche e filologiche* 9, no. 15 (2004): 531–94; Christine Mitchell Havelock, *The Aphrodite of Knidos and Her Successors: A Historical Review of the Female Nude in Greek Art* (Ann Arbor: University of Michigan Press, 1995). Elite Roman women even had their portrait busts attached to copies of the naked body of the Knidia, likening themselves to the goddess.

31. On the iconicity of the Venus de Milo (or Venus of Milos), see analysis of Beyoncé's engagement in her 2018 music video "Ape$hit" in Cady Lang, "Art

History Experts Explain the Meaning of the Art in Beyoncé and Jay Z's 'Apesh-t' Video," *Time Magazine*, June 19, 2018, https://time.com/5315275/art-references -meaning-beyonce-jay-z-apeshit-louvre-music-video.

32. Helen McDonald, *Erotic Ambiguities: The Female Nude in Art* (London: Routledge, 2001); Susan Suleiman, ed., *The Female Body in Western Culture: Contemporary Perspectives* (Cambridge, MA: Harvard University Press, 1986).

33. Vinzenz Brinkmann, Renée Dreyfus, and Ulrike Koch-Brinkmann, *Gods in Color: Polychromy in the Ancient World* (San Francisco: Fine Arts Museums of San Francisco, Legion of Honor, 2017); Jennifer Stager, "The Unbearable Whiteness of Whiteness," *Art Practical*, January 16, 2018, https://www.artpractical.com/column/ feature-the-unbearable-whiteness-of-whiteness.

34. Doreen St. Felix, "What It Means When Beyoncé and Jay-Z Take Over the Louvre," *New Yorker*, June 19, 2019, https://www.newyorker.com/culture/culture -desk/what-it-means-when-beyonce-and-jay-z-take-over-the-louvre.

35. Denise Murrell, *Posing Modernity: The Black Model from Manet and Matisse to Today* (Yale University Press, 2018). On the construction of Western culture, see Kwame Anthony Appiah, "There Is No Such Thing as Western Civilization," *The Guardian*, November 9, 2016, https://www.theguardian.com/world/2016/nov /09/western-civilisation-appiah-reith-lecture; on whiteness as the default status for the nude see Charmaine Nelson, *The Color of Stone* (Minneapolis: University of Minnesota Press, 2007); Charmaine Nelson, *Representing the Black Female Subject in Western Art* (New York: Routledge, 2010).

36. Catherine Hodge McCoid and Leroy D. McDermott, "Toward Decolonizing Gender: Female Vision in the Upper Paleolithic," *American Anthropologist* n.s. 98, no. 2 (1996): 319–26.

37. Linda Nochlin, "Courbet's 'L'origine du monde': The Origin without an Original," *October* 37 (1986): 77–86. On the through line from the Venus of Willendorf to Courbet's painting, see Rainer Mack, "Reading the Archaeology of the Female Body," *Qui Parle* 4, no. 1 (1990): 79–97.

38. Eunice Lipton, "Representing Sexuality in Women Artists' Biographies: The Cases of Suzanne Valadon and Victorine Meurent," *Journal of Sex Research* 27, no. 1 (1990): 85–7. See Summer Brennan's forthcoming *The Parisian Sphinx: A True Story of Art and Obsession* (Boston: Mariner Books, 2022).

39. Saidiya V. Hartman, "Venus in Two Acts," *Small Axe: A Caribbean Journal of Criticism* 26, no. 1 (2008): 1. Murrell's recent exhibition and catalogue, *Posing Modernity*, argue that overlooked depictions of the Black female body were integral to the development of modernism.

40. Hartman, "Venus in Two Acts," 14.

41. Patricia J. Saunders, "Defending the Dead, Confronting the Archive: A Conversation with M. NourbeSe Philip," *Small Axe: A Caribbean Journal of Criticism* 12, no. 2 (2008): 68.

42. M. NourbeSe Philip, quoted in Saunders, "Defending the Dead," 71.

43. As Deborah Willis writes in the introduction to her edited volume dedicated to Baartman, the different renderings of Sarah's name, which the essays collected in her volume use interchangeably, reproduce colonial violence even as they attempt to

honor their subject. Deborah Willis, *Black Venus 2010: They Called Her "Hottentot"* (Philadelphia: Temple University Press, 2010), 4. Among the many rich essays in this collection, see especially Kellie Jones, "A. K. A. Saartjie: The 'Hottentot Venus' in Context (Some Recollections and a Dialogue) 1998/2004," in *Black Venus 2010*, 126–43. Willis's 2010 collection brings together prose, poetry, and visual arts to analyze and to honor Baartman's history while also crafting her future. The volume itself is a form of critical fabulation that crafts Sarah Baartman's archive from many sources.

44. Sarah Derbew, "(Re)membering Sara Baartman, Venus, and Aphrodite," *Classical Receptions Journal* 11, no. 3 (2019): 338.

45. On the cost of the exhibition and class-based dissemination of Baartman's story, see Robin Mitchell, "Another Means of Understanding the Gaze: Sarah Bartmann in the Development of Nineteenth-Century French National Identity," in *Black Venus 2010*, 37.

46. Robin Mitchell, *Vénus Noire: Black Women and Colonial Fantasies in Nineteenth-Century France* (Athens, Georgia: University of Georgia Press, 2020), 65.

47. See, for example, Frantz Fanon, *Black Skin, White Masks* (London: Pluto Press, 1986), especially chapter 7, "The Negro and Recognition," 210–22. In his 2015 text, *Between the World and Me*, Ta-Nehisi Coates describes this differentiation as necessary for the functioning of the American dream, a dream he ties to the dream of those who "believe themselves to be white." Coates writes to his son: "There is no them without you, and without the right to break you they must necessarily . . . tumble out of the Dream. And then they would have to determine how to build their suburbs on something other than human bones, how to angle their jails toward something other than a human stockyard, how to erect democracy independent of cannibalism." Ta-Nehisi Coates, *Between the World and Me* (New York: Random House Publishing Group, 2015), 105.

48. J. Yolande Daniels, "Exhibit A: Private Life without a Narrative," in *Black Venus 2010*, 63. This treatment also accords with the long history of medical racism, especially enacted toward Black women. Some of this is detailed in Rebecca Skloot's *The Immortal Life of Henrietta Lacks* (New York: Crown Publishing, 2010) and ongoing research on the practices of Marion Sims. For a contrast between artistic and medical plaster casts, see the exhibition *Bodies* in Las Vegas: https://luxor.mgmresorts.com/en/entertainment/bodies-the-exhibition.html.

49. Mitchell, "Understanding the Gaze," 41. Cuvier described the hypertrophy of the labia as her "apron." See also Kianga Ford, "Playing with Venus: Black Women Artists and the Venus Trope in Contemporary Visual Art," in *Black Venus 2010*, 99.

50. Jones, "A. K. A. Saartjie," 140. On p. 141, Jones notes that Baartman's remains were formally buried on National Women's Day in South Africa. The museum website seems to have erased their history of display. The same Musée de l'homme currently includes a Paleolithic figurine called the Venus de Lespugue: http://www.museedelhomme.fr/fr/musee/collections/venus-lespugue-3859.

51. Daniels, "Exhibit A," 64.

52. Karen Fields and Barbara J. Fields, *Racecraft: The Soul of Inequality in American Life* (New York: Verso, 2012).

53. Only when analyzing the full Venus spectrum does one understand the potential ambiguity surrounding this designation for the Paleolithic figurine.

54. See Theresa Brown, "An Unflinching Exploration of Trauma and Obesity," *American Journal of Nursing* 118, no. 6 (2018): 67; Craigan Usher, "The Body and the Traumatic Real," *Journal of the American Academy of Child and Adolescent Psychiatry* 57, no. 9 (2018): 703; Tiffany L. Carson, "Heavy Hunger: Managing Weight and Obesity in Black American Communities," *JAMA: The Journal of the American Medical Association* 322, no. 16 (2019): 1534–36; and Ann Jurecic and Daniel Marchalik, "On Obesity: Roxane Gay's *Hunger*," *The Lancet* (British Edition) 390, no. 10102 (2017): 1577.

55. See, for example, this Venus candle: https://otherwild.com/products/copy-of -beeswax-corncob-candler.

56. See examples like Yusef Komunyakaa, "Venus of Willendorf," *The Atlantic*, August 9, 2020 [September 1998], https://www.theatlantic.com/books/archive/2020 /08/poem-yusef-komunyakaa-venus-willendorf/615061, Rita Dove, "The Venus of Willendorf," *Poetry* 161, no. 1 (October 1992): 25, and Irving Penn and Maria Morris Hambourg, *Earthly Bodies: Irving Penn's Nudes, 1949–50* (Boston: Metropolitan Museum of Art in association with Little, Brown and Co., 2002).

57. Dove, "Venus of Willendorf," 25–7.

58. Aimee Dawson, "Facebook Censors Famous 30,000-year-old Nude Statue as Pornographic," *Art Newspaper*, February 27, 2018, https://www.theartnews-paper.com/news/facebook-censors-famous-30-000-year-old-nude-statue-as -pornographic.

59. Gay, *Hunger*, 3.

60. For example, in an interview with *Rolling Stone*, Gay explains that: "Writing about the body is a very vulnerable thing. I just didn't want to do it, but that is what told me this is what I should be writing." Britt Julious, "Roxane Gay: New Memoir Is 'about My Body and the Things That Happened to My Body,'" *Rolling Stone*, June 19, 2017, https://www.rollingstone.com/culture/culture-features/roxane-gay -new-memoir-is-about-my-body-and-the-things-that-happened-to-my-body-204081.

61. Monica Lewinsky, "Roxane Gay on How to Write Trauma," *Vanity Fair*, February 18, 2021, https://www.vanityfair.com/style/2021/02/roxane-gay-on-how-to -write-about-trauma.

62. Gay, *Hunger*, 16.

63. In *Vogue* magazine, Gay explains and explores the issue of stories and ownership: "It's like, please, this is my story, let me have my story, just as you have yours; because I want to hear your story and respect it, but you have to respect mine as well." Janelle Okwodu, "In *Hunger*, Roxane Gay Says What No One Else Will about Being Fat in America," *Vogue*, June 18, 2017, https://www.vogue.com/article/ roxane-gay-interview-hunger-memoir.

64. This act itself leads us to speculate on the difference between the "untruth" of critical fabulation as a contrast with the process of carving out authority over one's own story. Gay demonstrates agency over her own truth, while narratives about Baartman must to a large degree be imposed.

65. Gay, *Hunger*, 6.

66. See our earlier discussion of the way this very occupation of the subject position of the questioner became an unfortunate part of many interviews following the publication of Gay's book.

67. Gay, *Hunger*, 164. And this is of course paradigmatic of the social media public experience in general.

68. See, for example, David Lazar, *Truth in Nonfiction: Essays* (Iowa City: University of Iowa Press, 2008) and J. Alexander Bareis and Lene Nordrum, *How to Make Believe: The Fictional Truths of the Representational Arts* (Berlin: De Gruyter, 2015).

69. Adrienne Green, writing in *The Atlantic*, suggests that Gay relies on "repetitive descriptions of her rape and her brokenness in a way that might in other circumstances seem gratuitous, but which in *Hunger* serves to give readers some emotional insight into the unrelenting nature of trauma. Woven into this repetition is a ruminative preoccupation with strength, in all its varieties." Adrienne Green, "The Boldness of Roxane Gay's *Hunger*," *The Atlantic*, June 13, 2017, https://www.theatlantic.com/entertainment/archive/2017/06/the-boldness-of-roxane-gays-hunger/530067.

70. Gay, *Hunger*, 24.

71. Gay, *Hunger*, 28.

72. For other recent takes on this convergence, see Kate Douglas, *Contesting Childhood: Autobiography, Trauma, and Memory* (New Brunswick, NJ: Rutgers University Press, 2010); Dix Hywel, *Autofiction in English* (Cham, Switzerland: Springer International Publishing, 2018); and Margaret Sönser Breen, *Gender, Sex, and Sexuality* (Ipswich, MA: Salem Press, 2014).

73. Van der Kolk, *The Body Keeps the Score*.

74. Helen Morales, *Antigone Rising: The Subversive Power of the Ancient Myths* (New York: Bold Type Books, 2020), 66.

75. "Dissociation allows the person under attack to avoid experiencing the assault. Our rather stiff medical vocabulary terms this involuntary temporary paralysis tonic immobility. The feeling of leaving one's body and being alienated from it are well documented, as are their longer-lasting effects," Morales, *Antigone Rising*, 69.

76. Morales, *Antigone Rising*, 74–6.

77. Morales, *Antigone Rising*, 72.

78. Gay, *Hunger*, 40.

79. This invokes what Shoshana Felman and Doris Laub would call "testimony"; they assert that "to testify—to *vow to tell*, to *promise* and *produce* one's own speech as material evidence for truth—is to accomplish a speech act . . . [to address] what in history is action that exceeds any substantialized significance." Shoshana Felman and Doris Laub, *Testimony: Crises of Witnessing in Literature, Psychoanalysis, and History* (New York: Routledge, 1991), 5.

80. Gay, *Hunger*, 44.

81. See chapter 2 for our discussion of Chanel Miller's memoir *Know My Name* (New York: Viking, 2019), which also explores the aftermath of sexual assault.

82. Gay, *Hunger*, 36.

83. Gay, *Hunger*, 90–1.

84. Gay, *Hunger*, 5.

85. Gay, *Hunger*, 39.
86. Gay, *Hunger*, 40.
87. Gay, *Hunger*, 41, emphasis added.
88. Gay, *Hunger*, 164.
89. Silence has been previously identified as a tool for feminism. See Kathryn M. Hunter, "Silence in Noisy Archives: Reflections on Judith Allen's 'Evidence and Silence: Feminism and the Limits of History' (1986) in the Era of Mass Digitisation," *Australian Feminist Studies* 32 (91–92, 2017): 202–12; Amy Carrillo Rowe and Sheena Malhotra, *Silence, Feminism, Power: Reflections at the Edges of Sound* (New York: Palgrave Macmillan, 2013); and Vanessa Iwowo and Alessia Contu, "Images of Otherness: Postcolonial Feminism in Subaltern Silence," *Academy of Management Proceedings* 1 (2019): 17716.
90. Gay, *Hunger*, 265.
91. Gay, *Hunger*, 291.
92. We explore this silence more deeply in chapter 3 when we analyze feminist translations of canonical texts, but one connection we'd like to make here is to Anne Carson's translation of Sappho. In her translation, Carson emphasizes blank spaces in Sappho's work. These spaces were not created by Sappho but exist as a result of the archive's evolution through time, where it has lost pieces. Carson elects to render this loss—this silence—as aesthetic choice rather than a passive consequence of history. This active taking up of silence reminds us, in part, of Gay's choice.
93. Statuette of Venus; First century BCE; Material: rock crystal; Museum Number: The Getty Museum 78.AN.248. See Stager, "Unbearable Whiteness"; Patrick R. Crowley, "Crystalline Aesthetics and the Classical Concept of the Medium," *West 86th: A Journal of Decorative Arts, Design History, and Material Culture* 23, no. 2 (Fall–Winter 2016): 237–45.

Figure 2.1 *Two Women Beholding Two Paintings of* Judith Beheading Holofernes *by Artemisia Gentileschi*. In the exhibition Artemisia, organized by Laetitia Treves for the National Gallery of Art, London. 2020. Color Digital Photograph. Courtesy of the Museo di Capodimonte, Naples, the Uffizi Gallery, Florence, and the National Gallery of Art, London.

Chapter 2

Mapping Enclosure and Disclosure

In 2016, one of us was tasked with reviewing a new art book that combined image and text, Susan O'Malley's *Advice from My 80-Year-Old Self*. The difficulty was that the artist had tragically and suddenly died while pregnant the year before the book was published—a fact that was hard to disentangle from the reception of the text, especially given the book's ostensible positivity. "For a moment, let's do what will never be possible again," the review eventually began. "Let's look at [the book] outside of the tragic loss that has become its context."[1]

That same challenge—the entanglement of work and life (and its many variants)—is at the heart of this chapter. While in chapter 1 we examined the role of the archive in shaping the experience of women more generally, this chapter explores the way that archive for women tends toward a focus on the private details of personal lives rather than the public details of production and work. We ask what such focus means for women when they try to set boundaries around their bodies or their work while also noting that sometimes the process of setting boundaries may include curating the transmission of personal details.[2]

Although we do not wish to suggest that work and life—the "public" and the "private"—are, in the end, truly divisible, we nevertheless highlight the specific ways in which women's stories (and often the aspects of which most lend themselves to display, the most personal and intimate) become, due to the operations of spectacle and the foregrounding of the public body in culture investigated in chapter 1, a substitute focus for women's professional or creative contributions. "Reading" a work exclusively through a frame of biography or spectacle can distract from the other important contributions that work might wish to make.

And yet, if we excise biography, we also excise the human producers of works of art in various media—the writers, poets, painters, dancers, and so on—and the necessary entanglements of their lived experiences with their artistic production. In some ways, this is the work of formalism, a drive to focus on what is contained within a work—the turn of phrase or stroke of paint—so much as to emphasize those forms at the expense of their human producers and historical contexts. This approach has been understood as responding to an earlier dependence on biography to shape interpretation.[3] But these boundaries between formalism and biography are not actually so fixed. In considering the formalism of modern art, Aruna D'Souza asks:

> How is it that Modernism—an interpretive approach to art that purportedly considers *only* the analysis of an internally driven development of pure form in its discussions—has created so many artist-heroes, mythified geniuses who populate the field of twentieth-century art? (emphasis in original)

and concludes that the relationship between formalism and biography constitutes "the hidden biography of Modernism."[4] In the end, neither approach—biography or formalism—is, to us, sufficient to capture the complexity of the work-life dynamic, a dynamic we explore in this chapter as we chart the relationship between private and public through the lens of public feminism.

To do so, we begin with the life and work of seventeenth-century painter Artemisia Gentileschi, whose violent rape and the subsequent refraction of her work through a biographical frame have shaped her reception for centuries both through the silence around and the misattribution of her work following her death and her rediscovery in the twentieth century.[5] The feminist reception of Artemisia's work and life illuminates the complexities surrounding biography, self-fashioning, and disclosure. Later artists and writers addressed this problem directly through the practice of overlay, a process of placing a new filter over what was previously understood to be objective in order to claim their own stories. This practice undergirds feminist mapping, a specific use of overlay that foregrounds artists' and writers' subject positions even as it protests the imposition of biography as well as implicitly critiques it. Surveying work that overlays subjective experience onto delineations of space in forms of "mapping" helps us understand one aspect of the #MeToo movement: its cartographic framework. Examining #MeToo as a cartographic system of disclosure illuminates one of public feminism's central challenges: how to protest violence and oppression while controlling which private details to reveal. Understanding the map as a possible tool of connection and community across difference allows us to see mapmaking as a tool of liberation public feminists can use to rethink the entanglement of the private with the public.

BETWEEN PUBLIC AND PRIVATE

The exhibition *Artemisia* (December 2–January 24, 2021) organized by the National Gallery in London around the paintings of the eponymous Artemisia Gentileschi emphasized the history of Artemisia's rape by another painter when she was seventeen (Fig. 2.1).[6] Like the review of Susan O'Malley, the exhibit seems to have been intentionally designed to put the famous story of Artemisia's rape out front in order to move beyond it. The curator Laetitia Treves explains that Artemisia is "someone whose life story has somewhat overshadowed her art . . . the story of her rape has in many ways defined the ways in which art historians have talked about her for many many years now."[7] Such spectacle overtakes the important work Artemisia produced and marks a paradox also navigated by #MeToo, discussed later in this chapter: how to break the silence and speak such stories without letting them *become* the story.

Artemisia worked as a painter in seventeenth-century Italy (1593–1656). Her father, Orazio Gentileschi, was a well-known painter in the circle of Caravaggio who trained his four children to be painters. That Artemisia was trained as a painter despite her gender was possible because her father supported her training—which is also to say that her access remained tied to patriarchy. One might understand the National Gallery's choice to name their exhibition using solely Artemisia's first name as simultaneously an attempt to differentiate between the two Gentileschis (indeed much of Artemisia's work was initially attributed to her father Orazio, and she sometimes used a family name of Lomi), to elevate Artemisia to the single-named artist tradition in the Italian Renaissance that included Leonardo and Michelangelo, and to gesture to the single-named celebrity that Artemisia has more recently achieved (as in Beyoncé, Madonna, Rihanna, or Adele).[8] We have opted to perpetuate this single first-name celebrity in this chapter while recognizing the vexed position of choosing to be on a first-name basis with a historical figure (which also raises the gendered question of familiarity and titles, whereby women are much more likely to be called by their first names in professional contexts in which their male counterparts are deferred to by titles).[9]

When a fellow painter raped Artemisia, promised marriage, and then reneged, her father went to court not to jail his daughter's rapist for his crimes against her but to contest the reduction in her value that the rape had sustained.[10] Perhaps Orazio sought only vengeance for Artemisia, but legally that vengeance was achieved by pointing out the way she had been devalued as a familial asset.[11] Orazio's eventual victory in the case hinged on the finding that her value had, in fact, been decreased by the rape. The transcription of the rape trial is the first written record of Artemisia's words and demonstrates how her archive builds up around the violence she experienced.[12]

GENDER AND REPRESENTATION

While we have argued that biography clings to women in ways that differ from the operations of biography attached to men, this different treatment is compounded by the comparatively few names of women artists that reach us in modernity.[13] This problem reflects both the greater difficulty that women had in pursuing such artistic training and careers as well as the limitations of their reception in the archive. To address this structural problem of fewer names populating received histories, art historian Linda Nochlin wrote the groundbreaking "Why Have There Been No Great Women Artists?" (1971), an essay in which she critiqued the very basis for the question. Few names of women painters come to us from this period or most other periods of art history. Finding "hidden women" whose work might be elevated alongside men does not, Nochlin argued, resolve the structural problem, which results from a codified set of expectations that privileges patriarchal values. Nochlin cited (then) recent work on Artemisia Gentileschi among her examples of scholarship organized around adding women to the status quo.[14] She concluded: "Hopefully, by stressing the *institutional*—i.e. the public—rather than the *individual*, or private, preconditions for achievement or the lack of it in the arts, we have provided a paradigm for the investigation of other areas in the field" (emphases in original).[15] The structure that Nochlin seeks to dismantle is one organized around the individual genius artist whose name is recorded in connection with attention to their work.

Even when women are recorded and received through traditional art historical means, their work may not secure the same treatment as the work of male artists. For example, critic Jillian Steinheuer recently drew attention to the impact of age in the reception of women artists, opening her essay "Old Women" with the lines: "The best way to succeed as a woman artist is to be old. Not necessarily dead yet, but with the specter of death hanging over you."[16] Documenting the phenomenon by which working women artists may be safely discovered in their old age, Steinheuer suggests that there is little risk to investing in someone who has already produced decades of work and can thus be discovered, in some ways, already formed. Steinheuer goes on to capture the devastating response by these older artists to receiving their long-delayed dues, including gratitude that they will now be able to pay for home caregivers, for example, or the inability to know that their retrospective is happening due to memory loss.

Nor can women's work and its reception be collapsed into a uniform practice and reception. Steinheuer invokes the way surfacing the aging female body, as in Alice Neel's naked self-portrait at eighty, can still be experienced as a radical act due to the taboos around women's aging. Steinheuer also contrasts Neel's visual choices as a white woman, in many ways similar to Artemisia's self-portraits without clothes, to those of Black artist Emma Amos, who borrows the naked white body of Lucien Freud, twenty years her senior, from his 1993 self-portrait for her own painting done in 1994, "Work Suit." In Amos's painting, she wears Freud's naked body and her own face and stands, paintbrush at the ready, over a painting of a naked white woman. Amos, Steinheuer emphasizes, paints the differences in the way her own racialized body and body of work have been received in contrast to that of Freud, who at one time commanded the highest price of any living artist at auction and whom curators honored with a retrospective when he was still young enough to experience it with health and memories intact.[17]

These issues have become the focus of protest, including by the feminist collective Guerilla Girls, formed in the 1980s.[18] Anonymous and each wearing a rubber gorilla mask, the members of the collective, through their anonymity, explicitly reject the tyranny of individual biography undergirding value.[19] The collective drew on the trope of the female nude in the Venus tradition as discussed in chapter 1 for what became their iconic poster first released in 1985.[20] On it, a naked white woman wearing their eponymous gorilla mask reclines on a magenta coverlet against a bright yellow backdrop. Black text across the right side of the image asks: "Do women have to be naked to get into the Metropolitan Museum?" Below that, text (in mostly black with contrasting hot pink for statistics and the keywords "artists" and "nudes") reads: "Less than 5% of the artists in the Modern art wing are women, but 85% of the nudes are female."[21] That poster has been translated into Spanish and its statistics modified to critique other institutions. And these structures persist today, as the artist Mickalene Thomas recently emphasized in response to data about contemporary women artists: "It's like we're crabs: if one or two of us gets out of the bucket, it feels so exciting. . . . But what are we cheering? We should be protesting! . . . We got so settled after a little bit of growth instead of getting infuriated about the fact that it has not really changed."[22] The Guerilla Girls collective has remained active, as has the problem of disproportionate representation of male artists.

Alice Walker asks a different question about the structures governing artistic production in the context of the transatlantic slave trade in the 1972 essay that became the titular piece in her 1983 essay collection *In Search of Our Mother's Gardens: Womanist Prose*, a book that continues to shape scholarship.[23] For example, historian Martha Jones begins her book on Black women's fight for the right to vote by alluding to Walker's work with an introduction titled "Our Mother's Gardens," wherein she finds inspiration in the way Walker "went in search of how [Black women] survived and thrived in a world not always of their making."[24] Indeed, Walker requests that her readers imagine what happens when an artist does not even own herself:

> Did you have a genius of a great-great-grandmother who died under some ignorant and depraved white overseer's lash? Or was she required to bake biscuits for a lazy backwater tramp, when she cried out in her soul to paint watercolors of sunsets, or the rain falling on the green and peaceful pasture-lands? Or was her body broken and forced to bear children (who were more often than not sold away from her)—eight, ten, fifteen, twenty children—when her one joy was the thought of modeling heroic figures of rebellion, in stone or clay?[25]

Kaitlyn Greenidge continues this conversation about lost geniuses and artists in her 2016 opinion piece "My Mother's Garden," in which she extends Walker's argument into the paradox of contemporary poverty. Greenidge narrates how her mother plants a garden in an unused corner of the parking lot of the public housing unit where her family resides. This garden attracts the other children living in the same complex to tend and play yet eventually is deemed illegal by the complex's administrator. The administrator then orders the garden to be intentionally poisoned by the maintenance staff, a metaphor for the imprisoning system of public housing. When Greenidge's mother elects to go back to school so that she can eventually find a way to secure the resources to move away, the rules of the project prohibit her from retaining her family's housing while she is a student. The only way out is to lie, despite Greenidge's description of her mother as radically honest:

> It was an impossible choice: Obey the housing project's rules, don't go back to school, certain that path would mean no upward mobility and thus, no way to leave public housing. Or break the rules, work quiet and quick and hard, hoping the path she hacked in secret would allow some sort of escape.[26]

As Greenidge shows, such systems are designed to restrict escape and perpetuate exclusion and silence. And yet somehow all these narratives, from Nochlin to Walker to Greenidge, demonstrate the paradox of continued production and contribution by women despite the oppressive systems they are trapped within.

Mapping the history of women's creativity becomes challenging when approached from deep within our racist, patriarchal, and oppressive culture and history—and Artemisia's story is no exception. In the decades since

Nochlin's essay, Artemisia has remained a subject of art historical inquiry and museum exhibition. Over the past five years, she has also emerged as a rallying point for public feminism and a place where these questions converge.[27] Specifically, Nochlin's essay included a reproduction of a painting by Artemisia: *Judith Beheading Holofernes* (1614–1620). Nochlin's caption reads: "A banner for Women's Lib could be Artemisia Gentileschi's *Judith Beheading Holofernes*, one of this Roman painter's favorite subjects."[28] Indeed, this painting, of which Artemisia made at least two versions, *has* emerged as a banner for public feminism (a term different from but connected to the "Women's Lib" of Nochlin's second-wave feminist moment).

JUDITH BEHEADING HOLOFERNES

Writers and artists have engaged with the reception of Judith's story since as early as the fifth century CE. Propelled by feminist art histories and literary critical approaches to the biblical texts, this cross-disciplinarity emerged in the twentieth century as its own field of "Judith Studies."[29] For instance, using the example of Judith and the painting by Francesco Maffei of Judith carrying a sword and Holofernes's head in a bowl, art historian Erwin Panofsky analyzed different ways in which texts and art objects tell similar stories in order to introduce his theory of iconology.[30] Additionally, as far back as the twelfth century CE, many early modern male artists took up the subject, which became a workshop staple and a visual paradigm of overcoming tyranny.[31] Artemisia's father himself painted four versions. However, the approach of male artists diverges from that of Artemisia. Artists including Botticelli, Caravaggio, and Mantegna painted an almost dispassionate Judith; Artemisia takes us deep into the embodied experience of Judith's (and her maid Abra's) violent act.

The painting, done in rich jewel tones, depicts a story from the Book of Judith (Septuagint) in which the Jewish heroine Judith and her servant Abra behead the fictional Assyrian general Holofernes, who has cut off the water supply to their village Bethulia, in order to liberate her people.[32] According to the tradition, Judith seeks out Holofernes in his tent, seduces him, encourages him to drink to excess, and then, with Abra's assistance, severs his head from his body with a sword. Artemisia painted two different versions of *Judith Beheading Holofernes* (Fig. 2.1). One, now in the collection of the Museo e gallerie nazionali di Capodimonte, she painted roughly concurrently with the rape trial (*ca.* 1612–1613). This is the version that Nochlin selected to illustrate her essay. In it, Judith, dressed in a blue gown with the sleeves pushed up, leans into the thrust of her sword, which pierces Holofernes's neck as she pulls herself away from his body. Her left hand holds Holofernes's head back by his hair to expose his neck to her sword, the gold hilt of which picks up the gold embroidery threading through her dress. Her arms are stretched long, as though she seeks both the force to land her blow and the ability to maintain as much distance from his body as possible while doing so. Holofernes reaches up with his right hand to grab the bodice of Abra's red gown. Abra, whose help is required but whose name is not included in the painting's title, looks straight down at him and seems to lean into his body to keep him pinned for Artemisia's blade. Holofernes's blood runs in rivulets from beneath his body along the white sheets of his bed, trailing into the tuck of the sheet around the mattress and down toward the floor. In this painting, both women appear determined and fairly composed as they execute their enemy, remaining unstained by Holofernes's blood. The bloody sheets mark the success of Judith and Abra's execution of Holofernes, an act that protects both them and their village from the violence of rape that would likely have accompanied their enslavement by the Assyrian general had they not acted.

Artemisia's second version of *Judith Beheading Holofernes*, painted in 1620 and now in the collection of the Uffizi in Florence, tells the story somewhat differently.[33] In this second version, Judith wears a deep mustard yellow dress with red cuffs pushed up her arms to free them for her work. Artemisia has altered Judith's serene concentration in the earlier version to show her brows furrowed with the effort that a beheading demands. Judith again grasps Holofernes by the hair with her left hand to expose his neck to her sword, which she brings down with her right hand. She again keeps both arms straight to keep as much distance as she can between her torso and his, but in this version, Judith has also brought her right thigh across Holofernes's body to hold him down. Abra again presses him to the mattress with both hands and Holofernes again grabs the bodice of her gown, now blue. While rivulets of blood again run from beneath Holofernes's body and Judith's blade, blood also sprays from his neck where she stabs him, arcing across the canvas, her yellow gown, and Judith's and Abra's forearms as they restrain Holofernes. The golden hilt of the sword catches the yellow of Judith's gown and its iron blade pierces straight through Holofernes's neck, exiting along the mattress trailed by blood. A red velvet coverlet crosses Holofernes's body, echoing the bands of red at the arms of both women's sleeves and the spray of red from his neck.

This second version, painted after Artemisia had lived with the reverberations of the rape and public trial and after she left her native city, Rome, for Florence, is bloodier and much more visceral than the first. Some of its power comes from its far greater attention to the physical intensity of the beheading it depicts and its refusal of the more comfortable decorum of most depictions of this story. We do not wish to suggest that this intensity was shaped directly by any specific experience in Artemisia's life, yet we nevertheless believe that many factors in her life contributed to her artistic perspective. Rather than adjudicate the particulars of how or to what extent Artemisia's rape impacted her work or accepting the reductionist terms on which women's biographies often enclose their work, we seek, instead, to foreground the ways in which Artemisia herself sought to control her biography, her painting, and her reception—and the complexities this poses in modernity.

Throughout her practice, Artemisia blurred the boundaries between her own biography and her subject's mythology, including in her depictions of Judith. These autobiographical infusions do not, however, create a one-to-one correlation, either for Artemisia as a painter or for historians analyzing her work. Additionally, pursuing a reductionist mapping of Artemisia's story onto and into her paintings of Judith leaves no room for another figure in the scene—that of Judith's servant and assistant, Abra, for whom Artemisia's biography offers no historical counterpart. This effectively erases Abra from the reception of Artemisia's Judiths: she becomes merely the unnamed "maidservant." Although Abra is a mythological rather than a historical figure, her erasure and invisibility point to the layers of class that inflect women's visibility in the archive. At the same time, Judith's and Artemisia's stories emphasize that class alone does not protect women from sexual violence, gratuitous biographical frames, or archival erasure.

The biblical tradition records Abra's name, but in the visual reception of the Judith story, Abra's name drops out. She is, therefore, and by virtue of her class position, unnamed—despite her centrality to visual representations of the beheading.[34] Abra partners with Judith in this liberation, but art and history work to erase her from Judith's victory. In this exclusion, we see a microcosm of challenges faced by feminist movements more broadly. Abra's effacement in the context of the Judith tradition participates in the elevation of single heroines (in this case, Judith) that too often reinscribes patriarchal hero narratives as our default expectation from narrative more broadly. Indeed, Artemisia's own singular elevation threatens to enact a similar conformity, despite the undeniable challenges she faced. Failure to integrate differential class positions into feminist interventions has been—and remains—deeply divisive.

CONCEPTUALIZING RAPE

Decades after Panofsky, Nochlin also came to Judith's story through the specific work of Artemisia. In parallel to male artists' more decorous versions of the Judith story, Nochlin deemphasizes the rape and its embodiment in Artemisia's formal practice. Characterizing the rape as "the scandal of her alleged promiscuous relations with her teacher," she selects Artemisia's first, more serene version of *Judith Beheading Holofernes* to illustrate her essay.[35]

This glossing of rape as scandal and labeling of its victim as promiscuous have a long and storied history, one written into our archives, pedagogy, and feminisms. Cynthia Colburn and Ella Gonzalez have, for example, tackled the contentious practice of naming depictions of rapes in ancient Greek and Roman art where power structures entirely favored the rapists, who were often also gods, in their essay "How to Teach Ancient Art in the Age of #MeToo."[36] This practice continues to the present, reproducing violence. When we don't name rape, we risk teaching our readers and students that maybe it didn't really happen. However, dynamics around naming rape are evolving, as demonstrated by more recent work on Artemisia, including the National Gallery show that does not hesitate to name her rape.

In its reception, the rhetorical question of Nochlin's essay's title has been misinterpreted as a straightforward call to expand the canon by including more women artists. Some have taken her inclusion of Artemisia's first Judith as a directive to solve the problem of the dearth of celebrated women painters with Artemisia's work specifically. For example, the catalog accompanying the recent display of Artemisia's second, more visceral *Judith* at The Art Institute of Chicago opens with the following words from the director:

> Over the past forty years—ever since Linda Nochlin's groundbreaking 1971 essay . . .—scholars have strived to integrate women artists into the history of art and culture. As a result of this attention, Artemisia Gentileschi has emerged in the past decade as one of the most celebrated and studied of seventeenth-century artists.[37]

The director misunderstood Nochlin's essay to call for more exhibition of Artemisia's work on the grounds of her gender when, in fact, she had demanded a complete overhaul of precisely the disciplinary structures that had and continue to elevate Artemisia as a token woman artist. The justification for staging the show is therefore antithetical to Nochlin's argument, despite the fact that it uses her essay as a starting point for its development and presents its exhibition as an answer to her rhetorical question. Nochlin herself did not argue that a bumper crop of Artemisia studies changed the structures by which women artists have long been excluded.

The National Gallery anchored its exhibition with the second, bloodier version of Artemisia's *Judith Beholding Holofernes* and took a very different approach to the rape, trial, and aftermath that shaped Artemisia's production of this painting. The trial itself revictimized Artemisia, first by requiring that she face her rapist in the courtroom while she recounted the rape and next by forcing her to endure finger torture on the stand to assess her honesty. The testimony included a midwife who recounted her manual examination of Artemisia's vagina to determine that her hymen had been broken. In capturing such details, the records continue to revictimize and trigger readers even today.

Artemisia's paintings and her biography, especially the horrific account of her rape and the retraumatization of its legal aftermath, have been deeply entwined in accounts of her work. The National Gallery chose to address Artemisia's rape very directly: the curatorial team, led by Laetitia Treves, produced a 3.5-minute video, "Artemisia's rape trial," in which actor Ellice Stevens travels the map of Artemisia's biography—Rome, Florence, Naples, London—and traces the archive of Artemisia's rape in vivid detail.[38] Stevens stands in for Artemisia Gentileschi in the present, revisiting elements of Artemisia's biography and lived experience as well as recovering agency for the artist.

Stevens's appearance in these videos draws on her earlier performance as Artemisia in the play "It's true, it's true, it's true!" that premiered in 2018. Women perform all roles in the play, including those of male characters. The script employs the archived language of the Latin and Italian transcript of the trial to produce a "semi-verbatim courtroom drama of a seventeenth-century rape trial."[39] The reworking of the transcript fits within a larger pattern in the twenty-first century in which artists engage with the language of legal documents.[40] In the case of "It's true, it's true, it's true!" the director describes the play as a statement of solidarity with survivors of sexual assault and recounts that

> it was made over the summer of 2018, which was kind of the peak of what became known as the #MeToo movement and we were very much deliberately engaging with that, through this historical material, through the 17th century court documents and what we found is that so many of the tactics that were being used in the court to discredit Gentileschi and so much of the sort of discourse around her situation was being mirrored in real time in the press with some high-profile cases.[41]

This reaching across time to meet the present moment in an act of public feminism very much parallels the larger project of this book. Emphasizing this connection with the politics of the present, Artemisia and her rapist in the performance mime intercourse from opposite sides of the stage while a narrator recounts the many other men with whom the rapist counter-accuses Artemisia of having had sex.

In the exhibition video, Stevens visits the archivist in Rome who cares for the text that documents the account of the trial. Together they read the passage in which Artemisia is tortured on the stand and quoted as saying "A vero, a vero, a vero" (It's true! It's true! It's true!) as Stevens begins to cry. This moment in the video evokes Stevens' performance in the earlier play, during which she faced the audience in her taupe underwear splattered with gold jouissance and extended her palm for emphasis as she repeated those same words.[42] Next, the archivist in Rome pats Stevens on the shoulder and says to the actor "You are there. You are Artemisia now." This exemplary moment— whether between an actor and history or between a woman and the public who witnesses her accusation of rape—collapses boundaries and identities, but it also always has the capacity to spin in multiple directions, which may be why the issue of disclosure and boundaries is such a challenging one for women in general. Artemisia's ongoing reception demonstrates the process by which figures from the past can become focal points for contemporary feminist inter- vention, excavations of past experiences that help us better see the present.

THE PROBLEM OF BIOGRAPHY

To the extant *Natural History* written by the Roman author Pliny the Elder, we owe the names of over 350 ancient Greek and Roman artists. Although most of the artists whom Pliny names are men, several are women, including the portraitist Iaia of Cyzicus (first century BCE), credited with developing a practice of self-portraiture using mirrors and narrated by her male biog- raphers as a "perpetual virgin."[43] These twin tropes of the woman artist—a virgin and someone who uses a mirror to paint a self-portrait—emerge at least as early as Pliny's account and persist deep into the early modern period when Italian writers, drawing on the classical tradition and on Pliny in par- ticular, reproduced it. While mirrors emerged in the early modern period as symbols of naturalistic painting (the mirror of nature) and as universal objects of vanity (reflecting not the spiritual but the material world), in the context of women painters, they also construct ideas about feminine vanity.[44] Male artists also used mirrors for self-portraiture, but painting the self by means of a mirror reinforced this biographical emphasis on the woman artist's virginity not only through the deployment of a woman's object (the mirror) but also because its use precluded any involvement of another subject (artist or model) to produce the painting.[45] The self-portrait, like the virgin, thus maintains the boundaries of the body's purity.

In the early modern period, Giorgio Vasari wrote his deeply influential *Lives of the Most Excellent Painters, Sculptors, and Architects* (1550), which shaped the history of art's early focus on the triumvirate of these media and mentioned only a few women alongside hundreds of male artists.[46] Although he celebrates the great skill of the women he does name and situates them within a lineage of women artists from Greek and Roman antiquity, this praise does not offset their rarity. The mirror-wielding virgin persists as a trope in Vasari's descriptions of the few women artists on his pages. Subsequent art historical writers drew on Vasari's model, itself inflected by Pliny.

This biographical tradition, which Pliny and later art historians embraced, established the trope of the female artist to such a formulaic degree that Artemisia seems to have drawn upon this model in crafting her own biography.[47] Artemisia rewrote her biography in an effort to disentangle her own story from her father's, although both he and she drew on the esteem and market demand accorded to Caravaggio and his circle. As Sheila Barker recounts in the catalog of the National Gallery's Artemisia exhibition:

> A recently discovered biography written by Cristofano Bronzini (1580–1633) when Artemisia was in her twenties demonstrates that she took a proactive role in molding her public image, by feeding her biographer fabricated stories that accorded with rigid codes of feminine conduct and her society's mytho-heroic ideal of the artist.[48]

Bronzini's account omits any mention of the rape trial and fabricates elements of Artemisia's biography in order to conform to the narrative models of male artists while also mobilizing the self-proclaimed virginity of other women artists.[49] In Barker's analysis, Artemisia crafted her public image as well as Bronzini's early written account of it in part of what she describes as Artemisia's "campaign for visibility."[50] This analysis of Bronzini's biography of Artemisia suggests that as Artemisia sought to live life on her own terms within the confines of seventeenth-century Italian culture, she also crafted a narrative that conformed to the centuries-old model of the cloistered perpetual virgin, cementing control over the public versions of herself through redrafting her biography.

Artemisia's staging worked as a tool of self-promotion—and it also served to write for herself an artistic genealogy that excluded her father. In patriarchal systems, fathers often have a paradoxical role. Ostensibly they are given the power to protect their daughters, but through their interpellation as male citizens, they are also called to replicate harmful structural dynamics.[51] Given Artemisia's own loss of her mother at a young age, her substitution of the church mother, the abbess, in her artistic genealogy takes on a particularly matriarchal valence in response to her upbringing: "Much in the same way that [the convent story] situates Artemisia's artistic origins within a feminine, even matriarchal, matrix, the fictitious biography emphatically demonstrates that the Caravaggesque impulse in her art was the result of a woman's intervention, not her father's."[52] Artemisia's capacity to train as an artist depended on her own father's career as a painter as well as his permission and investment in her education, yet she rescripts her biography to edit out her father's role, a revision that takes on additional pathos when we consider that many of Artemisia's works were attributed to her father for centuries.[53] It is also worth noting in this context that Artemisia chooses to paint Judith, a story from a set of biblical texts considered by some to be apocrypha, while at the same time, in the material she seems to have fed Bronzini, she stages her own apocryphal biography. Elements of her biography staged for Bronzini—a stint in a convent, a proclivity with embroidery that drew the abbess' attention, her study from Caravaggio's work supplied by the abbess—not only laundered her reputation in the wake of the rape trial but also bypassed her father in her painterly relationship to Caravaggio.[54]

When women artists have been included in art historical explorations, their biographies and often their relationships with powerful men have shaped the discussion of their practices. This perpetuation of the biographical for women artists long after it had ceased to be the dominant paradigm within art histories that had prioritized social histories and cultural contexts was perhaps motivated by a bias that suggested women's work could not be recognized outside of the artist's subject position.[55] It is from this position of biography clinging to women artists that Artemisia's story has propelled her to recognition. While Artemisia, as Barker analyzes, sought to fashion her own biography in her lifetime, this self-fashioning contradicts the archival record of the rape. It was this archival documentation that feminist scholars returned to in the twentieth century, debating how to fit together the violent spectacle of this archive and Artemisia's painting in an ethical manner. Museums took on the mantle of these debates as they considered how to exhibit Artemisia's work and biography. Over time, other artists produced their own responses as well.

Repeated erasures of women of color and especially of Black women from waves of white feminism form part of the reception of Artemisia's Judiths and the subject of a 2022 exhibition at the Frick Pittsburgh, *SLAY: Artemisia Gentileschi and Kehinde Wiley* (April 16, 2022–July 10, 2022). This exhibition pairs Artemisia's Judith from the Capodimonte with Kehinde Wiley's *Judith and Holofernes* (2012).[56] Wiley, an artist to whom we return in chapter 6, painted Treisha Lowe, a Black woman based in Brooklyn, as Judith. Wiley's Judith stands alone in a blue Givenchy strapless gown, holding a severed white head by its long brown ponytail in her left hand and a sword in her right.[57] Through his painting, Wiley intervenes in the historically white feminist movement that rose up around Artemisia's Judiths, inviting beholders to consider the intersections of gender-based and racialized violence. By removing Abra from his version and thereby showing his Judith as figure acting alone, Wiley also puts additional pressure on the class politics of Artemisia's version.

In very recent years, building from these exhibitions and others, Artemisia's Judith has re-emerged in the internet age as a feminist icon precisely because of the sexual violence that Artemisia survived. Women wear stickers of Artemisia's work as a coded way to mark traumatic experiences, turning Artemisia's Judith into an icon of the #MeToo movement. Artemisia continues to be propelled into spaces of public feminism by these new engagements with her work and her biography, the boundaries of which remain vexed.

CONFRONTING THE PARADOX OF AUTOBIOGRAPHY

A technique some women artists and authors have used to confront the paradox of biography has been to overlay the personal on top of the "objective" or "neutral" (we place these terms in quotation marks to indicate that they are actually only objective in that they represent a socially agreed-upon delusion of objectivity). The word "overlay" refers to the process of setting one thing on top of something else, and it is used to describe techniques in both art and literature (for example, the Cambridge dictionary connects the word to the practice of adding a quality that changes the original object, as in: "Her new novel is overlaid with political concerns").[58] By foregrounding their own subject positions (a topic we investigate in chapter 3 on feminist translation), writers and artists can defend themselves against the imposition of that subject position and, in effect, marshal an implicit critique.

We are particularly interested in overlay in connection with feminist mapping, a practice by which a document or object previously received as objective (like a map of a location) can be overlaid with something personal and subjective. We view neither the map nor the personal as "objective" and instead employ a subjective understanding of feminist mapping that draws on approaches from cartographic theory. Such theories reject an empiricist understanding of maps as factual statements in favor of a critical understanding of maps as texts and cartography itself as idealization.[59] Through the process of overlay, feminist maps "read" their map texts while also filtering those texts through the overtly subjective. This overlay thereby changes the quality of the map, claiming, in some sense, its territory. At the same time, the purportedly neutral elements of the original map work to circumvent any weaponization of the personal. By placing the curated aspects of the personal in the public space of the map, they become, by association, validated. This process parallels the claiming of an archive (see, for example, our analysis of Roxane Gay's claiming of her story in *Hunger* in chapter 1) but moves into the realm of spatial relationships while still maintaining the possibility of silence—which, on a map, can be figured as emptiness or blankness. As we explore such relationships, we move between actual cartography and the metaphor of mapping to examine some of what feminist overlay mapping can do in the face of the imposition of the biographical. Such mapping can reveal connected subjectivities, and its spatial elements can track networks of relationships that allow a reader or viewer to understand both space and connections themselves in new and powerful ways.

In the twentieth century and beyond, examples of feminist mapping take a variety of forms, some relatively abstract. For example, in *Autobiography, 1964–Present*, Alison Pebworth connects her own life history to the intellectual and creative material that shaped, inspired, and coexisted with her own development as an artist. As an artist-in-residence with Recology (the recycling and trash collection company serving the San Francisco Bay Area), Pebworth foraged in the city's dump for objects from which to craft her autobiographical installation and her poetics of reuse. (We return to the idea of the trash dump and how one preserved Sappho's poetic fragments in chapter 4.) As one component of her installation, Pebworth created a bookshelf from a vintage wheelchair and on it arranged an autobiographical collection of books that had been discarded by city residents. It was not the contents of each book that produced her autobiography but their respective topics and publication years—each book both indexed that year and directedly addressed that life in some way. Among her selections were *The Gay Cookbook* (1965), *Women's Mysteries, The Power of Feminist Art* (1994), and Rebecca Solnit's *Infinite City* (2010), to which Pebworth contributed a number of images. The collection of books, regularly charting years, also plays with the idea of completion (as does "present" in the overall title of the exhibit, *Autobiography, 1964– Present*). Pebworth's piece appears to be a full capture, one book for every year, yet contains within it an interrogation of the very idea of what counts as finished. As Pebworth is still alive, more years are being added to her life without books being added to the display; the work thus interrogates the drive to collect "complete works" (for example, posthumously, as in the troubled example of Shakespeare's First Folio). Pebworth's work thereby trades on the illusion that the private story is fully known to create a "finished" version of the public story. Yet that public story, by its very nature, implies gaps, allowing Pebworth's work to participate in the system of linking women artists to biography while simultaneously critiquing it.

Pebworth's books, as discarded texts of her city, also create an overlay map arising from their origin. Ultimately, it is only possible for Pebworth to index her life because people within geographic proximity had discarded books, allowing her to connect her own experience with those of others as reflected in the reading material they had thrown out. Like the concept of negative exposure (in this case, where residents had discarded what no longer represented them), this connection allows Pebworth to situate herself in a larger geographical context. But if the project does shape a map, it is one that can be read on various levels, including the topographical—in that it captures a pattern of distribution that represents a larger city—and the subjective, as it is a type of mapping that centers on one person's individual experience. Finally, as a possible map, Pebworth's project does the work of "claiming" that maps often do, saying "this territory is mine" in a gesture of self-fashioning that mirrors that of Artemisia. While Pebworth lacks the civic power that the imperialist project of mapping suggests, she can publicly claim a version of the city as central to her own private identity in her overlay map. Likewise public feminists, we suggest, can use overlay maps to establish boundaries, whether around their biographical details or their bodies. They can also rethink maps to reimagine geographic and ideological space in feminist terms. This system of mapping and these dynamics of public and private will be central concerns for the remainder of this chapter.

Mapping onto the body itself can also be a way of demonstrating resistance to violations of its boundaries, whether through sexual assault or through public attention to the private details of one's life. As an example, we offer Chanel Miller's reclaiming of her own bodily autonomy by color-coding her nail polish to match her colored highlighting of the court documents of her case. Miller's sexual assault by a Stanford undergraduate student in 2015 and the subsequent trial in 2016 were widely publicized during those years and beyond. For most of that time, Miller was identified as Emily Doe to protect her identity. Her moving impact statement at the close of the trial, which some have argued participated in laying the foundation for the subsequent #MeToo movement we narrate at the end of this chapter, eventually evolved into her 2019 memoir, *Know My Name*. In her memoir, Miller publicly identifies herself as Emily Doe and thereby claims her experience.[60] During a public reading from the memoir (hosted in partnership between San Francisco Public Library, which selected the book as its "One City One Book" pick for 2021, and City College of San Francisco on March 16, 2021), Miller displayed blue and yellow nail polish.[61] Here is a reflection one of our students wrote about this choice:

> I noticed Ms. Miller's finger-nail polish colors: blue and yellow. She said when she re-read the transcripts from the trial, People v. Turner, that she had highlighted the defense's side in blue, hers in yellow. Much of what the defense side claimed about her, she said, was questionable at best or patently false. Because she had essentially color-coded the entire text, the lines of yellow that shone within the blue were like rays of hope. As an artist, the visual impacted her sense of not being washed away in a sea of blue. I thought this was a powerful maneuver.[62]

After the boundaries of her body were transgressed in her sexual assault, Miller reclaimed her body by marking it in parallel to the marks she made on the court documents. And after the boundaries of her truth were transgressed by the false accusations of the defense, Miller reclaimed her truth by high-lighting the true sections with the classic highlight color, yellow, allowing the truth to pop in contrast to the blue. Miller reframed both violations by map-ping their truths and lies onto her own body, a practice of overlay that thereby claimed her body in the same way that announcing her name claimed her story. This process of claiming and reclaiming through marking and overlay mapping is one tool that can be used powerfully by public feminists.

Feminist mapping can also be located in printed texts, which we here investigate in the context of a published overlay atlas, *Infinite Cities*.[63] As previously mentioned, Pebworth contributed to Rebecca Solnit's trio of atlases (released together in 2019, these volumes map San Francisco, New Orleans, and New York spatially as well as ideologically, although the San Francisco stand-alone version was first published in 2010) as one of the illustrators; Pebworth chose to draw on that collaboration in her bookshelf exhibit.[64] For Solnit's original San Francisco book, Pebworth contributed illustrations for the title and half-title page as well as a new version of a map she had created prior to collaborating with Solnit on *Infinite City*. Pebworth's earlier solo map, "Phantom Coast," is more directly spatial than any Solnit prints in her own volume, yet it is also untraditional.[65] In it, Pebworth captured in paint the progression of time that led to the evolution of San Francisco's Third Street coast. Capturing several distinct periods (coastal tribes, 4000 BCE–1776; Spanish expeditions, 1769–1775; Colonization, 1776–1821; Mexican rancho era, 1821–1849; and American conquest, 1845–1851), Pebworth overlaid the present coastal grid with the creeks, landmasses, and marshes lost to history. By grounding its topography in the temporal, the map records change and loss as well as the process by which our history haunts us.

When adapted for inclusion in *Infinite City*, Pebworth's map was modi-fied to fit on a printed page. It therefore foregrounds her iconography of the cast of characters of Third Street history (which appears in the painting on the scale of a map "key" but on the printed page as a column of person-ages). Yet despite the expansion of this cast, the mapping of locations and events on the coastline of the book's page is much more compact. The most notable change is that the beautiful hand-painted lettering was removed in favor of the typeset text that standardizes this map with the others in the atlas. Sometimes this also means that a graphic element in the painting—like Pebworth's rendering of an 1850s Chinese fishing village—was reduced to typed words. Thus while the book's map emphasizes the distribution of people (captured in its column), Pebworth's original version feels more personal and intimate—and more focused on time and change. In her essay accompanying the map, Solnit explains that Pebworth's original work is named "Phantom Coast" "because even the original coastline was lost amid the development. Every city is full of ghosts."[66] This admission aligns with Pebworth's own mapping of her biography through the ghosts of the books that shaped her—and that she shaped into her own exhibit (and, in the case of *Infinite City*, as a contributor).

Both Pebworth and Solnit drew on practices of material geography as old as the first known cartographic document charting the ancient Mediterranean and Middle East—a map known as the Madaba mosaic. Like their work, the mosaic maps space and also situates objects within that space. In the sixth century CE, a workshop of mosaic artists produced a map for the floor of the church of Saint George in Madaba, Jordan. The map was discovered in 1884 during renovations to the church.[67] As one of us has written elsewhere, mosaics (floors or walls crafted through the assemblage of colorful stone and glass cubes, or tesserae) are themselves a mapping technology.[68] Artists sourced the stone tesserae from the earth, making each cube a mark of its original quarry and geolocation. Opaque glass cubes were used for particularly vibrant colors, such as blues and yellows, and these were also produced using earthborn pigments manipulated with fire to create glass. When, for example, an artist shaped an image of a peacock in mosaic, the individual stones that made up the bird fashioned not only the image of a peacock but also a map of the materials from which the image of the peacock was rendered. The use of mosaic technologies to produce the image of a map thus presents a double map—both cartography and material geography. In the case of the Madaba map, artists laid down individual stones in order to express the spatial relationships between places of importance in the Middle East in the Byzantine period. The artists delineated places in part by spelling out their placenames in Greek letters shaped by stone tesserae and, for particularly notable places, depicting some element of their spatial presence from a bird's eye view or in profile.

Jerusalem, the capital of three religions, is the center of this map from which other places and spaces radiate. Within the segment of the map that depicts Jerusalem, the mosaic artists represented architectural structures that remain present in the city in contemporary times—the Damascus, Lions', Golden, and Zion Gates and the Church of the Holy Sepulchre. Regional cities such as Jericho, Bethlehem, and Ashkelon are also clearly marked. The map stretches from the Nile Delta to Lebanon and from the Eastern Desert (Egypt and Eritrea) to the Mediterranean Sea. Blue and green tesserae mark that sea, through which ships shown in profile navigate. Artists captured the terrain largely in earth tones. The map thus both represents and locates specific places while it incorporates elements common to a given region—such as gazelles, lions, rivers, and roads—establishing several dimensions to which future cartographic projects return.

MAPPING DISCLOSURE

In *Infinite City*, Solnit builds on a similar practice of material geography in the present, especially in terms of locating objects and marking boundaries. Although known for this cartography, Solnit is also a feminist; we assert that her work on overlay mapping has implications for public feminism more broadly. Solnit's work uses mapping in part to highlight and critique the role of men's actions in defining the experiences of women. When Solnit initially entered public conversations around issues directly related to feminism, her focus lay in the negative impact that excessive verbal posturing by men—now termed "mansplaining"—might have on women. Marketed as "a landmark essay that went viral, inspired the word 'mansplaining,' and prompting fierce arguments" by the publisher of the book the essay evolved into in 2014, Rebecca Solnit's "Men Explain Things to Me" (2008) began conversations among women that, as we will theorize later in this chapter, contributed directly to the public feminist projects of the Trump years and beyond.[69]

The 1944 George Cukor movie *Gaslight* inspired the contemporary term "gaslighting," which names the process by which an abuser undermines another person's reality by leading them to doubt what they know is true. This doubt eventually overtakes their perceptions in the broadest sense as victims of gaslighting begin to second-guess their ability to differentiate between what is real and what is suggested by their abuser. The term itself gained so much popularity following Trump's election that Oxford Languages named it a popular word of 2018.[70] Writing about Cukor's film in 2021, Bonnie Honig argues that "*Gaslight* helps us see how [Trump's constant tweeting] works as a device of disorientation, blocking access to the solitude and plurality that are the conditions of critical thinking and reflection."[71] Indeed, during the years of the Trump administration and beyond, public feminists demonstrated ways that aggressive and abusive discourse, often from powerful white men, contributed to the disorientation of women and others with less power.

At least as far back as 2008 when Solnit explained the seeds of what later came to be called mansplaining, the phenomenon was already being tracked. Solnit's essay begins with an anecdote in which a man at a party condescends to her about her book topic, explaining that an important book about the same topic had been released that same year (and yes, the "important book" turned out to be Solnit's own).[72] In response to such practices and as the Trump years wore on, public feminists took up Maxine Waters's mantle of "reclaiming my time" to combat this disorientation. The phrase, coined by Waters during a hearing to combat stalling and obfuscation by men, was a clever take on House floor practice that became an internet meme as women around the internet staked their resistance.[73]

To better understand Solnit's contributions to public feminism, it is help-ful to consider the foundational work she performed in *Infinite Cities* in what Jason Henderson calls a merger between cultural and critical geography.[74] We view her atlas as an example of overlay mapping that connects subjective experiences with delineations of space; in it, Solnit suggests that "what we call places are stable locations with unstable converging forces that cannot be delineated either by fences on the ground or by boundaries in the imagina-tion—or by the perimeter of the map."[75] These "unstable converging forces" include the personal and the subjective, which can be overlayed across "objective" boundaries to illuminate new intersections. Solnit's work in the atlases and beyond is to propose and then exceed such perimeters and forces, drawing boundaries that are variously serendipitous, literal, metaphorical, and paradoxical—or many of the above.

Solnit's atlases are in fact collaborative texts that bring together authors, illustrators, and cartographers to shape what feels like a new genre and to pair idiosyncratic maps with linked essays, despite the fact that the relation-ship between the maps and their corresponding essays shifts throughout the book.[76] Sometimes the maps explain the essays, sometimes the essays explain the maps, and oftentimes the relationship between the two works figuratively, more like poetry than linear prose. The atlases attempt to depict a finite sample of infinite ways to think about urban space. Some of the maps represent significant intellectual interests of Solnit's. For example, "Cinema City: Muybridge Inventing Movies, Hitchcock Making *Vertigo*" traces what seems at first to be a fanciful overlay but which Solnit fully theorized in her 2004 text *River of Shadows: Eadweard Muybridge and the Technological Wild West*. That book—which, incidentally, is the one that spawned the awk-ward conversation that inspired *Men Explain Things to Me*—draws a direct connection between Muybridge's nineteenth-century work in California to Hollywood, Silicon Valley, and the contemporary, post-tech boom culture of the late twentieth century and beyond.

Other overlay maps in the atlas are more fanciful. One of the most color-ful maps in a somewhat monochromatic collection, "Monarchs and Queens: Butterfly Habitats and Queer Public Spaces," is self-explanatory if one allows one's brain to think the way the book invites readers to think—that is, through wild and playful associations. On the other hand, "Right Wing of the Dove: The Bay Area as Conservative/Military Brain Trust" performs a serious cri-tique in pointing out the history the Bay Area would like to pretend does not shape its past and is one of the few non-"overlay"-style maps. The military industrial complex, complete with a quote from Cicero about the infinite cost of war, is not graphed in relationship to something ironically or paradoxically more liberal in order to show contrast.[77] Instead, the contrast is silent: it is the map of (liberal) San Francisco itself.[78]

Henderson's broadest critique of Solnit's project is her lack of references; according to him, her book contains "one critical omission: citations. The work contains many strong claims and arguments, and yet even a fellow traveler such as myself wishes to see these claims backed with evidence. This seems especially appropriate for an atlas."[79] Such a critique highlights the tension between academics and journalists—and Solnit primarily works in the broader field of journalism.[80] Of interest to us is Solnit's nonacademic approach to the concept of citation more broadly. Instead of employing a citational system that includes "evidence," she instead creates the entire book as a collaboration with those whom she might have cited—other authors, illustrators, and cartographers who contribute directly to the primary text. In chapter 4 of this book, we explore in greater detail the concept of feminist citation, but Solnit's book already demonstrates one iteration of this practice.

Ultimately, Solnit's interest in mapping seems to involve rethinking the map as a tool, making maps meaningful beyond their traditional associations through overlay and community. Henwood suggests that Solnit's rethinking functions as a countermapping project (see chapter 6 of our book for related work on countermonuments). Countermapping reveals previously hidden or occluded stories and can be used for activism; Manissa M. Maharawal and Erin McElroy define countermapping as "a set of critical cartographic and feminist data visualization practices that seek to render visible the landscapes, lives, and sites of resistance and dispossession elided in capitalist, colonial, and liberal topographies" and that also assist activist practice.[81] Henwood argues that through this practice, Solnit works deliberately to dismantle hierarchical power structures in favor of systems of connection. Solnit's use of "connective narratives counters the historical uses to which maps have been put," demonstrating this practice in action.[82] Yet, as with any "counter" project, an ethos that works against historical use necessarily also invokes that use in an effort to transcend it. Like the Madaba mosaic map, Solnit's craft involves overlaying representation with cartographic charting in order to claim spaces—to say "this is mine," though Solnit's "mine" is quite personal, encompassing not only places and spaces but also ideas and bodies. Maps, then, as theorized by Solnit, can be important instruments of feminist projects.

Some critics have recognized the influence of subjective or overlay mapping and its attendant domains on Solnit's feminist work as in *Men Explain Things to Me*. For example, the *Boston Globe*'s review of the book argues that Solnit's

> ability to make a landscape into a text is present in every piece of writing she's ever done, and especially here. Solnit understands that our minds are also landscapes, that they are uncharted territory and we must constantly have something left to discover within ourselves.[83]

This understanding hearkens back to Pebworth, whose shelves—populated by books that shaped her story—graph the tension between self and work that also underlies Solnit's radically subjective approach to mapping ideas and geographies. Solnit puts that approach to good use in *Men Explain Things to Me* as well, drawing on the 1970s "personal as political" model so critical to early twenty-first-century public feminist projects more broadly.[84] In this model, small experiences that individual women have—for example, that of facing "mansplaining"—become understood as a broader phenomenon when they are mapped by many individual voices chiming in to say they also have experienced the same issue.[85] This practice has been achieved in more recent times through tools like social media.

Solnit's intervention integrates well with the mobilized, layered, and iterative networks and (non)spaces of the internet in general and social media in particular. Solnit writes: "Maps are always invitations in ways that texts and pictures are not; you can enter a map, alter it, add to it, plan with it. A map is a ticket to actual territory."[86] The idea of a map as invitation to participate is not just a theory—it is also a practice. In fact, the work of #MeToo, a disclosure hashtag for survivors of sexual assault, may very well be seen this way: as the population of an overlay map, a GIS distribution of individual experiences which demonstrates prevalence to implicitly inspire change while often simultaneously explicitly demanding it.

#METOO AS OVERLAY MAP

One of the most profound interventions of the process of aggregating voices to demonstrate the impact of a structural problem—indeed, one of the most profound interventions of public feminism more broadly—is the #MeToo movement, yet its history has been complicated by a metamapping of race and celebrity onto its foundation. #MeToo's co-optation from its original creator Tarana Burke, a Black activist and educator, has been widely documented (and is touched on in the introduction to this book).[87] While Burke coined the phrase "me too," her intentions were quite distinct from the later social media movement: #MeToo

> wasn't built to be a viral campaign or a hashtag that is here today and forgotten tomorrow. It was a catchphrase to be used from survivor to survivor to let people know that they were not alone and that a movement for radical healing was happening and possible.[88]

In other words, "me too" was founded as a cue, a form of coded language survivors could use to find each other—and thereby find help.

On October 15, 2017, "me too" began to evolve. The evolution began with actor Alyssa Milano, whose initial tweet performed a request for individual voices to come together in aggregate. Specifically, Milano's Twitter post expressed what she saw as a critical missing piece of the conversation around sexual assault—the understanding of how common it is, the map of its distribution. "If all the women who have been sexually harassed or assaulted wrote 'Me too' as a status," Milano shared in an image attributed to a friend, "we might give people a sense of the magnitude of the problem."[89] Through this action, Milano implicitly formed and pre-populated an overlay map capable of visualizing the global scope and scale of sexual assault—one that would not be entirely constrained by geography and social relations due to the operations of the hashtag.

Critically, Milano did two additional things beyond simply sharing the idea. First, she invited her followers to participate directly, framing the image with her own invocation: "If you've been sexually harassed or assaulted write 'me too' as a reply to this tweet." One of the great selling points of social media to the public, in general, is the invitation it extends of a perceived connection to celebrities—a connection celebrities encourage by creating ways for their followers to participate actively in actions or conversations unfolding on their feeds.[90] Milano's invitation demonstrated this dynamic while also giving her followers a place to affirm their own existence. Second, Milano modeled such participation by replying immediately to her own post with "Me too." And as the responses came flooding in, Milano expressed support. "I'm standing with you" and "I'm sorry anyone ever hurt you" were some of the ways she encouraged more women to voice their experiences and to scale up an expanding aggregation of voices.

In her late 2021 memoir, *Unbound: My Story of Liberation and the Birth of the Me Too Movement*, Tarana Burke describes her experience watching the movement she had painstakingly built to create community and healing be adopted by white Hollywood the morning after Milano's tweet. At the same time, she recognized in the action a mutual need for healing:

> It was clear that all the folks who were using the #metoo hashtag, and all the Hollywood actors who came forward with their allegations, needed the same thing that the little Black girls in Selma needed—space to be seen and heard. They needed empathy and compassion and a path to healing. I wanted to be a part of making sure they had what they needed.[91]

While the experience of being excluded from the movement she founded was hurtful, Burke redoubled her efforts and continues this work today.

In 2017, the #MeToo hashtag did function to distribute ideas efficiently via social media. From celebrities with huge platforms to women with few, if any, followers, the idea of "me too" spread along with its articulation. Women began to tell their stories and amplify the stories of others. The stories became their own overlay map, using the "personal as political" model of small experiences aggregating to demonstrate broader phenomena that charted the prevalence of rape and sexual assault.[92] Individual tweets spoke out of silence until voices joined together in powerful demonstration (for context, the hashtag was posted almost 5 million times in the first 24 hours after Milano's post).[93] Like Solnit's "Right Wing of the Dove" overlay map, the contrast in the overlay was the implied map of the world itself. While the implied map is "silent" in this formulation, map-based imagery of the #MeToo distribution did overlay the hashtag onto traditional maps for ease of visualization.[94]

The mobilization of everyday people marking the scale of the crisis unfolded against another celebrity backdrop, that of Ronan Farrow's investigative journalism exposing decades of predatory behavior by movie mogul Harvey Weinstein as well as the many other people in power who facilitated and subsequently covered up Weinstein's abuse. Shortly after an article about Weinstein in the *New York Times* (October 5, 2017) by Jodi Kantor and Megan Twohey (with whom Farrow shared a Pulitzer Prize in 2018 for this combined work), Farrow published a series of essays in the *New Yorker*; a bestselling book recounting the long process of tracking Weinstein's abuses; a podcast of interviews with survivors; and most recently an HBO series, *Catch and Kill: The Podcast Tapes*, that interviewed many of the same survivors.[95] The initial reporting in early October 2017 in both the *New York Times* and the *New Yorker*, itself the result of many months of in-depth research that exposed decades of cover-ups, catalyzed the hashtag movement #MeToo that Milano subsequently initiated.

At the same time as these initiatives brought public attention to the problem, the #MeToo movement was plagued by issues around reception. In the end, its metamapping of celebrity may have proven distracting. For example, *Time* magazine, which the year before had chosen Donald Trump as its person of the year, in 2017 featured "The Silence Breakers."[96] This collective honor (perhaps referencing "The Whistle Blowers" of 2002) was meant in part to applaud the contributions of "hundreds of others, and of many men as well, [who] have unleashed one of the highest-velocity shifts in our culture since the 1960s," yet its editor-in-chief, Edward Felsenthal, credited "the galvanizing actions of the women on our cover" for the honor.[97] On that cover, Susan Fowler, Ashley Judd, Taylor Swift, Adama Iwu, and Isabel Pascual are featured with the subtitle "The Voices that Launched a Movement," while a disembodied elbow visible in the right corner of the frame is perhaps intended to stand in for the many other contributors not pictured, including Tarana Burke. The women on the cover undoubtedly contributed, but their contributions were one part of the project—and a part that skewed toward whiteness.[98] The problem of using emblematic figures to represent a larger group (one we analyze in depth in chapter 6) here initiated backlash.[99] An elbow was not enough. By choosing five women, *Time* missed the point of the map, which, even in Milano's terms, was created to show prevalence rather than to spotlight individual people or even specific stories. It was the aggregation, the network, that mattered most.

Ultimately, this practice of overlay—making the private public in a visible and networked way—makes a new kind of map, one that, like all maps, is imaginary, but that nevertheless shows the presence of women and their experiences. The map says: "We are here." Exposing the distribution of rape and sexual assault in such a visual way has undoubtedly made a difference that will reverberate into future conversations and policies. At the same time, this exposure was only possible because women fought against the notion that their biographies defined them, paradoxically by sharing and mapping their own private and subjective experiences through agency and choice.

The navigation of the line between our public work—whether activism or art, atlases or exhibits—and our private subject positions is challenging in special ways for women and for all who respond to the work of women. We must allow the blood on the canvas to mark us without dismissing it as someone else's story. We must map the millions of voices calling "me too" without depending on lurid details of millions of private stories or letting those details distract us from action and change. We cannot be called upon to share what is private and personal to us unless we wish to. It must be enough that we speak, whether with our voices or through our work.

NOTES

1. Leila Easa, "'Advice from My 80-Year-Old Self' by Susan O'Malley," *Art Practical*, February 9, 2016, https://www.artpractical.com/column/printed-matters -advice-from-my-80-year-old-self.

2. That women have been excluded from the public archive in large degree has meant that there is often very little of the non-personal for scholars to work with when engaging with women. That imbalance, in turn, puts even more pressure on those same thinkers to move back to the personal, demonstrating the circuits of patriarchy in action.

3. See Christopher S. Wood, *A History of Art History* (Princeton, NJ: Princeton University Press, 2019), 24, 385–6, 395–6.

4. Aruna D'Souza, "Biography Becomes Form: William Rubin, Pablo Picasso, and the Subject of Art History," *Word and Image* 18, no. 3 (2002): 126.

5. There are many layers to the feminist reception of Artemisia Gentileschi's work in the twentieth century, from interventions by Mary Garrard to more recent analysis

by Sheila Barker, which also track changes in the reception of her biography. A selection of these debates include: Mary D. Garrard, "Artemisia Gentileschi's Self-Portrait as the Allegory of Painting," *Art Bulletin* 62, no. 1 (1980): 97–112; Thalia Gouma-Peterson and Patricia Mathews, "The Feminist Critique of Art History," *Art Bulletin* 69, no. 3 (1987): 326–57; Norma Broude, Mary D. Garrard, Thalia Gouma-Peterson, and Patricia Mathews, "An Exchange on the Feminist Critique of Art History," *Art Bulletin* 71, no. 1 (1989): 124–7; Mary D. Garrard, *Artemisia Gentileschi: The Image of the Female Hero in Italian Baroque Art* (Princeton, NJ: Princeton University Press, 1989); Griselda Pollock, "Review of *Artemisia Gentileschi: The Image of the Female Hero in Italian Baroque Art*, by Mary D. Garrard," *Art Bulletin* 72, no. 3 (1990): 499–505; Elizabeth Cropper, "New Documents for Artemisia Gentileschi's Life in Florence," *Burlington Magazine* 135, no. 1088 (1993): 760–1; Elizabeth S. Cohen, "The Trials of Artemisia Gentileschi: A Rape as History," *Sixteenth Century Journal* 31, no. 1 (2000): 47–75; Sheila Barker, "The First Biography of Artemisia Gentileschi: Self-Fashioning and Proto-Feminist Art History in Cristofano Bronzini's Notes on Women Artists," *Mitteilungen des Kunsthistorischen Institutes in Florenz* 60, no. 3 (2018): 404–35. On biographies of Artemisia written up through the mid-eighteenth century, see Jesse Locker, *Artemisia and the Language of Painting* (New Haven: Yale University Press, 2015), 161–80.

6. Laetitia Treves and Sheila Barker, eds., *Artemisia* (London: National Gallery Company, 2020). Exhibition catalogue.

7. Laetitia Treves, "Artemisia's Rape Trial," *National Gallery of Art Online*, February 01, 2021 (London: National Gallery of Art, 2020), https://www.nationalgallery.org.uk/exhibitions/past/artemisia/artemisias-rape-trial.

8. Keith Christiansen and Judith Walker Mann, eds., *Orazio and Artemisia Gentileschi* (New York: Metropolitan Museum of Art, 2001). Exhibition catalog. Keith Christiansen, "Becoming Artemisia: Afterthoughts on the Gentileschi Exhibition," *Metropolitan Museum Journal* 39 (2004): 102.

9. See, for example, Stav Atir and Melissa J Ferguson, "How Gender Determines the Way We Speak about Professionals," *Proceedings of the National Academy of Sciences of the United States of America* 115, no. 28 (2018): 7278–83, doi:10.1073/pnas.1805284115. Or note the late 2020/early 2021 controversy around calling Dr. Jill Biden "doctor"; see Katie Kindelanvia, "Dr. Jill Biden Responds after Op-Ed Called for Her to Drop 'Doctor' from Name," *ABC News*, December 18, 2020, https://abcnews.go.com/GMA/News/dr-jill-biden-responds-op-ed-called-drop/story?id=74797472.

10. Treves "Artemisia's Rape Trial."

11. This legal recourse calls to mind the case surrounding the Zong (further explored in chapter 6), in which the idea of "value" underwrites a lawsuit in a profoundly inhumane way.

12. Letizia Treves, "Artemisia in Her Own Words," *National Gallery of Art Online*, February 01, 2021 (London: National Gallery of Art, 2020), https://www.nationalgallery.org.uk/exhibitions/past/artemisia/artemisia-in-her-own-words.

13. At the same time, questions about the extent to which biography should be returned to our conversation around male makers who are also abusers have become

part of contemporary conversations in the post-#MeToo world; in a November 2021 essay, Nandini Pandey suggests that "whether we can or should separate the art from the artist remains an open question. It affects all of us who study ancient cultures that normalized slavery, assault, and other practices we find reprehensible. What do we do, though, when the reprehensible actors include living Goliaths in our own fields?" Nandini Pandey, "Where Do We Draw the Line? Addressing Eminent Scholars' Imperfect Pasts," *LA Review of Books*, November 18, 2021, https://www.lareviewofbooks.org/article/where-do-we-draw-the-line-addressing-eminent-scholars-imperfect-pasts. On a separate note, to counter this structural problem of representation of the work of women, various feminist interventions have been mounted. One example of mobilizing social media to draw attention to women artists is "Herstory," helmed by Erika Gaffney (https://artherstory.net).

14. Linda Nochlin, "Why Have There Been No Great Women Artists?" *Art News* (January 1971; republished May 2015); R. Ward Bissell, "Artemisia Gentileschi: A New Documented Chronology," *The Art Bulletin* 50, no. 2 (June 1968): 153–68.

15. Nochlin, "Why Have There Been No Great Women Artists?"

16. Jillian Steinhauer, "Old Women," *Believer Magazine*, June 1, 2021, https://believermag.com/old-women.

17. Steinhauer, "Old Women."

18. For more about the Guerilla Girls, see https://www.guerrillagirls.com/projects, accessed February 9, 2021.

19. Rosalind Krauss uses the term "art history of the proper name" to indicate the power of names within histories of art, including and expanding beyond an individual's biography to capture their technique, formal choices, and other visible components of a named individual's practice around which histories build up. See Rosalind Krauss, "In the Name of Picasso," *October* 16 (1981): 5–22; this is also discussed in connection to biography in D'Souza, "Biography Becomes Form," 128.

20. "Do Women Still Have to Be Naked to Get into the Met Museum?" *Guerilla Girls*, February 01, 2021, https://www.guerrillagirls.com/naked-through-the-ages.

21. "Do Women Still Have to Be Naked?"

22. Steinhauer, "Old Women."

23. Alice Walker, *In Search of Our Mothers' Gardens: Womanist Prose* (San Diego: Harcourt Brace Jovanovich, 1983), 7.

24. Martha S. Jones, *Vanguard: How Black Women Broke Barriers, Won the Vote, and Insisted on Equality for All* (New York: Basic Books, 2020). Jones also highlights the structural inspiration provided by Walker's, explaining that "*Vanguard* gathers up Black women's stories in the spirit of Alice Walker's narrative-based approach 1983 essay collection, *In Search of Our Mothers' Gardens*" (7).

25. Walker, *In Search of Our Mothers' Gardens*, 402–3.

26. Kaitlyn Greenidge, "My Mother's Garden," *New York Times*, March 26, 2016, https://www.nytimes.com/2016/03/27/opinion/sunday/my-mothers-garden.html.

27. Angelica Frey, "How Judith Beheading Holofernes Became Art History's Favorite Icon of Female Rage," *Artsy*, April 4, 2019, https://www.artsy.net/article/artsy-editorial-judith-beheading-holofernes-art-historys-favorite-icon-female-rage;

E. Straussman-Pflanzer, *Violence and Virtue: Artemisia Gentileschi's Judith Slaying Holofernes* (Chicago, IL: Art Institute of Chicago, 2013).

28. Nochlin, "Why Have There Been No Great Women Artists?" 22.

29. Kevin Brine, introduction to *The Sword of Judith: Judith Studies across the Disciplines*, ed. Kevin R. Brine, Elena Ciletti, and Henrike Lähnemann (Cambridge: OpenBook Publishers, 2010), 4.

30. Erwin Panofsky, "On the Problem of Describing and Interpreting Works of the Visual Arts," trans. Jaś Elsner and Katharina Lorenz, *Critical Inquiry* 38, no. 3 (2012): 474; in addition to the translation, see also analysis of Panofsky's essay and book by Elsner and Lorenz, 497. Despite coauthoring with his wife, Dora Panofsky, Erwin was on record as believing women to be a necessary distraction; Emily J. Levine, "PanDora, or Erwin and Dora Panofsky and the Private History of Ideas," *Journal of Modern History* 83, no. 4 (2011): 756.

31. See, for example: Hirsaugiensis, *Speculum Virginum, ca.* 1190, British Library, London, MS Arundel 44; Ghiberti, *Gates of Paradise 1425–1452*, bronze (detail), Florence, Italy; Botticelli, *The Return of Judith to Bethulia*, 1472, Uffizi; Pollaiuolo, *Judith*, 1470, bronze with traces of gilding, Detroit Institute of Arts; Baldini, *Judith with the Head of Holofernes*, 1460–1485, engraving in blue-gray on ivory laid paper, Art Institute of Chicago; Mantegna and Campagnola, *Judith with the Head of Holofernes*, c. 1495/1500, tempura on poplar panel, National Gallery of Art, Washington DC; Donatello, *Judith Beheading Holofernes*, 1457–1464, bronze, Palazzo Vecchio; Michelangelo, *Judith and Holofernes*, Sistine Chapel (detail), 1509–1511, Vatican City; Vasari, *Judith and Holofernes, c.* 1554, oil on panel, Saint Louis Art Museum; Orazio Gentileschi, *Judith and her Maidservant with the Head of Holofernes*, 1621–1624, oil on canvas, Wadsworth Atheneum Museum of Art; Orazio Gentileschi, *Judith and her Maidservant with the Head of Holofernes, c.* 1608, oil on canvas, National Gallery Oslo, Norway.

32. Brine, "Introduction"; Deborah Levine Gera, "The Jewish Textual Traditions," 81–95, and Elena Ciletti and Henrike Lähnemann, "Judith in the Christian Tradition," 41–66, all in *The Sword of Judith: Judith Studies across the Disciplines*, ed. Kevin R. Brine, Elena Ciletti, and Henrike Lähnemann (Cambridge: OpenBook Publishers, 2010).

33. Yet another version of this theme with a different composition also by Artemisia Gentileschi is *Judith and Her Maidservant with the Head of Holofernes, ca.* 1623–1625, oil on canvas, Detroit Institute of the Arts.

34. Straussman-Pflanzer, *Violence and Virtue*, 11.

35. Nochlin, "Why Have There Been No Great Women Artists?" 22.

36. Ella Gonzalez and Cynthia Colburn, "How to Teach Ancient Art in the Age of #MeToo," *Hyperallergic*, September 5, 2018, https://hyperallergic.com/456269/how-to-teach-ancient-art-in-the-age-of-metoo. The authors later expanded their work into a deeper exploration of the foundations and ongoing impact of the #MeToo movement in the context of art history; Cynthia S. Colburn, Ellen C. Caldwell, and Ella J. Gonzalez, eds. *Gender Violence, Art, and the Viewer: An Intervention* (University Park, PA: Pennsylvania State University Press, forthcoming). See also Rebecca Levitan, "A Rape by Any Other Name: Against Teaching Abductions in

Greek Art," *Journal of the History of Ideas Blog*, June 6, 2019, https://jhiblog.org
/2019/05/06/a-rape-by-any-other-name-against-teaching-abductions-in-greek-art-2.

37. Straussman-Pflanzer, *Violence and Virtue*, 7.

38. Harriet Hall, "It's True, It's True, It's True: All-Female Play Based on Rape
Trial of Artemisia Gentileschi Strikes Uncanny Chord a Year On from #MeToo,"
Independent, October 30, 2018, https://www.independent.co.uk/arts-entertainment
/theatre-dance/features/its-true-its-true-its-true-play-metoo-artemisia-gentileschi
-diorama-theatre-tickets-a8608486.html.

39. "Edinburgh Showcase 2019: 'It's True, It's True, It's True' by Breach
Theatre," *British Arts Council*, July 16, 2019, https://www.youtube.com/watch?v
=5H4yc4E1nRU, accessed January 24, 2021. See also "It's True, It's True, It's True,"
Breach Theatre, https://www.breachtheatre.com/shows/its-true-its-true-its-true.

40. Our book engages with many different examples of art, literature, and
performance based on court documents, including trial transcripts and legal decisions.
Michael Leong's 2020 book, *Contested Records: The Turn to Documents in
Contemporary North American Poetry* (Iowa City: University of Iowa Press), 153–8,
theorizes this move to documents in contemporary poetry as a rejection of the lyric
and disclosure-based tradition of much later twentieth-century poetry (for more on
the lyric tradition in poetry, see our book's fourth chapter). In our current chapter, the
work that we explore that uses legal documents always connects those documents to
personal disclosure and the body itself.

41. "Edinburgh Showcase 2019."

42. "Edinburgh Showcase 2019."

43. Wood, *History of Art History*, 61. On the afterlife of this account in Boccaccio
(as Marcia), see C. Montes Serrano, "La contribución de Ernst H. Gombrich a la
Revista EGA," *EGA Expresión Gráfica Arquitectónica* 23, no. 34 (2018): 78–9.

44. Jodi Cranston explicates this concept in "Speculum cum macula: Materiality
and Desire," chapter 1 of *The Muddied Mirror: Materiality and Figuration in
Titian's Later Paintings* (University Park, PA: Pennsylvania State University Press,
2010), 21–45. On mirrors in the premodern world, see Maria Gerolemou and Lilia
Diamantopoulou, eds., *Mirrors and Mirroring: From Antiquity to the Early Modern
Period* (London: Bloomsbury, 2020).

45. As the National Gallery exhibition emphasizes, Artemisia could not join group
sessions with models attended by her male peers and so had to pay for a private model
when she wished to paint from one.

46. Frick, Carole Collier, Stefania Biancani, and Elizabeth S. G. Nicholson, eds.
Italian Women Artists: From Renaissance to Baroque (Milano: Skira, 2007), 19.
Giorgio Vasari, *Lives of the Artists: Biographies of the Most Eminent Architects,
Painters, and Sculptors of Italy*, translated by Betty Burroughs and Jonathan Foster
(New York: Simon and Schuster, 1946). Douglas Biow, *Vasari's Words: The Lives
of the Artists as a History of Ideas in the Italian Renaissance* (Cambridge: Cambridge
University Press, 2018). David Cast, ed., *The Ashgate Research Companion to
Giorgio Vasari* (Burlington, VT: Ashgate, 2014). David Young Kim, *The Traveling
Artist in the Italian Renaissance: Geography, Mobility, and Style* (New Haven, CT:
Yale University Press, 2014). Sally Quin, "Describing the Female Sculptor in Early

Modern Italy: An Analysis of the Vita of Properzia de' Rossi in Giorgio Vasari's *Lives*," *Gender and History* 24, no. 1 (2012): 134–49.

47. Barker, "The First Biography of Artemisia Gentileschi," 404–35.

48. Sheila Barker, "The Muse of History: Artemisia Gentileschi's First Four Centuries of Immortal Fame," in *Artemisia*, 62.

49. Barker, "The First Biography of Artemisia Gentileschi," 424.

50. Barker, "The First Biography of Artemisia Gentileschi," 417 and, on the legal case and its documentation, 414, n 41.

51. See especially Carol Gilligan and Naomi Snider, *Why Does Patriarchy Persist?* (Cambridge: Polity Press, 2018).

52. Barker, "The First Biography of Artemisia Gentileschi," 421.

53. On Italian women artists' dependence on their fathers for training in artistic practice, see Jordana Pomeroy, "Italian Women Artists from Renaissance to Baroque," in *Italian Women Artists*, 20.

54. Barker, "First Biography of Artemisia Gentileschi," 418.

55. This bias is not limited to women. In "the tiny white people in our heads," Brandon Taylor connects this overreliance on biography to the reception of Black creators by a white audience: "But something really weird happens with Black art where people grant biography primacy over the matter of the art. Where one's biography extends out ahead of the text and therefore everything one encounters in the text is filtered through biography. And not just biography, but the whole matrix of systems that act upon biography. That is: race, gender, sexuality, class, etc. A black man painting an apple has painted an apple, the italics denoting some set of complex signifiers and operations. I mean, the truth is that every rendering of an apple is an apple, being that to make art is to produce a record of one's own subjective experience of the world. But somehow, when it's Black art, our own subjective experiences are really a collective subjective experience. A kind of translation happens, and we become, somehow, objectified. At least in America. All that slavery and colonialism business." Brandon Taylor, "The Tiny White People in Our Heads; Black Subjectivity, Elaine de Kooning, Autofiction," May 11, 2021, https://blgtylr .substack.com/p/the-tiny-white-people-in-our-heads.

56. The Frick Pittsburgh, SLAY: Artemisia Gentileschi and Kehinde Wiley, April 16, 2022–July 10, 2022, https://www.thefrickpittsburgh.org/SLAY.

57. Marylynne Pitz, "SLAY shows Judith from very different points of view at The Frick," *Pittsburgh Post-Gazette*, April 08, 2022, https://www.post-gazette.com /ae/art-architecture/2022/04/08/frick-pittsburgh-art-slay-judith-holofernes/stories /202204080048.

58. Cambridge Dictionary, "Overlay," June 23, 2021, https://dictionary.cambridge .org/us/dictionary/english/overlay.

59. See, for example, Matthew H. Edney's framing of the empiricist delusion that "maps are statements of geographical fact, that a map's significance is defined solely by the quality and quantity of its factual content, and that cartography is the singular enterprise of reconfiguring the world onto paper," 84–5; Matthew H. Edney, "Academic Cartography, Internal Map History, and the Critical Study of Mapping Processes," *Imago Mundi* 66, no. supplement 1 (2014): 83–106.

60. On Miller's laying the foundations for #MeToo, see Concepción de León, "'It Will Always Be a Part of My Life': Chanel Miller Is Ready to Talk," *New York Times*, September 22, 2019, https://www.nytimes.com/2019/09/22/books/chanel -miller-know-my-name-emily-doe.html. For the memoir, see Chanel Miller, *Know My Name: A Memoir* (New York: Viking, 2019).

61. "One City One Book: Know My Name," *San Francisco Public Library*, March 18, 2021, https://sfpl.org/books-and-media/read/one-city-one-book-know-my-name.

62. Paula D'Oyen, "Response to Chanel Miller *Know My Name* Reading on March 16, 2021" (unpublished manuscript, March 18, 2021), typescript.

63. Please note that the larger collection of atlases (including San Francisco, New Orleans, and New York) is titled *Infinite Cities* while the individual atlas of San Francisco uses the singular, *Infinite City*.

64. Pebworth writes that she "created logo design, title and end paper drawings, and maps for Rebecca Solnit's Atlas Trilogy for San Francisco, New Orleans and New York City." Alison Pebworth, "Atlas Series Drawings," *Alison Pebworth*, March 18, 2021, https://alisonpebworth.com/section/467496-Atlas-Series-Drawings.html.

65. Alison Pebworth, "Third Street Phantom Coast Map," *Alison Pebworth*, March 18, 2021, https://alisonpebworth.com/artwork/4409679.html.

66. Rebecca Solnit, *Infinite City: A San Francisco Atlas* (Berkeley: University of California Press, 2010), 76.

67. Yiannis Meimaris, "The Discovery of the Madaba Mosaic Map," in *The Madaba Map Centenary, 1897–1997: Travelling through the Byzantine Umayyad period = al-Dhikrá al-miʾawīyah li-khārīṭat Mādabā : Khilāla al-ʿaṣr al-Umawī al-Bīzanṭī : Proceedings of the International Conference held in Amman, 7–9 April 1997* (Collectio maior; n. 40), ed. Michele Piccirillo and Eugenio Alliata (Jerusalem: Studium Biblicum Franciscanum, 1999), 35–44.

68. See Jennifer M.S. Stager, *Seeing Color in Classical* Art: Theory, Practice, and Reception from Antiquity to the Present (Cambridge: Cambridge University Press, 2022).

69. Rebecca Solnit, *Men Explain Things to Me* (London: Haymarket Books, 2015). See also Viviane Fairbank, "Why I Don't Read Rebecca Solnit," *The Walrus*, April 23, 2020, https://thewalrus.ca/why-i-dont-read-rebecca-solnit. Fairbank writes: "It wasn't until 2008, after a friend casually suggested that Solnit write an essay about the then-unnamed phenomenon of mansplaining, that Solnit caught the public eye as a *female* writer—as opposed to a writer who happened to be female."

70. "Word of the Year 2018: Shortlist," *Oxford Languages*, December 17, 2020, https://languages.oup.com/word-of-the-year/2018-shortlist.

71. Honig, *Shell Shocked*, 17.

72. Rebecca Solnit, "Men Explain Things to Me," *Guernica*, August 20, 2012, https://www.guernicamag.com/rebecca-solnit-men-explain-things-to-me/.

73. As Harris succinctly described in 2018: "Waters shut down his rambling and redirected him to her question again and again with the phrase 'Reclaiming my time,' a stone-faced invocation of House procedural rules. The Internet rejoiced, turning Waters' 'Reclaiming my time' into a widely shared meme." Harris, *Black Feminist Politics*, 202. As of the publication of this book, the phrase persists as a hashtag.

74. Jason Henderson, "INFINITE CITY: A San Francisco Atlas," *Geographical Review* 102, no. 2 (2012): 268.

75. Solnit, *Infinite City*, vii.

76. In fact, even the overlay format of the book's maps was executed through collaborations among Solnit, the cartographers and illustrators, and the art director and editors from University of California Press. For a narration of some parts of this collaboration, see Lia Tjandra and Dore Brown, "Behind-the-Scenes at UC Press: The Making of Rebecca Solnit's Atlas Series," *UC Press Blog: Where Bright Minds Share Bold Ideas*, April 03, 2021, https://www.ucpress.edu/blog/22817/behind-the-scenes -at-uc-press-the-making-of-rebecca-solnits-atlas-series.

77. Cicero, *Fifth Philippic*, chapter 5: "Nervos belli, pecuniam infinitam" ("The sinews of war, unlimited money.")

78. Oddly, Henderson describes this contrast without noting the omission of the first term: "In one of the boldest maps, the 'Right Wing of the Dove,' the Bay Area's leftist political history is juxtaposed against a long, complicated local history tangled with politically conservative think tanks such as the Hoover Institution at Stanford University" (Henderson, "Review of 'Infinite City,'" 268–9). It is almost as if the leftist political history is so very visible that Henderson almost forgets that it isn't an explicit plus part of the map.

79. Henderson, "Review of 'Infinite City,'" 270. For an example of a recent feminist, decolonial, and collaborative mapping project that does include citations, see the Anti-Eviction Mapping Project, *Counterpoints: A San Francisco Bay Area Atlas of Displacement and Resistance* (Oakland, CA: PM Press, 2021).

80. Our thanks to Rachel Brahinsky for this insight.

81. Manissa M. Maharawal and Erin McElroy, "The Anti-Eviction Mapping Project: Counter Mapping and Oral History toward Bay Area Housing Justice," *Annals of the American Association of Geographers* 108, no. 2 (2018): 381. Maharawal and McElroy build this framework within ongoing research on feminist cartography, on which see their citations on 381.

82. Daisy Henwood, "Ecofeminist 'Lines of Convergence': Remapping the American West in Rebecca Solnit's Savage Dreams," *European Journal of American Culture* 39, no. 1 (2020): 107.

83. "Cultural Studies: Here, Let Me Explain Mansplaining (and Rebecca Solnit) to You," *National Post*, May 10, 2014, https://nationalpost.com/life/cultural-studies -here-let-me-explain-mansplaining-and-rebecca-solnit-to-you.

84. Carol Hanisch's 1972 essay demonstrates how the structural nature of the power dynamics of patriarchy impacts individual women's experiences. This notion, in turn, fuels the process by which individual experiences can be aggregated to demonstrate structural problems. Carol Hanisch, "The Personal is Political," *Women of the World, Unite!* Writings by Carol Hanish. February 13, 2021, http://www .carolhanisch.org/CHwritings/PIP.html. See also Carol Hanisch, "The Personal Is Political," *Woman's World* 2, no. 1 (1972): 15 and 22.

85. See Jennifer Wilson, "No One Disagrees with Rebecca Solnit," *New Republic*, April 2, 2020, https://newrepublic.com/article/157136/no-one-disagrees-rebecca -solnit-memoir-feminism. Wilson writes: "At a time when feminism is about finding

others who have lived on the same frequency (#metoo, #yesallwomen), a thinker like Solnit, who gravitates toward identifying common denominators in the female experience (mansplaining, gaslighting, silencing, etc.) is primed to resonate."

86. Solnit, *Infinite City*, 8.

87. Richard Greggory Johnson and Hugo Renderos, "Invisible Populations and the #MeToo Movement," *Public Administration Review* 80, no. 6 (2020): 1123–6.

88. Hari Ziyad, "Tarana Burke Was Omitted from the Time Magazine Cover, so Let's Celebrate the Shit out of Her Today," *AfroPunk*, December 7, 2017, https://afropunk.com/2017/12/tarana-burke-omitted-time-magazine-cover-lets-celebrate-sht-today.

89. Alyssa Milano (@Alyssa_Milano). "If You've Been Sexually Harassed or Assaulted Write 'Me Too' as a Reply to this Tweet," *Twitter*, October 15, 2017, 1:21 p.m., https://twitter.com/alyssa_milano/status/919659438700670976.

90. For a study of the role of self-disclosure in strengthening parasocial interaction between celebrities and fans on Twitter, see Jihyun Kim and Hayeon Song, "Celebrity's Self-Disclosure on Twitter and Parasocial Relationships: A Mediating Role of Social Presence," *Computers in Human Behavior* 62 (2016): 570–7.

91. Tarana Burke, *Unbound: My Story of Liberation and the Birth of the Me Too Movement* (New York, NY: Flatiron Books, 2021), 12.

92. Hanisch, "Personal Is Political," 14–15.

93. However, in the years following #MeToo's emergence as a celebrity rallying cry, its impact, through arguably profound, has also been plagued by issues not only of representation but also around developing and sustaining its focus as activism. While 2017–2018 were strong years for the movement, its energy has since moved off of the internet and into the courtroom (for its prevalence in the courtroom, see Jocelyn Noveck, "For Top #MeToo Legal Duo, a Pandemic Year Brings No Pause," *Associated Press*, July 11, 2021, https://apnews.com/article/business-sports-football-health-government-and-politics-8446ed43b95ecd728a3ed662d8a3859c; for its tapering online energy, which often happens with the energy around celebrity news, see Karen Arriaza Ibarra, "Global Perspectives on the #MeToo Movement: From 'Big Noise' to 'Discrete Oblivion?'" *Interactions: Studies in Communication and Culture* 10, no. 3 [2019]: 153–8). In fact, historians have argued that the focus in the United States on the #MeToo movement shifted between 2017 and 2019 from an activist movement grounded in analyses of race and class to one viewed as a political one—and thereby divisive—within one calendar year (by 2019; see Elizabeth R. Earle, "'The Consequences Will Be with Us for Decades': The Politicization and Polarization of the #MeToo and Time's Up Movements in the United States," *Interactions: Studies in Communication and Culture* 10, no. 3 (2019): 257–71).

94. See a map of the globe overlayed with #MeToo incidents at "Me Too Rising: A Visualization of the Movement Using Google Trends," *Me Too Rising*, January 17, 2021, https://metoorising.withgoogle.com. See also "Tracking the #MeToo Movement across Social Media on a Map," *esri*, June 22, 2021, https://storymaps.arcgis.com/stories/f302610237df41cbbf9276c03c17ac45 and "Unsettled: Mapping #MeToo," *NPR and Iowa Public Radio*, January 16, 2021, https://www.npr.org/podcasts/666302911/unsettled-mapping-me-too.

95. Jodi Kantor and Megan Twohey, "Harvey Weinstein Paid Off Sexual Harassment Accusers for Decades," *New York Times*, October 5, 2017, https://www.nytimes.com/2017/10/05/us/harvey-weinstein-harassment-allegations.html; Ronan Farrow, "From Aggressive Overtures to Sexual Assault: Harvey Weinstein's Accusers Tell Their Stories," *New Yorker*, October 10, 2017, https://www.newyorker.com/news/news-desk/from-aggressive-overtures-to-sexual-assault-harvey-weinsteins-accusers-tell-their-stories; Ronan Farrow, "Weighing the Cost of Speaking Out Against Harvey Weinstein," *New Yorker*, October 27, 2017; Ronan Farrow, "Harvey Weinstein's Army of Spies," *New Yorker*, November 6, 2017, https://www.newyorker.com/news/news-desk/harvey-weinsteins-army-of-spies; and Ronan Farrow, "Harvey Weinstein's Secret Settlements," *New Yorker*, November 21, 2017, https://www.newyorker.com/news/news-desk/harvey-weinsteins-secret-settlements.

96. See Stephanie Zacharek, Eliana Dockterman, and Haley Sweetland Edwards, "The Silence Breakers," *Time Magazine*, December 18, 2017, https://time.com/time-person-of-the-year-2017-silence-breakers.

97. Felsenthal, quoted in Alissa Wilkinson and Emily Stewart, "*Time*'s 2017 Person of the Year is the 'Silence Breakers,'" *Vox*, December 6, 2017, https://www.vox.com/identities/2017/12/6/16741324/times-person-of-the-year-silence-breakers. For "the whistleblowers," see Gregory Heisler, "2002: The Whistleblowers," *Time Magazine*, March 5, 2020, https://time.com/5793757/the-whistleblowers-100-women-of-the-year.

98. Similarly, a cover for *The Envelope* grouped six white actors under the headline: "Actresses call for a change to the way many stories are told." For a discussion of this cover, see Stager "The Unbearable Whiteness."

99. See Ziyad, "Tarana Burke Was Omitted."

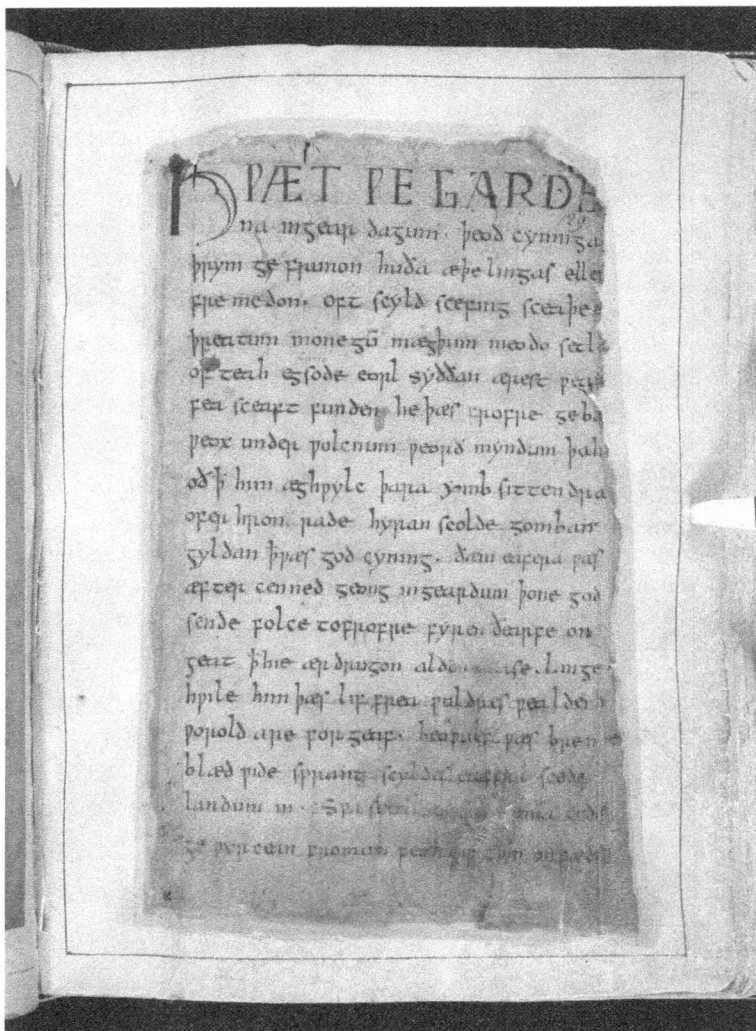

Figure 3.1 Opening Page of *Beowulf*, "Nowell Codex," Cotton MS Vitellius A XV.
© The British Library Board.

Chapter 3

On the Gendered Politics of Translation

On June 23, 2021, the Twitter account Translation Talk, staffed by a rotating set of curators, posted the following tweet: "Writer Nikolai Gogol on translation: 'The translator should be like glass: so transparent that you can't see him.'"[1] Hours later, poet and translator Sasha Dugdale tweeted her response: "The translator is many kilos of flesh, hair, bones, fingernails, teeth. Wherever she goes she leaves her fingerprints, dust, oils and smell."[2] We took one look at that paired set of tweets and recognized them as an epigraph for this chapter.

In fact, these competing images of translation were so visceral that they stayed on our minds. Glass, a translucent and shiny material that is almost intended to trick, to indicate "not hereness" despite its clear presence, served as a vivid contrast to the aspects of the body that endure long after death (bones, nails, teeth) as well as those that are fleeting but noticeable (fingerprints, dust, oils, and perhaps even flesh). The material aspects of the body have a persistent hereness, despite continual efforts by many to mask that effect (at the very least, in terms of smell and hair), and remind us that the translator's ideas originate from a specific body.

Debates around the role of the translator, especially in the context of feminist translation, have abounded. Theorizing translation's aesthetic, ethical, and political investments, Jhumpa Lahiri writes that translation "is more than one way of understanding reality. It displaces the solution of one [single] solution to anything—which is fascism. Translation completely cancels that out."[3] While feminist translators are not the only ones who reject the notion of "one solution" or the place of invisible neutrality claimed by translators of the past (and, in fact, many contemporary translators working from a variety of subject positions also favor a model of translation as interpretation), we nevertheless contend that the work of feminist translation rewards foregrounding this interpretive role.[4]

Perhaps attention to the identity of the translator does feminist work simply by dismantling the assumed default status of a cis white man helming the text, but some translators—as in the examples to follow in this chapter—identify their subject positions in ways that explicitly intervene in the reception of the text whether by attending to the intersections of class and gender embedded in the source language, by rendering a tired text newly contemporary, or by surfacing the complex world of a central female character in new ways.

We seek in this chapter to bring attention to a contemporary moment in translation that has coalesced over the last few years as women translators have taken on foundational male-authored texts, in part to connect them to the events of the present seen through a feminist lens. If in the previous chapter we investigated feminist mapping as a practice that can counter the imposition of biography around women artists, in this chapter we look at feminist translation as a practice of intervening in canonical texts through surfacing new words, characters, and ideas of both the source text and of the relationship of each translator to that text in the present. As such, we see the translational act as one of public feminism and are particularly interested in the way so many of its practitioners bring the conversation around it onto social media.

Specifically, our exploration focuses on three women translators who work within what has emerged as a watershed moment in feminist translation. The translators we examine in this chapter have published their translations of male-authored epics since the 2016 election in the United States, an additional circumstance that has generated momentum around and shaped the audience for their work by bringing so intensely to the surface patriarchal foundations of United States and broader Anglophone politics.[5] Newly public "grab-em-by-the-pussy" rhetoric forced open the eyes and ears of audiences of these translations, which probe the patriarchal structures undergirding a society that could and did elevate misogyny and rape culture to the highest political office. The translators we survey make specific connections between the work of translation and the contemporary political landscape.[6] They also move these connections into public dialogue through academic as well as popular channels like social media that allow what may have previously been seen as the hidden technical work of translation to circulate more widely. By entering contested conversations and spaces, these translators can, through acts of public feminism, break into and break down arenas previously controlled by men. And the moment already appears to have propelled future translations by women of canonical male authors, including the announced collaboration of Jhumpa Lahiri and Yelena Baraz to translate Ovid's *Metamorphoses* and Stephanie McCarter's forthcoming translation of the same text, both of which demonstrate the continued momentum of feminist translation into the 2020s and beyond.[7]

Within this broader context, Emily Wilson published her translation of the *Odyssey* in 2017, Maria Dahvana Headley published her translation of *Beowulf* in 2020, and Shadi Bartsch published her translation of the *Aeneid* in 2021. All three translators reexamine canonical texts from a subject position outside of the patriarchal structures within which these texts were originally produced—and which they have been used to uphold. All return a form of accuracy to the texts they explore by reexamining their source language and stripping patriarchal bias from it.[8] All center their subject position and the related contingency of their new text, reasserting their "I" in an explicit rejection of the rationalist discourse of pure language through a counterassertion that the translator's subject position cannot be effaced.[9] All were constrained by material circumstances, including the material circumstances of their source texts. And whether related or not—and despite the fact that the production of specific translations is often underexplored in academic contexts—all three seem to have gained the public eye in a way previous translators may not have, whether through interviews, events, or some of the trappings of social media stardom, allowing them to bridge the gap between academic and public feminist work.

FEMINIST TRANSLATION THEORY
AND THE MYTH OF PURITY

The approaches of the three translators we investigate in this chapter are grounded in the history of feminist translation. Writing this history, Luise von Flotow invokes Hélène Cixous's insistence that "women must write through their bodies, they must invent impregnable language that will wreck partitions, classes and rhetorics, regulations and codes" to emphasize the ways in which feminist translation recenters the body of the translator (as in the second of the tweets with which we begin this chapter).[10] Indeed, within the deep history of feminist translation, even being in the world as a woman has been theorized as an act of translation within worlds structured for men.[11] This constant state of translating has yielded various modes of feminist practice, including surfacing lost women writers and texts, writing in experimental forms, and intervening in difficult texts.[12]

With scholars and theorists of feminist translation, we rely on an assumption that the work of the translator is the production of a new text, not through the silent or hidden equation of one word to another, one language to another, but as authored by the translator in its own right—what some have named "retranslations" to emphasize the seriality and iterative nature of translating texts.[13] Yet historically, translation projects—especially those by men—have been considered or idealized as neutral, aligned with Walter

Benjamin's contention in "The Task of the Translator" that "real translation is transparent; it does not cover the original, does not block its light, but allows the pure language . . . to shine upon the original all the more fully."[14] Such ideals are deeply embedded in the myths of Western culture critiqued by theorists like Kwame Anthony Appiah, who identifies the desire of contemporary Anglophone societies to trace their history directly back to what Appiah terms the "golden nugget" of primarily ancient Greek and secondarily Roman culture.[15] The myth of pure language—like the Adamic language of pre-Tower of Babel imagined in the Christian Bible—aligns well with historical discourses of purity in language, art, and philosophy.[16] To preserve purity of heritage, text, and translation—the dream suggests—the translator must efface himself. At the same time, this self-effacement of the translator can be its own kind of privileged patriarchal fiction, identified as good but available only to some.[17]

In light of these performances of "purity" underwritten by the (male) translator's invisibility, the very act of women translating texts at the heart of what many imagine to be the canon of Western literature is powerful. Yet the path for women translators who reject these myths of purity can be vexed. One strategy they may use is to center the way that bringing a different subject position to bear on a text can produce a translation of greater accuracy—what Benjamin calls "fidelity"—that attends to the realities of the original text in ways that previous translators have overlooked or compressed.[18] For example, Anne Le Fèvre Dacier (Madame Dacier), a French woman living in the mid-seventeenth to eighteenth centuries who, having learned Greek and Latin from her father alongside her brothers, was one of the first women known to have translated Homer, engaged in public debate over the importance of accuracy (although she did not emphasize her gendered subject position in those debates).[19] This strategy may have protected translators like Dacier from potential criticisms, and indeed women translators may wield accuracy as a shield against attacks over the open subject positions they bring to bear on their work. Such protections may also be necessary given how critical it is that women get the opportunity to do this work. Without this work—without translation from noncentered subject positions—future translations may reinscribe patriarchal stories that perpetuate the exclusion of women and nonbinary people, an exclusion whose ultimate ramifications even include preventing future acts of such translation. Building from a friction between the translator's and author's subject positions, feminist translators intervene in patriarchal texts not only by recovering overlooked agency for nondominant actors within the text but also by resurfacing uncomfortable and violent truths that previous translations may have camouflaged.

One of the reasons to retranslate canonical texts is that these texts have played such an outsized role in the politics of patriarchy—and that politics has shaped earlier translations as well. While a powerful practice in the arsenal of feminist activism can be to trouble, deconstruct, and seek to replace canons of patriarchal texts, artifacts, and even culture, a second strategy is to reexamine those canons and to pull from them a series of stories that have been overlooked in order to illuminate the other voices that have always been there. This second strategy (engaging with the canon from subject positions historically excluded or disempowered by it) is not discontinuous with the first (moving beyond the narrow selection of canonical art and text to amplify other materials, modes, voices, and approaches), though they exist in some tension. The work we explore in this chapter aligns with the second strategy of working from within.

Navigating within the constructed Western canon takes on additional urgency given the Trumpian mobilization of classical heritage. Even at the end of 2020, we note the ongoing infatuation with Appiah's "golden nugget" of the Western tradition in Trump's declaration that the preferred style for federal buildings should henceforth be classical (or at the very least not modern).[20] Yet such conceptualization of what constitutes "classical" is itself often shaped by misunderstandings, sometimes directly created by the biases of historians and archeologists themselves.[21] At other times, the concept of the classical artifact is imbued with the violence of white supremacy.[22] When we break this cycle—when, for example, more women, especially feminists, translate canonical texts—the stories we tell may change. When women do not engage in this way, we get more of the dreaded same, as Emily Wilson's late-2020 article "Oh How Miserable" (following the release of three new translations of the *Oresteia* by white men) laments.[23]

MATERIAL CIRCUMSTANCES

The three translators whose work we trace in this chapter have begun to break that cycle. Yet doing so is far from simple. Critically, in order for a translator to produce a translation, many material concerns must be met—both the material concerns of the translator (sufficient time, money, and infrastructural support to do the work) and the material concerns of the source text, its journey through time inflected by the materials of the texts themselves (carbon inks, woven reeds, animal skin vellums, printed paper, digital types) and the hands that preserved, transcribed, and eventually archived them. While attention to the transmission history of their source text is customary in a translator's introduction or note, we also wish to highlight the less common attention and space the translators we consider in this chapter devote to the material support undergirding their own translation work. All three translators expose the circumstances that enabled their translations. Of the three translators considered in this chapter, two hold tenured university positions that formed the base from which their acts of translation were made possible. All worked under a publishing contract with an advance. The privilege of paid time to think and write has historically belonged so exclusively to elite white men that we name it as one of the factors that shapes the intersections of gender and class in the production of literary translations.[24] For example, Wilson writes:

> I am a single mother of three with a full-time job and a mortgage to pay on my own. There's no way I could have taken on this enormously challenging work just as an amateur pursuit, to keep in the desk drawer. I do this work because I love it. . . . But I couldn't do it without a structure that supports my work.[25]

So direct an acknowledgment of the material circumstances that must be met in order to produce the translation of an epic rarely appears in the introductions of male translators. Women have not, historically, been able to translate because they have not had the years of paid time that translation demands. Patriarchy and power, we argue, have thereby shaped both the material circumstances of the source text and of the translator's labor.

So many articles and headlines claimed Emily Wilson as the first woman to translate the *Odyssey*, the story of Odysseus's decade-long journey home to his kingdom and family in Ithaca after the Trojan war of the *Iliad*, that for a time she changed her Twitter bio to read "NOT the first woman to have translated the *Odyssey*."[26] Wilson has emphasized several reasons for her pushback against this "first woman" position: the erasure of women who had already translated the *Odyssey* into other modern languages (including Imme Dros into Dutch, Rosa Calzecchi Onesti into Italian, and Azra Erhat into Turkish) and the Anglophone hegemony that their erasure reinforced; the risks of tokenism whereby one woman might be considered quite enough, blocking rather than clearing the way for future women translators; and the fact that, as the default subject position, men's gender is never invoked in the coverage of their translations.[27] Wilson has also highlighted the collective work of other women's voices in her field, Classics, and in translation studies, work from which her own research benefited, situating her translation within a collective intellectual practice—which in the next chapter we will pick back up as a collective "lyric I."

Despite Wilson rejecting the label, interest in her version of the *Odyssey* surged in part because she is the first person who does not identify as male to have translated this ancient epic poem about "a complicated man" into English. One of us chose to read Wilson's translation during a cross-country move with her family not only to overlay the hero's misadventures with her own but also to hear this old tale "for our modern times" in a voice that she, despite decades of study in Greek and Latin, had not heard.[28] For her, the revelation that Wilson is not only a woman but also a mother, as are both authors of this book, deepened the significance of Wilson's epic—its very existence spoke to resilience and possibility in a career long inhospitable to mothers.

Bartsch is not the first woman to have translated the *Aeneid* into English— that task was taken up by Sarah Ruden in 2009 during a phase in translation prior to the watershed moment we are interested in here; her translation was, furthermore, produced outside of the frame of current social media practices. As a translator during this later moment, like Wilson, Bartsch foregrounds her subject position and the infrastructural support her project demanded:

> The support of two influential women let this translation see the light of day. They are my agent, Wendy Strothman at the Strothman Agency, and Hilary Redmon, Vice President and Executive Editor at Random House. They listened when I argued that a new translation was needed; they understood the rationale for this claim; and they found value in having a woman and a scholar of Latin translate a major work in the cultural history of the West. In more material terms, Wendy engineered an advance, and Hilary paid it—great teamwork.[29]

Headley also acknowledges the important role of her editor and emphasizes the enduring support of her agent, who "for ten years has been telling me I can do whatever I set my mind to."[30] Thus material circumstances include not only monetary support but also advocacy. In exposing the structural support translation demands, Wilson, Bartsch, and Headley also throw into sharp relief the extent to which earlier male translators have treated their structural circumstances as given—as transparent as they professed the translator himself to be. We argue instead that theorizing translation demands an account of the means by which translators labor.

Regarding her decision to translate *Beowulf*, Headley describes the moment when she was asked, in light of her novel *The Mere Wife* (which reimagines *Beowulf* in the modern, suburban United States and includes some short sections of the epic translated by Headley herself), when her translation of all of *Beowulf* would appear. Headley initially brushed off the question, claiming that she wasn't qualified, to which the questioner replied that she was as qualified as many who had already translated the text.[31] Confronting this very gendered moment of self-restriction, Headley writes: "Despite the significant work of female and other marginalized scholars, despite several excellent translations by women, the fact remains that *Beowulf*, at least for publication, has longstandingly been aggressively marketed as an off-limits area."[32] Headley also cites a formative conversation with Wilson on translation in the summer of 2018 as having motivated her own work. Similarly, another scholar, Johanna Hanink, took on the challenge of translating Thucydides, a "strangely masculine enterprise," shortly after Wilson's success.[33] Just as Wilson acknowledged the circle of women classicists whose work directly and indirectly informed her "first" translation, Headley acknowledges "every woman who's ever published a translation of *Beowulf*."[34] Each of these women translators recognizes the wider corps of women writers and translators within which their work is situated.

Just as patriarchal structures have shaped the material conditions by which a translator labors, so have they shaped the material circumstances by which a source text reaches the translator. While tracing the reception history of the source text is more familiar ground, when coupled with a frank assessment of the material conditions of the translator's labor, new light shines on the materiality of the text's transmission itself. As Emily Wilson's Homeric invocation to "find the beginning" invites us to do, tracking the transformations of a text prior to its modern translation forces us to wrestle with the many moments in which structural and differential power dynamics might inflect a text—and which texts are preserved and how they are preserved are two conditions at least somewhat driven by power.

For the *Odyssey*, the complexity of the text's reception history includes its ancient transmission from an epic deeply informed by centuries of oral performance by traveling *rhapsodes* ("story-stitchers") to a written text that reaches modern translators via preservation by ancient authors on papyri (Egyptian reed-paper, e.g., P. Oxy 1819 EES), through Byzantium (e.g., *Ilias Ambrosiana*, Cod. F. 205 P. inf., Bibliothecae Ambrosianae Mediolanensi, an illustrated Byzantine manuscript from the sixth century now housed in Milan), to the early modern printed book tradition (Florence: Nerlius, Nerlius, and Damilas, 1488).[35] Fragments of the *Iliad* and the *Odyssey* are preserved in various material contexts from antiquity, such as a third-century BCE clay tablet from Olympia with lines from *Od.* 14.7–13, a fourth-century BCE potsherd from the Black Sea region with lines from *Od.* 9.39, and various papyri or ceramic vessels with lines written or painted onto them. These fragments, however, all align with or amend source texts that were already known prior to their discovery. Whereas *Beowulf*, for example, has a single source text, texts of the *Odyssey* are only produced through the collection of many partial copies and citations over millennia. Unlike the fragments of Sappho to which we turn in the next chapter, Homeric texts remained in circulation from antiquity so that, as Robert Lamberton put it, the text interacted with "perhaps a hundred generations of readers"; these ancient readers from Alexandria, Pergamon, the Greek East, and the early modern Latin West have all shaped it in return.[36] Examining the material conditions of a given text's reception undermines straightforward narratives of authorship and ancestry.

Even Bartsch is working from a text that itself absorbs some of the ancient readers interacting with the *Odyssey*: Vergil cited both the *Odyssey* and the

Iliad in the *Aeneid*'s opening line of this foundation epic, and the two texts are complex influencers for the *Aeneid* more generally.[37] Just as Vergil draws on Homeric structures in his text, so does Wilson invoke the translators who worked on the *Odyssey* before her, signaling their presence in her new translation. No one, both examples remind us, writes or translates alone. Feminist translation in particular often highlights these layers of collaboration across time, sometimes all the way back to the source text.

Vergil's biographer, Suetonius, claims that on his deathbed in 19 BCE, Vergil asked his friend to burn the unpublished text of the *Aeneid*. His request, if it happened, must not have been honored, for shortly after his death Emperor Augustus, to whom the poem was dedicated and who might have commissioned it, circulated the poem.[38] This potentially apocryphal story demonstrates that while even the author could try to control the distribution of his own text, other hands might intervene against authorial wishes, especially when those hands wielded civic power. Either way, the poem has reached us centuries later. In the introduction to her translation, Bartsch does not reveal which version of the Latin text she used for her translation, though we note that one of the earliest extant illustrated manuscripts of the Aeneid, the Vergilius Vaticanus (fourth century CE), has now been digitized and made publicly available.[39]

Headley also cites the democratization of access that manuscript digitization has afforded those with a ready internet connection in her work on *Beowulf*, explaining that "this translation exists because of that access."[40] Such access makes it possible for more translators to approach the source text in a variety of ways—and for more readers to compare that text to its translations. On the other hand, Headley is working with a text that itself is materially troubled (Fig. 3.1). Unlike Wilson and Bartsch's breadth of at least partial source texts, there is only one version of the source text (the Nowell Codex), demonstrating some of the archival challenges we explored in chapter 1. As source text, the Nowell Codex was written sometime around the end of the tenth century by two scribes, each making their own set of mistakes and changes, including plugging metric gaps and inserting lacunae. Not only were parts of the poem presumably lost to memory prior to transcription but others were materially damaged in their subsequent history or marked by the translators and librarians who have encountered the text over time. Of course, the fact that this text was preserved in any way is remarkable in itself. As material objects, source texts must be protected if they are to be eventually transmitted or replicated in digital form. Institutional infrastructure preserves material conditions of certain texts but not others (in chapters 2 and 4, we examine unprotected texts that sometimes even end up in the trash). Digital formatting begets new archival life for a text, but it does not solve the problem of which text was housed in the first place (through practices that, in certain ways, ensure that we keep recirculating the same canonical texts). Such choices create opportunities for transmission but not always opportunities to rethink what can and cannot be circulated in the first place. Questions of which texts are preserved, how such texts are protected and archived, and what such material issues say about the status of the texts are critical for feminists to investigate.

The material circumstances of each of these texts—from their early readers and scribes to the scholia and emendations made throughout their collection in archives and their receptions—offer each translator a source text that has been shaped by centuries of hands, structures, and materials. In addition to the element of chance, the survival of an ancient author's text depends on the kind of power they held in their lifetimes, on how power holders contemporary to its production received their work, and on how later stakeholders in positions to make decisions about and to fund the excavation and preservation of documents take up that work. Dominant powers have thus shaped source texts while modern material contracts and conditions—university jobs, publishing contracts, broadband, and digitization—have shaped their translations. In light of millennia of misogyny during which women have been more likely to hold at best marginalized, noninfrastructural power, patriarchal structures have marked text, translator, and translation.

SUBJECT POSITION

Once material challenges have been accommodated, translators must contend with their own subject positions. Translations by men are more likely to present their products as more neutral. For example, in his 1965 translation of the *Odyssey*, Richmond Lattimore explains that he followed "the formulaic practice of the original" but that his memory "failed at times" and that he "allowed [himself] some liberties."[41] The woman translators we explore in this chapter who published their work between 2017 and 2021 present a different vision of the translator's role, one embraced by many feminist translators before them. For example, in her "Translator's Note" to the *Odyssey*, Emily Wilson theorizes the "gendered metaphor of the 'faithful' translation whose work is always secondary to that of a male-authored original," establishing her own position in vexed contrast to that myth.[42] Wilson goes on to suggest that we require a new way to think about the work of translation, arguing that her "translation is, like all translations, an entirely different text than the original poem. Translation always, necessarily, involves interpretation."[43] Even this—the suggestion that the work of translation is to interpret—is a feminist assertion that centers the value (and contingency) of labor. The other translators in this chapter join Wilson in positioning each translation as a new text. As we circle their retellings, we set the groundwork that allows us to look at poet Alice Oswald's radical reimagining of the *Iliad* in chapter 6.

Identifying her subject position in her Translator's Note to the *Aeneid*, Bartsch argues that Latin literature was written by and for men and that most of the professors with whom she trained were also men. Like Wilson, she recognizes her own text as a new version of its source and her subject position as tantamount to shaping that source, explaining that

> all translators bring a certain worldview with them, and to date, this view has been mostly a male, European-American point of view. Perhaps, then, it is not insignificant that I grew up as a foreigner in other people's countries (including Indonesia, Iran, and the Fiji Islands as well as Europe)—not as a refugee, but an outsider to the dominant culture, an observer rather than a participant.[44]

Bartsch contends that her subject position allows her to rethink characters and inflections that male translators, too steeped in the world that they are translating—one written by and for them—have overlooked. In this sense, being a woman and thus an outsider to the text allows Bartsch to see otherwise and, in so seeing, to offer what she argues is a more accurate translation.

In what is perhaps the most radical example of self-positioning, Headley reveals her individual subject position from the start. Her translation is

> done by an American woman born in the year 1977 . . . a person who, if we were looking at the poem's categories, would fall much closer in original habitat to Grendel and his mother than to Beowulf or even the lesser denizens of Hrothgar's court.[45]

Among other identifiers, Headley centers her age, nationality, gender, and class position, implicitly suggesting that they make a difference in her vision of the text. What she sees in the text must of course be shaped by how she sees, in general, the world—and her experience within it—in a personal and idiosyncratic way.[46]

Finally, it is important to reiterate that these translators create some tension in acknowledging their own subject positions while also raising the ideal of accuracy in translation (which may, as discussed earlier, be a protective measure). We have analyzed previsouly the way that Bartsch sees "accuracy" as a by-product of her outsider status; Wilson and Headley also imply accuracy as a goal. Wilson sees moments when the original Greek has been recast based on the biases of translators (for example, in the derogatory use of "sluts" discussed later in this chapter), while Headley determines that the word translators have used to describe Grendel's mother as a "monster" is elsewhere used to describe a person of nobility (also discussed later in this chapter). In these examples, a feminist recasting emerges from the original language of the text when it is stripped of the subsequent patriarchal biases of male translators.

POETICS AND LANGUAGE

Each translator had to develop strategies for working within the confines not only of the source language but also of the source's verse and poetic structures more generally. The structural constraints of each poem offer a metaphor for the structural constraints within which any translator who is outside of mainstream systems of power must operate. They must stay within the bounds of the poetic system, but within those bounds each word choice has the potential to become a watershed.

Wilson translates the *Odyssey* from Homeric Greek's dactylic hexameter into English's iambic pentameter—the poetic meter of so many canonical male writers—"Chaucer, Shakespeare, Milton, Byron, Keats, and plenty of more recent anglophone poets."[47] The role of tonal oral performance in the development of the poem likely contributed to the frequent repetition of epithets throughout. Rather than select one translation for each epithet and repeat it, Wilson modifies each epithet slightly in relation to its surrounding context, so "when rosy-fingered Dawn came bright and early" appears also as "when newborn Dawn appeared with rosy fingers."[48] Wilson aims to produce a metered text in plain speech that is readable and varied while avoiding artifice and slang.[49]

Where Wilson varies the epithets, Bartsch, facing the same challenge, selectively cuts formulaic phrases in order to free up additional space within her translation.[50] Bartsch describes the pressure that Latin's more compressed word requirements put on her English meter, which she matches to Vergil's six beats using a combination of six- and five-beat iambs that she describes as the "beating heart of the poem."[51] She also emphasizes the fidelity of her pace, alliteration, and assonance in English to Vergil's Latin and avoids metaphors that the Latin itself does not produce.[52] Bartsch's formal choices prioritize pace and shape an English poem that resonates with the brisk pace of the Latin.

Wilson and Bartsch make what could be seen as opposite choices as they pursue their goals as translators. Wilson's substitution of different phrases for the same repeated epithet in her translation creates multiplicity in language, while Bartsch's removal of certain repeated epithets creates tight pacing. And yet both choices contrast markedly with Headley, who liberates herself from the constraints of regular meter and embraces both archaic words and modern slang wholeheartedly.[53] Considering these varied choices in relation to each other demonstrates something about translation itself. Each of these translators is working within the formal constraints of moving between two languages and therefore makes a set of choices about what to prioritize. While the "invisible translator" model we examined earlier in this chapter implies that there is only one way to translate a text, comparing different translation choices to each other demonstrates that every translator makes a set of interventions that may be visible or invisible depending on our ability as readers to perceive those decisions.

In the case of Headley, for seasoned readers this perception will likely be immediate. While Headley makes multiple contributions to the context of the epic poem, it is perhaps her vision of its first word that will startle experienced readers the most. "Hwæt," often translated as "behold" or "listen!" but also as "yes!" or "so," in Headley's version becomes "bro!" Her text thus begins with an invocation for "bros" to pay attention to the epic adventure ahead. This move reflects many of Headley's broader choices as a translator, one of which is to fully explore the possibilities of contemporary language, including slang, even when translating a text from the sixth century CE. Yet the term "bro" has a complicated history. Originating as Black slang (short for "brother") in the twentieth century, it became more generalized in the 1970s due to white appropriation (of which Headley subsequently plays a part).[54] Later, in 2013, Oxford University Press' OxfordWords blog argued that the label "bro" refers to the person using the term as much as the person it addresses, implying that the type of person who would use such language must themselves be captured by it.[55] This reading suggests that the narrator in Headley's translation is the "bro" as much as is the listener—and that the label may even extend to Headley herself.

Indeed, part of the way Headley's text becomes a public feminist project lies in her co-optation of the public language of social media (and perhaps the appellation "bro" is a part of this). For example, Wealhtheow, Queen to Hrothgar, is described as "hashtag: blessed" when she passes the goblet to honor Beowulf before his confrontation with Grendel.[56] "Hashtag: blessed" refers not to actual social media hashtags, which would be rendered through the hashtag symbol (#blessed), but instead to the way that such descriptions have entered our ordinary speech so that "hashtag" signals that you are about to describe or comment on something, calling audience attention almost in the same way that "bro!" does. Additionally, as further discussed in our introduction and throughout our book, hashtags create a network—a community of listener–readers interested in the same topic—representing a way Headley shapes an audience for her translation.[57]

Headley employs slang throughout her translation of the epic. Unferth, who initially belittles Beowulf, later in the text "unexpectedly stanned for Beowulf" after Beowulf's defeat of Grendel.[58] "Stanned," a portmanteau of "stalker" and "fan" that was popularized with Eminem's 2000 song "Stan" and spread and evolved into current usage from there, is especially interesting in light of the kennings—figures of speech common in Old English verse that combine two separate words to create, through metaphor, compounds (such as "sky-candle" for sun)—to which Headley is highly attentive in the original text.[59] Kennings are not the same as portmanteaus—instead of collapsing words together by removing letters, they suggest analogy by comparing a two-word compound with the thing the words evoke. Both operations demonstrate the need for new language to fully capture specific new experiences.

Along with new language comes other kinds of new forms; as with "bro," Headley even inserts hip hop sensibility into the poem. When advising Beowulf after his initial victory, Hrothgar explains that he's "dropping knowledge now" and, at the end of the poem, the narrator concludes that Beowulf "was the man."[60] It is hard to imagine Headley's translation being possible before *Hamilton*, Lin-Manuel Miranda's global phenomenon musical of 2015. We recognize, however, that the tension between appropriation and amplification of hip hop sensibility is present in both *Hamilton* and Headley's text. Both are subject to critique on those grounds, though another reading might see Headley (and, for that matter, *Hamilton*) using Black culture intentionally to fight the text's or subject matter's white patriarchal history, despite the problematic appropriation such a strategy entails.

Headley does, overall, seek to counter a white supremacist model. For example, although Beowulf is an epic organized around what it might mean to be a good king ("that was a good king" repeats throughout), in Headley's hands this story of elite nobles "feels populist"—an impression Headley crafts through the aforementioned contemporary language and slang she mobilizes as well as her nods to the linguistic codes of social media.[61] In other words, her text avoids rarified language and attempts instead to be accessible and current as well as to speak in the linguistic systems with which she assumes her readers are conversant. Those linguistic systems, furthermore, are complex—social media, like the situation of translation, is bound by its own formal constraints (whether 280 tweet characters, image requirements, or other restrictions). Indeed, social media is partially defined by the very fact that it allows access while at the same time restricting the form that access can take. Similarly, Headley's work, while attempting to invite access, is also constrained by the dictates of her source.

RESURFACING WOMEN

Another important contribution these translators make is to shift the focus of their texts slightly in order to allow other characters less typically focused on to appear more clearly. Specifically, each of these translators draws out from her hypermasculine text women who have been there all along but whom previous translators have not rendered with as much nuance or emphasis as their male protagonists have been rendered. While other translators have cast female characters in the text monolithically, these women translators produce what one could call a more "accurate" text by recovering specificity around what it meant to be a woman in these past societies and narratives.

Wilson attends to the many distinct kinds of women shot through the *Odyssey* in contrast to previous translators who collapsed so many of the differences across the women in this man's epic. Wilson describes herself as having reckoned with the women of the *Odyssey*—not only with Penelope, whom other male translators have written as Odysseus's equal (in class position, yes; in gender, no), but also with women across the various classes woven into the epic—from enslaved girls and women to free nonelite women to elite wives and daughters of kings like Penelope and Nausicaa to the goddesses (minor, like Circe and Calypso, and major, like Odysseus's champion, Athena, and enemy, Hera).[62] Most significant among Wilson's interventions on the level of the word is her choice to name the enslaved people whose labor undergirds the elite world of the epic poem. Where previous translators have chosen the comfortable euphemisms of low-wage labor—"maid," "fieldhand"—Wilson translates several different ancient Greek words (including *doulos, therapōn, tamia*) with the English "slave." As an example, where Lattimore glosses over Nausicaa's slaves, writing that "beside her two handmaidens with beauty given from the Graces slept on either side of the post with the shining doors closed," Wilson writes "Slaves were sleeping outside her doorway, one on either side; two charming girls with all the Graces' gifts."[63] All together, Wilson's translation includes over 200 instances of the word "slave" (in comparison to 5 for A. T. Murray's translation for the Loeb Classical Library), a choice that exposes the quotidian dependence of ancient Mediterranean societies on enslaved labor and also the historical glossing of that dependence with the more palatable language of service. Given the impact of the *Odyssey* over its centuries of translation and reception, such glossing has likely allowed readers to defer direct confrontation with systems of exploitation that undergirded antiquity while emulating them in modernity.[64]

In the end, all of the characters in the epic are bound by class positions to their painful roles—a dynamic that is especially apparent in Wilson's bold recasting of what is arguably the text's most gruesome scene, one that hinges on the translation choice of a single word. Wilson rewrites the scene in which Odysseus slaughters the enslaved women raped by the men who had vied for his throne (the so-called suitors). An earlier popular translator Robert Fagles positioned Odysseus as condemning the motives of the women in a patriarchal translation in which he called the enslaved girls "sluts."[65] In a Twitter thread, Wilson traces her encounter with this choice and others like it: "Many translations import misogynistic language when it isn't there in the Greek. In Fagles's best-selling version, 'You sluts—the suitors' 'whores!' Lombardo: 'Sluts.' Lattimore: 'Creatures.' Fitzgerald: 'Sluts.' Pope's is the best: 'nightly prostitutes to shame.'"[66] Wilson counters these readings, suggesting that Odysseus's motives are more complicated and unpacking the pain and suffering in a scene previously translated with bombast. Resisting the operations of spectacle we tracked in chapter 2, Wilson explains that she aims "to invite genuine empathy rather than an objectifying thrill."[67] By recognizing that the enslaved women in the household could not freely consent to sex with the suitors, Wilson translates the pathos of their slaughter.[68] Odysseus, the returned king, cannot allow the women raped by the suitors to live without undermining his masculinity and status; Penelope, his wife, does not intervene in their slaughter even though she would also have been forced into sex with whichever of the suitors had won the right to replace her husband had he not come home. Most importantly, the unnamed enslaved girls whom Odysseus kills for their lack of freedom had no rights over their bodies in life and could not prevent their own murder in the hall of the house where they were enslaved. Fagles's choice to name these girls "sluts" is a willful misunderstanding of the circumstances of their rape and also an offensive condemnation of the sex women may or may not choose to have. The choice also justifies Odysseus's slaughter of these girls and women on the grounds of their supposed promiscuity to fifteen years of Anglophone readers.[69] Wilson reclaims the enslaved girls' humanity.

And then there is the issue of the privileged women in the text, including Penelope and Athena. While Wilson has expressed her lack of interest in revisiting the strand of scholarship that seeks to find Penelope's voice in favor of a deeper exploration of "unelite" women, this translation nevertheless intervenes in interesting ways with both characters.[70] Wilson asserts that "opacity" is "the most important feature of Penelope's characterization."[71] This interpretation accords with Wilson's comfort with nuance in general as well as her attention to complexity in the text more broadly.[72] Wilson engages with the ongoing scholarly conversation around whether or not Penelope recognizes Odysseus earlier than she lets on and therefore helps him by setting up the challenge of the bow and the axes, reading the intention behind two strands of feminist assertion. One of these is that Penelope knows and therefore has more control than we might otherwise realize. The second is that Penelope does not know, but only because of the patriarchal and divine systems working against her knowing, though she would otherwise have the intelligence to know. The implication of this line of reasoning is that these competing theories can exist precisely because Penelope is defined as unknown by the text itself. Such a reading remains in contrast to that of male translators like Richmond Lattimore, who flatly states that "Penelope knew nothing of the plot."[73]

Commenting on the Robert Fagles translation for which he provides the introduction, Bernard Knox acknowledges the possibility of a reading based on Penelope's recognition but claims that such a reading "runs into an immoveable obstacle in Book 23," when Penelope refuses to recognize her husband after he directly reveals himself to her.[74] Knox does consider that the refusal could represent a counteroffensive by Penelope when her gambit to delay a marriage with the weaving and unweaving of her father-in-law's future shroud is discovered, but does not seem to acknowledge that not immediately admitting to a recognition of her husband could be another way Penelope uses the tools women in her position are given in what Bonnie Honig theorizes as feminist refusal.[75] Penelope cannot fight, expel the suitors herself, or rule Ithaca, but she can delay, create standards of untenable competition, and control the moment she admits to knowing her husband so that it unfolds on her terms. In fact, her own position as a married woman whose husband is absent may be a preferable one to what she will face when Odysseus finally returns and reasserts his authority, so it makes sense that she might want to control the speed at which this narrative progresses. Wilson does not go as far as to suggest this, but through her choices as a translator in emphasizing Penelope's unknown motivations, Wilson instead makes room for a variety of competing interpretations. Indeed, in her "Translator's Note," she argues that "simplicity of diction can also make clear feelings that are far from simple—as in the scene when Penelope and Odysseus meet for the first time after he kills her suitors, when she has not yet recognized him as her husband."[76] If Wilson's intervention does nothing other than complicate interpretations of Penelope, she has already succeeded in her effort to reframe.

As a final note, Wilson's characterization of Athena's independent power also stages a powerful intervention. In book 3, Athena, who is moved to help Telemachus's quest, prays to Poseidon for the hero's success and safe return home but eventually manages to secure the desired outcomes of the prayer on her own without Poseidon's help. Male translations of this moment emphasize different aspects of this feat: Lattimore writes that Athena "herself was bringing it all to completion"; Fagles describes how Athena "brought it all to pass."[77] The use of "all" (*panta*) in these translations refers to the completion of the task, explaining that everything Athena asked for had happened. In Wilson's translation, the "all" is shifted so that it describes Athena acting entirely with her own power: Athena "made her prayer come true all by herself."[78] For Wilson, the "all" signifies Athena's capacity; for Lattimore and Fagles it refers to the outcome of her action. This small shift is itself a form of intervention that empowers the female character it describes.

Likewise, Bartsch states succinctly and directly in a manner perhaps made possible by Wilson's explicit and longer engagement with the language of enslavement and sexual violence:

> I have not softened features of antiquity that are unpleasant to us today: female slaves are not "maids," and they are given away as prizes for games without further comment. Jupiter is a rapist, of both boys and young women. The hero Aeneas may be pious, but that doesn't stop Turnus from calling him a "half-man" (in fact, the charge of effeminacy was a common Roman view of "soft Asiatic types" in Vergil's own day).[79]

Bartsch does not shy away from expressing the reality typically avoided by translators—that ancient power holders could be enslavers, rapists, anti-Eastern, homophobic, or any combination thereof.

With respect to the feminism of her translation, Bartsch frames her intervention in terms of bringing back into the text dimensions that have not been amplified by male translators, such as the importance of Dido, Queen of Carthage. Bartsch argues that previous translators have downplayed Dido's status because of her "Eastern" (Phoenician) identity, her Punic kingdom (with which the Romans later went to war), her love and rage, and "of course she is a woman."[80] Even in antiquity, Bartsch reminds us, men debated Dido's role,

> but her point of view is as justified as any other voice in the *Aeneid*, and it should not be disqualified as "female"—as it was already a century after Vergil, when the satirist Juvenal remarked on how sick he was of erudite women who defended Dido over dinner! (*Satires* 6.434–35)[81]

As this passage demonstrates, women in antiquity engaged with and commented on the *Aeneid* and debated Dido's status, aligning Bartsch with a long tradition of women who have focused on the story. Following that tradition, Bartsch tracks the intersecting misogyny and xenophobia that have shaped Dido's reception and amplifies Dido's heroic status in the text.

As argued at the start of this chapter, Headley is also interested in recovering lost voices in the narrative, announcing in her introduction that her hope is to revise the identities of the female characters in the poem as well as to illuminate their inner workings.[82] One way Headley accomplishes this is by reimagining the unnamed character of Grendel's mother, narrating her own childhood history to demonstrate the importance of this choice. As a child, Headley was fascinated by an image she saw of Grendel's mother and assumed her to be the center of the story—a powerful warrior. As an adult looking back, Headley is unable to locate the specific image so vivid in her memory and even wonders if what she originally saw was actually a representation of Judith beheading Holofernes, the subject of Artemisia Gentileschi's work discussed in our previous chapter. This memory is grounded in Headley's understanding of how very much women and girls seek powerful role models and how presumed encounters with such role models are baked into even our earliest ideations. Much to Headley's surprise when she later reads the text, Grendel's mother is deemphasized and cast as "to many people, an extension of Grendel rather than a character unto herself, despite the significant ink devoted to her fighting capabilities."[83] This example demonstrates the notion of "accuracy" we have sought to develop in this chapter: Grendel's mother is already there inside the original text with lines that perform accolades to her power, yet her role has—in the centuries of reception of the original poem—been diminished or overlooked. Additionally, she is characterized in many translations (and in essays like J. R. R. Tolkien's "Beowulf: The Monsters and the Critics") as a monster. Returning to the language of the original text, Headley easily finds evidence that the mother should instead be seen as a "formidable noblewoman," though Headley also questions why Grendel's mother has to be either/or.[84] This reframing of Grendel's mother through a feminist critique can be situated in the lineage—and criticism—of the work of Sandra Gilbert and Susan Gubar, who, in their 1979 groundbreaking feminist text *The Madwoman in the Attic*, suggested that we imagine women as mad—or monsters—when they represent a liberated version of ourselves (or when they are, in Headley's words, "only doing as men do: providing for and defending oneself)."[85]

Ultimately, all three translations force us to confront the possibility that some of the patriarchal forces in a text are not inherent to it but have instead been added on through the accretions of mostly male translators over time. The women-authored translations discussed here perform important work in refocusing our attention on female characters and the language with which they are described, allowing us to view foundational texts in a more nuanced—and even-handed—way.

SHAPING AN AUDIENCE

A parallel across the woman-authored translations we analyze in this chapter is their interest in shaping their audience.[86] For the translators profiled here, the practice of such shaping can happen in multiple temporal relations to the text itself. On Twitter and other social media platforms, authors can engage their audiences before, during, and after the period of their book's publication to, for example, emphasize specific translation choices in tweets, as in Wilson's scholia, or in Headley's or Bartsch's threads about their practice or their books in general.[87] This engagement moves the work of feminist translation into the realm of a public feminist dialogue.

The interest these three translators develop in storytelling on such platforms parallels their translations' interest in storytelling itself. Each story moves between its diegetic world and its extradiegetic one, captured neatly in translation. Women translators, at least in the case of the three we profile here, are particularly attentive to both the story and the story about the story in their process of translation. Perhaps the social media world in which public feminists exist has even shaped this interest to some degree. And the source texts of the *Odyssey*, the *Aeneid*, and *Beowulf* are tales that very much concern themselves with the concept of storytelling. In each text, heroes both tell their own stories and listen to stories recounted about them; in each, the suggestion is raised of poems being written about them or their loved ones, whether during the time of the text or in the future.[88] And in some cases, the texts integrate reception practices even into their unfolding; in the context of the *Aeneid*, Nandini Pandey sees the power of storytelling as distributed across the text's diverse audiences, arguing that Roman artists and authors such as Vergil built flexibility into their work in anticipation of different receptions that would go on to shape it.[89] Given these emphases in the source texts themselves, the contribution of the women translators includes framing or highlighting the concept of storytelling and connecting that concept to its importance to public feminist platforms.

Wilson's translation of the end of the first stanza of the *Odyssey* emphasizes the idea of locating a story specifically at its starting point while some popular alternative translations by men focus instead on getting the process of telling started. Lattimore (1965) asks Muse (*Mousa*) to "speak, and begin our story" and Fagles (1996) requests Muse to "launch out on his story . . . start from where you will."[90] In contrast, Wilson asks Muse to "find the beginning," a choice that emphasizes knowing exactly what the story is, as finding the beginning also requires Muse to differentiate between what counts as the story and what is simply extraneous.[91] Likewise, Vergil's engagement with the Homeric formulation, already a complex extradiegetic storytelling in its use of the *Iliad* and the *Odyssey* as influencer texts, Bartsch renders: "Remember for me, Muse. Tell me the reasons" (line 8).[92] "Remember" for Bartsch does similar work to Wilson's "find," for memory is also a process of excavation. While the examples by male translators take the story for granted and request simply that the telling commence, Wilson sees part of the work as knowing what counts as the starting point for a sequence of events that may proceed with some degree of causality, and Bartsch centers the process that starting requires.

Locating and defining the story also requires constructing and shaping its audience and teaching that audience how to listen, a practice mediated through women in the figure of the muse (or the voice of the writer, translator, or rhapsode for which the muse surely stands in). When the start of the story or the inspiration for its telling is controlled by a female muse, she empowers its beginning, calling the story to order. In this light, the muse might herself be thought of as a precursor to public feminism. The *Odyssey* begins with an imperative directed to Muse (generally translated as "tell me") while *Beowulf* begins with an imperative directed at its audience to listen (see the "Poetics and Language" section of this chapter for a rundown of some standard choices for translating "hwæt," the first word of the text). Thus the earlier text invokes its audience/reader through a voyeuristic move ("observe me request the story from Muse") while the later one calls together its audience through a direct request ("it's time to focus on this story"). The remainder of the *Odyssey* is therefore implied to be the result of Muse speaking through that narrator to the audience, though there are some odd moments of shifting address (as when the narrator addresses Eumaeus directly in book 14) and books 9–12 are framed as Odysseus telling his story to the Phaiakians. For the most part, the audience is passively constructed through the voyeurism of listening to narrator/Muse, though the modeling within the text of the appropriate process for receiving tales may also help shape and instruct the audience/ reader—as does the start of book 13 when, after the conclusion of Odysseus's tale, the Phaiakians are described as "silent, spellbound."[93] Similarly, Aeneas tells his story to Dido and the Punic court in book 3 of the *Aeneid*: "Such was the god-sent fate Aeneas told / his spellbound audience, such his voyage. / Ending it at last like this, he fell silent."[94] Both texts thereby instruct their audience in how to listen directly through the choices their translators make in their opening lines.

Beowulf operates differently, particularly due to Headley's choice in using "bro," a move that already, from the first word, stages an interpretation. The text is, in part, a form of peacocking or "flexing" (Headley's term) to be read with the understanding that the story is not just a story but also an assertion of masculine identity and community—a casual, boast-filled conversation designed to draw the attention of an audience of peers. In making this choice, Headley shifts the very first word of the text away from what could be characterized linguistically as a simple locutionary interjection ("so") into one that is a direct appellation ("bro!"). Both variations function as "speech acts" in the sense that J. L. Austin theorizes them: words that perform an action. "So" and "bro" make a move similar to throat clearing (and both are very directly related to the variant "listen"), the piece Austin terms "locution." Austin also claims that locution results in "illocution" (what the speech actually does) and "perlocution" (what happens as a result of the speaking).[95] In this model, the locution "so" carries with it an illocution ("listen up") and the ideal perlocution is that the audience listens or the reader pays careful attention. But when the locution is "bro," the illocution is more complicated—a specific male and nonhierarchical audience is constructed and asked to listen, and the ideal perlocution is therefore a complex concatenation of a listening community coming together. Headley captures this idea expertly:

> The entire poem, and especially the monologues of the men in it, feels to me like the sort of competitive conversations I've often heard between men, one insisting on his right to the floor while simultaneously insisting that he's friendly. "Bro" is, to my ear, a means of commanding attention while shuffling focus calculatedly away from hierarchy.[96]

Such a capture—and one that is so different from an invocation to a female muse—also begs the question of how Headley's intervention could possibly count as a feminist one. We suggest that by focusing on the masculinity of *Beowulf*'s construction of male community and its status as a text written for men and about men, Headley draws attention to what is implicit but historically less observed—that we are watching masculine culture as it assembles and unfolds, often to the exclusion of women. It is precisely into that masculine circle that Headley inserts herself as a translator, demonstrating her feminist intentions and politics.

Headley will continue to use "bro" in the text in two major ways: first in the diegetic world as a form of address the characters make to each other (for example, Beowulf uses it to salute Hrothgar in line 454 and Unferth uses it to slight Beowulf in line 504) and second in the extradiegetic as a reminder of the narrator's connection to those hearing/reading the story (for example, the narrator in line 837 recounts: "Bro, I've heard when dawn broke, soldiers / stampeded to the ring-hall"; and in line 2752 prepares the listener/reader with: "Bro, here's how the story goes"). The fact that the word is used both ways connects the work of the writer/orator to the quotidian task of bringing together male–male communities (through posturing but also through confronting risk and death), though the second usage, narrator to reader, also functions to remind the reader that they are encountering a story (diegesis), something Headley keeps front and center.[97] Such stories, she implicitly suggests, shape cultural values in profound ways, and we should keep a watchful eye on them.

The relationship built with "bro" allows the narrator to directly address the reader in order to illuminate the tension between direct experience and encountering tales—and the trust required to maintain faith in the second. For example, in lines 1028–29, the narrator states: "I mean, personally? I've never seen anything / like it, so many treasures sliding down the table"— and the reader presumably accepts this assertion based on the previously established trust.[98] Such trust also allows the narrator to announce meaning through community. In line 2291, the narrator reminds us that "we all know stories / like this one," suggesting that an interpretive community with shared understandings about meaning has successfully been created, one that is similar to the potential interpretive communities that receive hashtags through social media.[99] This one word—"bro"—therefore does remarkable work throughout the text, ensuring that, through her choices in translation, Headley, like Wilson, will imply that her text functions as a telling of and as a simultaneous interpretation of the story that also shapes its audience.

COMMENTING ON/REFLECTING THE NOW

In addition to these translations that emerge in a moment of heightened attention for work by women translators, other women writers have produced backstories for women characters who appear in these ancient myths. For example, Madeleine Miller's fictional *Circe* (2018) and Natalie Haynes's *The Children of Jocasta* (2017) and *Pandora's Jar: Women in the Greek Myths* (2020) foreground the women often in the background of Greek tragedy and myths in retellings published during the same time period we explore in this chapter.[100] Even Headley's fictional retelling of *Beowulf* set in the twenty-first century, *The Mere Wife* (2018), preceded and led to her translation of *Beowulf*. That these works of fiction cluster during this time period demonstrates the depth and variety of interest in the worlds of women they recover, often through a public feminist lens. These interventions also align in some ways with Hartman's practice of critical fabulation (discussed in chapter 2), although they aim to fill lacunae in drama and myth rather than in historical archives.

Such work implicitly seeks a window to our contemporary world, evidenced by Wilson's translation of line 1.10 about the imperative to "tell the old story for our modern times." Surprisingly, while one might think this is merely generally true—that the texts are applicable to our contemporary world because they deal with power or battles—it is also quite specifically true in terms of current crises. This, in part, may account for the growing momentum of such translations and backstories during the Trump years and beyond. For example, Wilson writes that "Homer's concerns—with loyalty, families, migrants, consumerism, violence, war, poverty, identity, rhetoric, and lies—are in some ways deeply familiar" and argues that her translation can "help us reconsider both the origins of Western literature, and our infinitely complex contemporary world."[101] The *Odyssey* is thus presented as an important tool to assist us in addressing our contemporary issues, and it seems to fit specifically into a post-2016 election world. Bartsch likewise emphasizes not only Aeneas's status as a refugee from Troy but also his transition to a violent conqueror of the Indigenous ruler Turnus at the end of the *Aeneid*, drawing out two strands of modern geopolitics—refugee crises and Indigenous rights—that run through the old text.

Headley is similarly clear that part of her interest in her Old English text is in using it to comment on specific contemporary issues, writing that "as much as *Beowulf* is a poem about Then, it is also (and always had been) a poem about Now, and how we got here."[102] In her acknowledgments, Headley lists a string of poets whose similar transformations of canonical and epic material inspired her own, including Anne Carson and Danez Smith (we analyze the work of Carson in chapter 4 and that of Smith in chapter 6).[103] Smith's poem "not an elegy" directs the reader: "think: once, a white girl / was kidnapped & that's the Trojan war."[104] This invocation of Troy exposes the hypocrisy of a society that believes itself to be founded on principles it applies inconsistently to a degree that suggests genocide. Headley's reference itself implies that she was open to a variety of ways to engage powerfully with the canon in the context of our modern world.

Smith's use of the *Iliad* to comment on the murder of Black people in contemporary culture may be a practice Headley seeks to emulate as she connects her larger concerns around colonialism and its wide-ranging effects to specific contemporary crises, from Trump's imprisoning of refugees to school shootings to the dominion of amazon.com and its embedded capitalistic and exploitative market priorities. Her introduction therefore ends in a prayer of sorts, which is also a rationalization for her translation:

> That is, in my opinion, the reason to keep analyzing texts like *Beowulf*. We might, if we analyzed our own long-standing stories, use them to translate ourselves into a society in which hero making doesn't require monster killing, border closing, and hoard clinging.[105]

Headley holds up her text up as a mirror, asking readers to consider what they see when comparing contemporary society to its standard. In this way, by remaking foundational texts, feminist translations can help us imagine a way of remaking the world.

NOTES

1. Translation Talk (@translationtalk), "Writer Nikolai Gogol on Translation: 'The Translator Should be like Glass: So Transparent That You Can't See Him,'" *Twitter*, June 23, 2021, 6:36 a.m., https://twitter.com/translationtalk/status/1407693949234450437.

2. Sasha Dugdale (@SashaDugdale), "The Translator is Many Kilos of Flesh, Hair, Bones, Fingernails, Teeth. Wherever She Goes She Leaves Her Fingerprints, Dust, Oils and Smell," *Twitter*, June 23, 2021, 11:50 p.m., https://twitter.com/SashaDugdale/status/1407954237170937863.

3. Walker Kaplan, "Jhumpa Lahiri Is Writing a New Translation of Ovid's *Metamorphoses*," *LitHub*, May 18, 2021, https://lithub.com/jhumpa-lahiri-is-working-on-a-new-translation-of-ovids-metamorphoses-for-the-modern-library.

4. On the history of this position within feminist translation, see von Flotow, *Translation and Gender*, 35–6. Lola Sánchez, writing the article "Translations That Matter: About a Foundational Text in Feminist Studies in Spain" in a 2014 special issue of *Signs*, "Symposium: Translation, Feminist Scholarship, and the Hegemony of English," argues that "all translations are a rewriting that—whether consciously or unconsciously—transforms the original . . . whoever is translating can do nothing other than interpret the original and propose a version of it in light of his or her own understanding of the world" (*Signs* 39, no. 3 [Spring 2014], 571). In our argument, we build heavily on a long and ongoing conversation about the work of translation, especially feminist translation, and provide here some selected resources for further exploration. For the idea that translation deconstructs language itself, see Gayatri Chakravorty Spivak, "Translating in a World of Languages," in *Profession 2010*, ed. Rosemary G. Feal (New York: Modern Language Association, 2010), 35–43. For the danger of the hegemony of the English language, see Esther Allen and Susan Bernofsky, eds. *In Translation: Translators on Their Work and What It Means* (New York: Columbia University Press, 2013). For feminist translation more recently, see collections like Olga Castro and Emek Ergun, eds. *Feminist Translation Studies: Local and Transnational Perspectives* (New York: Routledge, 2017), and José Santaemilia, ed. *Gender, Sex and Translation* (New York: Routledge, 2005).

5. We must note here that, in the case of Beowulf, male authorship is assumed but not assured. The version of the text we have comes from a scribal tradition rather than one with a historically recorded author, shifting notions of agency and complicating the status of feminist translation to some degree.

6. For example, Emily Wilson, writing about three recent translations of the *Oresteia*, argues that translation has a particularly critical role in this time period: "In 2020, thinking about gender inequality, tyranny, grief, liberation, rage, action and reaction, generational change, and the proper function of norms and the rule of law has a new urgency." Wilson, "Ah, How Miserable!" Maria Dahvana Headley asserts in her translation that "as much as *Beowulf* is a poem about Then, it is also (and always had been) a poem about Now, and how we got here," a comment we explore in more depth later in this chapter. Maria Dahvana Headley, *Beowulf: A New Translation* (New York: Farrar, Straus and Giroux, 2020), ix–x.

7. Lahiri and Baraz's text is forthcoming from Penguin Random House Modern Library; McCarter's is forthcoming from Penguin Books. We also note renewed attention to translation in this moment in contexts beyond the constructed "Western canon," as in the recent section of *Small Axe* devoted to "Translating the Caribbean," which printed the first English translation of José Lezama Lima's 1941 essay "Julián del Casal," translated by poet and translator Robin Myers. José Lezama Lima, "Julián

del Casal (1941)," trans. Robin Myers, *Small Axe* 23, no. 3 (November 1, 2019): 131–54. For another example, see Allison Caplan's introduction to and translation of "Blowers of Sun-Excrement: Nahua Lost-Wax Gold Casting in the Florentine Codex Book 9, Chapter 16," *West 86th: A Journal of Decorative Arts, Design History, and Material Culture* 28, no. 2 (2022): 215–231. We understand intersectional feminism as a basis for public feminist practice; therefore, translation, which allows conversation across fields of study, genre, and context, must be at the heart of this work.

8. The operation of "accuracy" has been leveled against translators with marginalized subject positions, so the reclaiming of accuracy by these women translators is itself an implicit critique of patriarchal structures.

9. This position is distinct from that of a woman translator translating a woman-authored text, as in the case of Anne Carson's translation of Sappho, *If Not, Winter: Fragments of Sappho* (Sappho, *If Not, Winter: Fragments of Sappho*, trans. Anne Carson [London: Virago, 2003]), which we explore in chapter 4. Unlike Wilson, Headley, and Bartsch, Carson does not reject the rationalist discourse or the fantasy of pure language, perhaps in recognition that the at least partial alignment of her subject position and Sappho's might seem to allow for the kind of transparency so easily assumed by male translators of male-authored texts.

10. von Flotow, *Translation and Gender*, 29; Cixous, "Laugh of the Medusa."

11. von Flotow, *Translation and Gender*, 12.

12. von Flotow, *Translation and Gender*, 12–34. We distinguish the recovery explored in our chapter from recovery feminism more broadly, which focuses on inviting into the canon previously overlooked books by women authors. Talia Schaffer coins the term "recovery feminism," defining it as "the practice of salvaging texts that have been lost to history." Talia Schaffer, "Victorian Feminist Criticism: Recovery Work and the Care Community," *Victorian Literature and Culture* 47, no. 1 (2019): 63. Writing elsewhere, Schaffer warns that recovery feminism can rely on problematic notions of gender essentialism as well as a need as feminist writers to save actual women when writing about characters: "Victorianist feminist criticism still retains essential or biological 'women' as its subject, an untenable assumption now that gender is widely recognized as a constructed, intersectional category. The identificatory elements of recovery feminism, while personally satisfying, nonetheless perpetuated a kind of simplistic biographic ascription. It allowed a slippage from the work to the author. If one was feminist, suppressed, subversive, endangered, then perforce the other was too, and saving the work was tantamount to saving the person." Talia Schaffer, "Feminism and the Canon," in *The Routledge Companion to Victorian Literature*, ed. Dennis Denisoff and Talia Schaffer (New York: Routledge, 2020), 278. In the place of this ethos, Schaffer suggests drawing from an ethics of care: "Instead of seeing ourselves as saviors of a silenced victim, we can imagine ourselves into a care relation with the text—which might mean reparative readings, readings designed to respect the other regardless of whether we agree with its politics. We might, then, think of ourselves not as the agents of heroic rescue, but, rather, as carers keeping the welfare of the text at heart. . . . We might, in other words, end with the desire to care for the dead, and recognize that if we read as caregivers, we can work toward their 'recovery' in a whole new way." Schaffer,

"Victorian Feminist Criticism," 82–3. In our work, we endeavor to replicate this ethics of care.

13. von Flotow, *Translation and Gender*, 46. This conception was evident in the 2021 controversy over the German translation of Amanda Gorman's "The Hill We Climb," the poem that took the United States—and indeed the world—by storm after Gorman read at Joe Biden's 2021 inauguration. In the aftermath of the inauguration, when people around the world were impatient to read Gorman's poem in their own language, controversy brewed, and critics weighed in about the importance of having Black translators translate a poem that deeply focuses on the Black experience. Alex Marshall, "Amanda Gorman's Poetry United Critics. It's Dividing Translators," *New York Times*, March 26, 2021, https://www.nytimes.com/2021/03/26/books/amanda -gorman-hill-we-climb-translation.html.

14. Walter Benjamin, "The Task of the Translator," in *Illuminations*, ed. Hannah Arendt, trans. Harry Zohn (New York: Harcourt Brace Jovanovich, 1968), 78. We note that a number of writers engaged with feminist translation address other aspects of Benjamin's text but not necessarily his contention about maintaining the invisibility of the translator.

15. Appiah traces the origin of this desire to a concept originated in the Middle Ages of "the transfer of learning" (*translatio studii*). Appiah, "There's No Such Thing." To listen to the entire lecture, see Appiah, "Mistaken Identities," https://www .bbc.co.uk/sounds/play/b081lkkj.

16. Antoine Berman, *The Age of Translation: A Commentary on Walter Benjamin's "The Task of the Translator" = L'âge de la traduction: la tâche du traducteur de Walter Benjamin, un commentaire*, trans. and intro. Chantal Wright (Abingdon: Routledge, 2018), 31. von Flotow, *Translation and Gender*, 46–7, historicizes the model of foundational Adamic language, pointing out that both Luce Irigaray and Karen Littau have engaged with the other myth of the world's various languages—that of Pandora—to think through the plurality afforded by language and translation.

17. While we make this claim about transparency in patriarchy, there are others who elect transparency for completely different reasons. For example, in contexts like that of translating what has previously been a historically invisible Indigenous text as a non-Indigenous person, a translator might pursue something akin to transparency in order to surface as much of an Indigenous language and text as possible. This choice would not reflect a conflation of the translator's and writer's subject positions but instead have as its goal to foreground the language of the original text. As Indigenous and Indo-European languages have been treated and circulated differently—and, for example, an English translation will be read far more widely than its source text—this approach can help to redress such power imbalances. For a recent example, see Caplan, "Blowers of Sun-Excrement."

18. Benjamin, "Task of the Translator," 78.

19. Anne Le Fèvre Dacier, *L'Illiade d'Homere* (Paris: Chez Rigaud, 1711). Glenn Most and Alice Schreyer, eds., *Homer in Print: A Catalogue of the Bibliotheca Homerica Langiana at the University of Chicago Library* (Chicago: University of Chicago Press, 2013), 4, 234–5, 238. See also British Museum 332543001 for a frontispiece of Dacier's book depicting the "Personification of Heroic Poetry."

20. Zachary Small, "Trump Makes Classical Style the Default for Federal Buildings," *New York Times*, December 21, 2020, https://www.nytimes.com/2020/12/21/arts/design/trump-executive-order-federal-buildings-architecture.html.

21. On classicism and its discontents, see Andrew Stewart, *Classical Greece and the Birth of Western Art* (Cambridge: Cambridge University Press, 2009), 1–6.

22. For the connection between Trump's architecture directive, white supremacy, and the failed coup of January 6, 2021, see Lyra Monteiro, "How a Trump Executive Order Aims to Set White Supremacy in Stone," *Hyperallergic*, January 23, 2021, https://hyperallergic.com/614175/how-a-trump-executive-order-aims-to-set-white-supremacy-in-stone.

23. Do yourself a favor and read a bit more of Wilson's delightful prose: "It was with a sinking feeling that I learned that at least three new translations of the *Oresteia* had recently appeared. I plunged into an even deeper gloom when I realised that two of them are by elderly white men, both emeritus professors, and the other is by a younger white man, not an academic. These are the two demographic categories from which the vast majority of modern English translators of Greco-Roman texts emerge. . . . If we are going to have endless retranslations of the same old texts—which is not self-evidently a good thing—we might hope that at least some of them would be done by classicists who are younger, or less white, or less male . . . in this particular case, the similarities between these three translations, especially in the paratextual material, suggest a partial correlation between the translators' social positions and their readings of the *Oresteia*." Wilson, "Oh How Miserable!" For more academic feminist takes on what it means when women translators approach such texts, see Emily Wilson, "Found in Translation: How Women Are Making the Classics Their Own," *The Guardian*, July 7, 2017, https://www.theguardian.com/books/2017/jul/07/women-classics-translation-female-scholars-translators, and Bess Myers, "Women Who Translate," *Eidolon*, August 5, 2019, https://eidolon.pub/women-who-translate-7966e56b3df2.

24. On the intersections of race and gender discrimination in archives, museums, universities, and publishing houses, see Mary Louise Kelly, "#PublishingPaidMe: Authors Share Their Advances to Expose Racial Disparity," *NPR*, June 8, 2020, https://www.npr.org/2020/06/08/872470156/-publishingpaidme-authors-share-their-advances-to-expose-racial-disparities and La Tanya S. Autry and Mike Murawski, "Museums are Not Neutral," https://www.museumsarenotneutral.com.

25. Interview with Emily Wilson for the *Uncommon Muse* as cited in Jennifer Stager, "A Mother's Odyssey: The Journey to Integrating the Roles of Scholar and Mother," *Eidolon*, August 31, 2018, https://eidolon.pub/a-mothers-odyssey-9c1c6ea218b9.

26. Jessica Bao, "Emily Wilson: Not the First Woman to Translate the *Odyssey*," *34th Street*, October 22, 2019, https://www.34st.com/article/2019/10/emily-wilson-penn-classical-studies-translation-the-odyssey-macarthur-foundation-genius-grant-fellowship, and Emily Wilson (@EmilyRCWilson), "I Put 'NOT the First Woman to Publish a Translation of the Odyssey' on My Twitter-Bio, After Seeing It Asserted for the Gazillionth Time. Here is Why," *Twitter*, October 2, 2019, 9:03 a.m. https://twitter.com/EmilyRCWilson/status/1179426687047614464.

27. Thanks to Dr. Mackenzie Zalin for helping us to determine the names of these women who have translated the *Odyssey* from ancient Greek into a range of modern languages.

28. Stager, "A Mother's Odyssey."

29. Shadi Bartsch, Acknowledgments to Vergil, *Aeneid*, trans. Shadi Bartsch (New York: Random House, 2021), xii.

30. Headley, *Beowulf*, 139.

31. Headley's eventual translation both demonstrated her deep scholarship and great humility; as one critic comments, "the lack of scholarly apparatus [in Headley's translation] is deceptive: Headley has studied the poem deeply and is conversant with some of the text's most obscure details." Ruth Franklin, "A 'Beowulf' for Our Moment," *New Yorker*, August 24, 2020, https://www.newyorker.com/magazine /2020/08/31/a-beowulf-for-our-moment.

32. Headley, *Beowulf*, 137. In the tradition of Children's Defense Fund President Marian Wright Edelman's powerful quotation "you can't be what you can't see," this acknowledgment reminds one of us of a passage in Nnedi Okorafor's 2011 novel *Akata Witch* (New York: Viking Books, 2011). After the novel's main character participates in a soccer tournament typically restricted to boys, another female student comments: "I always wanted to play, but I didn't know I *could*. At least the girls who come after you will know now" (265, emphasis in original). For more on Edelman in the context of women in tech, see Anneke Jong, "You Can't Be What You Can't See: How to Get More Women in Tech," *The Muse*, March 06, 2021, https://www.themuse .com/advice/you-cant-be-what-you-cant-see-how-to-get-more-women-in-tech.

33. Johanna Hanink, "The Twists and Turns of Translation," *Eidolon*, February 4, 2019, https://eidolon.pub/the-twists-and-turns-of-translation-33f1272dffa8.

34. Headley, *Beowulf*, 138.

35. Emily Wilson, Introduction to Homer, *The Odyssey*, trans. Emily Wilson (New York: W.W. Norton, 2018), 7–11. Peter Gainsford, "Not 'The Oldest Written Record of the *Odyssey*,'" *Kiwi Hellenist*, July 12, 2018, http://kiwihellenist.blogspot.com /2018/07/not-oldest-written-record-of-odyssey.html. For a recent exploration of the collection and transmission of Homeric texts, see Most and Schreyer, *Homer in Print*. For the Johns Hopkins papyrus fragment with the *Odyssey*, see Johns Hopkins Special Collections: Homer, *The Odyssey*, X–XII (several fragments), P. Oxy 1819 EES, 192.

36. Robert Lamberton and John J. Keaney, eds., *Homer's Ancient Readers: The Hermeneutics of Greek Epic's Earliest Exegetes* (Princeton, NJ: Princeton University Press, 1992), vii–xxii.

37. Alessandro Barchiesi, *Homeric Effects in Vergil's Narrative* (Oxford: Princeton University Press, 2015), 115–31; Bartsch, Introduction, xxi–xxii.

38. Bartsch, "Introduction," xlii.

39. Manuscript of the *Aeneid* Vat.lat.3225: https://digi.vatlib.it/view/MSS_Vat .lat.3225. And also Vergilius Romanus, Vat.lat.3867: https://digi.vatlib.it/view/MSS _Vat.lat.3867.

40. Headley explains that "it was a cotton-gloved privilege to view the original manuscript of *Beowulf*. Now a click, and there you are, looking at handwriting a thou- sand years old: 'Hwæt. We Gardena in geardagum, þeodcyninga, þrym gefrunon.'

Not only is the original accessible to anyone with an internet connection, so are a huge number of translations and volumes of evolving scholarship, many long out of print. This translation exists because of that access." Headley, *Beowulf*, xv.

41. Richard Lattimore, Introduction to *The Odyssey of Homer*, trans. Richmond Lattimore (New York: Harper Perennial, 1967), 22–3.

42. Wilson, "Introduction," 86. In this chapter we are foregrounding a contemporary Anglophone woman translating a masculinized ancient epic—Homer's *Odyssey*. In contrast, Hélène Cixous mobilized her practice of feminist rewriting to claim a feminine, maternal, and personal role for Homer when she named her chronicle of the final six months of her mother's life "Homère est morte," which her English translator rendered "Mother Homer is Dead." Hélène Cixous, *Homère est morte* (Paris: Éditions Galilée, 2014) and Hélène Cixous, *Mother Homer is Dead*, trans. Peggy Kamuf (Edinburgh: Edinburgh University Press, 2018).

43. Wilson, "Introduction," 86.

44. Bartsch, "Translator's Note," xlix.

45. Headley, *Beowulf*, xv–xvi.

46. At the same time, Headley claims that viewing Beowulf as a "masculine text" is "somewhat unfair," so her subject position may be nearer to her text than the other translators we explore feel to their texts (Headley, *Beowulf*, xxiii).

47. Wilson, "Introduction," 82.

48. Homer, *The Odyssey*, trans. Wilson, 151 and 148.

49. Wilson, "Introduction," 87 ("I have tried to keep a register that is recognizably speakable and readable while skirting between the Charybdis of artifice and the Scylla of slang.")

50. Bartsch, "Translator's Note," li–lii.

51. Bartsch, "Translator's Note," l–li.

52. Bartsch, "Translator's Note," lii–liv.

53. These choices have produced some consternation, prompting even a supportive critic to remark that "Headley's version is more of a rewriting than a true translation." Franklin, "'Beowulf' for Our Moment." We wholeheartedly disagree with this contention and note instead the restrictions implicit in its framework—restrictions that, if perpetuated, limit translators who wish to translate the context as well as the content of canonical works.

54. Alexander Abad-Santos, "How the Bro Became White," *The Atlantic*, October 9, 2013, https://www.theatlantic.com/culture/archive/2013/10/how-encino-man-changed-race-bros/310146/.

55. The original blog post is no longer online; for a more recent version, see Katherine Connor Martin, "How Brothers Became Buddies and Bros," *Oxford University Press Blog*, April 30, 2016, https://blog.oup.com/2016/04/brothers-buddies-bros-oed-update.

56. Headley, *Beowulf*, 29.

57. This mirrors Roxane Gay's shaping of an audience explored here in chapter 1 and perhaps creates a pattern in this historical moment, especially in the age of social media, of women expressing anxiety around their own personal reception.

58. Headley, *Beowulf*, 64.

59. For more on Eminem's song and the evolution of "stan" as a verb, see Anne-Derrick Gaillot, "When 'Stan' Became a Verb," *The Outline*, October 26, 2017, https://theoutline.com/post/2425/when-stan-became-a-verb.

60. Headley, *Beowulf*, 75 and 136. Other academics are not as charmed; for example, writing insightfully in the *New York Review of Books*, English professor Irina Dumitrescu suggests that Headley's work will age awkwardly and that her overuse of "bro" starts to feel like a gimmick. Irina Dumitrescu, "Dudes Without Heirs," *New York Review of Books*, December 3, 2020, https://www.nybooks.com/articles/2020/12/03/dudes-without-heirs.

61. Headley, *Beowulf*, xix. And yet populism may be its own minefield after Trump co-opted it in service of white supremacy.

62. Emily Wilson, "A Translator's Reckoning with the Women of the *Odyssey*," *New Yorker*, December 8, 2017, https://www.newyorker.com/books/page-turner/a-translators-reckoning-with-the-women-of-the-odyssey.

63. Homer, *The Odyssey*, trans. Wilson, 197 (6.15–20). Notably, Wilson's translation compresses some of the language around the artistry and material splendor of Nausicaa's quarters, a strategy that keeps the emphasis on the enslaved women she aims to foreground. Recovering material color in Homer, however, is another feminist strategy that counters the historical erasure of color and materials from Homeric texts in order to make Homeric Greek conform to Neoclassical misconceptions about the absence of color in the ancient Mediterranean, on which see Jennifer Stager, "The Materiality of Color in Ancient Mediterranean Art," in *Essays in Global Color History*, ed. Rachael Goldman (New Jersey: Gorgias Press, 2016), 97–120, and Jennifer M.S. Stager, *Seeing Color in Classical* Art: Theory, Practice, and Reception from Antiquity to the Present (Cambridge: Cambridge University Press, 2022).

64. For perspectives on this connection to the transatlantic slave trade, see Roland Quinault, "Gladstone and Slavery," *Historical Journal* 52, no. 2 (2009): 363–83, and David Waldstreicher, "Ancients, Moderns, and Africans: Phillis Wheatley and the Politics of Empire and Slavery in the American Revolution," *Journal of the Early Republic* 37, no. 4 (2017): 701–33.

65. Homer, *The Odyssey*, trans. Robert Fagles, with an introduction by Bernard Knox (New York: Viking, 1996). See also Yung In Chae, "Women Who Weave," *Eidolon*, November 16, 2017, https://eidolon.pub/women-who-weave-c3a8dd322447.

66. Emily Wilson (@EmilyRCWilson), "Many Translations Import Misogynistic Language When It Isn't There in the Greek," *Twitter*, March 8, 2018, https://twitter.com/emilyrcwilson/status/971823043512360960?lang=en.

67. Wilson, "Introduction," 86.

68. Determining "accurate" meanings of contested words can be a tautological practice, especially in the context of translation. While we may think of a word's definition as immutable, the definitions for each word are actually gleaned from the ancient literature in which they appear and are thus shaped by the reception of ancient texts over time. Often a single word has several possible dictionary meanings from which the translator must make a selection. In this case, Wilson chose to use the word "slave" where others have sought alternatives to that violent history. Anne Thompson, responding to Simon Goldhill's review of an edited volume on

the ancient Greek dictionary Liddell and Scott in the *Bryn Mawr Classical Review*, offers some of the complexity of that dictionary's own transmission history: "Unlike the fresh start made for The Oxford Latin Dictionary (on which full-time work began in 1933), the first edition of Liddell and Scott (1843) was based on a German work (also not entirely original), and was revised through several editions until the ninth (1940, known as LSJ or LSJM), and later with a Supplement that was in its turn also revised (1968 and 1996)." Thus even definitions inscribed in dictionaries may themselves be translations, glosses, and etymologies, complicating the work of literary translation that may rely on them. Anne Thompson, "Response: Thompson on Goldhill on Stray, Clarke and Katz, Liddell and Scott: The History, Methodology, and Languages of the World's Leading Lexicon of Ancient Greek," *Bryn Mawr Classical Review*, 2021.06.35, https://bmcr.brynmawr.edu/2021/2021.06.35.

69. This practice aligns with the training of an audience or reader that we discuss in the "Shaping an Audience" section of this chapter. For now, we note the way that patriarchal systems are perpetuated through the training of an audience in acceptable forms of reception as well as in language use and meaning more broadly. As Luce Irigaray writes: "If we speak the same language, we reproduce the same history." Luce Irigaray and Carolyn Burke, *This Sex Which is Not One* (Ithaca, NY: Cornell University Press, 1985), 205; also cited in an alternate translation by the author in von Flotow, *Translation and Gender*, 9–10.

70. Wyatt Mason, "The First Woman to Translate 'The Odyssey' into English," *New York Times*, November 2, 2017, https://www.nytimes.com/2017/11/02/magazine /the-first-woman-to-translate-the-odyssey-into-english.html.

71. Wilson, "Introduction," 89.

72. For example, Wilson's translation of the *Odyssey*'s first line, "Tell me about a complicated man," breaks with the tradition of English translations to characterize Odysseus as having many paths (or ways or choices) to instead show him as complicated as a *character*, a reading Wilson solidifies in her introduction when she asserts that Odysseus "seems to contain multitudes." For Wilson's comment on the multitudes she believes Odysseus contains, see Wilson, "Introduction," 5.

73. Lattimore, "Introduction," 2.

74. Bernard Knox, Introduction to Homer, *The Odyssey*, trans. Robert Fagles, with an introduction by Bernard Knox (New York: Viking, 1996), 55. The relationship between Robert Fagles and Bernard Knox is interesting to us. As a poet, Fagles elects to partner with Knox, a scholar, to produce the paratext for his translation. This situation differs from Emily Wilson's, as Wilson is a scholar also practicing the work of poetry and therefore occupies both roles in her own text.

75. Bonnie Honig, *A Feminist Theory of Refusal* (Cambridge, MA: Harvard University Press, 2021), especially 1–13 for an outline of this theory.

76. Wilson, "Introduction," 86.

77. Homer, *The Odyssey*, trans. Lattimore, 68 (3.62) and Homer, *The Odyssey*, trans. Fagles, 109 (3.70). Additionally, A. T. Murray for the Loeb Classical Library 104 renders the line "Thus she prayed and was herself fulfilling it all." Homer. *The Odyssey*, trans. A. T. Murray. Loeb Classical Library 104. Cambridge, MA: Harvard University Press, 1919, 84–5.

78. Homer, *The Odyssey*, trans. Wilson, 137 (3.62).

79. Bartsch, "Translator's Note," lvii.

80. Bartsch, "Introduction," xlv.

81. Bartsch, "Introduction," xlvi–xlvii.

82. Headley, *Beowulf*, xxiii.

83. Headley, *Beowulf*, viii.

84. Headley, *Beowulf*, xxv and xxvii.

85. Headley, *Beowulf*, xxvii. Constructions of women as monsters date back to Greek antiquity, the Bible, and some Mesopotamian texts. We also highlight the parallels in the "monsterization" of Grendel's mother and the jailing of women who kill their rapists in self-defense. For more monster theory, see the collection Jeffrey Jerome Cohen, ed., *Monster Theory: Reading Culture* (Minneapolis: University of Minnesota Press, 1996) as well as Jeffrey Weinstock, ed., *The Monster Theory Reader* (Minneapolis: University of Minnesota Press, 2020), and Asa Simon Mittman and Marcus Hensel, eds., *Classic Readings on Monster Theory* (York: Arc Humanities Press, 2018). For the jailing of women who kill their rapists, see "Locking Up Women for Killing Their Rapists," *The Appeal*, January 30, 2020, https://theappeal.org/the-appeal-podcast-locking-up-women-for-killing-their-rapists. Finally, contemporary Victorian scholars do not universally accept Gilbert's and Gubar's formulation; Talia Schaffer calls "the idea that Victorian women were 'lost,' silenced or made mad or demonic by a world that refused to accommodate her" regressive. Schaffer, "Feminism and the Canon," 279.

86. Many of the creators we profile in this book express the same need. We have traced it in the work of Roxane Gay (see chapter 1) and will see it in the projects of writers and artists we explore in subsequent chapters. Perhaps under patriarchy, women creators focus on shaping an audience as they know too well the consequences they face otherwise. And perhaps this need is intensified when creators work in the era of internet comments. For an example of a completely different analysis of the way texts train audience reception, see Lyn Innes, "No Man Is an Island: National Literary Canons, Writers, and Readers," in *Islanded Identities: Constructions of Postcolonial Cultural Insularity*, ed. Maeve McCusker and Anthony Soares (New York: Rodopi, 2011), 189–206.

87. Emily Wilson shares her own wrestling with Homer's Greek in her Twitter Scholia (Emily Wilson, "Scholia Tweets," *Emily RC Wilson*, January 12, 2021, https://www.emilyrcwilson.com/emilyrcwilson-scholia); for commentary on Wilson's practice, see Dan Chiasson, "The Classics Scholar Quietly Redefining What Twitter Can Do," *New Yorker*, March 19, 2018, https://www.newyorker.com/culture/rabbit-holes/the-classics-scholar-redefining-what-twitter-can-do. For examples of Headley (@MARIADAHVANA) and Bartsch (@ShadiBartsch) using Twitter to share their choices, see https://twitter.com/mariadahvana/status/1314267812307767297 and https://twitter.com/ShadiBartsch/status/1301426855447232514.

88. Examples of the heroes telling their own stories include Odysseus telling his tale to the Phaiakians in books 9–12; Aeneas telling his story of the fall of Troy to Dido's court in book 2; and Beowulf telling the story of his defeat of Grendel in lines 1651–76 on pages 72–3 (and retelling it, adding in the defeat of Grendel's

mother, in ll.2000–2151, 87–93). Examples of the heroes listening to stories about themselves include the story the Phaiakian bard tells in book 8 of the past conflict between Odysseus and Achilles, prompting Odysseus to cry; Aeneas listening to stories of Shades in book 6; and the story produced when Unferth "run[s] his mouth" in a cutting tale about Beowulf in lines 504–27 on pages 24–5, after which Beowulf "drops some truth" about the same story in lines 532–80 on pages 25–7. Examples of the heroes or loved ones being immortalized in verse include Agamemnon telling Odysseus in book 24 that perhaps a poem might be written about Penelope; and a poet beginning to compose the playfully self-referential *The Tale of Beowulf* in lines 867–915 (39–41) before Beowulf even returns from defeating Grendel. Additionally, in the *Aeneid*, Aeneas reminds his men in book 1 that "perhaps someday even the memory of [your survival] will bring you pleasure," which does not invoke a future text but does follow a similar operation of suggesting a future memory of the present moment (ll. 202–3, 10).

89. Nandini B. Pandey, *The Poetics of Power in Augustan Rome: Latin Poetic Responses to Early Imperial Iconography* (Cambridge: Cambridge University Press, 2018), 114.

90. Homer, *The Odyssey*, trans. Lattimore, 1.10; trans. Fagles, 1.11–12.

91. Wilson treats us to a delightful extended Twitter thread on this choice: "I've been asked/praised/scolded/mansplained/ ad norovirus nauseam about my rendition of the first line of the Odyssey," *Twitter*, March 19, 2019, 1:27 p.m., https://twitter.com/EmilyRCWilson/status/1108057446180945923. For an exhaustive comparison of the proemic verse of a huge range of translations of the *Odyssey*, see Wikipedia, "English Translations of Homer," March 2, 2021, https://en.wikipedia.org/wiki/English_translations_of_Homer#Late_20th_century_(1976–2000).

92. Virgil, *Aeneid*, trans. Bartsch, 3. On the complex weavings of Homeric poetry in Vergil, see Pandey, 26-27.

93. Homer, *The Odyssey*, trans. Wilson, 316.

94. Virgil, *Aeneid*, trans. Bartsch, 73, lines 716–18.

95. J. L. Austin, *How to Do Things with Words*, ed. J. O. Urmson and Marina Sbisà (Cambridge, MA: Harvard University Press, 1975), especially "Lecture IX," 109–20.

96. Headley, *Beowulf*, xxi.

97. For the basics of interpretive communities in reader response theory, see Stanley Eugene Fish, *Is There a Text in This Class? The Authority of Interpretive Communities* (Cambridge, MA: Harvard University Press, 1980). For the creation of communities through the operation of nationalism, see Benedict Anderson, *Imagined Communities: Reflections on the Origin and Spread of Nationalism*, rev. ed. (London: Verso, 2006). On the range of Augustan theories of reader response, see Pandey, 14-16.

98. Headley, *Beowulf*, 46.

99. Headley, *Beowulf*, 99.

100. Madeline Miller, *Circe* (New York: Little Brown, 2018); Natalie Haynes, *The Children of Jocasta* (London: Mantle, 2017); Natalie Haynes, *Pandora's Jar: Women*

in the Greek Myths (London: Picador, 2020); Maria Dahvana Headley, *The Mere Wife* (London: Picador, 2018).

101. Wilson, "Introduction," 91 and 79.

102. Headley, *Beowulf*, ix–x.

103. Headley, *Beowulf*, 139.

104. Danez Smith, *Don't Call Us Dead* (Minnesota: Graywolf Press, 2017), 68. A briefer and earlier version of Smith's poem was published online under the title "Not an Elegy for Mike Brown," *Poets*, 2014, ://poets.org/poem/not-elegy-mike -brown. Kenneth Goldsmith—whose performance poem "The Body of Michael Brown" sparked outrage after his 2015 performance of it at Brown University and is an example of what happens when a translator with a misaligned subject position attempts to make their translator's perspective into the glass with which we began this chapter—commented on the same tragedy but in a vastly different way. Priscilla Frank, "What Happened When a White Male Poet Read Michael Brown's Autopsy as Poetry," *HuffPost*, March 17, 2015, https://www.huffpost.com/entry/kenneth -goldsmith-michael-brown_n_6880996. Credit: Danez Smith, excerpts from "not an elegy" from *Don't Call Us Dead*. Copyright © 2017 by Danez Smith. Reprinted with the permission of The Permissions Company, LLC on behalf of Graywolf Press, Minneapolis, Minnesota, graywolfpress.org.

105. Headley, *Beowulf*, xxxiv.

Figure 4.1 PSI XIII 1300: Third- to Second-Century BCE Ostracon from Egypt, Preserving Four Stanzas of Sappho fr. 2 (Voigt). *Source*: Ink on fired terracotta. Now in the collection of the Laurentian Library, Florence. Photograph by Sailko for WikiCommons.

Chapter 4

The Collective Lyric I

Inspired by *extreme lyric I*, a performance written and produced by Hope Mohr Dance in connection with Anne Carson's translation of Sappho (to which we turn later in this chapter), we have titled this chapter "The Collective Lyric I." Though the "lyric I" of poetry has been previously theorized as singular and subjective, we here explore how it can be understood as underwritten by collectives.[1] This same tension between we and I exists in public feminism more broadly as each public voice, while often encountered as an individual I, always intersects with collective politics.[2]

In general terms, this chapter expands upon the concerns of our previous chapter. While in chapter 3 we traced patriarchal subject positions in canonical literature and the way women translators can rework them through a feminist translational lens, starting in this chapter and continuing for the next two, we seek options that push beyond patriarchal, colonialist, and capitalist systems to provide models for public feminism more broadly. In their acknowledgment of the debt they owe to translators who have come before and their implicit collaboration with their original texts, the woman translators of the previous chapter demonstrate momentum toward the practice of the collective I that we theorize here—despite the implicit requirement they face to navigate the singular "I" of authorship that has been constructed around the writers they translate.[3] We argue that, through the embrace of a plural I, feminist translation as a practice takes what may be understood as singular (i.e., the rarified writing of a canonical author) and makes it more accessible and knowable by many, partially reworking the singular "I" that has been a primary mode of patriarchal culture.

As we build on the foundation of chapter 3 and move from epic into lyric to look again at translation—and now also metatranslation—we examine possibilities inherent in nonpatriarchal dynamics like those that occur when writers employ feminist citational practices or when a translator and originator's subject positions align, enacting something like the concept of a plural lyric I. We suggest that such dynamics serve as models for public feminism. To trace them, we consider Anne Carson's translation of Sappho into English as well as Hope Mohr Dance's metatranslation of Carson's translation into dance, tracking the accumulation of touches a body of work like Sappho's can receive through time—touches that turn its translation and reception into something like collective work.

We draw on Hope Mohr Dance's notion of the collaborative, embodied "lyric I" for several reasons. In contrast to a previously held conception of lyric as a marker of singular subjectivity, scholars of modern and ancient poetry now recognize the plurality of voices held within the lyric I.[4] Even the categories of lyric and epic, previously theorized separately, speak to each other. For example, as J. J. Winkler argues, Sappho positions her lyric I to subsume Homeric third-person epic.[5] Additionally, scholars now recognize the singular lyric I and the plurality of the tragic chorus as adjacent subject positions that inflect each other, disrupting fixed boundaries between singular and collaborative voices.[6] Marjorie Perloff emphasizes the interplay between individual and community that we return to: "The chorus, this *we* that speaks as an *I*, reminds us that subjective intimacy in a lyric poem is compromised by the numerous, anonymous undergrounds the word *I* holds within it."[7] The possibility of a plurality of voices even within the "I" (a plural "I" that is opposed, for example, to the masculinized "single genius" that Perloff elsewhere so amusingly mocks) aligns well with the model of translation investigated in the previous chapter.[8] Women translators often see their work as, in part, retranslations underwritten by the contributions of others who have come before them—in short, individual projects that rely on communal contribution.[9]

The authors of this book benefit from the same "I–we" relationship in our own work. We see mirrored in Carson's relationship to Sappho something of our literary collaboration as feminists from different disciplines reaching across literature and objects. This plurality is visible not only in our duet but also in this book's weaving together of different disciplinary threads and centuries of interlocutors. We choose this familiar, feminized metaphor of weaving with intention, for the craft of weaving has a deep history as women's craft, and yet the vibrant textiles that women wove and weave leave so much less of a visible trace than, for example, monuments in stone built to endure.[10] Even the word "craft" has a feminized history until recently associated with a more quotidian artistry than the single genius artist. And yet weavers, like quilters, have often produced their work in community.[11] In such communal settings, each person might weave a textile just as each person might write a sentence in a text, but the subtle voices and prompts of fellow weavers also work their way through the cloth, not always marked by a definitive change of hands. Thus, as we examine such collaborations and imagine the collective lyric I, we move among historical epochs, emphasize subjectivity, and honor the collective in part captured by the idea of the chorus as well as the connections among writers, translators, and readers.

THE COLLECTIVE "I" IN THE ACADEMY

For us, this investigation begins with the collective practice of academic citation. Just as a writer's and translator's subject positions inflect their work, so do theoretical interlocutors and academic analysis, posing a complication for feminist practices and the related pursuit of citational justice. In her book *Tragic Bodies*, Nancy Worman offers the following commentary for the male-authored theorists of aesthetics and the sensorium with which her work engages: "If this sounds suspiciously male in its scheme, I aim to follow feminist and queer theorists such as Eve Sedgwick, Donna Haraway, Elizabeth Grosz, and Vivian Sobchack, in putting their insights to provocative use."[12] Elsewhere in a book that takes its title from one of only two women characters in the entire Platonic corpus, *Diotima at the Barricades* (2016), Paul Allen Miller surveys the repeated and deep engagement of twentieth-century French feminists such as Simone de Beauvoir, Hélène Cixous, Julia Kristeva, and Luce Irigaray with Plato and Platonism, often partially mediated by earlier Platonist engagements by famous men such as Sigmund Freud, Jacques Derrida, and Jacques Lacan.[13] Miller invokes the question of his own gender in relation to the gender of his women subjects, themselves deeply engaged with the work of male philosophers, with two rhetorical questions: "But then who am I? Am I not just another Socrates appropriating women's voices for my own purposes?"[14] Offering several responses to his own question, Miller includes an argument aligned with Worman's—that Cixous's "women's writing" and Kristeva's "women's time" can be as easily located in the writing of men as of women and nonbinary people, an approach that aligns with Judith Butler's argument for the performance of gender. Miller's exposure of the buried patriarchal lineage of feminist luminaries demonstrates the deep need in the academy to locate and implement alternative genealogies.

A critical alternative to traditional citational practice—which so often recycles the same authority figures from the past, many of them men—is that of citational justice.[15] This practice deliberately highlights the work of women and other underrepresented contributors in a simple feminist framework advocated by academics who note urgency in citational absence. On August 27, 2021, twelve women scholars from a variety of fields published a treatise in *Inside Higher Ed* that decried inadequate or missing citations of women and people of color, linking citational marginalization with more general academic marginalization of these populations, and in October 2021 *Diacritics* released a special issue edited by Annabel Kim investigating the topic "Citation, Otherwise."[16]

Scholars like Sara Ahmed and others have provided a framework for this fight. In *Living a Feminist Life*, Ahmed argues that feminism is not a set of ideas but a lived practice that is "at stake in how we generate knowledge; in how we write, in who we cite."[17] Moving the conversation between the workplace in general and the academic world more specifically, Ahmed demonstrates that fighting academic sexism is "not optional: it is what makes feminism feminist. A feminist project is to find ways in which women can exist in relation to women; how women can be in relation to each other."[18] While not without its challenges, feminist citation builds a network among women and others marginalized under patriarchy that expresses interdependence and intellectual gratitude while also stepping off the ever-present plinth of patriarchal lineages and power.[19]

The foundation upon which Ahmed builds her "citational policy" of citing "those who have contributed to the intellectual genealogy of feminism and antiracism" (instead of what she calls the "institution" of white men) is her understanding of "white men as a cumulative effect rather than a way of grouping together persons who share a common attribute" and her warning that "we cannot conflate the history of ideas with white men [despite the fact that] ideas are assumed to originate from male bodies."[20] How, indeed, might women and other marginalized scholars operate in an academic system predicated on the work of those who have come before when that work is, by definition, embedded in patriarchy? Only by shifting the narrative.[21] As a powerful example of such shifting, Jennifer Nash outlines in a 2021 essay on citation and Black feminist praxis the ways in which Black feminists have sought to undo violence, remember (un-forget) people and history, and practice care through citation. Nash then asks whether the very territorialism of citation itself, grounded in identifying and crediting an author, might reinforce the structures this praxis seeks to dismantle. While Nash's approach could ultimately dismantle the apparatus of citation, less revolutionary approaches may provide at least steppingstones. If citation is, in Ahmed's terms, "feminist memory," then it may slowly lead to alternative lineages.[22] In some cases it already has.

Online public feminist collectives have raised a powerful voice in this conversation, including Cite Black Women, founded by Christen Smith in 2017 to

> motivate everyone, but particularly academics, to critically reflect on their everyday practices of citation and start to consciously question how they can

incorporate Black women into the CORE of their work [because] as Black women, we are often overlooked, sidelined and undervalued. Although we are intellectually prolific, we are rarely the ones that make up the canon.[23]

In other words, critics who suggest that women scholars or scholars of color do not produce sufficient work to cite are not paying attention—or are actively avoiding engaging with this body of work.[24] Scholarship by marginalized researchers has also been (at least initially) dismissed because it does not always look like the traditions of scholarship those in positions of power recognize; for example, prior to his keynote lecture at the Modern Language Association convention in 2020, Viet Thanh Nguyen tweeted: "In 1992, my English department chairman told me I couldn't write a dissertation on Vietnamese American literature. In 2020's Modern Language Association Conference, I'll speak on the Presidential Plenary—on Vietnamese American literature."[25] Over time, what is recognized as acceptable scholarship can change and evolve, especially when we intentionally shift academia's focus. Citations grow from citations; we must purposefully plant their seeds.

At their core, feminist citational practices represent one way to center women and keep their contributions foregrounded in an academic context that often excludes them. Cite Black Women, like many of the feminist movements we analyze elsewhere in our book, relies on the tools of social media, in particular hashtags, to spread its message and to network with other feminists. As explored in the context of Headley's #blessed in chapter 3, the social media hashtag may represent the ultimate in networked citational possibility. When ideas become hashtags, their relational potential is immediately apparent. In many senses, it is the hashtag itself more than social media that embodies the practice of public feminism and demonstrates its potential to break us free of our exclusionary networks and evoke the power of the collective. Whether forged by the hashtag or formal academic citation practices, networks of citation amplify our intellectual communities and block the zeitgeist of academic patriarchy. We might understand feminist citation as one kind of collective undergirding the lyric I.

THE COLLECTIVE IN TRANSLATION

We now turn to Anne Carson's translation of Sappho, *If Not, Winter*, and from citation to translation, two actions we imagine as metaphorically connected.[26] Both practices involve a merging, for a time, of agendas, as well as a baton pass of ideas. Especially in the case of work like Sappho's that comes to us through a vexed archive—full of losses but nevertheless also assembled through multiple systems of recovery (including, as discussed later in this chapter, fragments we have today only due to other writers who cited Sappho)—we see the accumulation over time of touches, actions of preservation, translations, retranslations, and metatranslations, all despite (or perhaps because of) the fact that we still have only fragments of Sappho's oeuvre.[27] Those systems of recovery, taken together, exemplify the work of the collective: work Sappho enacted in her own time and that many have continued since.

In part due to the ongoing feminization of the notion of the collective more generally, we argue that public feminism can reclaim the collective, and that the construction of the collective lyric I thereby acts as feminist practice—one that, in the case of Carson's translation, is facilitated by a woman translator working on a text by a woman.[28] Some of the histories of feminist translation practices have engaged specifically with this act of bringing women writers to new audiences by choosing to translate their work.[29] Within this tradition, translating Sappho has been an important staging ground; Carson comes to the fragments with that history of retranslations in the background in another sense of the collective lyric I in action.[30]

Yet in comparison to the translators surveyed in the previous chapter, Carson adopts different strategies with respect to both the transparency of the translator and the subject position of the poet herself. If we have argued in chapter 3 that Wilson, Bartsch, and Headley offer feminist translations that are shaped by the lived experience of these women's subject positions, then Carson's earlier translations of Sappho's collected fragments proceed along different lines. Carson intentionally pulls her lived experience and identity out of the focus.[31] Indeed, multiple commenters have noted with wry humor that Carson's "Note About the Translator," like the author bios on the back jackets of her poetry books, consists of a single sentence: "Anne Carson lives in Canada."[32] At the same time, Carson's success as a poet may be implied by these terse interventions, which seem to indicate that she is not interested in explaining herself to those who do not already know her work. Perhaps that authority itself ensures that she need not assert her presence in other ways.

Also unlike Wilson, Headley, and Bartsch, Carson does not reject the rationalist discourse or the fantasy of pure language but tries instead to remove traces of her voice from the poems, a goal that is particularly notable since she is a poet in her own right as well as a translator. Rather than asserting her subject position in her translator's introduction, Carson writes:

> In translating I tried to put down all that can be read of each poem in the plainest language I could find, using where possible the same order of words and thoughts that Sappho did. I like to think that, the more I stand out of the way, the more Sappho shows through. This is an amiable fantasy (transparency of the self) within which most translators labor.[33]

The amiable fantasy itself recalls the invocation of glass with which we opened our previous chapter, yet we locate some play between Carson's characterization and the book itself. First, Sappho's language is not entirely plain, so rendering it in this way makes a choice that trades some details of the rich material world Sappho captures in favor of a version that instead spotlights the materiality of Sappho's transmission through time, discussed later in this chapter.[34] Next, Carson's direct voice emerges powerfully in other sections of the text; according to Emily Greenwood: "It is in the notes that C. makes her own poetic voice felt."[35] The paratext, a place where Carson connects with readers and provides context that allows them to encounter Sappho's work more deeply, becomes a space that enacts the dynamics of the collective and demonstrates Carson's intervention.

Removing the translator nevertheless remains a fantasy, even for a poet like Carson who makes this erasure a goal. There is irony in Carson's claim to having sought "transparency of the self," for her translation has had such an afterlife as *her* work—for its crisp, modern language and for the ways in which she mobilizes blank space. Carson, whose project innovates in its handling of Sappho's fragments so that each is treated as poem unto itself, no matter how brief (a practice we discuss later in this chapter), uses blanks to disrupt our expectations of what does or doesn't count as a poem. In the end, some of her most feminist contributions unfold in her troubling the very boundaries of poetry itself.[36]

SAPPHO'S LYRIC I

Sappho is one of few female writers from ancient Greece whose writing survives, making her a clear choice for a translator hoping to translate a woman writer from antiquity.[37] In the late seventh and early sixth centuries BCE, Sappho lived and wrote her lyric poetry in and around the island of Lesbos in the Northeastern Greek islands. Like many of the historical women considered in this book, Sappho's poetry only survives—indeed her career as a poet may only have been possible—because of her elite class position.[38] This class position complicates our engagement with her reception as she achieves fame in part due to it, but she is also repeatedly marginalized because of her gender and the hovering question of her sexuality. Even Sappho was concerned with how her story would be told, staging her text for the future. As she wrote in Fragment 147, "someone will remember us / I say / even in another time."[39]

While modern readers most frequently encounter Sappho's words on the page, in Sappho's time a lyric poet would have played the lyre to accompany the poetic lines. Visual depictions of Sappho from antiquity often show her holding a lyre, and she invokes this accompanying lyre in her poetry. For example, Sappho's Fragment 118 reads in Carson's translation "yes! radiant lyre speak to me / become a voice" and Fragment 176 *"barbitos, barōmos, barmos* / lyre lyre lyre."[40] Both visual and textual invocations of the lyre present the instrument as an embodied object that collaborates with Sappho, so that even when she performs solo, she is not alone.[41] Critics have highlighted the isolation and loss that many of Sappho's fragments capture, most vividly in Fragment 31, and yet these pictures of loss have also been portals of connection for readers across time. The aloneness that Sappho evokes itself constructs the broader social world within which it might be felt.[42]

Sappho's poems center the embodied, often intimate or personal, experiences of women; they are designed for public performance for an audience. These poetic performances enact a tension between the private world of female friendship, desire, loss, and love that they bring to life and the public nature of performance itself, even for a small audience. In engaging these relationships, they demonstrate the collective I in action.

Analyzing the "explosion of confident, self-possessed lyric 'I's (in contrast to the Olympian objectivity and detachment of Homer, if not Hesiod) between 700 [and] 450 BCE," Leslie Kurke cites the role of writing, which "provided the means to fix poetry and song as text and thereby preserve them."[43] It is not, Kurke argues, that Greek poets of this period suddenly started to use "I" in what some have understood as a moment of poetic self-discovery but that poets were newly able, through the reintroduction of writing into the Greek world, to inscribe their lyric I's.[44] Recorded in a moment of radical political change across the Greek-speaking world and composed for performance with musical accompaniment as analyzed by Kurke, lyric poems were performed in two important and opposing contexts: the symposium (an elite male drinking party) and the marketplace (the center of the democratic city). Kurke argues that "the pervasive, self-assertive 'I' is not merely a historical and generic mirage: it is rather an epiphenomenon of political and social contestation and resistance."[45] Such contestation forms the social context of Sappho's lyric poetry, but her lyric I is always also conditioned by her gender. While lyric poetry in the hands of male poets engaged public political contests, Sappho crafted intimate, private female worlds of, by, and for women.[46] Engaging with J. J. Winkler's earlier reading of Sappho alongside Homer, Kurke demonstrates the ways in which Sappho, for example in Fragment 16, elevated the language of female erotic desire above and against the "bro cultures" (to borrow Headley's term examined in chapter 3) of war and weapons described in Homer with her caustic capture: "Men think weapons are beautiful, but they don't realize that their attraction to weapons is itself erotic."[47] Similarly, Sappho engaged and subverted the lyric I of archaic Greek male poets who contested aristocratic and democratic political structures in their poems, both of which regulate women's desires and bodies.

In addition, scholars have recently argued that Sappho composed both monodic (solo) and choral (performed by a chorus) poetry, the latter specifically for all-female choruses.[48] Seeing the possibility of plural voices in Sappho first required scholars to move beyond notions of pure genre that had historically kept solo and choral compositions apart.[49] Timothy Power has argued that we should understand Sappho's poetry as parachoral—that is, steeped in choral sounds and rhythms—even when she composes for solo performance, and that even a single performer might evoke the multiplicity of the chorus to mobilize what Kurke has named "choral value."[50] Just as the subject positions shift within some poems, so might genres shift from singular to plural or from monodic to parachoral. And this parachorality in lyric finds its complement in the lyric meter and plurality embedded in the chorus in tragedy.[51] Ultimately, within her singular lyric I, Sappho contains many voices.

The processes by which Sappho's public performances come to us on the page trace the (patriarchal) idiosyncrasies of the material archive (see chapter 1 for a discussion of the archive in general and chapter 3 for a discussion of the materiality of source texts), vexed by specific material issues around recovery. Textual objects—and their limitations—have shaped the reception and transmission of Sappho's embodied poetry. As mentioned earlier in this chapter, in a fascinating variation of the concept of feminist citation practice, Sappho's poetic fragments have been recovered in part through citations of her by ancient male authors.[52] Other fragments reach us from iterations recorded on papyri, on a fired ceramic ostracon, and on parchment (Fig 4.1). Unlike texts of Homer and Vergil, which remained in circulation and were therefore continuously copied and recopied, Sappho was celebrated in antiquity (Longinus, for example, quotes four stanzas of Fragment 1 in *On the Sublime*), but the rise of Christianity suppressed her work, and it fell out of favor due to her love of women.[53] Already in the second century CE, a tradition of two Sapphos—one a poet and the other a lesbian—had emerged in an effort to rescue her meter from her biography.[54] Although he had little access to her poetry when writing in the fourteenth century CE, Boccaccio picked up on an ancient tradition of Sappho as the tenth muse of poetry and included her in his text *Famous Women* (*De mulieribus claris*) in 1362.[55] All of these different modes also have a material history. For example, the means by which Sappho's words are preserved—pressed marsh reeds, carbon black ink, dust, fired clay, among others—all inflect the way her work is transmitted and how it persists through time. This materiality is markedly different from the sensorium of her performances.

People living in the Egyptian city of Oxyrhynchus under Roman rule used papyrus, a thick paper made by weaving and pressing the innermost fibers of the tall stems of the aquatic flowering sedge *cyperus papyrus*, which grows wild along the banks of the Nile River.[56] The etymological source of the English word "paper," papyrus was a surface on which many ancient scribes recorded texts with a dark plant-based ink. Over centuries people writing in Coptic, several dialects of ancient Egyptian, ancient Greek, Latin, Arabic, Hebrew, Aramaic, Syriac, and Pahlavi (Middle Persian) copied professional letters, receipts, tax returns, contracts, and other records of everyday life onto papyri. Once finished with a given text, its reader threw it into the town dump, building up a library of discarded texts of various types and in various languages over time. Amid the contents of the Oxyrhynchus dump—just as Alison Pebworth discovered at the dump in San Francisco as narrated in chapter 2—were hundreds of books and documents. These include work by authors whose words had not been preserved elsewhere; their discovery and excavation in modernity radically reshaped the archive of available ancient texts.[57]

Among the materials of the dump were papers on which people wrote some of the ancient Greek poems of the sixth-century BCE Greek lyric poet Sappho. Eleven fragments of Sappho's poetry lay buried in the dump for centuries, her song and music transferred to ink on woven dried plant stems. The dry Egyptian desert held her words mixed together with so many other people's words, textual objects that the ancient Egyptian people living in the town wished at some moment to record and eventually chose to discard. Paradoxically, these eleven fragments survive because they were once thrown out.

Discovered by Egyptians in the nineteenth century and excavated by two British men, the archive of papyri from Oxyrhynchus is now held at Oxford. The formation of this archive thereby reflects the colonial aspects of early archaeology. This nineteenth-century journey of Sappho's texts, like the journeys of so many antiquities, stages a British or Anglophone claim to Sappho's archive. In doing so, it loosens any ancient Egyptian heritage claim despite the essential role of local discoverers in preserving Sappho's work.

Critically, the preservation of the trash at Oxyrhynchus greatly expanded Sappho's corpus of fragments after early Christian scribes had sought to erase her because her life violated their norms for women.[58] As trash, Sappho's words were beneath the notice of those who might censor her. Invisibility can be a survival strategy, as the history of iconoclasm, witch hunts, and doxing of public feminists demonstrates. The stink of trash may repel those who might have destroyed her work, and yet hiding therein offers no guarantee of later discovery. In Sappho's case, luck was on history's side, yet perhaps additional fragments remain undiscovered elsewhere—possibly disintegrated, possibly preserved for future serendipity.

Although we do not know why Sappho's fragments were discarded in the Oxyrhynchus dump specifically and many other texts discarded there were not considered transgressive, the metaphorization of the trash dump as a place to put the work of those who transgress norms calls to mind the idea of women's bodies as messy. This concept has been critiqued in modernity in the work of artists like Sarah Levy, who in 2017 painted a portrait of Trump using her menstrual blood in response to Trump's referencing Megyn Kelly's vagina with the phrase "blood coming out of her wherever."[59] Such constructions contrast with the sanitized representation of women's bodies in some histories of art and literature, which itself draws on the idea of women's bodies as leaky vessels requiring containment (further investigated in chapter 5). Writing of her awakening feminist rage at what artistic tradition had done to female forms, the twentieth-century performance artist Carolee Schneemann attributed this violence to the disjunction between the artistic idealization of that form and the "stinking" reality of actual female bodies.[60] To bring these ideas back into the context of the trash metaphor, perhaps the reclamation of the woven reed paper fragments suggests a recovery of some of the "unruliness" (to use Gay's term as discussed in chapter 1) connected to women's bodies—and trash itself might be a potential site of collective consciousness.

Another fragment of Sappho's poetry travels to us not on a papyrus recovered from a dump but written on a fragment of pottery called an ostracon (Fig 4.1). An Italian antiquarian purchased the ostracon in Egypt and brought it to Florence, where the papyrologist and philologist Medea Norsa published it in 1957.[61] Carbon black ink on a piece of broken, fired ceramic pottery likely written down in the second century BCE records sixteen lines of a poem now known as Fragment 2. The poem captures the sensory delight of the temple set amid an apple grove—the frankincense burning on the altars, roses, rippling water, the rustle of leaves—and then invokes the goddess of love, Aphrodite, who features throughout Sappho's known corpus. Once again, we are lucky to know this. Even Norsa's access to this work was limited by similar material circumstances to those we explored earlier in the chapter—unlike her Protestant and Catholic male counterparts in both Britain and Italy, Norsa was regularly denied promotions, most likely because of her gender and Jewish heritage, yet she was able to contribute despite her more marginalized role in a male-dominated profession.[62]

Tracking this sort of discrimination in the archive is, as discussed in chapter 1, particularly fraught: unless it takes a legal form, much discrimination is invisible. In this section, we have thereby benefited from public-facing work on Twitter led by Sarah Bond, who connected us to papyrologists Roberta Mazza and Katherine Blouin. Upon seeing this public exchange, Judith Peller Hallett also reached out to share her recent work on Norsa. These scholars helped us deepen our archival documentation of Norsa's history, particularly around the question of her double discrimination as a Jewish woman.[63]

This very sequence of events exemplifies just the sort of public feminist collaboration—even among those who have never met—that we believe can expand possibilities for scholarship and increase access to hidden histories.

An account of Norsa's life, written a decade after her death, indicates that her funeral was very modest in comparison to the typical celebration of a male scholar's life, suggesting that, despite her acknowledged expertise in papyrology, widespread recognition eluded her even in death.[64] Building on a tradition that imagined Sappho as a schoolteacher, the author of the account closes his remembrances with a story of Norsa teaching his daughter how to read Greek from a papyrus fragment that she pulled out of her purse. The author wraps up his reminiscence with a quotation of Sappho's Fragment 75, "weaving twigs of dill with delicate hands," as though to compare Norsa's teaching with a papyrus to the weaving of dill Sappho describes.[65] Thus Sappho's poetry of community from antiquity is continuously mobilized and reconfigured across time—from Norsa to her eulogist to generations of scribes to the scholars who connected with us through Twitter and even to us as the authors of this book.

Additionally, throughout history, readers have come to Sappho's poetry seeking a way to speak from their own nonnormative subject positions. Along with a Jewish woman papyrologist and her momentary student (as in the example of Norsa discussed previously), a sampling of such readers might include queer women situating themselves within a lesbian lineage, Black women like Anna Julia Cooper mobilizing knowledge of Sappho to advocate for rights denied them by the law, and readers with intersecting identities who fall into multiple categories.[66] Thus, Sappho's work engages many different communities and connections in its reception. In them, we see a collective lyric I.

IN TRANSLATION: WORDS, SPACES, AND BRACKETS

The translator Anne Carson uses as her Greek source text the compendium of these poetic fragments on papyri, on the ostracon, and in different ancient quotations edited by Eva-Maria Voigt (1971). Carson translates 189 fragments of Sappho, rendering the ancient Greek on the left page and her translation in English on the right, allowing a reader to toggle between the two. The choice to include the Greek and English text on facing pages invites several different kinds of readers. A reader familiar with the Greek alphabet might recognize the words but not the ancient Aeolic dialect—or, with more specialized expertise, might evaluate the translation. For a reader who does not read Greek or its alphabet, the letters on the left-hand page "make strange" Sappho's native language, a reminder of the great distance between her time, language, and culture and those of her modern audience.[67] Or, as Emily Greenwood theorizes, the strategy communicates both the desire of Carson to remove herself as author figure from the translated page and the impossibility of doing so. According to Greenwood: "The arrangement of the volume in this way hints at the equivalence with the original text, which is the translator's impossible goal, while at the same time exposing the gaps between the Greek text and C.'s translation."[68]

Carson claims space for Sappho by giving most poems, no matter how fragmentary or brief, their own page. In fact, toward the end of her collection, Fragments 142–168A assemble into a block that foregrounds blank space. Each of these fragments is a translation of one to two lines of Sappho's original language on an otherwise blank page, creating the effect of words opening up into unmarked possibility as the collection itself winds down.[69] Such opening is anchored by Fragments 169–192, which are almost all translations of single words collected in groups of five per page.[70] In making these choices, Carson reimagines the relationship between fragment and full poem.[71] Carson's innovation suggests that fragments should generally be considered as full poems in their own right and not merely in relationship to other fragments. Though some critics might expect an interplay among multiple words for the operation of "poetry" to be enacted, Carson's departure from convention suggests that word selection is meaningful in itself.[72] The words Sappho used highlight where, in a universe of all possible words, she chose to place her attention—and Carson indicates that this matters too. This aspect of Carson's project is one we argue directly enacts the values of public feminism. By making more fragments count as full poems in their own right, despite their brevity, Carson expands the possibilities for approaching Sappho's oeuvre, implying that if we have so few poets who are women from Greek antiquity, we should elevate as many poems from them as we can. And once again, this move, in its shadows and echoes through time, suggests the ethos of the collective.

Carson's Sappho also takes up room through the embrace of the many gaps in the source text. By holding space for these gaps, which were created through the transmission of Sappho's work through time, Carson works within an earlier tradition of women translating Sappho like Yopie Prins and Diane Rayor. Prins and Rayor criticized male translators like Lattimore for the repairs they made to Sappho's fragments in a patriarchal mode—repairs that erased aspects of her woman's subject position and voice in the text.[73] In contrast to Lattimore, Carson uses [square brackets] to mark blank spaces, of which she writes:

> Brackets are an aesthetic gesture toward the papyrological event rather than an accurate record of it . . . Brackets are exciting. Even though you are approaching Sappho in translation, that is no reason you should miss the drama of trying

to read a papyrus torn in half or riddled with holes or smaller than a postage stamp—brackets imply a free space of imaginal adventure.[74]

Yatromanolakis identifies Carson's use of brackets as a strategy deserving further study:

> Recently, papyrological brackets in literary texts, either as scholarly signs or as a symbolic gesture towards (ancient) culture, have not received much attention by scholars working on archaic and classical lyric poetry. To be sure, brackets and other marks affect, and even enhance, the reading experience of ancient texts.[75]

The authors of this book theorize these brackets as a kind of wink, a communication between author and reader that seeks to share a more direct and immediate experience of the text's history.

Like Philip in *Zong!* (discussed in chapter 6), Carson uses the visual layout of the page to create meaning. Take, for example, her translation of Fragment 25:

]
]quit
]
]luxurious woman
]
]
]

While the page this poem unfolds on may initially look bare, it reflects Carson's aforementioned prioritization of the transmission of Sappho's text through time. These brackets claim space and ask the reader to encounter temporal and material gaps. As a translator, Carson eschews a practice that would fill these in and smooth over the lacunae of the contemporary experience of reading Sappho. Instead, she reminds us of the material conditions through which the text reaches us—and, in so doing, shares an experience with her readership.

For the fragments that have been recovered not on papyri but through quotations by other authors in a web of citation, Carson does not use brackets, making the type of text source visible on the translated page. She also often adjusts the spacing of the poem to produce visual movement, a choice she defends in light of Walter Benjamin's principle of "'intention toward language' of the original," outlined in the same short essay where he advocates for the translator's invisibility.[76] For Carson, the layout of her English translation on the page captures some of the "echo" of Sappho's Greek. So Fragment 128 becomes:

here now
tender Graces
and Muses with beautiful hair

and Fragment 114:

virginity
virginity
where are you gone leaving me behind?
No longer will I come to you
No longer will I come

Carson's movement, which foregrounds the way one line engenders the next, also echoes the relational network of citation investigated earlier in this chapter.

When Carson does group very fragmentary poems on one page as discussed previously, the attention she devotes to spatial concerns throughout the book suggests that she intends these fragments to both stand alone and piece together a new poem. For example, consider the following assemblage (Frs 184–188): "danger—honeyvoiced—Medeia—of the Muses—mythweaver."[77] Such choices may leave the reader wondering about the basis of assembling a logical narrative out of disconnected fragments—which, in many ways, is precisely Carson's (playful) point.

Ultimately, it is in Carson's careful attention to the structural and spatial concerns of the fragments that we might locate her translator's I as well as the basis for a collective lyric one. Her poems draw on modernist conventions that emphasize the unfolding of words in a pattern across the surface of the page and seem to imprint her authorial signature in their structural choices.[78] In the end, unlike the other translators considered in the previous chapter, it is not Carson's poetic voice but the placement and organization of Sappho's words that evokes this imprint. Carson's initial gesture of removing material circumstance from the text by removing her own voice is thereby repudiated by her return to materialism, which emphasizes questions of access, circulation, and history. By building the history of text's materiality into its form, Carson sets the stage for the more explicitly public feminist interventions of Hope Mohr Dance, discussed next. And the words themselves, passed from Sappho to Carson, connect to each other in surprising ways or lead, like steppingstones, from one image to the next, one reader to the next, and even one modality to the next.

RETRANSLATION INTO MOVEMENT

Carson does not replicate in English nor mention in her translator's introduction a metrical feature of Sappho's poetry known as the "Sappho stanza" or "Sapphics," a challenging meter of four Aeolic Greek lines—three long and one short, trochees and dactyls.[79] Sapphic meter was admired and adopted by many later Greek poets and in Latin by Catullus and Horace as well as taken up for its metrical challenge by European poets, translators, and even students testing their translation and composition skills against the measure of Sapphic meter. In the nineteenth and early twentieth centuries, women emulated Sapphic verse in their own poems as in the example of Renée Vivien, who composed French that deployed a Sapphic stanza in order to ally herself stylistically with a poet she understood as a queer forebearer. Vivien drew direct attention to this metrical allegiance to validate her queer identity in her poem "In the Sapphic Rhythm" (*Sur le rythme sapphique*).[80] Vivien also spent several summers on Mount Deer Island off the coast of Bar Harbor, Maine, in the company of Eva Palmer (Sikelianos) and Natalie Clifford Barney, with whom she created various Sapphic performances, including *tableaux vivants*.[81] The women's performances expanded beyond the specific meter of Vivien's poetry to imagine and express a fully embodied and sensorial Sapphic world. In contrast with Vivien's strict adherence to Sapphic meter in her poetry, Carson's versions of Sappho's meter have their own rhythms. It is just these rhythms around which Hope Mohr Dance, an international dance company, built their performance of *extreme lyric I*.

Written and choreographed by Hope Mohr and Maxe Crandall and performed by the choreographers alongside dancers Tara McArthur, Suzette Sagisi, Jane Selna, and Karla Quintero, *extreme lyric I* built from the embodied world of female subjectivity conjured in Carson's rendering of Sappho's fragments (see cover image). Hope Mohr Dance performed *extreme lyric I* at the Baltimore Museum of Art as part of the museum's "Vision 2020" programming, designed to recognize both the 100th anniversary of the Nineteenth Amendment and the women of color, especially Black women, for whom the right to vote did not come with the Nineteenth Amendment and for whom it remains under threat.[82]

Following the intensely physical performance, Mohr and Crandall discussed their approach to *extreme lyric I* in conversation with poet Dora Malech.[83] When asked about the particular role of Carson's translation—projected in Greek and English throughout the performance and from which the performers recited—on their choreography, Mohr replied,

> We built all of the dance . . . around individual fragments. A lot of the rhythms
> in the body come from the syllabic rhythms in the syntax. And I was thinking

a lot about breaks and ruptures and the white space. Carson loves the white space.[84]

The dancers translated Carson's brackets, marking in her text breaks in a papyrus, into abrupt and physically taxing movements. Single-word fragments took on staccato form, such as when each dancer recited "celery" one after the other as though passing a stalk quickly. That choice invoked practices like passing a baton or talking stick and made the spoken word into a kind of verbal object while also creating the kind of strangeness—why "celery," after all?—that forces an audience to really pay attention to the oddities of language more generally. The dancers' costumes, white leotards adorned with rich colors that varied across each performer, also evoked the material colors captured in Sappho's poetry, as in Fragment 92.[85]

]
]
]
]
Robe
And
colored with saffron
purple robe
cloaks/ crowns
beautiful
]
Purple
Rugs
]
]

In Carson's translation—and given Carson's commitment to maintaining the fragmentary nature of the poem as it has been received through history—this poem may feel underwhelming or even spare. Many of Carson's choices are indeed intentionally quotidian. Yet some of the power of the collaboration of Sappho's words in Carson's hands experienced in the performance of Hope Mohr Dance acted to bring all these choices to vivid life.

Just as in antiquity the tragic chorus and the lyric poet inflect each other, so did Hope Mohr Dance foreground the collaborative corps of dancers moving in relationship to each other, visualizing the plurality of the lyric I. In describing one of her motivations in creating *extreme lyric I*, Mohr said:

An interest of mine in making the piece was how we can lose the self through extreme states of embodiment and sensuality. And I was interested in exploring that not only through the solo body but through the body in relationship to other people . . . to me the idea of fracture, and rupture, and fragment, is very contemporary . . . I just wanted to bring it into a contemporary conversation with the body.[86]

In the performance, moving from fragmentation to connection, the female subjectivity captured by Sappho's poetry of women in community and in love with each other translated into the movements of the dancers in community with each other and the audience.

Originally designed to be performed in the round so that an intimate audience would be surrounded by the dancers, the performance in Baltimore demanded adaptation to a more traditional proscenium stage. The performance opened with Mohr and Crandall whispering "ssshhh, ssshhh" as a rhythmic call-and-response to silence while walking slowly through the aisles from either side of the seats to pass by and enclose the audience and create a temporary collective world shared by audience and dancers. Crandall described the process of building that intimate world in the contemporary present and the group's intention to engage with Sappho at that moment:

My challenge was that I wanted to engage with this text but I wanted to do it without nostalgia. And I mean that in a political sense. Hope had this idea about performing in the round and then when we came in here to adapt it, that's why we walked out and around [at the beginning]. We were using text in a performative way to form a space, to build a world within which we could work and use and experiment with Sappho in the now rather than like trying to take you back to an ancient world or something like that. We wanted to build a world here and now.[87]

The performance thus bent space and time, taking the audience back to the performance–context of the original fragments but within an entirely contemporary zone. That Mohr and Crandall built the dance not from the papyri but from Carson's translations of them further complicates the continuity and disruption of time the performance invoked and connects the choreographers' intervention to the very long history of layered touches of Sappho's words as part of a collective shaped by history. Moving from language to movement adds yet another layer.

In the performance, once they arrived at the front of the stage, Mohr and Crandall broke the silence they had engendered by speaking fragments of text about how Sappho has been characterized over time, evoking that (fictionalized) biography that clings to public women discussed in chapter 2. "Sappho is overcome with desire" meets "Sappho's body is breaking," then "Sappho is always turned on," "Sappho's body is leaking," "Sappho isn't happy" filled the room one at a time. Eventually, Mohr and Crandall each started to speak their assertions over the other, creating a cacophony or a vocal round of biographical projections from which only the repeated subject of each statement, Sappho, Sappho, Sappho, broke through. Eventually, Mohr closed the circle with the words "Sappho's heart is flying out of her chest" and a return to the "ssshhh, ssshhh."

Turning from biography to Sappho's own fragments, Mohr and Crandall next embraced in the center of the circle of dancers and proceeded to pass, with their voices, different very short fragments around the group. Building from the work that Carson does with these single- or few-word poems, the dancers tracked each fragment from the singular I to its plural by moving its sounds around their circle. The passing of the fragment until it verbally touched each performer exemplified the construction of a collective joined by language and more—by the individual word. Mohr called out the name "Fragment 191," and then each dancer repeated "celery, celery, celery" until Crandall closed the circle with "celery" in a variation of traditional call-and-response. Mohr led with "Fragment 189"; the dancers responded "soda." Mohr said "Fragment 132," and all of the dancers responded "sweat" in unison.

Twenty minutes in, Mohr and Crandall exited the stage and the focus moved to the other dancers—Quintero, McArthur, Sagisi, and Selna—who remained on stage beneath translucent sheets. As they danced, the English and Greek fragments of Sappho's poems projected onto the stage curtain behind them shifted. At this point in the performance, the poems had been evoked through voice, body, and textual projection, and their echoes filled the room. Within four minutes, the dancers removed their sheets to reveal the brightly colored adornments (each distinct) on their white leotards. The physicality of what followed pushed their bodies individually and collectively to the extremes of the performance's title—deep lunges and bends, contortions of feet, bodies pressed against bodies, and passages in which a single dancer repeated a particular beat and sequence or pairs twisted their limbs and torsos together. The weaving repetition of phrases threaded through the variation of other movements, creating an assembled collective despite individual differences. The spell was punctuated by a moment of levity when the background music changed to Tina Turner's *What's Love Got to Do with It?* and the corps exploded into movement. The sheer athleticism of this extended meditation on extremity staged an argument for the stakes of plurality. The collective does not just shelter each singular I—it amplifies it.

To complete the performance, the four dancers welcomed back Mohr and Crandall, who carried baskets of flowers onto the stage, and then the six performers together spoke as a chorus—a corps that is also a chorus—for the first time. Skipping over the first half of Fragment 94, which captures the

voice of a lovesick person who wishes to be dead, the dancers embodied the
voice of Sappho responding to the beloved:[88]

]and beautiful times we had.
For many crowns of violets
and roses
]at my side you put on
and many woven garlands
made of flowers
around your soft throat.
And with sweet oil
costly
you anointed yourself
and on a soft bed
delicate
you would let loose your longing
and neither any[
]nor any
holy place nor
was there from which you were absent
no grove[
]no dance
]no sound
[

In that moment, as it contemplated the loss of the beloved, the audience
figuratively and collectively became the beloved—another form of collective
I—anticipating the separation from the performers at the end of the
performance.

After the dancers spoke, each raised a flower petal to their mouth and
slowly ate it. The focus then shifted to all that the audience was losing with
the closure of the performance. The grove the performers created, the dance
in which the audience had been immersed, and the sounds that had structured
this performance since its opening "ssshhh" were about to evaporate, for
time's meter continues beyond the temporality of performance.[89] Yet the
collective I did, in some sense, go with the audience as it departed the
theater. It continues as history does, each new audience becoming part of its
accumulation.

We conclude this chapter by affirming the way that performance exemplifies
the collective plural I more generally. An individual performer might
connect with an audience and temporarily focus that audience's collective
attention. Individual performers also connect to other performers to become

corps. Shifting intimacies among performer and audience, performer and performer, and corps and audience draw all who are involved in and out of a collective created through a shared moment in time. Parallel to the dynamic of translation in which each iteration sheds new light on existing texts or that of citation in which intentionally foregrounding the work of those less often heard makes possible new forms of conversation, performance in different contexts and different temporalities allows us to know and understand within new frames. Not only is the work different in each iteration but we, its interlocutors, are also changed.

NOTES

1. This theorization is somewhat exemplified in reception of Sappho's work itself. As Yopie Prins traces, "Sappho seems to give birth to the Lyric I." Yopie Prins, *Ladies' Greek: Victorian Translations of Tragedy* (Princeton, NJ: Princeton University Press, 2017), 39.

2. As we theorize this plural lyric I, we also recognize its complement: the singular "they." Attempting to wrest the English language from its binary pronoun system, many have taken up the pronoun "they." The construction of a singular "they" has been traced back to at least 1375 in English, where it appears in the medieval romance *William and the Werewolf*. As a pronoun used in reference to an individual person (sometimes singular, sometimes plural), this pronoun may suggest the multitude of identities we all carry within us. Conversely, pluralities consisted of multiple individuals can, in the context of public feminism, at times be considered singular—connected in focus and purpose.

3. Although we refer to the reception of these authorial "I"s, Homer's status as an individual author has been much debated and called into question. For a point of entry into this conversation, see M. L. West, "The Invention of Homer," *Classical Quarterly* 49, no. 2 (1999): 364–82.

4. Theorizing the lyric in poetry is an extremely contentious project and beyond the scope of our chapter. As Jonathan Culler explains in *Theory of the Lyric* (Cambridge, MA: Harvard University Press, 2015), the widespread "conception of the lyric, as representation of subjective experience . . . no longer has great currency in the academic world. It has been replaced by a variant which treats the lyric not as mimesis of the experience of the poet but as a representation of the action of a fictional speaker: in this account, the lyric is spoken by a persona, whose situation and motivation one needs to reconstruct" (2). But even as far back as 1954, T. S. Eliot, in *The Three Voices of Poetry* (Cambridge: Cambridge University Press, 1954), argued that most poems contain more than one "voice" (he identifies three: the poet expressing personal thoughts, the poet addressing an audience with a message, and the poet creating a character). Perloff, in her review of Culler, highlights what she sees as Virginia Jackson's preferable framing that "the term lyric may well refer to the way we *read* a given poem rather than to its inherent nature." Marjorie Perloff,

"Review of *Theory of the Lyric*, by Jonathan Culler," *Nineteenth-Century Literature* 71, no. 2 (2016): 257, emphasis added). See also Virginia Jackson, "Lyric," in *The Princeton Encyclopedia of Poetry and Poetics*, 4th ed., eds. Stephen Cushman, Clare Cavanagh, Jahan Ramazani, and Paul Rouzer (Princeton, NJ: Princeton University Press, 2012), 826–34.

5. John J. Winkler, *The Constraints of Desire: The Anthropology of Sex and Gender in Ancient Greece* (New York: Routledge, 1990), 176.

6. Gregory Nagy uses the phrase "choral lyric song" to describe Sappho's lyric. See Gregory Nagy, "Genre, Occasion, and Choral Mimesis Revisited, with Special Reference to the 'Newest Sappho,'" in *Genre in Archaic and Classical Greek Poetry: Theories and Models; Studies in Archaic and Classical Greek Song*, vol. 4, eds., Margaret Foster, Leslie Kurke, and Naomi Weiss (Leiden: Brill, 2020), 31–54. On the intermedial roles of the chorus, see Claude Calame, "Choral Polyphony and Ritual Functions of Tragic Songs," in *Choral Mediations in Greek Tragedy*, eds., Renaud Gagné and Marianne Govers Hopman (New York: Cambridge University Press, 2013), 55–7.

7. Marjorie Perloff, "The 'I' of Lyric," *Boston Review*, December 6, 2012, http://bostonreview.net/forum/poetry-brink/i-lyric.

8. Perloff asks: "If genius theory is passé, if there is no such thing as unique style or authorial presence, why are these names so sacred? If Foucault has pronounced so definitively on the death of the author, why are we always invoking the name of the author Foucault? Again, if in the current climate we dare not claim canonical status for Beckett or Brecht, why does Walter Benjamin enjoy that status so readily?" Marjorie Perloff, "Language Poetry and the Lyric Subject: Ron Silliman's Albany, Susan Howe's Buffalo," *Critical Inquiry* 25, no. 3 (Spring 1999): 410.

9. Luise Von Flotow-Evans, *Translation and Gender: Translating in the "Era of Feminism"* (Manchester: St. Jerome Pub., 1997), 35–6. See also Emily Wilson's description of her translation process, involving a multistep process of using dictionaries to confirm connotations, collaborating with an editor who draws on past translations, and sharing with a broader community for their feedback as well. "Emily Wilson on Translations and Language," *Conversations with Tyler*, March 27, 2019, https://conversationswithtyler.com/episodes/emily-wilson.

10. The history of feminist translation often engages this metaphor of weaving and spinning; see von Flotow, *Translation and Gender*, 27. Consider also Jessica Marie Johnson's theory of null value (covered in chapter 1 of this book), which argues that you can find evidence for historically overlooked people in the gaps of the archive; this labor of recovery places demands on the researcher that more historically centered scholars do not face. In other words, finding the stories that have not been told requires work of a different nature and different tools than that of retelling known tales.

11. The quiltmakers of Gee's Bend, Alabama, offer one example of individual quilters making quilts in community and operating with collective principals as the Freedom Quilting Bee (1966–2012). For an exhibition of a selection of Gee's Bend quilts, see "She Knew Where She Was Going: Gee's Bend Quilts and Civil Rights," *Baltimore Museum of Art*, March 10, 2021–September 12, 2021, https://artbma

.org/exhibition/she-knew-where-she-was-going-gees-bend-quilts-and-civil-rights, accessed March 07, 2021.

12. Nancy Worman, *Tragic Bodies: Edges of the Human in Greek Drama* (London: Bloomsbury, 2020), 29.

13. Paul Allen Miller, *Diotima at the Barricades: French Feminists Read Plato* (Oxford: Oxford University Press, 2016); on Diotima 7–9; on the twentieth-century feminists, 1–51. Miller deems this genealogy particularly important because of the outsized impact these theorists have had on Anglophone scholarship in the humanities such that "the ancient world, in general, and Plato, in particular, function as our theoretical unconscious" (vii–viii). In a parallel to Worman's choice, von Flotow argues that other women translators working with masculinized texts regularly invoked the mantle of authority of feminist theorists such as Hélène Cixous and Julia Kristeva to support this choice of text. von Flotow, *Translation and Gender*, 36.

14. Miller, *Diotima at the Barricades*, 13.

15. In an inversion of the practice of citing male authority figures, von Flotow argues that feminist translator Suzanne Jill Levine sought a kind of authority to support foregrounding her own subject position in her translations of male authors in the established work of feminist theorists such as Domna Stanton, Julia Kristeva, and Hélène Cixous. von Flotow, *Translation and Gender*, 37.

16. 12 Women Scholars, "A Disturbing Pattern," *Inside Higher Ed*, August 27, 2021, https://www.insidehighered.com/advice/2021/08/27/entrenched-inequity -not-appropriately-citing-scholarship-women-and-people-color. Annabel Kim, ed. "Citation, Otherwise," *Diacritics* 48, no. 3 (2020). While the issue was released in 2021, it bears a 2020 issue date.

17. Ahmed, *Living a Feminist Life*, 14.

18. Ahmed, *Living a Feminist Life*, 14.

19. Citational justice can be more of a challenge in some fields due to structural issues preventing access by women and others to the kinds of work we would like to cite. One possible solution to this is to reach outside of one's given subfield to other adjacent sources—which also means that interdisciplinarity supports citational justice.

20. Ahmed, *Living a Feminist Life*, note 8 and pages 15–16. See also Roxane Gay's philosophy of art acquisition: "I prioritize work by Black artists, and then women artists and queer artists and artists of color. And then the very, very last thing I collect is white men. I think I have one piece by a white guy. I mean, they're fine . . . actually no, I have a couple pieces, but those are my priorities." Noor Brara, "Author Roxane Gay, Who Loves Art but Dislikes the Art World, Has Some Advice for Galleries: 'Stop Being Terrible,'" *Art Net News*, April 12, 2021, https://news.artnet .com/art-world/roxane-gay-collecting-interview-1958221.

21. Jennifer C. Nash, "Citational Desires: On Black Feminism's Institutional Longings," *Diacritics* 48, no. 3 (2020): 76–91.

22. Ahmed, *Living a Feminist Life*, 15.

23. "Cite Black Women," *Cite Black Women Collective*, April 12, 2021, https:// www.citeblackwomencollective.org/. For more on these issues, see Christa Craven, "Teaching Antiracist Citational Politics as a Project of Transformation: Lessons from

the Cite Black Women Movement for White Feminist Anthropologists," *Feminist Anthropology* 2, no. 1 (2021): 120–9. Of the resources Craven cites, we found these particularly helpful: Carrie Mott and Daniel Cockayne, "Citation Matters: Mobilizing the Politics of Citation toward a Practice of 'Conscientious Engagement,'" *Gender, Place, and Culture* 24, no. 7 (2017): 954–73; Andrea Eidinger, "Cultivating a Conscientious Citation Practice," *Unwritten Histories*, May 7, 2019, https://www.unwrittenhistories.com/cultivating-a-conscientious-citation-practice; and Rachael Pells, "Understanding the Extent of Gender Gap in Citations," *Inside Higher Ed*, August 16, 2018, https://www.insidehighered.com/news/2018/08/16/new-research-shows-extent-gender-gap-citations.

24. As narrated by Christa Craven, "Jessica Marie Johnson, author *of Wicked Flesh: Black Women, Intimacy, and Freedom in the Atlantic World* (2020), has also documented journalists taking original ideas from her tweets but consistently failing to credit her as the originator" (Craven, 5). Craven credits Hannah McGregor for this information (Hannah McGregor, "Citing Your Sources," *Secret Feminist Agenda*, March 15, 2019, https://secretfeministagenda.com/2019/03/15/episode-3-21-citing-your-sources/).

25. Viet Thanh Nguyen (@viet_t_nguyen), "In 1992, My English Department Chairman Told Me I Couldn't Write a Dissertation on Vietnamese American Literature. In 2020's Modern Language Association Conference, I'll Speak on the Presidential Plenary—On Vietnamese American Literature," *Twitter*, January 3, 2020, 4:18 p.m., https://twitter.com/viet_t_nguyen/status/1213253385874395136.

26. Citations from the text courtesy of Knopf Doubleday Publishing Group: "118 [yes! radiant lyre speak to me]," "176 [lyre lyre lyre]," "25 [quit]," "114 [virginity]," "184 [danger]," "185 [honeyvoiced]," "186 [Medeia]," "187 [of the Muses]," "188 [mythweaver]," "92 [robe]," and "94 [I simply want to be dead]." *If Not, Winter: Fragments of Sappho* by Sappho, translated by Anne Carson, copyright © 2002 by Anne Carson. Used by permission of Alfred A. Knopf, an imprint of the Knopf Doubleday Publishing Group, a division of Penguin Random House LLC. All rights reserved.

27. As Dimitrios Yatromanolakis puts it: "Transformations, metamorphoses in the classical tradition, conjectural reconstructions, then and now: what is Sappho's text, anyway?" Dimitrios Yatromanolakis, "Fragments, Brackets, and Poetics: On Anne Carson's *If Not, Winter*," *International Journal of the Classical Tradition* 11, no. 2 (2004): 267.

28. Just as recent years have witnessed a resurgence of interest in the unfinished work of twentieth-century feminisms, so has the Feminist Duration Reading Group returned to Italian feminist work of the 1970s to produce what they name "informal 'guerilla' translations of untranslated texts" through collective reading. Helena Reckitt, "Generating Feminisms: Italian Feminisms and the 'Now You Can Go' Program," *Art Journal* 76, no. 3/4 (2017): 101.

29. von Flotow, *Translation and Gender*, 30–4.

30. von Flotow, *Translation and Gender*, 57.

31. Writing about Carson's translation, Elizabeth Robinson describes this operation with subtlety: "The translator is doing a work of self-erasure. Whose

voice is speaking? The original draws the translator into an ever-receding text, for it is never possible to replicate it. Yet the translator is an agent who beguiles the primary text forward until both original and translation are remodeled in the interchange." Elizabeth Robinson, "An Antipoem That Condenses Everything: Anne Carson's Translations of the Fragments of Sappho," in *Anne Carson: Ecstatic Lyre*, ed., Joshua Marie Wilkinson (Ann Arbor: University of Michigan Press, 2015), 181–7.

32. For commentary on Carson's minimal biography, see, for example, Daniel Mendelsohn, "In Search of Sappho," *New York Review*, August 14, 2003, https://www.nybooks.com/articles/2003/08/14/in-search-of-sappho; Geoff Wisner, "Fragments of Sappho," *Words without Borders*, March 30, 2011, https://www.wordswithoutborders.org/dispatches/article/fragments-of-sappho; Melanie Rehak, "Things Fall Together," *New York Times Magazine*, March 26, 2000, https://archive.nytimes.com/www.nytimes.com/library/magazine/home/20000326mag-annecarson.html (who comments that "The only information given on the jacket flap of her books is the single sentence 'Anne Carson lives in Canada.'"); and Dennis Loy Johnson, "Make Big Money: Become a Canadian Poet," *MOBYlives*, June 18, 2001, http://www.mobylives.com/Griffin_Prize.html.

33. Anne Carson, *If Not, Winter: Fragments of Sappho* (New York: Alfred A. Knopf, 2002).

34. On the material splendor and colors of Sappho's fragments, see chapter 2 of Stager, *Seeing Color in Classical Art*.

35. Emily Greenwood, Review of *If Not, Winter: Fragments of Sappho* by Anne Carson, *Journal of Hellenic Studies* 125 (Cambridge: Cambridge University Press, 2005), 159.

36. Yatromanolakis, while interested in quite different aspects of Carson's contribution, nevertheless frames his interpretation similarly: "What poetry, or, more broadly, *poiesis*, may be is the underlying subject of this well-produced book by Anne Carson." Yatromanolakis, "Fragments, Brackets, and Poetics," 266.

37. Fragments of women writers working in Greek in the ancient Mediterranean include work by Corinna, Erinna, Praxilla Nossis, and Telesilla. On these see: Alcaeus, Anacreon, Bacchylides, Corinna, Ibycus, Sappho, Simonides, Stesichorus, and David A Campbell, *Greek Lyric* (Cambridge, MA: Harvard University Press, 2014), 38–67, 78, 374; Denys L. Page, *Greek Literary Papyri in Two Volumes I* (Cambridge, MA: Harvard University Press, 1942), 484–7; W. R. Paton and M. A. Tueller, *The Greek Anthology* (Cambridge, MA: Harvard University Press, 2014), 266–7, 362–3.

38. Leslie V. Kurke, "Archaic Greek Poetry," in *The Cambridge Companion to Archaic Greece*, ed. H. A. Shapiro (Cambridge: Cambridge University Press, 2007): 158.

39. Carson, *If Not, Winter*, 297.

40. Carson, *If Not, Winter*, 241, 348.

41. On the embodied object in ancient art history, see Milette Gaifman and Verity Platt, "Introduction: From Grecian Urn to Embodied Object," *Art History* 41, no. 3 (2018): 402.

42. Emily Wilson highlights the isolation of the speaking subject in Sappho's Fragment 31 in her review of Carson's translation as a counterpoint to feminist arguments for Sappho's collective practice: "Fragmentation is her subject, not just what happens to her work," Wilson writes, referring to fragmentation of the self. In contrast, we locate Sappho's collectivity in performance culture, in the social relations that she pictures (even from outside of them), and in the relationships to her text that bridge millennia. Emily Wilson, "Tongue Breaks," *London Review of Books* 26, no. 1 (January 8, 2004), https://www.lrb.co.uk/the-paper/v26/n01/emily-wilson/tongue-breaks.

43. Kurke, "Archaic Greek Poetry," 141–2.

44. Kurke, "Archaic Greek Poetry," 142. Kurke notes, for example, that one of the meters used by Alcaeus and Sappho is identical to the meter of the Sanskrit *Rg Veda*, thought to have been composed for oral performance sometime between 1400 and 1000 BCE.

45. Kurke, "Archaic Greek Poetry," 145–7.

46. Kurke, "Archaic Greek Poetry," 158.

47. Kurke, "Archaic Greek Poetry," 162; Winkler, "Sappho's Double Consciousness," in *Constraints of Desire*, 167–76.

48. Timothy Power, "Sappho's Parachoral Monody," in *Genre in Archaic and Classical Greek Poetry: Theories and Models; Studies in Archaic and Classical Greek Song*, vol. 4, eds. Margaret Foster, Leslie Kurke, and Naomi Weiss (Leiden: Brill, 2020), 82.

49. Power, "Sappho's Parachoral Monody," 84–5.

50. Power, "Sappho's Parachoral Monody," 91–7.

51. Marianne Govers Hopman, "Chorus, Conflict, and Closure in Aeschylus' *Persians*," in *Choral Mediations in Greek Tragedy*, eds., Renaud Gagné and Marianne Govers Hopman (Cambridge: Cambridge University Press, 2013), 67.

52. This citation practice creates a bifurcated history of Sappho, splitting one that focuses on her meter and technical aspects of her poetry, relatively independently of biography or even personhood, from another that focuses on constructing a biography from her fragments with little attention to her artistry. Margaret Reynolds, ed., *The Sappho Companion* (New York: Palgrave for St. Martin's Press, 2001), 18–19.

53. Kurke, "Archaic Greek Poetry," 158; Yopie Prins, "Sappho's Afterlife in Translation," in *Re-Reading Sappho: Reception and Transmission*, ed. Ella Greene (Berkeley: University of California Press, 1996), 36–7.

54. Reynolds, *Sappho Companion*, 74.

55. On the ancient tradition of Sappho as the tenth muse, see Reynolds, *Sappho Companion*, 67–78; Giovanni Boccaccio, *Famous Women*, ed. and trans. Virginia Brown (Cambridge, MA: Harvard University Press, 2001), 192–5; Alyssa Granacki, "Boccaccio's Sappho: Female auctoritas in 'De mulieribus claris' and 'Saphos,'" *Renaissance Society of America*, April 21, 2021, https://rsa.confex.com/rsa/21virtual/meetingapp.cgi.Paper/9754.

56. Oxford English Dictionary online, © 2021 Oxford University Press, s.v. "papyrus"; and University of Michigan Papyrus Collection, "Papyrus Making 101," https://apps.lib.umich.edu/papyrus_making/slides.html, accessed March 19, 2021.

57. Poxy: Oxyrhynchus Online. "Paper Wraps Stone?" http://www.papyrology.ox .ac.uk/POxy/oxyrhynchus/parsons4.html, accessed January 09, 2021.

58. Kurke, "Archaic Greek Poetry," 158.

59. Kate MacNeill, "Spilling Blood in Art: A Tale of Tampons, Trump, and Taboos," *The Conversation*, July 31, 2017, https://theconversation.com/spilling -blood-in-art-a-tale-of-tampons-trump-and-taboos-81455. Levy and others draw on an earlier feminist artistic tradition of painting with the vagina or working with menstrual blood, such as Shigeko Kubota's *Vagina Painting* (1965), which was painted using her vagina to hold the paintbrush and working with red paint as well as Carolee Schneemann's *Blood Work Diary* (1972), which was painted with blood. On more recent work in this tradition, see Julia Martinčič, "Let It Bleed: Art's Revival of Menstrual Blood," *The Guardian*, December 12, 2016, https://www.theguardian.com /lifeandstyle/2016/dec/12/let-it-bleed-arts-revival-of-menstrual-blood.

60. Worman, *Tragic Bodies*, 249. For more on Schneemann's practice in her own words, see Brandon W. Joseph, ed., *Carolee Schneemann: Uncollected Texts* (New York: McNaughton & Gunn, 2018).

61. Medea Norsa, "Dai papiri della Società Italiana," *Annali della R. Scuola Normale Superiore di Pisa. Lettere, Storia e Filosofia* 6, no. 1/2 (1937): 1–15, with a facsimile, pl. II.

62. James Keenan, "The History of the Discipline," in *The Oxford Handbook of Papyrology*, ed. Roger S. Bagnall (Oxford: Oxford University Press, 2011), 59–78; G. Fabre, "Medea Norsa ebrea?" *Analecta Papyrologica* 14–15 (2003): 337–50.

63. Sarah Bond @SarahEBond, "Not All of Sappho Comes to Us from Papyri," *Twitter*, August 28, 2021, 8:08 a.m., https://twitter.com/SarahEBond/ status/1431589417194504193; on Medea Norsa's precarity due to her gender, see Roberta Mazza, "Powerful Text-Things: Papyrology and the Material Turn," *Everyday Orientalism Online*, December 11, 2020, https://www.youtube.com/ watch?v=RGoWbzdY7RA. Notably, Luciano Canfora recounts that Norsa was the object of an attack by C. Gallavotti, on which see Luciano Canfora, *Il papiro di Dongo* (Milan: Adelphi edizioni, 2005), 714. Situating Norsa's role in publishing this ostracon within the broader context of recovering the work of women writers in ancient Greek and Latin, see Judith P. Hallett, "Introduction: Looking at Ancient Women Writers through Male and Female Lenses," in *Ancient Women Writers*, eds., Bartolo Natoli, Angela Pitts, and Judith P. Hallett (London: Routledge, forthcoming). Recounting the ways in which circles of papyrologists shared news of Norsa's well-being during World War II, James Keegan notes that papyrologist H. I. Bell published an academic article in 1945 that opened with news that he had received an offprint from Norsa and confirmation that "she was alive and well despite the current fighting in northern Italy in and around Florence," on which see Keenan, "History of the Discipline," 70.

64. Dino Pieraccioni, "Ricordo di Medea Norsa (dieci anni dalla morte)," *Belfagor* 17, no. 4 (January 1, 1962): 482–5.

65. Pieraccioni, "Ricordo di Medea Norsa," 485. Neither Anne Carson nor Diane Rayor include or translate Fragment 75 in their selections of Sappho's fragments.

66. Prins, *Ladies' Greek*, 25–6.

67. Wilson also emphasizes the strangeness of Homeric Greek and culture ("The tension between strangeness and familiarity is in fact the poem's central subject"), a position emerging out of French Classicism in the 1970s and Jean-Paul Vernant's call to "make strange" classical texts (Wilson, "Introduction," 4).

68. Greenwood, "Review," 158.

69. Carson, *If Not, Winter*, 286–341.

70. Carson, *If Not, Winter*, 346–55.

71. Carson, *If Not, Winter*, x.

72. This conversation draws from controversy and debate over how short a poem can be and still "count" as a poem. Examples of the shortest poem possible include "I--/ Why?" (Eli Siegel, 1925); "O, / So? (Anonymous, 1960s); "Me / We" (Muhammed Ali, 1975); "lighght" by Aram Saroyan, 1965 (which generated controversy after he received an NEA grant to fund what some readers felt was a waste of money; see Ian Daly, "You Call That Poetry?! How Seven Letters Managed to Freak Out an Entire Nation," *Poetry Foundation*, August 25, 2007, https://www.poetryfoundation.org /articles/68913/you-call-that-poetry); "i" (jwcurry, in which the dot of the i is the author's fingerprint); or *Guinness Book of World Records*: "M" with an extra hump (to perhaps symbolize letters of the alphabet evolving into language) also by Aram Saroyam (after which the *Book* stopped compiling records for such briefness, arguing that the competition for shortest trivializes the meaning of such work itself). And then there are also poems that provide blanks for language without including any actual language whatsoever, which themselves recall John Cage's controversial composition "4′33″," a score that directs musicians to refrain from playing their instruments for four minutes and thirty-three seconds.

73. von Flotow, *Translation and Gender*, 57.

74. Carson, *If Not, Winter*, xi.

75. Yatromanolakis, "Fragments, Brackets, and Poetics," 270.

76. Carson, *If Not, Winter*, xii.

77. Carson, *If Not, Winter*, 353.

78. Sources that make this claim about modernist aesthetics abound, but of particular interest is the argument that the layout of the poem on the page and the blank space that surrounded it was a necessary quality that distinguished modern "poetry" from "verse"; see Bartholomew Brinkman, "Making Modern 'Poetry': Format, Genre, and the Invention of Imagism(e)," *Journal of Modern Literature* 32, no. 2 (2009): 20–40.

79. On Sapphic meter, see Yopie Prins, "Sapphic Stanzas: How Can We Read the Rhythm?" in *Critical Rhythm: The Poetics of a Literary Life Form*, eds. Ben Glaser and Jonathan Culler (New York: Fordham University Press, 2019), 247–73.

80. This practice reclaims Sappho's meter—long embraced by male writers since the Roman era who prioritized her innovative meter over identity or sexuality—for lesbian writers. Gretchen Schultz, Introduction to *An Anthology of Nineteenth-Century Women's Poetry from France: In English Translation, with French Text*, ed. Gretchen Schultz (New York: Modern Language Association of America, 2008),

xi–xxviii. Renée Vivien, "Sur le rythme sapphique," in *An Anthology of Nineteenth-Century Women's Poetry from France: In English Translation, with French Text*, 354–5.

81. Artemis Leontis, *Eva Palmer Sikelianos: A Life in Ruins* (Princeton, NJ: Princeton University Press, 2019), 1–40.

82. This programming was held in conjunction with a workshop in the history of art, "Form Beyond the Aesthetic," organized by Jennifer Stager and hosted by the Baltimore Museum of Art as part of a series focused on women performers to honor the 100th anniversary of the ratification of the Nineteenth Amendment and to recognize the limitations of that amendment, which secured the vote primarily for white women.

83. Dora Malech, *Stet: Poems* (Princeton, NJ: Princeton University Press, 2018), https://www.doramalech.net/about.html.

84. Jennifer Stager, "Space as Form: Sappho Now," *Open Space*, April 9, 2020, https://openspace.sfmoma.org/2020/04/space-as-form-sappho-now.

85. Stager, "Space as Form."

86. Stager, "Space as Form."

87. Stager, "Space as Form."

88. Carson, *If Not, Winter*, 187.

89. Significantly, for many of the participants and audience members, the performance of *extreme lyric I* at the Baltimore Museum of Art on March 6, 2020, marked a last public gathering before our collective and, at the time of writing, ongoing sheltering in place due to the COVID-19 pandemic.

Figure 5.1 Carrie Spits into Ryan's Coffee in *Promising Young Woman* (2020). Screenshot by author.

Chapter 5

The Parabolic Curve

On March 16, 2020, our colleague Joni Spigler posted a narrative to a private social media account in which she described sitting outdoors in her garden:

> The radiant Sun hovered just above the rooftop of the house, and [my partner] sat between me and the Sun facing his mother. In the garden, myriad tiny spores and pollens and insects drifted and darted in the Sun's beams, sparkling like dust motes in a window's light.
>
> And as he spoke to his mother (who sat at least ten feet away), I could see the little droplets of breath and spittle flying out of [his] mouth into the light, launching about two feet out before falling again among their parabolic curves (and those were only the sparks I could see).
>
> I thought "This is what it is to stand in front of someone's face when they are talking to you: you stand under an invisible shower of moist word-sprayed particles and beams, all possibly deadly."[1]

Our title for this chapter, "The Parabolic Curve," takes inspiration from Spigler's lyrical description not only of the path of spit itself but also of the movement of risk and connection between people as well as something that, at the start of the COVID-19 pandemic, we had not yet fully realized for ourselves: that our fluids mingle in the air we breathe; that our choices affect others and that we are affected by the choices of others; that the pandemic had, in profound and paradoxical ways, split us apart as we sheltered in place—or could not shelter—while dramatically showing us how deeply interconnected our fates were. This interconnection became more profound with each passing week, though just as we recognize this interconnectedness, so too do we realize the disparity among individuals in terms of access to resources.

If chapter 4 narrates a vision of intentional feminist collectivity, this chapter traces some implications of interconnection, especially the kinds that are not chosen. Interconnection depends on circles of intimacy that arise from both positive and negative structures and circumstances, yet models outside of hierarchies can rearrange those circles. By providing these models or even simply exposing the power dynamics implicit within these structures, public feminism offers ways to think differently about interconnection, even in terms of our own bodies. For example, while many of us would likely consider bodily fluids like spit to belong to us, pandemic priorities necessitate an exploration of how they may affect others, creating both possibilities and warnings for public feminism. These explorations can make feminist notions of interdependent existence unavoidably visible by exposing the mechanisms of physical interconnection already in place, shedding light on both the present and the past. As we track engagements with the connectedness of bodily fluids in the historical past, we note how prescient these prior engagements feel from a COVID-19 perspective due to their politics around the individual body and the larger social contract they reveal, especially in terms of questions of what we do or do not owe each other. To better understand these politics, we will examine spit, bodily fluids, and viruses more generally to ask how contagions and ideas proliferate rapidly, how they become encoded politically, how their curves shape our lives profoundly, and how we can guard against their ultimate impact.

The producers of *Hamilton* released a filmed version of the Broadway hit in July 2020 for captive audiences streaming from home. These audiences noted various details of the release, among them the spit-filled performance of Jonathan Groff in the role of King George III. As he sang, Groff did not hesitate to let spit fly aggressively from his mouth and eventually settle in drool bubbles on his chin. This projecting spittle communicated King George's disdain for his subjects, played in the language of an abusive ex. Producer Jon Kamen reported that he offered to edit out the spit, but *Hamilton* creator Lin-Manuel Miranda declined, a move some critics have labeled "authentic."[2] Whether or not that decision was made in a post-COVID-19 world, the summer 2020 audience certainly experienced Groff's spit in that context. And from the vantage point of the pandemic, only the protection of watching from home shielded the audience/subjects from the contagion of King George's anger.

Later in the pandemic, such images grew even more vexed. In a tweet retweeted over 90,000 times, book publicist Cristina Arreola wrote on August 4, 2020: "I love masks. I can't believe I let y'all just breathe on me before," amusing readers with an idea that nonetheless felt quite reasonable at that moment in the pandemic.[3] Even later, on December 8, 2020, in an epic *New Yorker* essay titled "The Plague Year," which occupied about half of the magazine's printed pages, playwright Lawrence Wright created his own Spigler moment when reflecting on a rehearsal he had attended early in the spring from the vantage point of the end of the year:

> I have a memory of the preview performances which later came back to me, charged with significance. The actors were performing in the round, and slanted lighting illuminated their faces against the shadowy figures of audience members across the way. When one actor expostulated, bursts of saliva flew from his mouth. Some droplets arced and tumbled, but evanescent particles lingered, forming a dim cloud. At the time, I found this dramatic, adding to the forcefulness of the character. Later, I thought, "this is what a superspreader looks like."[4]

Of course, actual superspreader events turned out to look very different. Consider, for example, the September 26, 2020, Rose Garden celebration of Amy Coney Barrett's Supreme Court justice nomination, during which at least eleven people contracted the coronavirus.[5] Such events spread the virus because some participants refused to wear masks, maintain distance, or remain outdoors, choices that prioritized the individual's immediate desires over their collective impact.[6] Indeed, arbitrary markers of a shared political pact seemed to become metaphorized in antimasking itself, despite its conflict with individual self-interest (for example, in rejecting the protection masks may offer the wearer). This bizarre version of collectivity that harms both the self and the others with whom one shares space is not the public feminist kind. Ethics of care must undergird feminist collectives—care that extends to self and community.

In communities of care during the pandemic, testing became a necessary measure to curtail spread. Thus spit became something new—a substrate on which some forms of COVID-19 testing have been based. At the start of the pandemic, when most tests were swab-based, getting tested for the virus was a structural (supply chain and logistical) challenge. Even people who believed they were sick could not get tested unless they were having trouble breathing or experienced other symptoms that required emergency attention. We know now that early lack of access to testing contributed to the circulation of and associated mutation by the virus, which in turn produced more successful and virulent strains.[7]

A year later, COVID-19 testing—often in the form of spit testing—became more of a norm, although access was often determined by labor and was housed within institutions that had the means to invest in it. Within the privileged world of the university (and likely other workplaces), spit emerged as a kind of currency. On one of the authors' campuses, surveillance spit testing sites allowed staff, students, and faculty to make an appointment with an app, check in, collect a plastic tube, step into a sanitized space reminiscent of a voting booth, and then pull their mask down and drool about one and a half millimeters into the tube. Once a specimen was provided, a spit-checker, who was also responsible for spraying down each booth between visits, confirmed that the specimen was a large enough sample free of debris. Then each person placed their test tube in the vial tray next to the test tubes of other workers and walked out. In combination with an app asking health questions, weekly testing cleared a worker to move around campus while masked. While bodies thereby returned to their assigned professional roles, their spit remained in trays alongside the spit of others who performed different roles within the same institution. These spit tests were both flattening—in that everyone within a hierarchical workplace took the same test in the same way—and medicalizing. With the introduction of spit testing into work communities, we are potentially expanding experiences of surveilling the body in ways that might build connection across differences. Of course, the potential dark side of this surveillance testing is illuminated in its very name.

Though it might seem from our examples above that this moment—a moment of awareness, as if for the first time, of the physicality of bodies and their fluids—has itself become a genre, we argue that, at least during year two of the pandemic, it had not become enough of one. Instead, as mentioned above, mask wearing—a mitigation strategy that responded to the risk of spit—itself became politicized, prompting anthropologist Anand Pandian to tweet on January 11, 2021, following the social media clampdown on violent provocations on social media after the failed coup attempt at the Capitol on January 6, about the

> parallel between the conservative clamor over free speech and the deep opposition to pandemic masks. Both positions insist that you shouldn't have to worry about what your mouth expresses: whether the danger to others from a violent word or a viral particle.[8]

In this chapter, we worry precisely about that—the danger to others from our mouths and the processes by which humans use their mouths, along with other parts of their bodies, to threaten or protect others. While the pandemic exposed bodily fluids as actors on the human interaction stage and those fluids demonstrated our profound interdependence, community-driven choices to enforce pandemic-based restrictions enacted collective protection and care, though this care was far from universal. Interdependence also moves beyond the physical to inflect the world of ideas and vice versa; the reverberations of this process provide opportunities for the academic study of materialism and virality through a public feminist lens.

The imperfect and porous boundaries of the body have provoked anxiety throughout history. In confronting our interdependences (whether through wet-nursing or sex or other fluid sharing examples), cultures have recognized that they cannot entirely escape interconnection through the ideological bunkers of behaviors and identity, although of course structural problems shape how unevenly the impact of such connections can land. Norms around the sharing of fluids demarcate intimacy in various circles from romantic to familial to societal. We suggest that the operation of contamination, often aligned with the bodies of women, is a fundamental aspect of patriarchal society—one of the threats its system is designed to neutralize. While the containment of fluids in a pandemic expresses collective consciousness and care, the patriarchal containment of women's bodies is wholly different: a practice of regulation that produces power differentials that undergird oppression. The pandemic does, however, help us see how women's bodies can themselves be constructed as viral contaminants that threaten others. In the face of this threat lies the dream of invulnerability, sometimes figured in a fantasy of immortality—or even vaccination—that might protect the body from contagion. Reclaiming virality in light of this fantasy thus becomes a public feminist project. To explore it, we trace the apparatus of decentralization in redistributing power and contend that virality can be used as an important tool of feminist activism.

NEW MATERIALISM AND THE BODY

Embedded in the issue of contamination are questions surrounding the body. The notion of the self establishes an artificial boundary between the idea of the physical body and the experience of personhood, a boundary more recent analysis shows to be a fiction. Spit, for example, is a material of the body that also moves through the world beyond the body. Yet misunderstandings about the relationship between people and things persist—boundaries particularly troubled in stories like that of the late 2020 feminist revenge-porn film *Promising Young Woman (Fig. 5.1)*. A rape story that is also a bodily fluid story, the film demonstrates how transgressive an exchange of bodily fluids looks from a pandemic perspective, despite the fact that—as Spigler points out at the start of this chapter—we are already encountering the danger of such exchanges every day.

In an early scene of the film, a man, Ryan, walks into the coffee shop where the protagonist Cassie works and recognizes her from medical school.[9] He stumbles through a question-retraction-question about why Cassie is working in a coffee shop (and not, he implies, practicing medicine). Cassie does nothing to make Ryan—or, for that matter, the audience—more comfortable, a notable departure from the ways girls and women are coached to comfort others at their own expense. Growing more flustered at her failure to put him at ease, Ryan responds to her repeated query about whether he wants milk by saying "no, but you can spit in it if you want." Cassie looks directly at him, leans over the paper cup, and spits directly and audibly into his coffee before passing it across the counter (Fig. 5.1).

The scene is framed to highlight the materiality of the spit and its contamination—the camera subtly tightens its frame on Cassie's face; the spit is globular and prominent in its trajectory from Cassie's mouth into Ryan's cup. Of course, in some ways, this is a money shot—Cassie's spit a cypher for semen, a fluid figured as phallic presence—but Ryan responds according to the power dynamics implied by the spit.[10] After accepting the cup, Ryan looks up and asks: "Do you want to go out with me?" Incredulous, Cassie replies: "Seriously, I just spat in your coffee?" Ryan looks down at the lougie-filled cup and takes a sip.[11]

Spit plays several different roles in the scene, but above all symbolizes the colonization of one body by another—just, in this case, not the colonization we have come to expect in the standard patriarchal lexicon—and the feminist hero's reluctance to put male characters and the viewer at ease. Ryan invites Cassie to spit in his coffee in response to his rude questioning as a joke and because he assumes that propriety will prevent her from doing so. Cassie *does* spit in his coffee, both to refuse societal norms that insist that she not do so and to contaminate his coffee. Her spit contains the microbes of her body, and now so does Ryan's coffee. And yet when Ryan takes a spit-laden sip, his decision acquires the intimate charge of exchanging bodily fluids. At the same time, given the conventional nature of fetishism, dominance, and "swallowing" in phallocentric erotic discourse, the scene hangs in tension between feminine empowerment and persecution. In a film organized around rape and its long aftermath—and as a gesture that echoes conventions of other rape-revenge films like *I Spit On Your Grave*—Cassie's spit marks a way in which bodily fluids can transcend the boundaries of our bodies, whether spread through intimate, violent, or even quotidian means.[12]

This scene exposes the fiction that the insides of our bodies remain within what we understand as our body's boundaries—Cassie's spit leaves her body, is deposited in Ryan's coffee, and moments later enters his mouth.[13] Likewise, rape traverses bodily boundaries but by violent means. Some rape stories, including that of Artemisia as explored in our second chapter, suggest that the damage of rape can transform a person into a thing, at least from a legal perspective. Historical laws about rape establish this paradox, casting the person who is raped as a commodity whose value decreases when their boundaries are violated and leaving us to walk a fine line as we survey the landscape of feminist materialism. The challenge is to construct a framework that avoids viewing humans within the logic of objects even as it recognizes the material conditions for bodies and the active role that nonhuman things, or vital matter, play in bodies and embodied experiences.

The theoretical framework we refer to above, often called "new materialism," offers ways of thinking about the mutual inflections of humans and materials. This framework, which has roots in ancient Greek philosophy but has emerged as a crucial site of feminist and ecocritical engagement in recent decades, bears some relation to thing-focused theories by other names. Sarah Nooter aggregates the frameworks underlying these terms:

> Perhaps the most striking feature of new materialism is its endless semantic elasticity. It gives us objects, object agency, things, thingness, substance, stuff, viscosity, matter production, bodies (sort of), body parts, embodiment, prostheses, assemblages, capacities, autonomy, resistance, and irreducible alterity. The expanses encompassed by affect theory are no less capacious. Here we find emotions, feelings, senses, energies, vitality, vibrancy, presence, co-presence, convergence, compassion, sympathy, empathy, synchrony, co-existence, withholding, consumption, cannibalization, and digestion. We edge also toward the human as thing, the nonhuman and posthuman, to say nothing of OOO (Object-Oriented Ontology).[14]

Nooter's neat litany captures many of the vast points of engagement with new materialism—and some of the challenges of using its wide-ranging ideas as a framework.

Although we are interested in situating new materialism in its broader theoretical and historical context, the particular jumping-off point for this chapter's engagement with its ideas is Jane Bennett's work *Vibrant Matter: A Political Ecology of Things*. In its opening pages, Bennett lays out her methodology and distinguishes her approach and genealogy from that of Marxist materialism:

> I pursue a materialism in the tradition of Democritus-Epicurus-Spinoza-Diderot-Deleuze more than Hegel-Marx-Adorno. It is important to follow the trail of human power to expose social hegemonies (as historical materialists do). But my contention is that there is also public value in following the scent of a nonhuman, thingly power, the material agency of natural bodies and technological artifacts.[15]

This genealogy gestures to the deep history of materialism, dating back at least as far as to a group of ancient Greek philosophers active in the fifth century BCE, including Democritus. Bennett distinguishes her emphasis on vital materialism that destabilizes boundaries between human and nonhuman from the anthropocentric focus of the economic structures of

Marxist materialism.[16] Marx's dissertation addressed distinctions between Democritus and Epicurus, against whose version of naive materialism he later contrasts his own.[17] And so Bennett's invocation of Democritus and Epicurus deliberately aligns her materialism with this naive materialism.

Bennett, however, engages more deeply with the Latin reception of these early Greek philosophers in the work of the Roman author Lucretius's text *On the Nature of Things*.[18] Building on work by Empedocles (a contemporary of Democritus) and the later Stoic philosopher Epicurus, Lucretius describes atoms, seeds, or parts moving through the world, forming and reforming.[19] It is just such agentive matter that anthropocentric models occlude and that Bennett's vital materialism surfaces.

Although often mischaracterized along with some other new materialists as prioritizing the nonhuman over the human, Bennett seeks, in her own words, "to articulate a vibrant materiality that runs alongside and inside humans to see how analyses of political events might change if we gave the force of things more due."[20] Bennett analyzes vital matter in search of "more materially sustainable modes of production and consumption . . . motivated by a self-interested or conative concern for *human* survival and happiness."[21] Thus, for Bennett, foregrounding the interconnectedness of human and nonhuman "actants" (Bennett's word, drawing from Latour), enables humans to act from a place of more and better information about their own interdependence with both people and things.[22] Situated within an ecocritical and ecofeminist frame, Bennett's vital matter aligns with an expansive feminist new materialism; we see her engagement with an "out-side" (drawn from Thoreau's Wildness, or "strange dimension of matter," itself potentially influenced by the practice of formerly enslaved Black families who lived in Walden prior to Thoreau taking up residence there) as a mode of thinking beyond patriarchy.[23]

Anthropologist Daniel Miller provides a succinct summary of an alternative, but intersecting, strand of these ideas, connecting Hegel, Marx, Latour, and Gell, all of whom address the role of materiality in our lived experience while the latter two also emphasize matter's agency.[24] Miller argues that the less we are aware of a given thing, the more powerfully it acts on us and shapes our responses. For this formulation, Miller builds from art historian Ernst Gombrich's analysis of the frame in art, a border for the work that, Gombrich argues, disappears from our perception when it matches the work it frames. Expanding on this, Miller argues that objects have more power when their agency is less visible:

> The less we are aware of [things] the more powerfully they can determine our expectations by setting the scene and ensuring normative behaviour, without being open to challenge. They determine what takes place to the extent that we are unconscious of their capacity to do so.[25]

Miller employs this theory of the frame as an example of the very kind of silent agency by which objects act on subjects without their full awareness.[26]

Although unnamed in Miller's account, Derrida's theorization of the frame in *The Truth in Painting* focuses on how frames not only delineate the boundaries that surround what they frame but also establish an outside and inside of framed space in a formulation similar to that which we have investigated in trying to find pathways outside of patriarchal enclosure. Derrida's ideas are taken up in "Framing the Female Body," an essay that also draws together many of the concerns threaded throughout our own book; in it, art historian Lynda Nead connects the idea of the management of female bodies we explored in chapter 1, the Venus tradition of the female nude we traced in chapter 2, concerns around bodily fluids traversing boundaries of the body we seek to theorize in this current chapter, and the seemingly fixed boundary of the frame that delimits an inside and outside to a painting discussed previously. Nead argues that

> one of the principal goals of the female nude has been the containment and regulation of the female sexual body. The forms, conventions, and poses of art worked metaphorically to shore up the female body—to seal orifices and to prevent marginal matter from transgressing the boundary dividing the inside and outside, the self from the space of the other.[27]

In Nead's reading, this boundary might be located either in a physical frame surrounding a painting or in poses internal to the picture that function as frames, but neither boundary truly maintains the distinctions it purports to delimit. Instead, the frames serve as reminders of patriarchal regulation enforcing systems of bodily containment.

The agency of these frames also demonstrates what Bill Brown has called "thing power," in which objects that move out of their relationship with human use become, in consequence, "things" that can be finally apprehended by virtue of their newly acquired distance. Bennett's work also relies on the formulation of thing power.[28] And Miller's point about the inverse relationship between the invisibility and power of objects applies equally to social structures, which are themselves shaped by materials and material conditions. If social structures, like things, often maintain power through invisibility, identifying these forces takes on great importance. The less we name sexism and racism, for example, the more powerfully they may operate (though at other times, such social structures depend on brute force that is explicitly displayed rather than rendered invisible).

A robust postcolonial challenge to these materialist modes of thinking refuses to collapse boundaries between human and nonhuman, instead insisting that such conceptual boundaries are necessary on the grounds that they might serve as a check against the treatment of some humans *as* things through the violence of slavery and colonialism. Severin Fowles historicizes the material turn within anthropology—what he terms "the subjectification of the object world"—against the backdrop of postcolonial critique, arguing that "as human subjects increasingly protested against being treated like objects—anthropologists began to explore the advantages of treating (non-human) objects like (quasi-human) subjects."[29] This transfer of attention, Fowles argues, allowed established scholars to maintain power even as the world in which they practiced such scholarship radically and rapidly changed. Rightly highlighting the dangers of subjectifying objects, Fowles's critique of thing power warns against the type of inappropriate application of new materialist thinking that removes agency from, for example, rape victims. His argument does not, on the other hand, directly address the strand of feminist new materialism we are engaging with in our chapter, although Fowles does name Bennett's attention to nonhuman affect in his sole reference to her work. The feminist strand of new materialist thinking that concerns us here does not disavow human agency and therefore does not conflict with Fowles's arguments. Instead, vital materialist theories like those of Bennett foreground not the humanness of objects but the deep interconnections of matter, including bodily fluids and the people they make up and move through. Nevertheless, Fowles offers us necessary historiography.

Bennett tracks the protean movements of vital matter through her chapters to demonstrate how such matter acts and reacts relationally with human actors. In a section that reads as eerily prescient, Bennett works through Rancière's theory of disruption to argue that his focus on the effects of a given instance leaves open the possibility that civic disruption might arrive in nonhuman form—as the vibrant matter of, for example, a virus.[30] Although Bennett's points of reference are HIV and SARS, her emphasis on the vibrant matter that acts on humans and nonhumans takes on an acute urgency in the context of the COVID-19 pandemic. And what reads as prescience in the midst of that pandemic is also a reminder that virality and pandemics (also from the ancient Greek, *pan + dēmos* or "all" + "people") have been here before, but too often people have not seen themselves as vulnerable and therefore have not focused enough on researching and otherwise responding to them, presuming the virus to be someone else's problem.[31]

One of the authors' children, who is attentive to nonhuman actants, said of the virus and its enduring contagion and mutation that "it just wants to survive. Everything it is doing, it does in order to survive." In response to the COVID-19 virus' pursuit of survival, we remade our lives—retreating from collective social spaces and face-to-face community, covering our faces with masks, washing and rewashing our hands in an effort to dislodge the virus and wash it away. Imagining the virus as an active agent or embodied material presence has helped us respond to it. Indeed, the priorities of new materialism have proven especially useful in encouraging us to think about virality in material terms as the COVID-19 pandemic has tracked the movements and mutations of just such a "thing." Ubiquitous illustrations of its spiked protein shape make productively visible what we cannot actually see—a virus that is also an object moving through our spit, bodies, and communities.[32]

THE MILKY WAY: BREASTFEEDING, CLASS, AND CONTAGION

As we expand our exploration of bodily fluids to trace how the pandemic provides a framework to better see patriarchal constructions of the female body as a (leaky) container, we now return to Wilson's translation of the *Odyssey* (which we previously examined in chapter 3).[33] Like the mouth with which we began this chapter, other parts of the body can leak and move from private to public, yet not all fluids are figured through the same dynamics. While bodily fluids like spit and blood are viewed as potentially containing contagions, breast milk—like vaccination—can also potentially confer immunity through fluid sharing. And in the face of the threat of contagion, some writers and artists imagine immortality as ultimate protection. All of these dynamics are in play in this section's exploration of breast milk.

To begin, we focus on the embodied wet nurse living in and with the vibrant material world. Breast milk, like spit, is a bodily fluid that seems personal to our own body but that actually connects us. It is affected by environment and toxins but adjusts itself based on the needs of the infant.[34] It is internal to a bounded body but also external—and the act of extracting it transgresses, for a moment, the duality of internal/external and perhaps also of self/other.

The class-driven politics of breastfeeding—most especially around who is deemed appropriate to do it—have run through history as well as myth. One ancient Greek myth, for example, accounts for the creation of the starscape now called the Milky Way.[35] That story recounts that Zeus impregnated a mortal woman, Alcmene, who gave birth to Herakles. As a half-mortal, Herakles was not born with immortality. In order to secure it for him, the goddess Athena tricked Zeus's wife Hera into nursing Herakles in her sleep without her knowledge or consent, demonstrating that even a god's autonomy and body can be violated.[36] But when Herakles tugged too strongly at her nipple, Hera pulled him from her breast and the resulting spray of breast milk twinkled across the night sky as stars.[37]

Artistic depictions of breastfeeding are rare in ancient Greek art, but a few images from the ancient Mediterranean have been identified as depictions of

Herakles suckling at Hera's breast.[38] Those depictions can be divided into two distinct versions of the myth. The first, painted onto a ceramic vessel, depicts Zeus (or Athena) sneaking the infant Herakles to Hera's breast; the second, etched into a bronze mirror, depicts an adult Herakles suckling at Hera's breast before an audience of other gods.[39]

In an example of the first version, an artist painted the scene of a toddler standing between the knees of an adult woman dressed in a beautifully patterned embroidered dress. She has unclasped the right shoulder of her dress to bare her right breast, at which the child suckles. Another woman, perhaps Athena, faces the pair. Although their setting is only loosely delineated, a line of white dots traces under Hera and Herakles, perhaps evoking the twinkling stars of the Milky Way that they will soon produce. The artist who painted this ceramic vessel did not sign the work, and so John Beazley—in his massive archive that seeks to categorize the full corpus of ancient Mediterranean ceramics—created an artistic persona for the artist: "the Suckling Painter."[40] Beazley then attributed painted ceramics of other scenes to the same artist, even when they did not depict acts of wet-nursing, on the basis of his perception of their similar style. The demand to connect named artists with identified bodies of work crafts this painter as forever identified by the wet-nursing that their painting once captured.[41]

In an example from the second version, an image etched onto an Etruscan bronze mirror, an assembly of the gods surrounds a seated Hera. A thickly bearded, adult Herakles wearing the Nemean lion skin tied around his shoulders leans over Hera; she holds her right breast to his mouth. Although the imagery makes no direct reference to the Milky Way, a pattern of half circles runs around the edge of the mirror, not quite breasts and not quite stars. These images suggest that the story of Herakles feeding from Hera's breasts in order to secure his immortality circulated in conjunction with the naming of the galaxy and the Milky Way. Consistent across different strands of the myth is the power of Hera's breast milk to bestow immortality. This fantasy of the invulnerability of immortality shores up the body against the risk of contagion. Eventually, this death-defying milk from the body of the queen of the gods installed itself in the heavens as the sparkling stars by which ancient and modern travelers navigated—and continue to navigate—the globe.[42]

These are the very stars by which Odysseus and his sailors navigate the Mediterranean over the course of his journey in the *Odyssey*. Upon finally returning home to Ithaca, Odysseus reunites with the enslaved woman who wet nursed him, Eurycleia, with whom he shares a deep connection in some senses and an extreme power differential in others. Fluid-bonding through breast milk connects Odysseus as well as his son Telemachus, whom Eurycleia also nursed, to the enslaved woman, establishing circles of intimacy that complicate the clear class and gender boundaries between them.

Odysseus, however, simultaneously invokes their entangled and intimate histories while also emphasizing that if Eurycleia does not maintain her loyalty to him, he will not hesitate to kill her despite these ties. In Wilson's translation of book 19, Eurycleia recognizes Odysseus in disguise even when his wife Penelope seems not to. Odysseus responds:

> Nanny! Why are you trying to destroy me? You fed me at your breast! . . . Be silent; no one must know, or else I promise you, if some god helps me bring the suitors down, I will not spare you when I kill the rest, the other slave women, although you were my nurse.[43]

In this speech, Odysseus reminds Eurycleia not only that he enslaves her but also of the fluid bond they share. Later, Eurycleia assists the men she has breastfed with their revenge against the suitors and reclamation of Odysseus's throne.

Patrizia Birchler Emery has argued that enslaved wet nurses and nannies in ancient Greek culture were depicted as renunciants.[44] The iconography of women like Eurycleia routinely depicts them as old women—not in order to portray them in a realistic way but instead to convey the duration of their lives given over to this labor of care and to the demand that they renounce other aspects of their identities. This paradigm of women forced to nurse the infants of their enslavers establishes a practice that continues into modernity with real people. According to historian Maria Helena Pereira Toledo Machado: "The practice of placing master-class infants in the care of female captives to be breastfed by them was widespread, occurring in all of the slave societies of the Americas."[45] Additionally, in the specific context of nineteenth-century Rio de Janeiro, Cassia Roth has analyzed the commodification of enslaved women's breast milk in the practice of renting bondswomen to other families to nurse their children in return for capital paid to the enslaver.[46] Roth argues that the complexity of this situation unsettles traditional distinctions between Marxist production (masculinized labor) and feminist social reproduction (feminized care).[47] In this situation, the body of each enslaved wet nurse is the means of production (the production of milk) that produces capital for her enslavers; the commodity is not only her enslaved labor as wet nurse but also her material body as milk. Roth describes the escalation of this practice in the lead-up to abolition in Brazil as well as contemporary critiques of this practice by physicians on the grounds of what that milk might contain. Roth writes: "For physicians, the perceived dangerousness of enslaved women's milk went beyond the physical to encompass the moral and emotional."[48] In short, their objections did not concern the harm to the enslaved women and their own infants but rather what might transfer from their bodies to the elite infants they nursed. The idea that a woman's emotional state might impact her milk or transfer that emotion via the milk simultaneously recognizes the impact of emotions on the body and also figures them as material contaminants.

Although in radically different contexts and times, the structures normalized in the story of the *Odyssey* around enslaved women forced to wet-nurse the children of their enslavers may have had an enduring influence on such lived practices in modernity, as in the example of the women in Roth's study.[49] In adopting this practice, elite women outsourced the nutritional intake of their infants to women whom they did not recognize as equally human and who were less likely to be granted access to varied nutrition, to medical care, and, in modernity, to vaccinations. In cases where an enslaved wet nurse could nurse both her own child and the elite child whose parents had rented her or in whose home she was enslaved, the shared breast milk would have also produced a tie between both infants despite their radically different class positions and the violence by which such ties were created. Both infants would have taken in the same milk and both would have prompted changes in the wet nurse's body and milk, creating an unexpected circle of intimacy.

Yet while some fluids bond in unexpected ways, other fluids threaten to leak and contaminate. Historically, women have been feared for the leakiness of their bodily containers. That same fear motivates Odysseus when confronting the violation of his household by the suitors. Odysseus seeks to remove irrevocably the bodies of the enslaved girls following their possible contamination by the semen of the suitors. Telemachus contributes to this purification murder by insisting on the method by which they will kill the enslaved girls—by hanging. His logic in choosing this method of death, rather than the blade, is twofold: he both marks their deaths as different from the heroic deaths of warriors or objects of sacrifice and also contains the fluids of their bodies. Wilson connects Telemachus's intervention in keeping the enslaved girls' bodies intact in death in order to hold in their pollution with his own transition from boyhood to manhood.[50]

Ancient Greek artists often depicted the bloodiness of battles, athletic competitions, or sacrifices, from the spray of blood depicted on vase paintings to blood painted on architectural relief and inlaid copper blood on bronze statues.[51] In these contexts, the visible flow of blood could be associated with heroic acts and heroic deaths. By denying the enslaved girls death by stabbing, Telemachus also denies them any association through the flow of their blood with warriors, noble sacrificial daughters, or athletes. Enslaved in Odysseus's household, the murdered girls can neither freely refuse nor consent to sex with the suitors, and so they cannot escape contamination by the living semen of the dead suitors, through which the suitors could potentially live on. By executing this violent solution to the possible contagions held within the enslaved girls' bodily fluids,

Telemachus prioritizes containing this imagined virality over the girls' individual lives.

GOING VIRAL

In the face of the construction of women's bodies as viral threats, feminists can reclaim virality as a public feminist tool. Indeed, any conversation of virality must extend to the transmission of ideas and language as well as to the contamination and "going viral" upon which the modern world of social media—and indeed the internet at large—rests. We maintain that the trajectory of the internet has allowed some ideas to spread rapidly, though capitalism has at times co-opted this spread (while co-opting even hashtags themselves). Viral ideas, as they proliferate, have at times united vast swaths of people in a synchronous aim—even when that aim is centered in something small, like the resonance of a poem.

Three days after the June 12, 2016, Orlando nightclub shooting that killed forty-nine people in what at the time was the deadliest mass shooting by a single gunman in US history, poet Maggie Smith (who had already published two book-length poetry collections and multiple chapbooks) released the poem that would, in the poet's own words, become her "Freebird." "Good Bones," accepted by *Waxwing* literary magazine months earlier, immediately went viral, likely spurred on by the tragedy on whose heels it inadvertently followed. Retweeted by celebrities and profiled in magazines like *Salon* and *The Guardian*, the poem increased *Waxwing*'s readership by 50 percent in three days. After the November 2016 election, the poem experienced an additional resurgence as one of the three most forwarded poems on the "heavy poetry days" of November 10 and 11 (in the company of "Still I Rise" and "September 1, 1939").[52] Smith eventually titled her 2017 book of poems, a collection that included "Good Bones," by the same name. The BBC/Public Radio International called it "the Official Poem of 2016."[53] Clearly, the poem spoke to a moment, one in which readers were perhaps hungry for its accessible balance of comfort and realism.[54]

In its largest context, viral poetry, theorized by Jacquelyn Ardam as "internet poetry," became normalized in the years leading up to the period we explore in this book.[55] Consider, for example, the rise of Instagram poetry in general and Instagram poet Rupi Kaur's astonishing success more particularly—in print she outsells Homer 10 to 1.[56] Later, the 2021 inauguration of Joe Biden provided a platform for the immediate (and quantifiable) surge in popularity of poet Amanda Gorman.[57] Smith's work had its own patterns of recirculation; Ardam narrates that it "continues to circulate widely every time something horrific happens in the United States, which is frequently" and that it came to Ardam's own "attention in the wake of Trump's election, when I saw it all over Twitter and Instagram," clearly speaking to a moment of need.[58]

Still, the rapid circulation of "Good Bones" was notable even within the larger context in which the symbiotic needs of poetry and social media can produce poetic virality. The piece, a brief, seventeen-line repetitive poem, tries to make sense of the very burden discussed at the start of this chapter—our connection to and responsibility for others with whom we share the world. This central concern of public feminism is here figured in the relationship between parent and child. Though the specific parent and children imagined in this poem are ungendered, the emotional labor the poem describes in determining just how much reality to mete out to your offspring is typically gendered as women's work.[59] The poem unfolds in the tension between the private life of the speaker (who provides tiny hints of salacious details like "Life is short, and I've shorted mine / in a thousand delicious, ill-advised ways"), the unknown experience of the "children" (who are not characterized at all in the poem), and the voyeuristic eyes of the reader who is coyly cued to know just what the poem's vague terms—what exact ways are "ill advised"?—refer to.[60] By the end of the poem, that reader encounters the point: using the metaphor of a realtor walking a prospective buyer through a dump of a house with a good underlying structure, the speaker is trying to "sell [the children] the world" (even though that world is "at least half terrible"), especially through its final suggestion/request/imposition: "You could make this place beautiful."[61]

The poem employs flat dialecticism. Each revelation to the reader is balanced by a restriction of the children. Revelations that fall into the "positive" category are offset by "negative" ones and vice versa. Yet the poem splits on its enjambed line that ends with "I am trying," letting its reader imagine for an instant that this is true, that we *are* trying within the confines of our obligations to each other.[62] However, when the sentence continues onto the next line, we learn that such trying is linked to capitalism, to a "selling" of the world. Here, then, is a parable of culture: its rules and systems are broken but still balanced ("For every bird there is a stone thrown at a bird"), its realities both hidden and disclosed (especially through the work of mothering), its systems underwritten by market values, and its final conditional should probably be an imperative.[63] If we are to continue, new generations must make this place beautiful, for it won't fix itself. But why, if we cannot heal these rifts, must we imagine a future generation to do so? The poem figures transmission that may more rightly be understood as infection given the expectations it places on those who come next.

Of particular interest is the poem's focus on the metaphor of the house, a focus we connect to our investigations of the body in chapter 1.[64] While

Smith never uses the word "house" (substituting "shithole" and "place" instead), her final four lines imagine a realtor directing a buyer's gaze to see through a house's problems to its underlying titular "good bones."[65] The house as metaphor for the (shitty) world is not new, but its expression in the era of Trump has proven particularly apt, as evidenced by the award-winning 2019 film *The Last Black Man in San Francisco*. In that film, a young Black man named Jimmie cares for his childhood home in San Francisco—a structure he believes to have been built by his grandfather—despite the fact that his family can no longer afford to own it. Though a white couple resides in the house, Jimmie and his friend Mont sneak around to try to maintain it, fearing the couple has neglected it. When the actual owner of the house (the mother of one of the residents) dies, Jimmie learns that the house may be caught up in a fight between the two inheriting sisters and left empty for years. He and Mont reclaim the house as squatters and restore it with the original furnishings owned by his family when they occupied it. But as Jimmie struggles to hold on to the house that ties him to San Francisco, he eventually learns that his grandfather did not actually build the structure, shaking his own sense of belonging. On a bus one day, Jimmie tells two white women complaining about the city: "You don't get to hate San Francisco. You don't get to hate it unless you love it," expressing what the viewer assumes to be his own orientation toward the city that is metaphorically evicting him.

A symbol of gentrification and the displacement of Black San Franciscans over a period of decades, the house anchors Jimmie's existence in the city, where he recognizes that, of everyone in his family, he is the last who remains.[66] After he learns the truth that his grandfather was not the builder of the house, there is nothing left to anchor him to San Francisco. In a conversation with his aunt that echoes the Smith poem, Jimmie is treated to her powerful words: "I believe you can make this place yours. I really do. But if you leave, it's not your loss. It's San Francisco's. Fuck San Francisco."

Both the poem and the movie ask the next generation to clean up their messes—to take on the work of changing things, to find their place even as more knowledge brings more certainty that such places are highly destabilized, especially for the marginalized who are constructed as a contagion or threat to systems of power that continue to exclude them. But the movie that, unlike the poem, deals with the aftereffects of systemic racism imagines fighting back by articulating the reverse loss (not of people when they lose a place but instead to the place itself when its future departs). In constructing this, the film evokes a world in which transmission does not occur, in which infection stops because its carriers depart instead—but their departure is not figured as a victory. Instead, the exit of the next generation creates loss on all sides.

In the end, infection can burrow itself deep inside culture, down to our ideas, down to what we believe to be reality. The viral rise of public historian Heather Cox Richardson, whose lucid daily newsletters were initiated to combat the era of Trump's lies, reflects a widespread understanding of the danger of such misdirection.[67] Consider, for example, the evolution of Facebook (renamed Meta in late 2021). In a few short years, the company moved from calling the thought that it held culpability for the results of the 2016 election "a crazy idea" to the present day, when such responsibility is presumed.[68] In October of 2021, former Facebook data scientist Frances Haugen filed complaints against the company, alleging that the internal research she turned over to federal law enforcement demonstrated that Facebook "amplifies hate, misinformation and political unrest—but the company hides what it knows."[69] When the idiosyncratic filters of our networks translate news media, when the fastest way to spread inaccuracies is through viral meme culture that necessarily privileges provocative content, information—and thereby reality—splits on the fault line of bias. The line between fact and opinion becomes impossible to hold. The lie has already spread—and, more than ever, tech giants have consolidated the power to perpetuate this infection.[70] Facebook has staked its moderation hopes on artificial intelligence, gambling that moving content moderation to AI systems will solve this problem, yet research demonstrates that AIs can only replicate and amplify the same biases as the humans that program them.[71] Alarmingly, research performed in part by Timnit Gebru while at Google that demonstrated this exact problem may have led to her being forced out of that company. Gebru's experience shows how deeply these problems are entrenched in the tech world.[72]

And such infection, buried down to the level of language, rarely remains abstract, inert, or nonmaterial. Instead, it can lead directly to violence. For example, Meag-gan O'Reilly notes the impact of language and framing on the murder of Black men by police officers, asking, among other things, what happens when we say "murder" in the place of "death." She goes on to discuss the framing of coronavirus-related outcomes in Black communities:

> Language has been wielded for all sorts of oppressive purposes. Chief among them is its ability to frame worldviews, set definitions, and thus influence the treatment of people. . . . In light of COVID-19 death rates in the African-American community and the inequities in access to care, the health determinates are on full display. You hear the following terms: At-Risk, Vulnerable, Disproportionately, More likely to, Historically.[73]

O'Reilly argues that we must replace these terms with words that foreground what a person is over what they have experienced—as well as the role our systems take in shaping that reality. For example, instead of framing the impact of the coronavirus on Black communities as "disproportionate," we instead call it systematic, a calculated result of systems working as they have been designed (in other words, the feature, not the bug).[74] When our language refuses to acknowledge this—when it casts people of color as vulnerable victims instead of powerful actors whose autonomy has been violently oppressed—we spread pernicious ideas even through the words we use.

Yet infection, at least in the logic of "going viral," is sometimes a tool of empowerment. Like an mRNA vaccine that can spread a safe version or picture of a virus to build immunity, the spread of ideas can inoculate against their abuse or, at other times, create "safety in numbers" through a process of assembling a community of witnesses.[75] In chapter 2, we narrated the process by which #MeToo created a map of voices to demonstrate the prevalence of sexual assault and rape; here we trace a similar operation, that of enlisting enough observers to bring attention—and possibly justice—to unjust situations, a process we will examine through the Black Lives Matter movement of the summer of 2020.

The murder of George Floyd on May 29 by police officers initiated one of the most impactful movements in US history.[76] Our intention in raising Floyd's murder is to focus on the tools of public feminism marshaled in response, especially in light of the conditions of the pandemic—which, according to Black Lives Matter founder Opal Tometi, meant that people had time to attend rallies and to connect, on a personal level, with police brutality, as well as with a deepened understanding of the economic reality facing many Black Americans.[77] The combination of having time due to pandemic isolation and information due to viral online sharing is of particular interest to us. Sharing information on this murder and shaping a response to it depended as much on time and access as it did on the tools of social media and the platforms and premises of Black feminism.

A particularly important aspect of the Black Lives Matter movement— its reliance on dialogue—matches imperatives of Black feminist theory. In "The Social Construction of Black Feminist Thought," Patricia Hill Collins explains the primacy of dialogue.[78] Dialogue is underwritten by social connection—by networks. In conversation and discussion, knowledge validation occurs through connectedness via the exchange of ideas. As the outsourcing of knowledge validation to AIs increases, this theory feels particularly critical. In contrast to practices that privilege the individual locus of content production, Black feminist practice requires negotiation of knowledge validation through community, contrasting with a model of institutional policing such as Facebook moderation.[79]

Thus, when confronted with an epidemic of police violence targeting Black people, Black feminists mobilized the Black Lives Matter movement, a system of viral protest bolstered by community-based validation through dialogue. In the aftermath of the murder of Trayvon Martin in 2012 and specifically of George Zimmerman's acquittal of this murder in 2013, Alicia Garza, Patrisse Cullors, and Opal Tometi founded the movement. Tometi describes its founding as one of networking from the very start:

> Alicia writes a Facebook post. I reached out to her. I didn't know Patrisse at the time, but she puts a hashtag on it. I buy the domain name. And we start to use this hashtag as our umbrella language, and we share it with other community organizers in our network.[80]

Thus the story of the founding of a movement is also the story of the founding of a hashtag. From the start, this was a movement designed to go viral.

In the summer of 2020, a record number of protesters took to the streets (during a pandemic and without affecting spread due to careful masking and maintaining distance while in community) to stand up against the brutality that had led to the murder of George Floyd.[81] And yet despite these record numbers, despite the success of these protests, the leadership of the Black Lives Matter movement is essentially decentralized.[82] As Tometi explains: "Different chapters might take on different issues, but there is this throughline of valuing black life and understanding that we are not a monolith but being radically inclusive in terms of chapter makeup."[83] Over and over, individual cities and towns saw new faces—sometimes quite young ones—organizing events like the historic protest in San Francisco led by 17-year-old Simone Jacques and her friends that attracted up to 16,000 fellow protesters. Jacques explained:

> This entire time, people have been asking us, "Are you under an org?" They want to know, "Who is it?" We're just youth who grew up in the city. We're just people who care and love each other and love each other enough to take care of each other.[84]

Taken in total, these people taking care of each other—with their local events added to the events nearby, and in the next state, and in the nation, and in the world—became something much greater than the sum of their parts.

Garza, Cullors, and Tometi did not begin a movement they would seek to preside over. Instead, they began a conversation. From a Facebook post, they created a hashtag.[85] The hashtag became a rallying cry but it also, due to the virality of social media, became a simple tool that eventually provided a strategy that others could use—that anyone could use—to spread the word and to continue the work. In some ways, #BlackLivesMatter is *the* hashtag of the early twenty-first century: the one that showed the world what a hashtag was good for, producing what turned out to be the largest movement in US history, counting as many as 20 million people in its ranks.[86]

DISTRIBUTED LEADERSHIP AND THE COLLECTIVE

Also through the work of Black Lives Matter, we note the model of distributed leadership as one that returns the potential of the collective as theorized in chapter 4. Models that dismantle hierarchies can combat forced circles of intimacy (like that of enslaved wet-nursing), replacing them with intentional ones.[87] Consider, for example, the evolution of the leadership of Hope Mohr Dance Company (the company that created *extreme lyric I*, narrated in chapter 4). In 2021, the company announced a transition to a decentralized leadership system (their website explains that "HMD is currently in an ongoing process of transitioning to an equity-driven model of distributed leadership").[88] This shift suggests that innovation itself is not enough. To really create change, the entire structure that supports your innovation must also be rethought.

Using similar practices to those of Black Lives Matter, Mohr's collective disperses leadership into the hands of its company members in the co-op model. While often in dance, individual performers contribute choreography that evolves into a formal piece, even in a devised choreography model, these contributions are rarely highlighted, and frequently only the named choreographer receives credit.[89] This smaller example parallels a larger problem: in dance, as in all systems inflected by hierarchical power, certain voices receive more amplification or credit than others. One method, therefore, to combat structures of racism, sexism, and other forms of oppression is to redistribute power.

By dispersing power into the collective, Hope Mohr Dance Company fights the problem of hierarchy at its source (in a strategy analogous to long-running conductor-less Orpheus Chamber Music).[90] About this plan and through an arm of the company called "The Bridge Project," the organization writes:

> There is no such thing as a race-neutral arts organization; every arts organization is producing either racial inequity or equity. A commitment to institutional restructuring is an essential step in becoming a fully inclusive, anti-racist, multicultural organization . . . only in this way can we align our internal structures with the values that drive our programs.[91]

This final sentence is telling: it demonstrates that values must be simultaneously expressed through ideas *and* the structures that produce them. We think this model has potential for public feminism more broadly.

The virality of ideas, especially in the age of public feminism, will likely always produce some tension. When lies spread quickly, harm accelerates. At the moment of finalizing this book, for example, we face a doubling down on the individual and its rights before overwhelming evidence that this boundedness is fiction. Anti-maskers push laws preventing regulation, protests ignite against pandemic protection measures, and the COVID-19 virus continues to spread. Yet other forces, especially in the form of scientific truths, push back against misinformation and slowly change minds. When truth is mobilized, historic successes can unfold and perhaps, ultimately, healing can begin as many small, local circles assemble into a larger whole.[92]

Like the parabolic curve this chapter started with, ideas can fly out of the mouth, arc in the sun, and fall flat to the ground. They can lose their energy and put no one at risk. Yet sometimes ideas become their own pandemics, infecting multitudes before their violent toll overwhelms us. And sometimes they become movements, bringing us together and enlarging the circle of people to whom we feel connected enough to share if not our bodily fluids, then at least our voices—and our fists.

NOTES

1. Joni Spigler, "The Radiant Sun Hovered Just above the Rooftop of the House," *Facebook*, March 16, 2020.

2. Rachel Labonte, "Lin-Manuel Miranda Refused CG Removal of Hamilton's King George Lip Spit," *Screen Rant*, July 23, 2020, https://screenrant.com/hamilton-movie-king-george-spit-jonathan-groff-remove.

3. Cristina Arreola (@C_Arreola), "I Love Masks. I Can't Believe I Let Y'all Just Breathe on Me Before," *Twitter*, August 4, 2020, 6:24 p.m., https://twitter.com/c_arreola/status/1290820843233259522.

4. Lawrence Wright, "The Plague Year: The Mistakes and the Struggles behind America's Coronavirus Tragedy," *New Yorker*, December 28, 2020, https://www.newyorker.com/magazine/2021/01/04/the-plague-year.

5. Ann Gerhart and Lucio Villa, "Rose Garden Ceremony Attendees Who Tested Positive for Coronavirus," *Washington Post*, October 3, 2020, https://www.washingtonpost.com/graphics/2020/politics/coronavirus-attendees-barrett-nomination-ceremony.

6. For more on coronavirus spread in Congress, see Claudia Grisales and Audrey Carlson, "Congress and COVID-19: Members' Cases and Quarantines," *NPR*, February 8, 2021, https://www.npr.org/2020/04/15/833692377/how-the-coronavirus-has-affected-individual-members-of-congress. The pandemic phenomenon of spitting or coughing as a form of assault, which in some cases resulted in charges, emerged around this time as well. See Tiffini Theisen, "People Who Claim to Have Coronavirus and Spit, Cough on Victims Face Variety of Charges," *Orlando Sentinel*, April 9, 2020, https://www.orlandosentinel.com/coronavirus/os-ne-coronavirus-people-charged-with-spitting-coughing-in-faces-20200409-ps5dgw64pfeobhthwvr6mhbuuy-story.html.

7. Ed Yong, "Where Year Two of the Pandemic Will Take Us," *The Atlantic*, December 29, 2020, https://www.theatlantic.com/health/archive/2020/12/pandemic-year-two/617528.

8. Anand Pandian (@anandspandian), "There's a Precise Parallel Between the Conservative Clamor over Free Speech, and the Deep Opposition to Pandemic Masks. Both Positions Insist That You Shouldn't Have to Worry About What Your Mouth Expresses: Whether the Danger to Others from a Violent Word, or a Viral Particle," *Twitter*, January 1, 2021, 9:21 a.m., https://twitter.com/anandspandian/status/1348683516876386306.

9. For reviews of the film, see Chris Hewitt, "Jittery Comedy *Promising Young Woman* Has Serious Issues on Its Mind," *Star Tribune*, January 14, 2021, https://www.startribune.com/jittery-comedy-promising-young-woman-has-serious-issues-on-its-mind/600010537; Carmen Maria Machado, "How *Promising Young Woman* Refigures the Rape-Revenge Movie," *New Yorker*, January 29, 2021, https://www.newyorker.com/culture/cultural-comment/how-promising-young-woman-refigures-the-rape-revenge-movie; Philippa Snow, "In *Promising Young Woman* Revenge Is a Dish Served Lukewarm," *Frieze*, January 19, 2121, https://www.frieze.com/article/promising-young-woman-revenge-dish-served-lukewarm; and Dennis Harvey, Review of *Promising Young Woman* (film), *Variety*, January 26, 2020, https://variety.com/2020/film/reviews/promising-young-woman-review-1203480660. (This last is the infamous review for which *Variety* later apologized after Harvey suggested Margot Robbie might be better for the role than Carrie Mulligan—a move Snow argues signifies simply that Harvey thought Mulligan wasn't hot enough.)

10. In an essay in *Mother Jones*, Maddie Oatman argues that rape-revenge narratives, of which *Promising Young Woman* is one, can never transcend the trap that "vengeance replicates the same power structure the avenger wishes to hold accountable" in part because most of these narratives reproduce the phallic cycle of plot conventions themselves (growing tension, climax, release)." Maddie Oatman, "Hollywood Loves Rape-Revenge Plots. But What Story Are They Really Telling?" *Mother Jones*, July 22, 2021, https://www.motherjones.com/media/2021/07/hollywood-loves-rape-revenge-plots-but-what-story-are-they-really-telling.

11. Emerald Fennell, dir., *Promising Young Woman*, 2020 (Universal City, CA: Universal Pictures Home Entertainment).

12. For more on rape-revenge narratives, see Alexandra Heller-Nicholas, *Rape-Revenge Films: A Critical Study* (Jefferson, NC: McFarland, 2011), and Jacinda Read, *The New Avengers: Feminism, Femininity, and the Rape-Revenge Cycle* (Manchester: Manchester University Press, 2000).

13. As Mary Douglas theorizes, "Spittle, Blood, Milk, Urine, Faeces or Tears by Simply Issuing Forth Have Traversed the Boundary of the Body." Mary Douglas, *Purity and Danger* (1966), as quoted in Lynda Nead, "Framing the Female Body" (1992), in *Feminism—Art—Theory: An Anthology, 1968–2014*, 2nd ed., ed. Hilary Robinson (London: Wiley-Blackwell, 2015), 323. Nead finds in Douglas an articulation of the way in which purification is used to control perceived threats from the body.

14. Sarah Nooter, "The Materialities of Greek Tragedy: Objects and Affect in Aeschylus, Sophocles, and Euripides," *Bryn Mawr Classical Review*, 2019.11.03, https://bmcr.brynmawr.edu/2019/2019.11.03.

15. Jane Bennett, *Vibrant Matter: A Political Ecology of Things* (Durham, NC: Duke University Press, 2010), xiii.

16. Bennett, *Vibrant Matter*, 17–19.

17. Karl Marx, "The Difference between the Democritean and Epicurean Philosophy of Nature, 1841, with an Appendix," cited in Bennett, *Vibrant Matter*, 129n51, and Paul Schafer, ed., *The First Writings of Karx Marx* (Brooklyn, NY: Ig Publishing, 2006).

18. Bennett, *Vibrant Matter*, 17.

19. Bennett, *Vibrant Matter*, 17–22.

20. Bennett, *Vibrant Matter*, viii.

21. Bennett, *Vibrant Matter*, x.

22. Bennett responds at length to the critique of vital materialists dismantling the subject-object divide, arguing that at times this divide is essential to prevent suffering, at other times it enables choices that lead directly to human suffering (e.g., the climate crisis), and finally that the hierarchy inherent within it has often shored up hierarchies within humans. Bennett, *Vibrant Matter*, 12.

23. Thoreau was drawn to Walden by the model of formerly enslaved Black families, including the family of Brister Freeman, who lived there before Thoreau and may have influenced Thoreau's utopian thinking. (Courtney Lindwall, "Black Walden Came First, Thoreau After," *Natural Resources Defense Council*, February 01, 2021, https://www.nrdc.org/stories/black-walden-came-first-thoreau-after.) Bennett also aligns her vital matter with work by a range of ecofeminist writers. Bennett, *Vibrant Matter*, xiv.

24. Daniel Miller, *Materiality* (Durham, NC: Duke University Press, 2005), 1–15.

25. Miller, *Materiality*, 5.

26. Miller, *Materiality*, 5. See also Verity Platt and Michael Squire, *The Frame in Classical Art: A Cultural History* (Cambridge: Cambridge University Press, 2017).

27. Nead cites Derrida's theorization of the frame, a discourse active in Gombrich's account and drawn on by Miller. Nead, "Framing the Female Body," 324.

28. Bill Brown, "Thing Theory," *Critical Inquiry* 28, no. 1 (2001): 1–22.

29. Severin Fowles, "The Perfect Subject (Postcolonial Object Studies)," *Journal of Material Culture* 21, no. 1 (2016): 12.

30. Bennett, *Vibrant Matter*, 104–7.

31. For example, the earliest history of the AIDS epidemic demonstrates the way in which public perception of a threat shapes medical investment in a solution. At the same time, the two crises unfolded quite differently. Sarah Schulman describes the contrast between the public attention paid to the very beginnings of the AIDS/HIV epidemic and of the COVID-19 pandemic: "What's interesting, when you compare AIDS with COVID, you know, COVID is a collective public experience that we're all having on television. People are talking about it in their families. AIDS, on the other hand, was like our private nightmare. Our battle was to get it into the public and that was the biggest fight." See "ACT UP: A History of AIDS/HIV Activism," interview on "It's Been a Minute with Sam Sanders," *NPR*, June 18, 2021, https://www.npr.org/2021/06/16/1007361916/act-up-a-history-of-aids-hiv-activism.

32. For the narrative of structural biologist Sai Li's early look at the shape and form of the virus, see Carl Zimmer, "The Coronavirus Unveiled," *New York Times*,

October 9, 2020, https://www.nytimes.com/interactive/2020/health/coronavirus
-unveiled.html.

33. For early theorizations of the female body as leaky, see, among many others, Margrit Shildrick, *Leaky Bodies and Boundaries: Feminism, Postmodernism, and (Bio)ethics* (London: Routledge, 1997), and Elizabeth Grosz, *Volatile Bodies: Toward a Corporeal Feminism* (Bloomington: Indiana University Press, 1994), the latter of which inscribes the notion of "seepage" as fundamental to patriarchal constructions of women's corporeality.

34. See, for example, Dominica A. Gidrewicz and Tanis R Fenton, "A Systematic Review and Meta-Analysis of the Nutrient Content of Preterm and Term Breast Milk," *BMC Pediatrics* 14, no. 1 (2014): 1–14.

35. The name for the band of stars still known today as the Milky Way (from the ancient Greek *galaxias kyklos* or "milky circle") comes to us from ancient Greek philosophical texts. Aristotle (*Meteorology* 345a12-346b8) summarizes the views of pre-Socratic philosophers (the Pythagoreans, Anaxagoras, and Democritus again) and his own explanation. While none of these are tied to the Herakles myth, they all imply a relationship between breast milk and the Milky Way that is largely obscured today, and they all demonstrate the centrality and importance of breastfeeding despite attendant anxieties around its materiality. The first known textual reference appears in the work of Hellenistic tragedian Lycophron of Chalcis. On breastfeeding, see C. W. Marshall, "Breastfeeding in Greek Literature and Thought," *Illinois Classical Studies* 42, no. 1 (2017): 185–201.

36. Variations on the myth shift not only Hera's consent but also Herakles' age, ranging from infant to adult.

37. A. J. Rutgers, "Hera and Herakles," *Numen* 17, no. 3 (1970): 245–6.

38. On the rarity, see Julie Laskaris, "Nursing Mothers in Greek and Roman Medicine," *American Journal of Archaeology* 112, no. 3 (2008): 461. See also Larissa Bonfante, "Nursing Mothers in Classical Art," in *Naked Truths: Women, Sexuality, and Gender in Classical Art and Archaeology*, ed. A. Koloski-Ostrow and C. Lyons (London: Routledge, 2000), 174–7.

39. British Museum 1846,0925.13; National Archaeological Museum of Florence, found in Volterra (Etruscan). See also Tom Rasmussen, "Herakles' Apotheosis in Etruria and Greece," *Antike Kunst* 48 (2005): 30–9.

40. The subjects of the painting are not announced by identifying inscriptions on the vase, so the identification of this woman with Hera and this baby with Herakles also came about only through the connoisseur's ascription.

41. On connoisseurship and the creation of artistic personae, see Jeremy Melius, "Connoisseurship, Painting, and Personhood," *Art History* 34, no. 2 (April 2011): 288–309, and Richard Neer, "Connoisseurship and the Stakes of Style," *Critical Inquiry* 32, no. 1 (2005): 1–26.

42. Later, painters in early modern Europe embraced this origin story of the stars of the Milky Way. For example, the Venetian Jacopo Tintoretto painted *The Origin of the Milky Way* (1575) such that the spray of breast milk shoots up toward the galaxy and each individual stream of milk terminates in a bright yellow star. Peter Paul Rubens also painted *The Birth of the Milky Way* (1636–1638). Fascinatingly,

Rubens inserted the face of his own wife, Hélène Fourmant, as Hera, as though to claim that a living woman was producing the very stars. Svetland Alpers notes that for this painting, Rubens and others drew on a story referred to obliquely but not retold in Ovid. L. Burchard and Nationaal Centrum voor de Plastische Kunsten van de XVIde en XVII de Eeuw, eds. *Corpus Rubenianum Ludwig Burchard: An Illustrated Catalogue Raisonné of the Work of Peter Paul Rubens Based on the Material Assembled by the Late Dr. Ludwig Burchard in Twenty-Six Parts* (London; New York: Phaidon, 1968), 98l.

43. Homer, *The Odyssey*, trans. Wilson, 440.

44. Patrizia Birchler Emery, "De la nourrice à la dame de compagnie: le cas de la *trophos* en Grèce antique," *Paedagogica Historica* 46, no. 6 (2010): 751–61.

45. Maria Helena Pereira Toledo Machado, "Between Two Beneditos: Enslaved Wet-Nurses amid Slavery's Decline in Southeast Brazil," *Slavery and Abolition* 38, no. 2 (2017): 320.

46. Cassia Roth, "Black Nurse, White Milk: Breastfeeding, Slavery, and Abolition in 19th-Century Brazil," *Journal of Human Lactation* 34, no. 4 (2018): 804–9, and Cassia Roth, *A Miscarriage of Justice: Women's Reproductive Lives and the Law in Early Twentieth-Century Brazil* (Stanford, CA: Stanford University Press, 2020).

47. Cassia Roth, "Disembodied Reproduction: Enslaved Wet Nurses, Stratified Reproduction, and Commercial Advertisements in Nineteenth-Century Rio de Janeiro," presentation at *Critical Conversations on Reproductive Health/Care: Past, Present, and Future*, Johns Hopkins University, February 3, 2021, https://hopkinshist oryofmedicine.org/events/reproconvo2021.

48. Roth, "Black Nurse, White Milk," 805.

49. Emily Wilson's translation, discussed in chapter 3, draws attention to the particular violence of this structural paradigm through her attention to the granular class positions of women in the *Odyssey*. Homer, *The Odyssey*, trans. Wilson.

50. Homer, *The Odyssey*, trans. Wilson, 86–9.

51. Examples of blood painting include depictions of the sacrifice of Polyxena (e.g., British Museum 1897.0727.2), the painted relief sculpture of a dying warrior on the pediment from the Temple of Athena Aphaia on Aegina, and the copper inlay down the face of the Terme Boxer. See Brinkmann, Dreyfus, and Koch-Brinkmann, *Gods in Color*.

52. Nora Krug, "Maggie Smith and the Poem That Captured the Mood of a Tumultuous Year," *Washington Post*, December 23, 2016, https://www.washingtonpost .com/entertainment/books/maggie-smith-and-the-poem-that-captured-the-mood-of-a -tumultuous-year/2016/12/22/a652b43c-c3a6-11e6-9578-0054287507db_story.html.

53. Lidia Jean Kott, "This Is the Official Poem of 2016," *The World*, December 31, 2016, https://www.pri.org/stories/2016-12-31/official-poem-2016.

54. In fact, Jacquelyn Ardam includes "Good Bones" in her category of poems specifically written to soothe their readers. Jacquelyn Ardam, *Avidly Reads Poetry* (New York: NYU Press, 2021), 95.

55. Ardam's category of "internet poetry" refers to "poems of all sorts that have circulated widely on the internet. They may be created especially for a social media

outlet (like the poems of Rupi Kaur and Instagram), or they may be poems first published in print journals, magazines, chapbooks, or books . . . that have had second or third lives on Instagram or Pinterest, in email inboxes or on Twitter. It is a term that has to do with circulation, not with form." She goes on to say that "the internet, and social media particularly, is where so much of poetry happens these days." Ardam, *Avidly Reads Poetry*, 94.

56. See Faith Hill and Karen Yuan, "How Instagram Saved Poetry," *The Atlantic*, October 15, 2018, https://www.theatlantic.com/technology/archive/2018/10/rupi -kaur-instagram-poet-entrepreneur/572746.

57. See Celine Castronuovo, "Amanda Gorman Captures National Interest after Inauguration Performance," *The Hill*, January 21, 2021, https://thehill.com/homenews /news/535325-amanda-gorman-captures-national-interest-after-inauguration -performance: "According to analysis by Axios based on social media data provided by NewsWhip, Gorman had [a high number of] interactions on social media, receiving more than 4,000 likes, comments or shares per article shared across platforms." See also Marina Watts, "Poet Amanda Gorman Gains 300K Twitter Followers after Inauguration Recitation," *Newsweek*, January 20, 2021, https://www.newsweek.com /poet-amanda-gorman-gains-300k-twitter-followers-after-inauguration-recitation -1563135.

58. Ardam, *Avidly Reads Poetry*, 95.

59. As Talia Schaffer writes, "Modern care ethicists are not interested in essentialist identification of their subjects, but rather on the work of caregiving—a form of labor that has for centuries been intimately associated with women." Schaffer, "Victorian Feminist Criticism," 81.

60. Maggie Smith, *Good Bones* (Massachusetts: Tupelo Press, 2014), 75. Credit: Maggie Smith, excerpts from "Good Bones" from Good Bones: Poems. Copyright © 2017 by Maggie Smith. Reprinted with the permission of The Permissions Company, LLC, on behalf of Tupelo Press, tupelopress.org. As Ardam points out, Smith may have overassumed her readers' familiarity; Ardam theorizes on Twitter that the poem is "is for Gen X + Boomers only." Jacquelyn Ardam (@jaxwendy), "It turns out that yes, I *will* be entering into some light generational culture wars in my book, and I have decided to define myself (born in 1982) as an elder millennial. This is in reference to Maggie Smith's 'Good Bones,' which I have decided is for Gen X + Boomers only," *Twitter*, June 12, 2021, 5:27 p.m., https://twitter.com/jaxwendy/ status/1403871510247268353.

61. Smith, *Good Bones*, 75. Ardam traces resistance to this imposition on the next generation, a resistance she herself shares, in her chapter "Internet Poems: To Soothe," in *Avidly Reads Poetry*, 87–113.

62. Smith, *Good Bones*, 75.

63. Smith, *Good Bones*, 75.

64. The connection between women's bodies and houses has been variously explored in art and literature. For example, the curators of *Women House* juxtapose mid-twentieth-century paintings by Louise Bourgeois with more contemporary feminist artists to demonstrate "the formal association between the female body and the architecture of the house . . . [and] show the extent to which women were

still being absorbed or devoured by the home, which it was their role to nourish and support." Camille Morineau and Lucia Pesapane, eds., *Women House* (Washington, DC: National Museum of Women in the Arts, 2018), 180.

65. Smith's use of "shithole" reads differently after her poem's publication in the context of Trump's infamous comments about "shithole countries" in 2018. See Ali Vitali, Kasie Hunt, and Frank Thorp, "Trump Referred to Haiti and African Nations as 'Shithole' Countries," *NBC News*, January 11, 2018, https://www.nbcnews.com/politics/white-house/trump-referred-haiti-african-countries-shithole-nations-n836946.

66. For more on this displacement and its corresponding creative resistance, see the work of Rachel Brahinsky, including "Tell Him I'm Gone: On the Margins in High-Tech City," in *A Political Companion to James Baldwin*, ed. Susan McWilliams (Lexington: University Press of Kentucky, 2017), and "The Story of Property: Meditations on Gentrification, Renaming, and Possibility," *EPA: Economy and Space* 52, no. 5 (January 5, 2020), https://doi.org/10.1177/0308518X19895787.

67. Edward Luce, "Historian Heather Cox Richardson: 'Now People See What's Happening. Thank God!'" *Financial Times*, July 16, 2021, https://www.ft.com/content/08f3728c-bbff-493f-aa66-a1aa35dd3924.

68. For Facebook's refusal to take responsibility in the 2016 election, see Aarti Shahani, "Zuckerberg Denies Fake News on Facebook Had Impact on the Election," *NPR*, November 11, 2016, https://www.npr.org/sections/alltechconsidered/2016/11/11/501743684/zuckerberg-denies-fake-news-on-facebook-had-impact-on-the-election.

69. Scott Pelley, "Whistleblower: Facebook Is Misleading the Public on Progress against Hate Speech, Violence, Misinformation." *CBS News*, October 4, 2021, https://www.cbsnews.com/news/facebook-whistleblower-frances-haugen-misinformation-public-60-minutes-2021-10-03.

70. For Facebook's struggles with curating news and distinguishing between biased and unbiased content, see Nicholas Thompson and Fred Vogelstein, "15 Months of Fresh Hell Inside Facebook," *Wired*, April 16, 2019, https://www.wired.com/story/facebook-mark-zuckerberg-15-months-of-fresh-hell.

71. Nicholas and Vogelstein, "15 Months of Fresh Hell," and Karen Hao, "We Read the Paper That Forced Timnit Gebru Out of Google. Here's What It Says," *MIT Technology Review*, December 4, 2020, https://www.technologyreview.com/2020/12/04/1013294/google-ai-ethics-research-paper-forced-out-timnit-gebru.

72. On the other hand, Gebru was able to reach others using the tools of public feminism, including social media. For the story of Gebru being forced out, see Hao, "We Read the Paper."

73. Meag-gan O'Reilly, "Systems Centered Language: Speaking Truth to Power during COVID-19 while Confronting Racism," *Medium*, June 5, 2020, https://medium.com/@meagoreillyphd/systems-centered-language-a3dc7951570e.

74. O'Reilly, "Systems Centered Language." On racism as a product of white supremacy working as it is designed, see David G. Embrick and Wendy Leo Moore, "White Space(s) and the Reproduction of White Supremacy," *American Behavioral Scientist (Beverly Hills)* 64, no. 14 (2020): 1935–45; https://doi.org/10.1177/0002764220975053.

75. For theories of witnessing we have leaned on in this chapter, see Felman and Laub, *Testimony*.

76. For the narrative of Floyd's murder, see Evan Hill, et al., "How George Floyd Was Killed in Police Custody," *New York Times*, updated April 20, 2021, https://www.nytimes.com/2020/05/31/us/george-floyd-investigation.html.

77. Isaac Chotiner, "A Black Lives Matter Co-Founder Explains Why This Time Is Different," *New Yorker*, June 3, 2020, https://www.newyorker.com/news/q-and-a/a-black-lives-matter-co-founder-explains-why-this-time-is-different.

78. Patricia Hill Collins, "The Social Construction of Black Feminist Thought," *Signs* 14, no. 4 (1989): 745–73.

79. Collins, "The Social Construction," 763.

80. Chotiner, "A Black Lives Matter Co-Founder." See also Christopher J. Lebron, *The Making of Black Lives Matter: A Brief History of an Idea* (Oxford: Oxford University Press, 2017).

81. Matt Berger, "Why the Black Lives Matter Protests Didn't Contribute to the COVID-19 Surge," *Healthline*, July 8, 2020, https://www.healthline.com/health-news/black-lives-matter-protests-didnt-contribute-to-covid19-surge.

82. See Chotiner, "A Black Lives Matter Co-Founder," in which Tometi explains that the movement "has always been somewhat decentralized."

83. Chotiner, "A Black Lives Matter Co-Founder."

84. Amy Graff, "17-year-old Mission District Teen Leads Protest of Thousands in San Francisco," *SF Gate*, June 3, 2020, https://www.sfgate.com/news/slideshow/Simone-Jacques-Mission-District-protest-203235.php.

85. Jordan Zakarinjan, "How Patrisse Cullors, Alicia Garza, and Opal Tometi Created the Black Lives Matter Movement," *Biography*, January 27, 2021, https://www.biography.com/news/patrisse-cullors-alicia-garza-opal-tometi-black-lives-matters-origins.

86. Larry Buchanan, Quoctrung Bui, and Jugal K. Patel, "Black Lives Matter May Be the Largest Movement in U.S. History," *New York Times*, July 3, 2020, https://www.nytimes.com/interactive/2020/07/03/us/george-floyd-protests-crowd-size.html.

87. Similarly, Talia Schaffer has speculated that digital humanities tools can disrupt some hierarchies inside canonical formations: "Not only are texts far more available but their hierarchies get disrupted, for when a database calls up *Jane Eyre* and a temperance tract with equal facility and in identical formats, that powerfully suggests equivalent interest. Digitization makes all texts into data, and for a casual reader skimming information on a screen, no data looks more canonical than any other." Schaffer, "Feminism and the Canon," 280. Writing elsewhere, Schaffer imagines that "in the digital era, we occupy an alternative chronology, in which we envision ourselves not as strenuously excavating the last disintegrating relics of the past, but rather as choosing among multiple simultaneous virtual texts, severed from markers of time or space." Schaffer, "Victorian Feminist Criticism," 63.

88. "Company," *Hope Mohr Dance*, May 01, 2021, https://www.hopemohr.org/company.

89. For the dancer's perspective on the labor conditions of individual dancers, see Emily Hansel, "Relearning Agency: A Dancer's Call for Collective Action," *Life*

Chapter 5

As a Modern Dancer, January 1, 2021, https://blog.lifeasamoderndancer.com/2021 /01/relearning-agency-a-dancers-call-for-collective-action.html, and Emily Hansel, "Cultivating Healthy, Equitable Workplaces for Dancers," *Life As a Modern Dancer*, April 4, 2021, https://blog.lifeasamoderndancer.com/2021/04/cultivating -healthy-equitable-workplaces-for-dancers.html. For issues in devised choreography, see Jenny Roche, "Dancing Strategies and Moving Identities: The Contributions Independent Contemporary Dancers Make to the Choreographic Process," in *Contemporary Choreography: A Critical Reader*, 2nd ed., ed. Jo Butterworth and Liesbeth Wildschut (Milton Park: Routledge, 2018), 150–64.

90. "About Us," *Orpheus*, April 13, 2021, https://orpheusnyc.org/about/about-us. Other similar organizations, including Intersection for the Arts, have announced that they are moving toward this model.

91. "Commitment to Distributed Leadership," *Bridge Project*, April 13, 2021, https://www.bridgeproject.art/distributed-leadership.

92. As one small example of this, see "Arkansas Governor OKs Ban on Local, State Mask Mandates," *Associated Press News*, April 29, 2021, https://apnews.com /article/arkansas-coronavirus-government-and-politics-health-95afbfae283a1105b7a b96d9c14eb9ff, and Josie Fischels, "Arkansas Governor Wants to Reverse a Law That Forbids Schools to Require Masks," *NPR*, August 4, 20218, https://www.npr.org /2021/08/04/1024939859/arkansas-governor-reverse-law-let-schools-require-masks.

Figure 6.1   One of the Authors and Her Daughter Reflected on the Surface of a Section of Maya Ying Lin's *Vietnam Veterans Memorial*, Washington, DC. February 2nd, 2021. Black granite. Photo: author.

Chapter 6

Scaling Loss, Listing Names

Perhaps fittingly, our final chapter focuses on mourning. Thus far we have surveyed the ways women do and do not control their archives in chapter 1; the mapping of the personal/biographical onto the production of women in ways both oppressive and liberating in chapter 2; the practice of resurfacing feminist qualities from patriarchal texts through translation in chapter 3; the model of a feminist collective and the practice of feminist citation in chapter 4; and the positive and negative interconnection and contagiousness of bodies and ideas in chapter 5. Now, at the end of this journey, we look at loss and how it is understood and memorialized. Specifically, this chapter examines the power of lists. While listing has been an implicit feature of previous chapters—we might view the archive as a collection of lists and can certainly theorize the list-like qualities of hashtags—we argue that listing individual names as a form of protest and memorialization became a special focus of public feminism during the Trump and pandemic years.

A chain-link fence circles the reservoirs in Silver Lake, a neighborhood in East Los Angeles. On June 6, 2020, Angelenos gathered by the reservoir to produce "Say Their Names: Silver Lake Memorial."[1] They ripped long strips of fabric in a variety of colors and wove them through fence links to spell out 259 names of Black people killed by police: Michelle Casseaux, Philando Castille, John Crawford, Amadou Diallo, David Dowdy, George Floyd, Terrance Franklin, Charles Goodridge, Darren Hunt, Tony McDade, Nina Pop, Walter Scott, and the list continues. To produce it, the organizers consulted two databases: "The Counted" and "Mapping Police Violence."[2] The memorial also drew on the #SayHerName campaign launched in December 2014 by Kimberlé Crenshaw, the African American Policy Forum, and the Center for Intersectionality and Social Policy Studies to bring attention to Black women and girls murdered by police.[3] By merging art with text and listing and reciting names as a form of protest, the installation attempted to bring visibility to the individuals themselves instead of the state-sponsored violence of their deaths.[4]

Memorializing loss by drawing attention to individual people rather than aggregating them into emblematic representation, a tradition we explore later in this chapter, is an impactful practice in the arsenal of public feminism—especially when the emphasis is on the general public in contrast to the few, the famous, or the powerful. The mode of public feminism enacted in Crenshaw's campaign, the Silver Lake memorial, #SayHerName, the Vietnam Veterans Memorial (discussed later in this chapter), and countless others around the globe works by giving visibility to an individual name, often as part of a list. This practice takes many forms: names painted on protest placards, letters affirming solidarity with mourners posted on the internet, and fabric strands woven through fence links, among others. Feminist lists seek to perform a fundamental recovery not only of names in the now but also of the very status of lists in the archive.[5] Their ensuing monuments ask an audience to think about how many individual people make up any possible group and to affirm that each represented individual matters deeply.

And yet lists also group individuals into a collective, raising questions about how to focus on one name when so many are necessarily included. We therefore believe that the individual and the group are simultaneously engaged by listing practices. While list-based monuments entail a return to the individual, they also situate individuals within a collective, and often decentralized, framework. Thus, while in chapter 5 (and our earlier chapters) we focused on collectivity and decentralized leadership, in this chapter we return to the individual within the collective at the level of the name—each name spoken and remembered in the context of some collective—and often violent—experience or loss, the parameters and definitions of which are always under scrutiny. In this way, the list itself may be seen as particularly feminist in the way that it promotes nonhierarchical representation, especially in resistance to patriarchal modes embodied in figural monuments as investigated later in this chapter.

Additionally, public feminist naming practices seek to amplify the lost in their individuality instead of focusing on the forces or people who harmed them. As previously mentioned, the social media campaigns #SayHerName and the related #SayTheirNames use this strategy to protest Black lives lost to police violence. Although efforts to deplatform perpetrators have been a focus of public action, public and media attention may still highlight the perpetrators of such violence through news reports and online dialogue, erasing the lives and individuality of the victims.[6] #SayTheirNames, like campaigns responding to mass shooter violence, rejects this erasure by returning focus to the individuals who have been unjustly killed, seeking to include many, even when the list is tragically long, as in the example of the installation at Silver Lake.

This feminist tradition of naming has a surprisingly deep, though often deemphasized, history. In this chapter, our intention is to capture that history, resurfacing it (as the translators in chapter 3 resurfaced voices from patriarchal texts) and tracing its ongoing place in the public conversation about loss and memorializing. Through this practice, as we have argued in our previous chapters, we give public feminism a history, planting its roots through the centuries and through its many forebearers.

FIGURAL MONUMENTS

We start with the more widely understood narrative: a certain vision—a story perhaps—of monumental history that charts power from Greek and Roman antiquity to today. In this narrative, patterns of figural representation predominate, especially when it comes to monumentalizing the powerful and the dead. Figural monuments designed to memorialize a single person were often erected after that individual's death, functioning less to mourn the deceased and more to celebrate the political world he had embodied—a practice that encodes and perpetuates systems of patriarchal and civic power.[7] Although each specific local context reveals cultural and political differences, similar patriarchal figural monumentalizing practices have been maintained across centuries and cultures.

Twenty-first-century work in the field of classics has explored the resonance between nineteenth-century Confederate monuments and the robust ruler-portrait tradition from ancient Rome.[8] This work tracks a lineage from, for instance, the portrait statue of Emperor Augustus of Prima Porta or the gilded horse-drawn chariot of Emperor Marcus Aurelius still visible in Rome to Confederate and other figural monuments in the United States and the United Kingdom. As Sonja Drimmer argues: "Two millennia of European and American history could be told through a genealogy of equestrian monuments to men, from Marcus Aurelius to Gattamelata, from Confederate generals to Kehinde Wiley's exhilarating riposte, 'Rumors of War' (2019)."[9] Connecting such a history from the ancient Roman empire to modern Anglophone empires situates the self-fashioning of British and US imperialist and neoimperialist governments into a model that they understood as neoclassical.[10] In fact, this retrospection had a broader geotemporal footprint, as the ancient Egyptian obelisks populating many European and American cities make visible and which the Egyptianizing example of the Washington Monument (1848–1884 CE) in DC sought to emulate.[11] Designed to maintain systems of power and silence, these modes of neoclassical self-fashioning demand the contemporary work of critique and ultimately fallism: the practice of tearing down monuments to white supremacy.[12]

Such work is resonant for public feminists and other activists who seek to oppose corrupt systems of power. As Verity Platt has argued in her article on fallism, acts of removal "are not simply acts of destruction: they should rather be understood as moments of what the philosopher Bruno Latour has called 'Iconoclash,' generating new images that can be powerful agents of social change."[13] These new images might be created by the fallen statue itself, the empty plinth its removal leaves behind, or even the photographs and videos that capture the process of demolition. Further, not all removal happens in the context of immediate activism; some occurs after months or years of protest in the sedate form of state-sponsored actions that respond to protest from a later moment.

As an extension of these explorations and actions, we offer a parallel history with an equally deep precedent by tracking a nonfigural monument tradition from ancient Athens to contemporary times. While not the dominant narrative, its lineage has been part of monumental practice for centuries. Through naming, language, and the poetic power of the list, this practice engages a more diverse set of voices and offers a more living and flexible system of monumentalizing that aligns with the concerns and goals of public feminism more broadly.[14]

COUNTER MONUMENTS

An ongoing challenge that producing monuments presents is how to represent the loss of many. Consider, as examples of catastrophe that join those of Silver Lake, the losses of the Holocaust, the Vietnam War, and September 11, 2001. While the scale and circumstances of these atrocities are distinct, their casualties represent numbers larger than the human mind can easily grasp and thereby present unique challenges to memorialization. Efforts to capture large-scale traumas may prioritize absence over presence by highlighting blank or negative spaces like empty plinths or the darkness surrounding a beam of light in contrast to the filled-in or occupied spaces of figural representation. James Young has theorized this practice as counter monumentality, using as an example Sol Lewitt's *Black Form—Dedicated to the Missing Jews* (1987), an empty plinth built from black concrete blocks rather than traditional white marble or monochrome bronze to represent the blank space left by the 6 million Jews murdered in the Holocaust.[15] Lynn Meskell has named a related practice—that of negative heritage, "which operates between the dual poles of transformation and erasure, depending on the context."[16] In an essay that navigates multiple politics of removal, including some that employ the arguments marshaled by fallism, Meskell describes Ground Zero, the site of the September 11, 2001, terrorist attacks that resulted in the collapse of the World Trade Center towers, and decries the recasting of the site, which remains a burial ground, as a museum that collects and displays associated artifacts.[17] Although Meskell does not address it in her essay, an alternative to the practice of displaying objects is the collectively produced *Tribute in Light* (2002–present), which now marks the site, projecting beams of light skyward where the twin towers once rose. These light beams memorialize lost lives and structures without permanently replacing them or commodifying their ruins.

A more traditional artistic response to the challenge of memorializing loss has been to create emblematic representations in accordance with the figural tradition—to take all of the dead and compress them into a few figures that stand in for the totality of loss, as in Rowan Gillespie's *Famine* (1997) in Dublin and George Segal's *Gay Liberation* (1980–1992) in New York City. These examples are distinct from the equestrian monument tradition that elevates specific individuals, but equestrian monuments (of which Confederate monuments are an example) may also stand in for larger military and political losses and thus implicitly represent a larger group. Kehinde Wiley's *Rumors of War* (2019) both emerges from and responds to this equestrian practice.[18] Wiley's bronze sculpture, commissioned by the Virginia Museum of Fine Arts, presents an unnamed young Black man with short dreadlocks seated astride a horse and clad in a hoodie, ripped jeans, and high tops. The museum label tells visitors that Wiley's "bronze sculpture commemorates African American youth lost to the social and political battles being waged throughout our nation."[19] Prior to this sculpture, Wiley was most famous for his Neo-baroque paintings centering Black subjects and especially for his 2018 painting of US President Barack Obama.

Mobilizing a related politics to his painterly practice but here in bronze, marble, and glass, Wiley's monument appropriates the pose and material of the equestrian portrait of Confederate general J. E. B. Stuart in response to the Confederate monuments lining Monument Avenue in Richmond, Virginia. Such a strategy echoes (or reacts to or against) the monument tradition of elevating a single public figure in marble or bronze (what Drimmer names Wiley's riposte) but translates it into the realm of everyday life and the rhetoric of protest as a figural monument that protests its own genre. On the one hand, Wiley's statue claims the associated power undergirding the equestrian figural tradition for contemporary Black men. At the same time, the impact of Wiley's statue also creates a site-specific counter monument. When unveiled in 2019, the Confederate monuments to which it responded still stood. Now, empty plinths mark the spots where Confederate statues were removed in the summer of 2020.[20] Wiley's intervention accelerated the change that led to the removal of Confederate statues as well as increased global awareness of this sculptural legacy. Although initially produced as a critique of these monuments, *Rumors of War* now stands alone, a victory won through protest and a structural change to the city that in turn changes the meaning of the statue itself. Wiley's decision to leave his figure unnamed in deliberate contrast with the named Confederates marking the avenue allows the figure to do emblematic work; however, despite this anonymity, the openness of the unnamed figure raises questions about who is being represented and who may be excluded, especially given the clear gendering of Wiley's subject.

As these examples show, artists face difficult choices when they attempt to monumentalize a large number of people. They may select emblematic figural representation as Wiley does, or they may attempt to represent individuals as in #SayTheirNames. As soon as figuration is employed, however, many are immediately excluded—and, so often, that means women and others outside of systems of patriarchal power.[21] In contrast, naming or list monuments resist traditional figuration, yet each name marks and invokes a life. While list-based monuments may be similarly civic and patriarchal (and, indeed, some of our ensuing examples like the *Iliad*, Athenian casualty lists, and the Vietnam Veterans Memorial primarily feature men), they nevertheless offer a more flexible form whose construction and interpretation may be driven by the possibilities of protest and mobilized by public feminists.

Such monuments represent the relationship between individuals and their larger communities and work in the overlap between sculpture and poetry. The Silver Lake #SayHerName fabric installation onto chain-link fence is an example of this overlap—the graphic elements of its fabric lettering function as an art object that is also textual, invoking poetry in the way that its lines, letters, and spaces relate to each other. Residing in this overlap, list-based monuments are profoundly different from the single figural monument in the dominant historical narrative, although both perform memory work. In place of the single figure, these alternative monuments mobilize lists, names, and networked scale to mark the loss of many—and are therefore especially suited to representing vast loss.

LIST MONUMENTS

List-based monuments trace back at least to the ancient Greek practice of carving casualty lists into stone pillars. Confronted with significant casualties of Athenian citizens during the Persian Wars, ancient Greek artists changed how they memorialized their dead, turning away from figural gravestones that marked individual burials.[22] In his monograph on the treatment of the war dead in fifth-century BCE Athens, Nathan Arrington has narrated a civic strategy that shifted toward public cemeteries, sometimes with communal graves, as well as to annual casualty lists carved into marble pillars.[23] These Athenian casualty lists were produced and renewed annually, with the names of the dead organized by Kleisthenic tribe, allowing beholders to locate each person relationally.[24] Arrington argues that this visual strategy emphasized shared sacrifice rather than individual valor to reinforce these losses as experienced collectively for a common goal.[25] The system of individual grave markers encouraged mourners to tend to each grave site and mourn their own dead, whereas casualty lists invited those who read them to see their beloved's name and recognize it in relation to the surrounding names of others who had died.[26] No longer dispersed as individual names on grave markers, these lists both gathered in the fallen and also marked each death within the group. The governing intention driving the production of such casualty lists may have been to emphasize collective grief. However, in emphasizing multiple levels of scale—the civic community, the Kleisthenic tribal group, and each individual name—these lists both recorded and broadcast the totality of loss, demonstrating its impact on multiple and intersecting communities within the collective.[27]

In her monograph on lists in ancient Greece, Athena Kirk analyzes the way that list-based memorial strategies maximize the impact of a visceral experience of mass loss while recognizing the individuality of each of the dead.[28] Arguing for a transmedial approach to lists and exploring them across various textual genres and material instantiations, Kirk theorizes ancient Greek list making as a genre unto itself that interweaves visual and verbal strategies.[29] Reevaluating the ancient Greek *apodeiknumi* (to show, display, or inventory), Kirk argues that the verb form narrates the simultaneous show and tell of list practices and defines its noun form, *apodexis*, as "an enumerative display with words."[30] Kirk locates precursors of apodexis in archaic poetic practices—including the Homeric Catalogue of Ships, which counts and thereby elevates elite men while also evoking quantities beyond those possible to name, and the Hesiodic *Catalogue of Women*, whose typologies compress, sort, and value women as commodities—and suggests that a synthesis of such practices shape those that undergird later funerary monuments like the casualty lists.[31] As Kirk shows, such apodeictic monuments deploy this strategy of simultaneous visual and verbal display, thereby structuring Greek historiography and archivism.[32]

Arrington and Kirk have demonstrated the significance of a different kind of public practice in fifth-century BCE Athens, the height of (democratic imperial) classicism within the modern imagination. Tracking apodeictic monuments back to ancient Greece counters the history of art written with predominantly figural monuments to male power holders as its scaffolding. This theorization of apodeictic monuments informs our understanding of list-based monuments more broadly. The poetic possibilities of apodeictic monuments have long been crucial to the construction of memory and should therefore be examined more closely, starting with the very recent monument of the *New York Times* cover that captured the first wave of deaths from COVID-19.

INK AND PAPER LISTS

On May 24, 2020, the *New York Times* printed the names, ages, residences, and a single phrase epitaph for 1,000 of the first 100,000 Americans who had died of COVID-19 across the front page and fold of its daily paper.[33] "Mary Virginia McKeon, 64, Chicago, 'Devoured art in every medium.' Albert Petrocelli, 73, New York City, 'Fire chief who answered the call on 9/11.' Latasha Andrews, 33, New Jersey, 'Always first to offer help to those in need.'" So read the phrases that tried, in centimeters, to capture a life and a loss. This printed list of names staged its impact in part through its sheer volume of continuous text. So many lives lost, and it was only May.

Six columns of black text on soft gray newspaper ran beneath the horizontal headline in black ink—"U.S. Nears 100,000 Deaths, an Incalculable Loss"— and wrapped the fold. On any other day, a variety of articles would be pieced together, each with its allotment of column inches and headlines, creating an irregular grid. In contrast, the repeated, regular intervals of the six columns registered May 24's difference. Instead of patchwork, the memorial evoked stanzas of poetry, forcing us to think about words on a page and the blank space—or lack thereof—surrounding them.[34]

The *New York Times* cover entered the world not from the vantage point of reflection but *in medias res*—capturing a fraction, as it turned out, of the mass casualties that the United States would face.[35] Through this change in format, the front page moved beyond reporting to what it is today: a list-based monument to COVID-19 loss. As such, the cover does many different types of work—by listing names, it showcases each individual; by using selective examples (1,000 out of 100,000), it is also emblematic. At the same time, it is diverse: within the selection of 1,000 names, the editors chose people of different genders, geographies, and ages. Finally, as the monument was synchronous with the losses it represented—much like the AIDS Memorial Quilt, comprising 48,000 panels that accumulated over time—it sought to effect political change. Indeed, the AIDS quilt intervened in an ongoing crisis. Its very collaborative construction demanded that viewers recognize how many different people the virus had impacted as well as brought this diverse group of mourners into community with each other and with the dead. And yet the quilt also produced an aesthetic object that some critiqued for sanitizing the violence of these deaths. Activists like Larry Kramer of Act Up argued that the quilt worked to make death beautiful and the HIV/AIDS epidemic palatable in ways that delayed instead of promoted change.[36] Despite this critique, some combination of the public attention given the AIDS quilt and the response to activists like the Act Up collective inspired the allocation of more funds for medical research, which in turn drove the medical advances that now allow people with HIV to live full lives. The *New York Times* cover performs similar activist work, drawing attention to a problem in order to inspire action by naming the previously nameless dead.

Among other challenges, the front page intends to solve a problem of comprehension: how to grasp both the size of the number and the individuality its toll represents. While the cover's headline narrates the single story told by these columns—the pandemic had by that date claimed nearly 100,000 lives in the United States—that number is too large for easy visualization or comprehension, even when excerpted as 1,000 names. To give order to this unfathomable number, an interpunct—a black dot—separates the epitaph of the previous person from the name, in bold font, of the next person, and these microhistories flow together down each column, suggesting both separation and interconnectedness (as the virus also does). The interpuncts evoke footnotes or asterisks, each of which would typically indicate more to come but which here mark finality or, like full stops, the hard stop at the end of a life.[37]

Each interpunct invites the reader to pause. Into the space of that pause wells up a small moment of grief before the next name.[38] Together with the excerpted words, these contemporary interpuncts even evoke poetic quotation, the style by which we would represent, in formal writing, lines of verse in running prose by separating each line with slashes. Yet if we removed all language, we would see only a grid of six column dividers populated by an irregular pattern of interpuncts: 1,000 to represent 100,000. In fact, this dot strategy was later employed by the February 2021 *New York Times* cover, published when the United States neared half a million COVID-19 deaths. That cover printed almost half a million dots organized chronologically, each dot representing one individual person.[39] Beginning with a few dots puncturing the mostly white space of the section devoted to the start of the pandemic, the graphic concludes with so many dots pushed together that its bottom appears as a nearly black band.[40]

The 2020 cover's layout eschews figural representation of the dead, marking each person not with a representation of their bodies but instead in four textual ways: name (first and last), age, place of death, and an epitaph excerpted from their obituary as it was printed in their local paper.[41] As a publication, the *New York Times* is known for producing robust obituaries of famous people after they die, updating these in preparation before tragedy occurs. Yet in the context of the pandemic, the paper turned to a different strategy, gathering and aggregating local obituaries in order to capture the scope of pandemic deaths. The grim new context of the pandemic thereby forced the paper to shift practice in response to the scale of the tragedy and to focus on writing an aggregated obituary of collective loss rather than an individual story of elevated status.

Notably, the epitaphs aggregated by the paper are fragments—incomplete sentences—and they have also been relocated from their local origin to a space meant to denote the nation as a whole. As these epitaphs vary in length—five words, eight words, sometimes more—they create their own patterns within the columns on the page like uneven breaks in quoted lines of poetry. The printed page makes a fractal of sorts—letters to words, words to columns, columns to page—that figures the relationship of individual to community to nation.[42] The overall organization of the page addresses such relationships in a nuanced way while also equalizing the dead in connection with each other. Yet this equalizing effaces differential pandemic impacts: the cover gathers names equally across gender even though COVID-19 has proven more fatal to men and fails to mark out how, in the face of federal misdirection and abdication of responsibility to states and individuals, geography, as well as class, race, and gender, has driven deaths.[43] In addition, the cover records only the names of those who died directly from COVID-19, not from its sequelae—poverty, closed schools and childcare centers, and delayed medical diagnoses and treatments for other diseases.

The cover also performs metacommentary on COVID-19 loss more generally, exposing the structures by which economic precarity of all forms produces vulnerability in both individuals and organizations. For example, by listing the names of people who might not otherwise be mentioned in a publication like the *New York Times*, the cover implicitly acknowledges its power as an institution that typically excludes everyday people and their personal lives from its main pages. Moreover, by excerpting obituaries from local papers, the *Times* cover elevates the work of small publications struggling against conglomerate presses. Such papers are the most at risk amid the economic precarity that the pandemic has deepened, even as the era of Trump valorized attacking the press more generally.[44] By memorializing each individual person through an excerpt, the cover also affirms the importance of each local paper.

As a monument, the hard copy *Times* cover emphasizes transience in the medium of fine and fragile newspaper, ubiquity through the paper's mechanical reproducibility, and circulation through the networks of community built by its physical circulations and recirculations.[45] Unlike a static stone structure with a figural component occupying a prominent public space—unlike the typical memorializing sculpture—the fleeting paper record evoked even in the language that surrounds it ("a daily" to describe a newspaper; the etymology of "journal" from the French "jour," meaning "day") fits with an unchecked pandemic that continues to move through our communities as we write.

MIRRORED LISTS

The *New York Times*' list-based approach to monumentalizing the dead aligned, in a different medium, with Maya Lin's iconic Vietnam Veterans Memorial, dedicated on the National Mall in Washington, DC, on November 10, 1982 (Fig. 6.1).[46] Lin, a first-generation Asian-American woman and twenty-one-year-old undergraduate student at Yale University, won the juried contest of anonymous submissions for the monument's commission administered by the Vietnam Veterans Memorial Fund. Lin's chevron of shining black granite emerges directly from the earth, rises 10 feet, and extends more than 246 feet in length. In keeping with the juried contest's stipulations that the memorial include the names of the fallen, 58,318 names of US soldiers who died in the Vietnam War were cut into its stone.[47] Lin organized the names in chronological order of each death, spanning two decades of war. The names of those who died on the same day are listed alphabetically within that unlabeled group. Only the dates of the first (1957) and final (1975) years in which US soldiers died in active combat are marked on the monument, but the internal chronology of the war is captured simply by the progression of names. Each alphabetic group delineates a single day of loss so that the viewer notes a new day when confronted with a new alphabetical cycle.[48] Grouping the names in this way (instead of by birthday or alphabetically from start to finish) reminds the viewer that even the name they may be there to witness was part of a group of fellow soldiers who perished during the same twenty-four hours.[49] Although different from the organization by tribe of the annual Athenian casualty lists, Lin's day-by-day chronological organization drawn out over the eighteen years of active combat performs similar work for mourners by bringing each name into communities of fallen.

One of the most feminist aspects of the monument is the way it demands the viewer to confront their own place in such loss—along with their own future. The high shine of the granite slabs of Lin's wall reflects each visitor so that a beholder sees not only the sharp cut of names into black granite but also their own image mirrored by the monument's surface. This reflection implicates each viewer for a brief moment in the systems of military violence that produced so much death, connects their body with the list of names beneath their silhouette, and reminds them of their own future death.[50] The carved names invite touch, and many visitors trace individual letters with their fingers or rub pencils over scraps of paper pressed against part of the list to bring home a rubbing of a name or several names.[51] Unlike the nearby

Lincoln Memorial (1922), where a monochrome portrait sculpture of the former president sits within a white marble temple, Lin's commission includes
no figural representation or plinth, hallmarks of traditional memorials; in
the immediate moment after the design was revealed, many veterans, politi-
cians, and pundits responded in dismay at what they perceived as Lin's lack
of traditionalism. While the terms of the contest stipulated that the architect
incorporate a list of names, Lin might have chosen to pair a figural form with
a list displayed on a plaque or plinth instead of foregrounding the list as the
memorial's primary focus. Lin's memorial thereby eschews the white marble
figural form that has come to characterize such monuments and thus seemed
to deny veterans the heroization of past war memorials. Critiques of the monument were compounded by Lin's youth, gender, and race, none of which had
been known before she was selected by anonymous competition.[52] And the
very controversy over the reception of the memorial seemed to replicate the
controversy about the unpopular and protracted war itself.[53]

Lin's memorial drew bipartisan criticism that mobilized the image of
a police report on a traffic accident to critique its reliance on names and
lists—established tools of administrative bureaucracy—and questioned the
memorial's status as simultaneously high and low art.[54] For some, Lin's
disavowal of tradition failed to appropriately honor the fallen through its
refusal of ornamentation. For others, like the right-wing novelist Tom Wolfe,
Lin's aesthetics aligned her with left-wing, antiwar, elite practitioners of
minimalism and so also failed to appropriately honor the fallen on the grounds
of the monument's elitism.[55] Though seemingly opposed, both critiques reject
Lin's radical departure from existing monuments.

Published on October 15, 1982, Wolfe's op-ed, "Art Disputes War: The
Battle of the Vietnam Memorial," maligned art movements and left-wing
elite academics.[56] Dramatizing paradigm shifts in art school instruction in the
twentieth century, Wolfe claims that

> janitors were instructed to throw out the plaster casts, those thousands of
> Corinthian capitals and Esquiline vases and whatnot that students had been
> using as models for drawing. For that matter, the hell with drawing itself . . .
> Modernism was abstract.[57]

This image of faculty at elite institutions instructing working-class employees
to dispose of the models with which artists had traditionally trained served
Wolfe's political agenda in casting the stripped-down simplicity of Lin's list-
based monument as anti-prole—simultaneously elite and communist. Wolfe
contends that

> statues of heroic soldiers were the most inutterably bourgeois of all. . . .
> You could put a gun at the temple of one of the new breed [of artists] and

you couldn't make him sculpt a realistic figure of a soldier to put up on a pedestal.[58]

Furthermore, these were just the sort of people—trained at Harvard, Yale, and MIT—Wolfe argues, who judged the competition for the Vietnam Veterans Memorial and selected Lin's proposal. In a move that perpetuates long-standing anti-Islam rhetoric, he calls these judges "art mullahs."[59] Thus Wolfe characterizes those who selected Lin's proposal as elitist and anti-proletariat as well as Eastern and effete, tapping into enduring Orientalist tropes that also played into anti-Asian bias churned up during the war itself and directed against Lin.

In the face of this outcry, the Vietnam Veterans Memorial Fund commissioned a second monument of three men in combat gear cast in monochrome bronze (*Three Soldiers*, 1984).[60] Its artist, Frederick Hart, had also participated in the original contest and been passed over for Lin's monument. His more traditional figural monument includes the first representation of a Black man on or surrounding the National Mall, pitting this "first" against the "firsts" of Lin's monument. This idealized trio stands within feet of the chevron in an effort to embody and offset the nonfigural list and is another example of the compression of the many into the few discussed at the start of this chapter. The return to figuration satisfied some of the complaints against Lin's alternative approach, but it is the wall itself that has emerged as an icon in subsequent years. Despite Wolfe's op-ed and the associated outcry, the Vietnam Veterans Memorial's dedication immediately quelled its critics, and the memorial emerged as a site of mourning and remembrance.

Among the laudatory descriptions of the Vietnam Veterans Memorial after its dedication were comments during a Senate committee meeting in which Daniel Smith of the National Park Service referred to "the aesthetic qualities that make this memorial, in the eyes of many, one of the most emotionally moving memorials ever built," and Senator Tom Daschle commented that "the Wall has proven to be an amazing instrument for healing."[61] Nowhere in the extended committee notes is any reference to the early controversy over the monument; instead, speakers consistently affirmed its singular importance and success. The wall has been so popular that several grassroots organizations have created replicas of the memorial for veterans and others who cannot make the pilgrimage to DC.[62] Lin's memorial has therefore become the subject of reproductions and scaled-down copies of just the sort Wolfe claimed elite art professors had been instructing their cleaning staff to throw out in the early twentieth century.

Lin's aniconic and feminist approach refused to elevate and monumentalize a catastrophic and controversial war, instead grounding, narrating, and naming its human losses. Critically, however, her monument only records the names of those who died in combat, not those who died while conscripted but not

actively fighting or those who were damaged by the war but died after its conclusion. It also records the names of just eight women. Further, Lin chose not
to expose differences of class, race, and rank among those who served in her
list, instead implicitly suggesting that the veterans were equal in the moment
of death. Debate over the parameters of who should or should not be eligible
for inscription continues, and the subsequent additions of a commemorative
plaque (2000) for those who died after the war and a Vietnam Women's
Memorial (1993—also a figural monument depicting, in part, a female nurse
tending to a wounded male soldier) sought to expand beyond what the list could
capture.[63] This expansion remains in tension with the impact of the monument
itself, some of which stems from Lin's creativity within the constraints of the
competition's guidelines, constraints that these additions wholly circumvent.

Yet even list monuments face limits in accounting for the full scope of
loss and trauma. As we have narrated, state-sponsored list monuments, from
the Athenian casualty lists to the Vietnam Veterans Memorial, tend toward
monumentalizing the names of men. At the same time, in such monuments
we see a trajectory that leads to opportunity: as old forms of imperialism and
hierarchal structures of power decline, new spaces for feminism emerge.

BLANK SPACES AND POETRY

Speaking of her intent in listing the names of the US soldiers in chronological
order of their deaths, Lin said that she wished to make the list read "like
an epic Greek poem."[64] Notably, while Lin sought a different form from
the classical figural monument for her memorial, she nevertheless found
resonance with ancient Greek poetic practices, perhaps because poetry
employs a more deconstructive strategy of representation. This resonance
also aligns with the synergy between archaic poetic practices and the ancient
Greek casualty-list monuments theorized by Athena Kirk and discussed
earlier. Lin's system of arrangement, bookending her start and finish dates
but providing no other numerical reference points and instead allowing a new
alphabetical cycle to indicate a new day, itself suggests the basic operation of
poetry—that is, to allow combinations of letters of the alphabet to represent
and suggest a multitude of forms (and, in this case, to register protest).

The poet Alice Oswald trades on both of these concepts, rewriting a Greek
epic poem by exposing its essence as a combination of letters in her 2011
work *Memorial: A Version of Homer's Iliad*, a poem she describes as an "oral
cemetery."[65] While this rewriting cannot be strictly classified as translation,
it nevertheless shares many strategies with the texts explored in chapters 3
and 4.[66] To produce the first section of her work, Oswald strips the ancient
poem of all but the names of its dead in what she calls her "reckless dismissal

of seven-eighths of the poem," creating a blackout or erasure poem that lists these names in block capitals:

PROTESILAUS
ECHEPOLUS
ELEPHENOR
SIMOISIUS
LEUKOS
DEMOCOON
DIORES
PIROUS
PHEGEUS
IDAEUS[67]

Oswald extracts the list of casualties from the poem to showcase the poetics of naming the dead. We might understand her work as a kind of unweaving of narrative aimed at representing something new and different that was also already within the text. While she conjures each man, the block letters of their names—organized by moment of death as described in the poem—provide, like Lin's organization around the moment of death in the real time of the Vietnam War, a new form of monument: visual, poetic, but quite far from the traditional figural monumentalizing discussed earlier in this chapter.[68]

By listing just these names, Oswald has removed all words that do something to the narrative (verbs, nouns other than proper nouns, etc.). What remains is pure sign—names that do not themselves take action but merely evoke it, as if the surrounding text itself has passed away, its block capitals evoking the incised script of a tomb's epitaph. Like the practice of the translators surveyed in chapter 3 who translated epics through their feminist subject position, the strategy of removing the storyline and leaving just the names creates a feminist interpretation of the canonical poem itself, one suggesting that all we learn from the narrative of war is the names of the dead, the tally of the lost. And as a name typically indexes the person—but in this case, the presence of a name also marks that person's absence from the world of the living—the names in this section of the poem invoke an occupation of space as well as a blank. The source poem's historical place as part of the oral tradition means that in performance, temporal space can be given around these names—a rhapsode reciting the *Iliad* might pause, perhaps even for a significant duration, to create a memorial effect (a "moment of silence"). In Oswald's textual version, she has fewer tools to control time and must exploit white space to achieve this same effect.

Oswald's contention that her methods are "compatible with the spirit of oral poetry, which was never stable but always adapting itself to a new audience, as if its language, unlike written language, was still alive and kicking" suggests a fascinating operation wherein she creates a text in the spirit of speech acts that destroys most of the possible speech, leaving instead only the sign of the sign.[69] In the end, the name, not the body, endures; yet in Oswald's work, its meaning as a "positive" inscription is, of course, underwritten by the blank "negative" space surrounding it, invoking absence and loss.

NAMING OVERWHELM

Foregrounding names, as many of the monuments in this chapter do, can be a strategy to bring attention back to individuals themselves. A variation of that strategy, the anti-elegy, purports to reject the name of the individual in order to protest the continual repetition of the same tragic circumstances that replicate violence onto person after person.[70]

The murder of Michael Brown in 2014 catalyzed what has since unfolded as years of protests against the unrestrained and systematic application of violence in police interactions with Black people, protests including the broader work of #BlackLivesMatter (discussed in chapter 5) as well as those that have taken the form of art and literature, among other modalities. Danez Smith's poem "not an elegy" is one of these protests. Included in Smith's 2017 poetry collection *Don't Call Us Dead*, the poem is an expansion of Smith's earlier poem published online. That poem, "not an elegy for Mike Brown," was written on August 9, 2014, the night of eighteen-year-old Brown's murder by a white Ferguson police officer. Smith reports writing the poem in twenty minutes in a frenzy of what they called fury and initially posting it to Facebook from which it spread.[71]

The original poem began with this line: "I am sick of writing this poem."[72] In it, Smith narrates the feeling of repeating the same elegy over and over as more and more Black people are lost due to police violence and white supremacy more generally. Even in the evolution of the title, originally "not an elegy for Mike Brown" and later simply "not an elegy," we see Smith demonstrating frustration with listing names or memorializing individuals when the circumstances of their deaths continue to repeat.

Smith concludes that this very feeling—of watching yet another child be murdered—is what Blackness itself is:

is that what being black is about?
not the joy of it, but the feeling

you get when you are looking
at your child, turn your head,

then, poof, no more child.

that feeling. that's black.[73]

Despite its overt denials, the poem elegizes Michael Brown and other murdered Black people. Given the widescale scope of the loss the poem confronts, Smith's expression of overwhelm at trying to capture each individual person is a strategy—one of anti-listing. This strategy also mirrors that of the second *New York Times* cover previously discussed, in which the list of the dead became so overwhelming that their representation moved out of language and into dots. At the same time, the poem attempts, like the AIDS quilt and the first *New York Times* cover, to motivate action in readers. Smith is in effect saying that the problem is too big for poetry—but in a poem that expresses this painfully and beautifully. The paradox of a poem expressing what it cannot express is paralleled by the impossibility of trying to locate justice in the face of systematic and targeted violence and injustice. Thus Smith's rhetorical move of decrying the poem's elegiac genre is designed to make the reader question—and ultimately change—the circumstances that make this so.

This rhetorical move occurs in at least two places in the poem. When Smith contrasts the feeling of hopelessness and rage at losing another child (the feeling they call "Blackness") with "not the joy of it," they echo the title's denial. By stating that the poem is not an elegy for Michael Brown, it becomes both a protest of the circumstances that resulted in his murder as well as, of course, an elegy. And by stating that being Black is not about "the joy of it," the poem becomes a protest for the circumstances of Black life that prevent joy by also invoking its joy. These denials are not only to be read literally but also are intended to motivate the reader to question and take action. The expression of overwhelm is thereby a strategy that perhaps feels like one of the few that remain—to motivate people who have actively or implicitly allowed the same patterns to continue to repeat.

Smith's poem has had an afterlife in the years since it was written. Now included in school curricula, the poem teaches students about Ferguson more broadly.[74] This circulation is perhaps a step toward Smith's broader goal. Emphasizing overwhelm at a growing list of names draws attention to the problem, foregrounding the iterative nature of unjust loss in order to inspire action and change.[75]

NAMING THE UNNAMED

A different process must take place, however, when records do not name the dead. In M. NourbeSe Philip's book-length poem of 2008, *Zong!*, Philip "untells" the horrific fact-based narrative of her text's titular slave ship.[76] During its 1782 transatlantic journey, the *Zong*'s captain threw more than 130 enslaved people overboard to drown, believing that the loss of their economic "value" could be compensated via an insurance claim. Philip's book mobilizes constraint, erasure, and the cut-up tradition in poetry by using only the 500 words of the ensuing legal decision *Gregson v. Gilbert*—the text she calls the "mother document"—to engage with the horror of this massacre.[77] This feminist, anticolonialist, anticapitalist strategy of using the text of the oppressor to articulate protest has much in common with the other public feminist projects described elsewhere in our chapters (see especially chapter 2).[78]

The text evokes drowning spatially in the form of a concrete poem—words cast across its pages, unmoored—and breaks up words from the mother document, allowing the poem to devolve into fragmentation, first to the word, then to the syllable, and finally to the letter. Such fragmentation expands what *Zong!* can do: breaking up the larger words allows Philip to use and invoke French, Latin, Shona, and Yoruba (among other languages) as well as write in phonemes and individual letters. Additionally, as Meilani Clay points out, this breaking up of words allows Philip to directly invoke African American Vernacular English:

> When Philip writes "this be," she is using AAVE's "habitual be" to call attention to the fact that "this" massacre within the context of "this" larger human atrocity that "was" the institution of slavery will forever stand as something that has happened, in some ways is happening, and as far as we know will happen again, which is the unique frame of time represented by the habitual be.[79]

With this intervention, Philip projects the past onto the future in an act of prolepsis, suggesting that without change, we will never move out of this habitual time.

The constraint of using the language of the legal decision as the basis for imagining the life of the murdered mirrors the colonialist and supremacist imposition of language more generally, yet some scholars have argued that Philip's poetic deconstruction of such language does, in some ways, imagine an "outside" of the master's house.[80] Michael Leong has suggested that, while many contemporary conceptual poets turn to documents as source materials for poems, such techniques are perhaps especially well-suited to "respond[ing] to racial traumas" as reexamining documents through a poetic lens can create "conceptual elegies, poems that are able to redouble their sense of 'afterness' via redocumentation into powerful acts of mourning."[81] In Philip's case, access to language, history, and documentation itself is limited by what was and was not preserved through time.

History does not record the names of the people who were murdered by the ship captain when they were forced from the *Zong* into the sea. Philip's text, then, faces the challenge of capturing or listing a group of people whose names have been lost, (white)washed away. Jessica Marie Johnson has named such gaps in the archive "null values." She writes: "Instead of pausing at empirical silence or accepting it at face value, surfacing silence in the empirical, imperial archive as having a value—a null value—imbues absence with disruption and possibility."[82] Philip both recognizes the null value in the absence of names for those killed on the *Zong* and chooses to overwrite it with her own version of potential names, following a practice related to what Saidiya Hartman has named "critical fabulation." Hartman describes such fabulation as a mode of writing whose "intention . . . isn't anything as miraculous as recovering the lives of the enslaved or redeeming the dead, but rather laboring to paint as full a picture of the lives of the captives as possible."[83] Rather than fabulate a story (which the mother document already tells), Philip instead fills the archival gap with names. To name the *Zong* dead, Philip researches Yoruba names and lists what could be historically accurate options in the first section of her book, five or six names at the bottom of each page in tiny font representing both traditional male and traditional female names.[84] "Masuz Zuwena Ogunsheye Ziyad Ogwambi Keturah" reads page 3, mirroring the footnote quality of the *New York Times* names while also anchoring the bottom of Philip's page of poetry and drowning beneath it. Philip's footnote practice continues throughout the entire first book of her text, "Os." In the second book, "Sal," Philip maintains the same "footnote" line at the bottom of the page but removes the names underneath it, preserving instead blankness and empty space. From the third book onward, there is no footnoted space whatsoever, enacting loss.

At the end of the fourth book, "Ferrum" (the very last section of the text printed in black ink), Philip again lists names, this time in the same size as her regular font but in cursive, evoking signatures, the voices of the dead signing off. "Bektemba Agbeke Gbolahan Fasuyi Abifarin Olurun" announces the first line of the name-list verse.[85] Philip fabulates these names to honor the real people whose lives are the basis for her poetic text.

Writing about a different text in which a name also marks murder, Marta Figlerowicz and Matylda Figlerowicz theorize signatures as signifying both individual agency and the broader systems that destroy it. The authors articulate their theory of "multilingual style" through the example of the signature of a man as evoked by its Spanish spelling on court documents that use only the Basque variant of his name:

> Legally, the signature seals the man's fate. And yet, it also becomes a stylistic mark . . . a sign of his capacity to conform to a recognisable writerly aesthetic as well as of his separateness from the regime by whose hands he is about to die.[86]

The complex relationship between the signatures Philip captures is similarly layered. Fabulated Yoruba names honor real people, yet their manifestation as signatures (especially in the context of a project underwritten by a legal document written in English that captures their murder) creates various forms of presence and absence: the names are fabulated rather than historically accurate, their presence in the poem marks their absence from the world of the living, and their participation invokes compliance while censuring both the document and the murders.[87] The form of this section, however, reveals an additional purpose. As concrete poetry in the shape of an inverted triangle, the section creates a monument in the form of an empty plinth, shaping the named into a platform upon which this history stands.

Despite bestowing names, Philip's work does not engage in the poetics of scale that many monuments for mass casualties do.[88] Though she does employ the strategy of the list, the separation of sets of names onto different pages and their citation on her plinth page (in which 22 "signatures" stand in for more than 130) means that these lists do a different type of work than do those in Lin's monument or the ancient Greek casualty lists, though they employ an excerption strategy similar to the *New York Times* cover. As an intervention in the ongoing conceptualization of the horrors of the transatlantic slave trade and its aftermath, Philip's text must do both individual and emblematic work as she is writing within a specific instance and its broader context. Katherine McKittrick demonstrates that the status of Black bodies as commodities inflects what the historical record does and does not preserve, arguing that

> a black archival presence not only enumerates the dead and dying, but also acts as an origin story. This is where we begin, this is where historic blackness comes from: the list, the breathless numbers, the absolutely economic, the mathematics of the unliving.[89]

Philip's lists thereby give life to absences in the archive of the history of the people aboard the ship as well as history more generally, while at the same time highlighting the absences central to both.[90]

Working in tension between telling and untelling while also capturing a polyphony of voices, Philip's text moves forward and backward, articulating, revising, recirculating, and fading in and out. Christina Sharpe theorizes this cyclical repetition as emblematic of work that navigates the paradoxes of Black survival and expression in the wake of slavery.[91] Because of the text's capture of these paradoxes, we *see* this book almost as much as we read it, watching words line up formally at the start until in "Zong! #26" they assemble into a block paragraph that exposes the words of the mother document for its profound inadequacy. Once the reader experiences the block, the words begin to expand and eventually explode across the page until the final palimpsest section in which they simultaneously accumulate and fade out. Throughout this process, instead of a "complete story," the reader sees the impact of text on the page, the rips the words make in blankness, their tiny wounds.

The final section of the book, "Ebora," dissolves even further as the text moves from dark black ink to very light gray, leaving a palimpsest—the ghost of words more shadow than ink, augmented with strikethroughs and over-writing. This use of faded grayscale intervenes in the monumental tradition whose materials tend toward monochrome in shiny bronze or white marble and connects Philip's practice to that of several other creators discussed in this chapter: Sol Lewitt's black platform, the *New York Times*' black ink on gray paper, and the gray letters cut into Maya Lin's reflective black granite.[92] All of these are visually distinct from the traditions invoked by the Lincoln Memorial's monochrome white marble or Wiley's repurposing of mono-chrome bronze to mount his critique, and they propose a feminist alternative to the violent systems undergirding traditional monuments. By rejecting the solidity of the patriarchal monument, grayscale makes visible that which it marks. These haunting grays are superimposed on top of our words (in Philip), written across our own reflections (in Lin), and printed across our skin (through newsprint transfer).

RETURN TO EMBODIMENT

The list-based monuments we have traced in this chapter tell a different history than that of the conventions of the figural tradition. This alternative lineage leaves room for more voices and directions. Though they may not be perfect, list-based monuments decenter some systems of power that have dominated for centuries, replacing their tradition with a more flexible, open, and activist praxis that public feminism can take up.

As a final demonstration of this flexibility, we turn to performance, a subject we have only briefly touched on so far in this chapter. Performances marshal the dynamics of embodiment and its systems of potentiality, but they also present new challenges—especially when they are themselves transla-tions of texts that capitalize on blank space (see chapter 4 for an extended example of this). Likewise, in performance of *Zong!*, Philip faces a dilemma: "Do you read the fragments across the spaces for comprehension and mean-ing, or do you honour the spaces and read the fragments as they exist, which I have written elsewhere is a threat to cohesion?"[93] This question identifies one of the perils of the blank space as a tool for memorializing: What if it is skipped over? Blank space, after all, can invite skipping by its very nature.

Yet blankness can also make an important contribution to meaning, as in Johnson's "null value."[94] We can never tell a full story. This limitation is particularly violent in the case of the *Zong*, in which individuals acting within capitalist systems of property murdered the named and, in doing so, excised their names from the archive. Yet we can, as Philip does, nevertheless mobilize blankness as a form of resistance, retaining possibility and space.

Another way to lift up blank space is to fold multiple actors or monuments together in a ritual of embodiment. We close this chapter with one such ritual. In 2014, forty-three college students from Ayotzinapa Rural College for Teachers in the Mexican state of Guerrero were disappeared by security forces.[95] No trace of the students has been found. They are presumed dead. In 2016, Luis Sierra and Cecilia McDonagh, third-grade Spanish-immersion teachers at Alvarado Elementary School in San Francisco, California, taught their students—including one child of each author of this book—this history. Over the course of the fall, each elementary student painted a portrait of one of the missing students, crafted a papier-mâché mask layered with colorful strips of Mexican textiles and miniature photographic prints, and built a rain stick percussive instrument to strap across their chests. Each mask was cast directly from a different child's face and so bears an indexical trace of its model while also merging each living child with the dead student they embody.[96] Then, in a haunting performance, forty-three US third graders put on clothing made of textiles that matched the masks to dance the story of these aspiring teachers. In their costumes, it was no longer possible to differentiate one child from the next. As the performance progressed, the students read in French and English an excerpt from Antoine de Saint-Exupéry's *The Little Prince* in which the prince watches forty-three sunsets in one day.[97] In the book, this accumulation of sunsets refers to the forty-three sunsets required by the Nazis to capture France. In the performance, the sunsets return the teachers from Ayotzinapa to the cycles of nature by metaphorizing each of them as an individual sunset (forty-three sunsets for forty-three teachers) while also representing their disappearance in the way the sunset represents an ending in time. This multilingual performance brought together the historically and geographically separate traumas of the German invasion of France during World War II and the Holocaust with the state-sponsored disappearance of the Ayotzinpa teachers, demonstrating the process by which one monument can evoke another in layered traumas, much like the way layers of paper constitute papier-mâché.

In the final minute of the performance, the children ceased their percussive beat and stood still in two rows. Then each child spoke a single name aloud, one after the next: Alexander, Dorian, Israel, José, Miguel Angel. As discussed earlier in this chapter, speaking names out loud performs protest and mourning, and this performance engaged that power while also adding the element of embodiment.[98] The resulting spoken list joined the two traditions of figural and list-based representation: for a brief moment, the deceased person and the person speaking each name were united so that the figural was brought back into the process of monumentalizing through performance. As Philip says, "the bones of the undead *can* find a resting place within us" through ceremony (emphasis in original).[99] The children conjured each of the forty-three students into the room and embodied them, blurring time, age, nationality, language, and space. The performance enabled figure and list to occupy what had until that moment remained mystery and absence. In the children's bodies and voices, time folded for a second to create a new, brief synchronicity—and another form of feminist protest.

Like these children—like so many of the artists and creators we have explored in this chapter—we might inscribe, fabulate, or chant the names of our dead in memoriam—and we claim such practices as public feminist ones. However, list-based monuments demand not merely that we see, touch, or hear those who have died but also that we recognize our own implication in these incalculable losses even as we mourn. As feminist praxis, they demand in the present that we work to reform our possible futures, and they determine what we can create and overwrite.

We might mobilize the blank spaces of the plinth, on the page, or in beats between the words we chant, working within constraints we must constantly seek to refigure. Between these collected blank spaces flow lists of names. Each list forges scale from individuation. Each name, even when marked only by interpunct or ribbon, brings us forward.

ITERATION

The figural monument tradition foregrounds a deep history of sculpting and elevating a single masculine body. That body might refer to a specific historical figure whose past public impact—as a political figure, a military general, or a civic actor—the statue marks in the present, or that body might stand in for and compress many bodies into itself as an individual symbol marking a group. In either of these modes, the figural monument mobilizes its familiar history to elide difficult or traumatic particulars under the mantle of heroic idealization.

List monuments, in contrast, unfold and expand in an effort to capture the scale of loss while simultaneously holding on to each individual name. While comprehending a single emblematic figure or a small group may feel comfortable, even familiar, confronting large numbers quickly overwhelms. Yet resisting this overwhelm is critical, whether by highlighting it or by fighting it. If we wish to recognize tragedy and injustice and to combat the circumstances that might lead to their reoccurrence, we must honor humans as individuals and not subsume them into the broader events surrounding their deaths.

Recognizing the parallel lineage of the list monument may itself function as a practice of social mourning, returning individuals to our focus while also reminding us that they have been with us all along. Like the artists whose graffiti and light projections onto the Confederate statue revise and reclaim the meaning of such work by, in effect, writing over it (Fig 0.1), we seek to metaphorically write on top of history itself, revealing narratives that have always been there but have been overlooked.[100] While attention to the figural has been more pronounced, the quieter act of memorializing by naming is a deeply rooted historical practice that produces a unique understanding of the cyclical process of loss. By their very nature, list monuments suggest expandability, acknowledging the ongoing and unfinished business of mourning. Their successes may well lie in their open-endedness, for the work of grieving is ever iterative.

NOTES

1. The organizers called their work "art" and intended the names to be spoken by passersby. They named more than 100 people but were limited by size: "And if the reservoir was 10 times as big, we would still have an abundance of names left over," said project co-organizer Eli Caplan. "We may hear about the George Floyds, the Breonna Taylors. But for each of those, there are hundreds and hundreds of other names that get lost. This is a way to acknowledge them." Deborah Vankin, "A 2.2 Mile L. A. Memorial Says Their Names: George, Breonna, Corey," *Los Angeles Times*, June 8, 2020, https://www.yahoo.com/now/2-2-mile-l-memorial-223946602.html.

2. R. Daniel Foster, "Silver Lake Expands Its 'Say Their Names' Project," *Cultural Daily*, June 24, 2020, https://www.culturaldaily.com/silver-lake-expands-its-say-their-names-project.

3. African American Policy Forum, "#SayHerName Campaign," https://aapf.org/sayhername, accessed February 01, 2021.

4. "Stacey Mann said she takes the title of the artwork seriously." As people have walked by, we've been asking them: "Please say their names, say their names out loud." Vankin, "2.2 Mile L. A. Memorial."

5. See Katherine McKittrick, "Mathematics Black Life," 17 for the relationship between the commodification of the Black body and the production of lists in the archive. McKittrick's work is discussed later in this chapter.

6. Although such work remains unfinished today, during the twentieth century, media attention began to shift from the perpetrator to the victim. For more on this historical shift, see Chris Greer, "News Media, Victims, and Crime," in *Victims, Crime,*

and Society: An Introduction, 2nd ed., ed. Pamela Davies, Peter Francis, and Chris Greer (London: Sage Publications, 2017), 21–2.

7. As in, for example, the bust of Pericles erected on the Acropolis in Athens by his sons after his death in the fifth century BCE. For one Roman marble copy of the fifth-century bronze original, see British Museum 1805,0703.91. While ancient ruler portraits of women and nonbinary people are comparatively rare, in examples where women have ruled and are monumentalized—such as the female pharaoh of ancient Egypt, Hatshepsut—they adopt the visual codes of patriarchal power. In Hatshepsut's case, this included her depiction wearing a ceremonial pharaonic beard. Kara Cooney, *The Woman Who Would Be King* (New York: Crown, 2014); Mary Beard, *Women and Power: A Manifesto* (New York: W. W. Norton & Company, 2017).

8. Jennifer Trimble presented the talk "Modern Statue Destructions and Ancient Roman Damnatio Memoriae" at Johns Hopkins University on September 29, 2020. She cited both Young and Meskell as well as Kehinde Wiley's *Rumors of War* (2020). In addition to her 2020 *Scientific American* piece, Verity Platt presented "Classicism and the Statue Crisis in the Age of Black Lives Matter" at the University of California, Los Angeles on October 28, 2020. At New York University on October 29, 2020, Hallie Franks, Ann Macy Roth, Patricia Eunji Kim, and Eric Varner presented a roundtable titled "Monuments and Memory."

9. Sonja Drimmer, "Seeing the Bigger Picture on Public Memorials to Women," *Hyperallergic*, November 27, 2020, https://hyperallergic.com/601877.

10. The December 2020 Executive order "Promoting Beautiful Federal Architecture" made this connection to neoclassicism explicit: "President George Washington and Secretary of State Thomas Jefferson consciously modeled the most important buildings in Washington, DC, on the classical architecture of ancient Athens and Rome. They sought to use classical architecture to visually connect our contemporary Republic with the antecedents of democracy in classical antiquity, reminding citizens not only of their rights but also their responsibilities in maintaining and perpetuating its institutions." Exec. Order No.13967, Section 1 (December 18, 2020). In addition, as public historian Heather Cox Richardson reported, members of the House of Representatives split largely along party lines 285–120 to remove statues of Confederates from the US Capitol—meaning over 40 percent of congresspeople voted to retain these statues. Among those were "Representative Mo Brooks (R-AL), who told the insurrectionists on January 6 before they stormed the Capitol 'Today is the day American patriots start taking down names and kicking ass,' issued a statement titled: 'CONGRESSMAN MO BROOKS DEFENDS STATES' RIGHTS, RIPS INTOLERANT SOCIALISTS WHO SEEK TO TAKE DOWN CAPITOL STATUES THEY DON'T LIKE.'" Heather Cox Richardson, "June 30, 2021," *Letters from an American*, June 30, 2021, https://heathercoxrichardson.substack.com/p/june-30-2021.

11. Cynthia S. Colburn and Ella Gonzalez drew attention to this broader ancient monument footprint in their presentation "The Complex Biographies of Ancient Political Sculptures and their Relevance Today" (paper presented at the annual meeting of the Archaeological Institute of America, online, January 2021). Of interest to us in this chapter is the modern circulation of ancient Egyptian obelisks. The

one-upmanship of the Washington Monument—an obelisk's obelisk—demanded a different construction technique in order to achieve its height. Using white marble, granite, and bluestone gneiss blocks to reach a height of 169.046 meters instead of the single block of granite that characterized the engineering of ancient Egyptian obelisks, the monument could be built taller by being built less elegantly. After the Roman annexation of Egypt, Roman emperors transported at least fifteen obelisks to Rome and Florence, on which see Susan Sorek, *The Emperors' Needles: Egyptian Obelisks and Rome* (Exeter: Bristol Phoenix Press, 2010), xiii–xiv. Turkey, France, England, the United States, and Israel are among the countries housing ancient Egyptian obelisks. For more on this, see Molly Swetnam-Burland, "'Aegyptus Redacta': The Egyptian Obelisk in the Augustan Campus Martius," *Art Bulletin* 92, no. 3 (2010): 135–53; Bob Brier, "Saga of Cleopatra's Needles," *Archaeology* 55, no. 6 (2002): 48–54.

12. But as Caroline Randall Williams reminds us in her 2020 opinion piece, monuments can be bodies as well as objects: "I have rape-colored skin. My light-brown-blackness is a living testament to the rules, the practices, the causes of the Old South. If there are those who want to remember the legacy of the Confederacy, if they want monuments, well, then, my body is a monument. My skin is a monument." Caroline Randall Williams, "Opinion: You Want a Confederate Monument? My Body Is a Confederate Monument," *The New York Times*, June 26, 2020, https://www.nytimes.com/2020/06/26/opinion/confederate-monuments -racism.html.

13. Verity Platt, "Why People Are Toppling Monuments to Racism," *Scientific American*, July 3, 2020, https://www.scientificamerican.com/article/why-people-are -toppling-monuments-to-racism.

14. Our understanding of list-based monuments owes much to Athena Kirk's analysis of apodeictic monuments in ancient Greece, discussed below. See Athena Kirk, *Ancient Greek Lists*.

15. James E. Young, "The Counter-Monument: Memory against Itself in Germany Today," *Critical Inquiry* 18, no. 2 (1992): 267–96. The cube was originally positioned near baroque architecture in a public space that might have otherwise lifted up an equestrian monument to a monarch. See counterpoint: Thomas Stubblefield, "Do Disappearing Monuments Simply Disappear?: The Counter-Monument in Revision," *Future Anterior* 8, no. 2 (2011): xii–11.

16. Lynn Meskell, "Negative Heritage and Past Mastering in Archaeology," *Anthropological Quarterly* 75, no. 3 (2002): 570–1.

17. Meskell, "Negative Heritage," 560–1.

18. *Rumors of War* takes its name from the biblical passage Matthew 24:6: "And ye shall hear of wars and rumors of wars: see that ye be not troubled: for all these things must come to pass, but the end is not yet." (King James Version). See Susan Stamberg, "'Rumors of War' in Richmond Marks a Monumentally Unequal America," *NPR*, June 25, 2020, https://www.npr.org/2020/06/25/878822835/rumors -of-war-in-richmond-marks-a-monumentally-unequal-america.

19. Virginia Museum of Fine Arts, "Rumors of War," https://www.vmfa.museum /about/rumors-of-war, accessed April 4, 2021.

20. The last Confederate equestrian monument, to Robert E. Lee, was removed on September 8, 2021, following a judicial ruling by the Virginia Supreme Court allowing its removal by the state. See Whittney Evans and David Streever, "Virginia's Massive Robert E. Lee Statue Has Been Removed," *NPR*, September 8, 2021, https://www.npr.org/2021/09/08/1035004639/virginia-ready-to-remove-massive-robert-e-lee-statue-following-a-year-of-lawsuit.

21. An example of this is the figural additions to Maya Lin's aniconic Vietnam Veterans Memorial discussed later in this chapter. For example, Frederick Hart's representation of three soldiers was added to increase inclusion, but some have cited the figural work as instead excluding; according to Marita Sturken, many "mistakenly assumed that these constituents [Air Force pilots, Navy seamen, and Native Americans who requested representation through additional statues] feel left out of the wall. It would appear, however, that it is Hart's statue that makes them feel excluded." Marita Sturken, "The Wall, the Screen, and the Image: The Vietnam Veterans Memorial," *Representations* 35 (1991): 142n31.

22. Nikos Axarlis, "Plague Victims Found: Mass Burial in Athens," *Archaeology*, April 15, 1998, https://archive.archaeology.org/online/news/kerameikos.html.

23. See Nathan T. Arrington, *Ashes, Images, and Memories: The Presence of the War Dead in Fifth-Century Athens* (New York: Oxford University Press, 2014), 91–124, esp. 92–4 and fig. 3.1. In some examples, the lists were topped by a figural scene of cavalry or foot soldiers in battle (Arrington, *Ashes, Images, and Memories*, 102–3).

24. Arrington, *Ashes, Images, and Memories*, 92–100.

25. Arrington, *Ashes, Images, and Memories*, 95.

26. On mourning practices at the gravesite for individual burials, see Seth Estrin, "Memory Incarnate: Material Objects and Private Visions in Classical Athens, from Euripides' *Ion* to the Gravesite," in *The Materialities of Greek Tragedy: Object and Affect in Aeschylus, Sophocles, and Euripides*, ed. Mario Telò and Melissa Mueller (London: Bloomsbury, 2018): 111–32.

27. Arrington notes that while the majority of those listed were citizens, the lists also included the names of noncitizens and enslaved men. The collective civic community produced by these lists thus transcended citizenship. Arrington, *Ashes, Images, and Memories*, 97. Athena Kirk argues that even in their physical design, these monuments do the affective work of mourning, suggesting that the "arrangement and the intervening spaces serve as a way to recover the lost dead spatially, while the prominence of each tribe's name verbally repatriates them to their native localities." Kirk, *Ancient Greek Lists*, 76. The tradition of making annual casualty lists began in Athens sometime before the earliest dated example of 464 BCE, earlier in the epigraphic record than other regular inscribed accounts such as the Athenian Tribute Lists or inventories from the Parthenon and other treasuries.

28. Kirk, *Ancient Greek Lists*, 73–7.

29. Kirk, *Ancient Greek Lists*, 3.

30. On *apodeiknumi* and *apodexis*, see Kirk, *Ancient Greek Lists*, 91 and 119; on Kirk's intervention in the traditional meaning of the noun form, see Kirk, *Ancient Greek Lists*, 102–7.

31. Kirk, *Ancient Greek Lists*, 20–30; 48–77.

32. Kirk, *Ancient Greek Lists*, 91–109; 140–6.

33. Our focus is the print paper and its form rather than the digital version. While most people now access individual articles digitally, as an object of mourning, this newspaper invited purchase of the physical form. However, an interactive digital list remains available at the *New York Times*: "An Incalculable Loss," *New York Times*, last updated May 27, 2020, https://www.nytimes.com/interactive/2020/05/24/us/us-coronavirus-deaths-100000.html. See also: Russ Choma, "Sunday's Heart-Wrenching New York Times Cover Marks Almost 100,000 Coronavirus Deaths in the US," *Mother Jones*, May 24, 2020, https://www.motherjones.com/politics/2020/05/new-york-times-cover-sunday-coronavirus-death-toll-memorial.

34. A recent example of attention to visual poetics, the grid, and blank space is on the Rakish Light site, "Conversation with the Taxman about Poetry by Vladimir Mayakovsky, 1926, translated from the Russian by James Womack," July 2020, http://rakishlight.com/projects.

35. The newspaper would print subsequent COVID-19-inspired covers, including one at the approach of half a million deaths, discussed below.

36. Tracie Hunte, "The Ashes on the Lawn," *Radiolab*, December 17, 2020, https://www.wnycstudios.org/podcasts/radiolab/articles/ashes-lawn. The podcast also highlights another parallel between the HIV/AIDS epidemic and the COVID-19 pandemic in the form of Anthony Fauci, whose role in the pandemic as the head of NIAID matched the exact same job and title he held in the 1980s during the AIDS epidemic.

37. Additionally, the use of interpuncts may gesture to the ancient Greek and Roman carvers who also used interpuncts to separate words carved into stone, as on the Marathon casualty list from Eua-Loukou and on the Pantheon in Rome. C. M. Keesling, "The Marathon Casualty List from Eua-Loukou and the Plinthedon Style in Attic Inscriptions," *Zeitschrift für Papyrologie und Epigraphik* 180 (2012): 139–49; P. Saenger, "Physiologie de la lecture et séparation des mots," *Annales* 44, no. 4 (1989): 943–50; P. Saenger, *Space between Words: The Origins of Silent Reading* (Redwood City, CA: Stanford University Press, 1997): 9–12.

38. The English term derives from the Latin *pungere*, meaning "to prick." We might understand each interpunct marking the shift from one person's epitaph to the next as intended to prick the viewer as with a pin—one tiny gesture to the pain of loss each name marks.

39. This strategy also invokes art that excerpts only the punctuation of a written work, perhaps to compare it to another work. See, for example, Adam J. Calhoun, "Punctuation in Novels," *Medium*, February 15, 2016, https://medium.com/@neuroecology/punctuation-in-novels-8f316d542ec4.

40. Nancy Coleman, "On the Front Page, a Wall of Grief," *Times Insider*, February 21, 2021, https://www.nytimes.com/2021/02/21/insider/covid-500k-front-page.html.

41. The digital version, in contrast to the print paper, includes small gray figural markers for each individual memorialized in the issue. When one moves the cursor over a gray silhouette, text related to a single individual appears in hypertext,

suggesting that the editors understood that, in its digital form, the list could not sustain its lack of figural representation.

42. And yet the pandemic is global by design or nature. While social structures, existing inequalities, and government-driven responses are deeply national and varied, the overall virus is transborder and transnational. The *New York Times* cover records and monumentalizes the specific situation of the United States in contrast with the far fewer deaths recorded by many other nations.

43. For one example, see "Health Equity Considerations and Racial and Ethnic Minority Groups," Centers for Disease Control and Prevention (CDC), updated April 19, 2021, https://www.cdc.gov/coronavirus/2019-ncov/community/health-equity/race-ethnicity.html.

44. Penelope Abernathy, "The Loss of Local News: What It Means for Communities," *Expanding News Desert*, November 8, 2020, https://www.usnewsdeserts.com/reports/expanding-news-desert/loss-of-local-news and Andrew Buncome, "Trump is the Biggest Threat to Press Freedom in US in My Lifetime, Says Dan Rather," *The Guardian*, October 6, 2020, https://www.independent.co.uk/news/world/americas/us-politics/dan-rather-interview-trump-press-freedom-fake-news-journalism-60-minutes-cbs-b811406.html.

45. This memorial, at once quotidian and exceptional, emerged from the print plant. Aluminum plates, lasers, soy inks, blades, mist (to maintain the 72 degrees and 50 percent humidity required), and fourteen miles of conveyor belts all produce the sensory world of paper production—the sounds of machines and people working in tandem, the smell of ink as it saturates paper, the touch of condensing mist, the heft of the damp paper, and the sight of finished papers, one after the next, far more than 100,000. Each paper circulates these names, enacting encounter after encounter with each reader that allows the memorials to complete their circuit—from local to national and then back, at last, to local. For more on this process, see Terence McGinley, "What the Cyan! How the *New York Times* Gets Inked," *New York Times*, May 23, 2017, https://www.nytimes.com/2017/05/23/insider/new-york-times-printing-plant-press.html.

46. For video of veterans visiting Lin's Memorial in 1982, see *Veterans Attend Dedication of the Vietnam War Memorial ca. 1982*, Part 1, WPA Film Library. On objections raised to Lin's memorial, especially the racist critique of its color and the antifeminist critique of its plinth-less connection to the feminized earth, see Sturken, "The Wall, the Screen, and the Image," 122–3.

47. Paul Spreiregan, "The Vietnam Veterans Memorial Design Competition," in *Architectural Competition: Research Inquiries and Experiences*, ed. Magnus Rönn, Reza Kazemian, and Jonas E. Andersson (Stockholm: Axl Books, 2010), 578–600; "Rear Window: Maya Lin and the Vietnam Memorial," *teleSUR*, December 14, 2014, https://www.dailymotion.com/video/x2dt2wl. Originally, the memorial included 57,939 names, but 379 have subsequently been added. On the chronology and diversity of the names, see Sturken, "The Wall, the Screen, and the Image," 127.

48. The monument does not mark the deaths of any Vietnamese soldiers and civilians or deaths of US soldiers from traumas connected to the war that took place after the final ceasefire agreement in 1975. On these omissions see Sturken, "The Wall, the Screen, and the Image," 127.

49. To aid visitors in finding a particular name among the thousands, the Vietnam Veterans Memorial Fund published a key to the names listing them in alphabetical order with their location on the wall marked in *Vietnam Veterans Memorial, Directory of Names* (Washington, DC: Vietnam Veterans Memorial Fund, 1991).

50. Our thanks to Karen Cox for this insight.

51. For images of touch and rubbings, see T. Morrissey, *Between the Lines: Photographs from the National Vietnam Veterans Memorial* (Syracuse, NY: Syracuse University Press, 2000).

52. Anne M. Wagner, "Once Upon a Time: The Vietnam Memorial at Age Twenty-Five," *Threepenny Review* 112 (2008): 19.

53. Elizabeth Wolfson, "The 'Black Gash of Shame'—Revisiting the Vietnam Veterans Memorial Controversy," *Art 21*, March 15, 2017, https://art21.org/read/the-black-gash-of-shame-revisiting-the-vietnam-veterans-memorial-controversy.

54. Wolfson, "Black Gash of Shame."

55. Wolfson, "Black Gash of Shame" and Tom Wolfe, "Art Disputes War: The Battle of the Vietnam Memorial," *Washington Post*, October 13, 1982, https://www.washingtonpost.com/archive/lifestyle/1982/10/13/art-disputes-war-the-battle-of-the-vietnam-memorial/89ef84dc-00d8-42ce-bfa8-318f51ea15c5.

56. Wolfe, "Art Disputes War."

57. Wolfe, "Art Disputes War."

58. Wolfe, "Art Disputes War."

59. The word "mullah" means "chiefly in Turkish-, Persian-, and Urdu-speaking regions: a person who is learned in Islamic theology and law; a Muslim cleric. Frequently as a title." *OED online*, "mullah," accessed June 2021.

60. On masculinist ways of being and Hart's additional figural memorial, see Sturken, "The Wall, the Screen, and the Image," 126–8.

61. *Memorial to Honor Armed Forces, Requirements for Name on Vietnam Veterans Memorial, Memorial to Martin Luther King, Jr., and Center for Vietnam Veterans Memorial: Hearing on S. 268, S. 470, S. 296, S. 1076, before the Subcommittee on National Parks of the Committee on Energy and Natural Resources*, 108th Cong. (June 3, 2003).

62. John Devitt devised a traveling wall that first exhibited in 1984; the Vietnam and All Veterans of Brevard (VVB) formed in 1985 to create a portable replica at three-fifths scale; Pittsburgh University also designed a half-size replica on their campus. For some examples, see http://www.themovingwall.org, http://www.travel-ingwall.us, and https://www.psuvetmemorial.org.

63. For ongoing debates in government concerning space on the mall, the parameters of naming, and demand for an educational center, see *Memorial to Honor Armed Forces, Requirements for Name on Vietnam Veterans Memorial, Memorial to Martin Luther King, Jr., and Center for Vietnam Veterans Memorial: Hearing on S. 268, S. 470, S. 296, S. 1076, before the Subcommittee on National Parks of the Committee on Energy and Natural Resources*, 108th Cong. (June 3, 2003).

64. Although the source interview remains unknown, multiple publications attribute this intention to Maya Lin, the first of which appears to be "America Remembers," *National Geographic Magazine* 167, no. 5 (1985): 571. See also

Sturken, "The Wall, the Screen, and the Image," 127, and Robin Wagner-Pacifici and Barry Schwartz, "The Vietnam Veterans Memorial: Commemorating a Difficult Past," *American Journal of Sociology* 97, no. 2 (1991): 406.

65. Alice Oswald, *Memorial: A Version of Homer's Iliad* with an afterword by Eavan Boland (New York: W. W. Norton & Company, 2013), ix. Thank you to Athena Kirk for directing us to this poem. Our focus is on its first section—the list of names. The second produces biographies for each name, while the third translates similes from the ancient Greek.

66. Oswald writes that her text "is a translation of the *Iliad*'s atmosphere, not its story" (Oswald, *Memorial*, ix). In the book's afterword, Eavan Boland claims translation as an important site of contemporary poetics: "Of all the conversations that have sustained poetry in the last half century, few are as rich or exciting as the one about poetic translation. Memorial enters this conversation at a steep angle, sparking fresh insight and questions." Eavan Boland, Afterword to Oswald, *Memorial*, 87–8.

67. Oswald, *Memorial*, x and 1.

68. Carolin Hahnemann also notes the comparison between Lin and Oswald, connecting it to equalizing the dead: "Abandoning the epic's narrative focus on a handful of heroes, she gives equal treatment to all the dead, blurring social distinctions, and in many cases even rendering it impossible for the reader to tell which side a man was fighting on." Carolin Hahnemann, "Feminist at Second Glance? Alice Oswald's *Memorial* as a Response to Homer's *Iliad*," in *Homer's Daughters: Women's Responses to Homer in the Twentieth Century and Beyond*, ed. Fiona Cox and Elena Theodorakopoulos (Oxford: Oxford University Press, 2019), 90–1. See also Carolin Hahnemann, "Book of Paper, Book of Stone: An Exploration of Alice Oswald's *Memorial*," *Arion* 22, no. 1 (2014): 1–32, for an exploration of Oswald that also discusses Lin and the Athenian casualty lists.

69. Oswald, *Memorial*, x.

70. An example of a variation of this is Layli Long Soldier's "38" from *WHEREAS* (Minneapolis, MN: Graywolf Press, 2017), in which Soldier writes about the way the rules of language and grammar walk lines between clarity and obfuscation in order to also write about the murder of 38 Dakota men by the US government in 1862. The speaker and the reader encounter this murder as too horrifying to conceptualize with clarity except, perhaps, through the clarity of the poem itself.

71. The poem was later included in Split This Rock's *The Quarry: A Social Justice Poetry Database*, https://www.splitthisrock.org/poetry-database, accessed February 18, 2021 and reprinted on Poets.org. For the circumstances of its initial writing, see Carey Reed, "'There Still Is a Lot Stacked against Us': Ferguson Inspires Year of Art," *PBS Arts*, August 9, 2015, https://www.pbs.org/newshour/arts/still-lot -stacked-us-ferguson-inspires-year-art, accessed February 18, 2021.

72. Smith, *Don't Call Us Dead*, 67. Credit: Danez Smith, excerpts from "not an elegy" from *Don't Call Us Dead*. Copyright © 2017 by Danez Smith. Reprinted with the permission of The Permissions Company, LLC on behalf of Graywolf Press, Minneapolis, Minnesota, graywolfpress.org.

73. Smith, *Don't Call Us Dead*, 68.

74. See, for example, the crowd-sourced syllabus assembled by Marcia Chatelain, professor of history and African American studies at Georgetown University: "How to Teach Kids about What's Happening in Ferguson: A Crowdsourced Syllabus about Race, African American History, Civil Rights, and Policing," *The Atlantic*, August 25, 2014, https://www.theatlantic.com/education/archive/2014/08/how-to-teach-kids -about-whats-happening-in-ferguson/379049.

75. For a haunting additional example of this, see Michael Leong's research on the publication history of page 134 of Claudia Rankine's *Citizen*, on which Rankine records an ever-growing list of memorials of Black lives cut short by police violence. The first printing included one name, the eighth printing included nine names, the nineteenth printing included twenty-six names, and the project tragically continues. Michael Leong, *Contested Records: The Turn to Documents in Contemporary North American Poetry* (Iowa City: University of Iowa Press, 2020), 153–8.

76. In Philip's words: "You take these hard facts, this desiccated fact situation of Gregson v. Gilbert—and you reintroduce those emotions and feelings that were removed." Quoted in Saunders, "Defending the Dead," 66.

77. M. NourbeSe Philip, *Zong!* (Middleton, CT: Weslyan University Press, 2008), 200.

78. As cofounder of the Black Lives Matter movement, Alicia Garza, names in an interview with Keeyanga-Yamahtta Taylor, white feminism's ambivalence about capitalism means that it has not always embraced other movements like anticapitalism (nor has Marxism always embraced feminism), producing deep limitations. Guided by Black feminist thought, we believe that only through partnership with other movements can feminism push us toward deeper systems of justice. Keeyanga-Yamahtta Taylor, "Alicia Garza," in *How We Get Free*, ed. Keeyanga-Yamahtta Taylor, 121–2. On the background to and development of the Black Lives Matter movement, see also Keeanga-Yamahtta Taylor, *From #BlackLivesMatter to Black Liberation* (Chicago, IL: Haymarket Books, 2016), especially 153–220.

79. Meilani Clay, "Response to Philip" (unpublished manuscript, last modified November 20, 2020, typescript).

80. See, for example, Kate Siklosi, "'The Absolute/of Water': The Submarine Poetic of M. NourbeSe Philip's *Zong!*," *Canadian Literature* no. 228/229 (Spring/ Summer 2016): 111–30 and Anne Quema, "M. NourbeSe Philip's *Zong!*: Metaphors, Laws, and Fugues of Justice," *Journal of Law and Society* 43, no. 1 (2016): 85–104.

81. Leong, *Contested Records*, 144 and 152.

82. Jessica Marie Johnson, *Wicked Flesh: Black Women, Intimacy, and Freedom in the Atlantic World* (Philadelphia: University of Pennsylvania Press, 2020), 134–5.

83. Hartman continues: "This double gesture can be described as straining against the limits of the archive to write a cultural history of the captive, and, at the same time, enacting the impossibility of representing the lives of the captives precisely through the process of narration." Hartman, "Venus in Two Acts," 11.

84. Philip explains that "The Africans on board the *Zong* must be named. They will be ghostly footnotes floating below the text—'underwater . . . a place of consequence.'" Philip, *Zong!*, 200.

85. Philip, *Zong!*, 173.

86. Marta Figlerowicz and Matylda Figlerowicz, "Multilingual Style," *Textual Practice* 35, no. 6 (2021): 1015–16.

87. As Patricia Saunders explains: "Black subjects have always had to view the Law suspiciously because they were always already situated outside of the law (as property, nonhuman, chattel). But the paradox is that there is no 'outside of the law,' since it frames the social and political structures in which we exist in order to make sense of [the fact] that you have to explode it from inside, and connect it to its origins, its buried pasts." Saunders, "Defending the Dead," 67.

88. Although the deaths of more than 130 people are felt on every page, the one historically known case of the *Zong* stands in for the many other slave ships and the ongoing trauma of the transatlantic slave trade more generally.

89. McKittrick, "Mathematics Black Life," 17.

90. As mentioned earlier in this chapter, the feminist list works against this history to recover listing practices as a mode of protest. Such recovery might well enact such a seismic shift. And yet, as the appropriation of such lists by institutions and corporations makes clear, what those writing and chanting intend as recovery could end up as mere reification.

91. Christina Sharpe, *In the Wake: On Blackness and Being* (Durham, NC: Duke University Press, 2018), 19; 35–41.

92. For a deeper exploration of the misunderstanding of this whiteness, see Stager, "Unbearable Whiteness."

93. Paul Watkins, "We Can Never Tell the Entire Story of Slavery: In Conversation with M. NourbeSe Philip," *Toronto Review of Books*, April 30, 2014, https://torontoreviewofbooks.com/2014/04/in-conversation-with-m-nourbese-philip.

94. Philip explains that "in the case of the *Zong*, the log book was lost, so from the beginning there were lacunae in the story, in the text, which becomes a metaphor for what I am talking about the impossibility of telling the entire story, and the problematic about the desire to do so." The one section of the book that Philip says cannot be read out loud is the very final palimpsest section in which words disappear into silence, suggesting once again the challenges inherent in representing silence (or blank space) in various media. Watkins, "We Can Never Tell the Entire Story."

95. Lucina Melesio, "Case of 43 Ayotzinapa Missing Students Unresolved Five Years On," *Al Jazeera*, September 26, 2019, https://www.aljazeera.com/features/2019/9/26/case-of-43-ayotzinapa-missing-students-unresolved-five-years-on.

96. On the practice of painting portraits from death masks, see Aby Warburg, *The Renewal of Pagan Antiquity* (Los Angeles: Getty Research Institute, 1999): 218.

97. "'Un jour, j'ai vu le soleil se coucher quarante-trois fois!' Et un peu plus tard tu ajoutais: 'Tu sais . . . quand on est tellement triste on aime les couchers de soleil . . .' 'Le jour des quarante-trois fois tu étais donc tellement triste?' Mais le petit prince ne répondit pas." Notably, while the French text has *quarante-trois*, the first English translator of the book, Katherine Woods, changed this number to forty-four, perhaps to recognize the age at which Saint-Exupéry died—but this choice erased the author's intention. Antoine de Saint-Exupéry, *The Little Prince*, trans. Katherine Woods (New York: Reynal & Hitchcock, 1943), 25. Ultimately, Woods's change seems to have been reabsorbed by subsequent French versions, such as the Gallimard edition

of 1999, which has her *quarante-quatre*. Antoine de Saint-Exupéry, *Le petit prince* (Paris: Gallimard 1999 [1945]), 29.

98. Kimberlé Crenshaw, "The Urgency of Intersectionality," *TEDWomen*, November 14, 2016, https://www.ted.com/talks/kimberle_crenshaw_the_urgency_of_intersectionality?language=en.

99. Describing what happens when she performs her work *Zong!*, M. NourbeSe Philip argues that "the bones of the undead *can* find a resting place within us. Each time I perform *Zong!*, it manifests as Ceremony. Drawing on the brilliant essay by the Caribbean novelist, George Lamming, on the Ceremony of the Dead he witnessed in Haiti, I would agree with him that there is a sense in which the living and the dead share an interest in the future, albeit in different ways." Watkins, "We Can Never Tell the Entire Story."

100. On multimedia artistic interventions as a means of protesting the Robert E. Lee statue in Richmond, see Ezra Marcus, "Will the Last Confederate Statue Standing Turn Off the Lights?" *New York Times*, June 23, 2020, https://www.nytimes.com/2020/06/23/style/statue-richmond-lee.html.

Figure 7.1   Lead Soloist De-Rance Blaylock Sings "I'm Covered" in Antigone in Ferguson. Photo credit: Gregg Richards, Courtesy Theater of War Productions.

Epilogue

This project emerged out of friendship and shared feminist commitments and was catalyzed by the collapse of time and space in the global pandemic, a collapse that brought many people "virtually close" (with all the attendant caveats about just what sort of closeness—partial, disorienting—we were experiencing). Such closeness had ramifications beyond any individual collaboration; one example of the shifting landscapes of pandemic closeness emerged as teachers and performers learned to navigate different ways of staying connected, creating new opportunities to create and share virtual performances. Among the in-person performances pivoting to virtual spaces was a series of collaborative plays produced by the organization Theater of War, which pairs a table read of a play—often an ancient Greek tragedy—with a facilitated discussion about themes of trauma that emerge from it.[1] These readthroughs connect experienced and often famous actors with community members and amateur singers and performers.

On August 9, 2020, the sixth anniversary of Michael Brown's murder in Ferguson, Missouri, Theater of War hosted a virtual performance of *Antigone in Ferguson* (which had previously been performed in person), joining together readings from Sophocles's play *Antigone* with choral song (Figure 7.1).[2] The play centers around a teenage girl, Antigone, who is committed to burying her brother despite the new king, her uncle, having outlawed these funeral rights. Feminists of many generations have embraced Antigone for this determination. Her fierce defiance of the restrictions she faces makes her a public feminist icon, exemplifying resistance.[3] The virtual performance of her story was introduced by Congresswoman Cori Bush and interwove commentary on the performance by family members who had lost children to police violence and who perhaps occupied some part of Antigone's subject position.

Speaking of herself and fellow "mothers of the movement" during the performance, Gary Hopkins Jr.'s mother, Marion Gray-Hopkins, said: "Antigone was very much like us. . . . We are standing strong and we're not backing down regardless."[4] These mothers and other activists identified with Antigone's commitment to caring for the body of her dead brother (and, through that care, his afterlife and memory) as well as with her strength in the face of institutionalized patriarchal power (represented by her uncle King Creon of Thebes) even at the expense of her own life. Antigone's lament, much like our own, has power beyond grief not only to mourn the dead but also to demand political change.

Writing of the practice of lament as encompassing both mourning and justice seeking even in the twofold definition of the verb "to grieve," Bonnie Honig argues that

> grieving in the double sense of that term, lamenting her losses but also litigating a wrong, Antigone's dirge moves beyond the courtroom of grievance and the sentimentalism of grief to seek out publics that Creon aims to repress and marginalize on behalf of his own view of public order. She may yet inaugurate new publics still.[5]

This analysis highlights what makes Antigone a particularly apt model for public feminism—she acts in public against the institutionally held power of her uncle in order to right what she considers wrong. During the performance, in virtual connection with Antigone, the audience joins her in inaugurating new orders figured as new publics.

In addition to the power Antigone marshals, she also grieves her loss. Theater of War writer and director Bryan Doerries has described the way Antigone's inability to bury her brother's body defers her grief—an experience to which many in the show's audience may relate. Tragic performances streamed live for audiences of fellow citizens afford those audiences access not only to the shared themes of the tragedy but also to a shared space to grieve. In bringing *Antigone in Ferguson* into our collective living rooms and inviting each audience member into the tragedy's chorus, this performance and its metacommentary by mothers and relatives of the movement shares deferred grief over the growing list of primarily Black men and women murdered by police violence.

While the operation of catharsis intended to frame the experience of Greek tragedy feels insufficient in the face of the lived experience of lost loved ones, the coming together of differently affected communities to join in witnessing performance events like *Antigone* gives some idea of what the future might hold in terms of virtual community. As a practice of mourning, catharsis feels safe: one can walk away unscathed. But becoming virtually close may implicate participants more directly—and may even allow them to be more chorus than audience.[6] Perhaps this dynamic provides a glimpse of how to bring disparate communities together in the future, even if only for a moment.

The same phenomenon of being virtually close has made possible the book you are now reading. The condition that, in some ways, prompted the inception of this book—that its two collaborators found themselves suddenly equally as close to each other as to their neighbors despite being geographically separated—is also the condition of public feminism in the twenty-first century. More and more, internet-based technologies are connecting people around the globe through shared experiences, shared disclosures, shared mourning, and shared accomplishments. Public feminist tools can bring communities together, even when disparate. They can shape the archive. They can separate the personal from the public. They can resurface women and nonbinary people's experiences from patriarchal systems and give them the tools and motivation to come together to cite allies whose voices deserve amplification. They can highlight the connections that bind us all. They can memorialize the dead, naming and remembering each. And they can, through our increasingly networked world, bring individuals virtually close. But these connections are underwritten by history. To fully explore the potential being equally close has for public feminism, we also need another look at the past from a feminist perspective.

The second half of our book attempted to investigate the idea of an "outside" of the systems and -isms we live within. While the very notion may be an ideal, practices like those of feminist citation suggest straightforward ways we might get closer to imagining it. In the largest sense, by seeking an outside, public feminists work toward a dissolution of the very containment that an inside/outside binary upholds.

From the community captured by Sappho's fragments to the power of contemporary global hashtags, public feminists have confronted and resisted oppressive structures for millennia, and their projects continue today. They demand in the present work that reforms the future even as they honor what has come before. They draw power from communities and networks yet remember and return focus to the individual. They claim agency and work toward change, straddling real and virtual spaces to lift a panoply of voices. While the future, as always, presents us with the unimaginable, the ideas and debates of public feminism push us onward.

NOTES

1. Theater of War Productions, "Theater of War," https://theaterofwar.com/projects/theater-of-war, accessed January 24, 2021.

2. Theater of War Productions, "Antigone in Ferguson: Online Premiere," https://youtu.be/Z6v5KpKqv6I, accessed August 9, 2020.

3. See, for example, S. E. Wilmer and Audrone Zukauskaite, eds., *Interrogating Antigone in Postmodern Philosophy and Criticism* (Oxford: Oxford University Press, 2010), and Fanny Söderbäck, *Feminist Readings of Antigone* (Albany: State University of New York Press, 2010). Other critics have resisted this notion; for example, Judith Butler endeavors to distance Antigone from feminist politics. Judith Butler, *Antigone's Claim: Kinship between Life and Death* (New York: Columbia University Press, 2000), 2–3.

4. Marion Gray-Hopkins, "Antigone in Ferguson: Online Premiere," https://youtu.be/Z6v5KpKqv6I, accessed August 9, 2020, 1:37–1:45.

5. Bonnie Honig, *Antigone, Interrupted* (Cambridge: Cambridge University Press, 2013), 120.

6. Perhaps *Antigone in Ferguson* forges this connection for its virtually close audience through a mechanism of shared grief; in a different context, Nafeesah Goldsmith theorizes the draw of Greek tragedy for those who have experienced deep loss as "pain recognizes pain." Nafeesah Goldsmith and Emily Allen-Hornblower presented "The Hurts of the Past, the Wounds of the Present: Reading the Classics to Elucidate Mass Incarceration" (talk at the Classics Department at Johns Hopkins University, Baltimore, MD, November 11, 2021).

Bibliography

12 Women Scholars. "A Disturbing Pattern." *Inside Higher Ed*, August 27, 2021. https://www.insidehighered.com/advice/2021/08/27/entrenched-inequity-not-appropriately-citing-scholarship-women-and-people-color.

Abad-Santos, Alexander. "How the Bro Became White." *The Atlantic*, October 9, 2013. https://www.theatlantic.com/culture/archive/2013/10/how-encino-man-changed-race-bros/310146.

Abernathy, Penelope. "The Loss of Local News: What It Means for Communities." *Expanding News Desert*, November 8, 2020. https://www.usnewsdeserts.com/reports/expanding-news-desert/loss-of-local-news.

"About Us." *Orpheus*, April 13, 2021. https://orpheusnyc.org/about/about-us.

"ACT UP: A History of AIDS/HIV Activism." Interview on "It's Been a Minute with Sam Sanders." *NPR*, June 18, 2021. https://www.npr.org/2021/06/16/1007361916/act-up-a-history-of-aids-hiv-activism.

African American Policy Forum. "#SayHerName Campaign." https://aapf.org/sayhername. Accessed February 1, 2021.

Ahmed, Sara. *Living a Feminist Life*. Durham, NC: Duke University Press, 2017.

Allen, Esther, and Susan Bernofsky, eds. *In Translation: Translators on Their Work and What It Means*. New York: Columbia University Press, 2013.

"America Remembers." *National Geographic Magazine* 167, no. 5 (1985): 552–73.

Anderson, Benedict. *Imagined Communities: Reflections on the Origin and Spread of Nationalism*. Rev. ed. London: Verso, 2006.

Anti-Eviction Mapping Project. *Counterpoints: A San Francisco Bay Area Atlas of Displacement and Resistance*. Oakland, CA: PM Press, 2021.

Appiah, Kwame Anthony. "Mistaken Identities." "The Reith Lectures." *BBC*, November 8, 2016. https://www.bbc.co.uk/sounds/play/b081lkkj.

Appiah, Kwame Anthony. "There Is No Such Thing as Western Civilization." *The Guardian*, November 9, 2016. https://www.theguardian.com/world/2016/nov/09/western-civilisation-appiah-reith-lecture.

Ardam, Jacquelyn. *Avidly Reads Poetry*. New York: NYU Press, 2021.

Ardam, Jacquelyn (@jaxwendy). "It Turns Out That Yes, I *Will* Be Entering Into Some Light Generational Culture Wars in My Book, and I Have Decided to Define Myself (Born in 1982)...." *Twitter*, June 12, 2021, 5:27 p.m. https://twitter.com/jaxwendy/status/1403871510247268353.

Arendt, Hannah, ed. *Illuminations*. Translated by Harry Zohn. New York: Harcourt Brace Jovanovich, 1968.

"Arkansas Governor OKs Ban on Local, State Mask Mandates." *Associated Press News*, April 29, 2021. https://apnews.com/article/arkansas-coronavirus -government-and-politics-health-95afbfae283a1105b7ab96d9c14eb9ff.

Arreola, Cristina (@C_Arreola). "I Love Masks. I Can't Believe I Let Y'all Just Breathe on Me Before." *Twitter*, August 4, 2020, 6:24 p.m. https://twitter.com/c _arreola/status/1290820843233259522.

Arriaza Ibarra, Karen. "Global Perspectives on the #MeToo Movement: From 'Big Noise' to 'Discrete Oblivion?'" *Interactions: Studies in Communication and Culture* 10, no. 3 (2019): 153–8.

Arrington, Nathan T. *Ashes, Images, and Memories: The Presence of the War Dead in Fifth-Century Athens*. New York: Oxford University Press, 2014.

Atir, Stav, and Melissa J. Ferguson. "How Gender Determines the Way We Speak about Professionals." *Proceedings of the National Academy of Sciences of the United States of America* 115, no. 28 (2018): 7278–83. https://doi.org/10.1073/pnas.1805284115.

Austin, J. L. *How to Do Things with Words*. Edited by J. O. Urmson and Marina Sbisà. Cambridge, MA: Harvard University Press, 1975.

Autry, La Tanya S., and Mike Murawski. "Museums are Not Neutral." https://www .museumsarenotneutral.com.

Axarlis, Nikos. "Plague Victims Found: Mass Burial in Athens." *Archaeology*, April 15, 1998. https://archive.archaeology.org/online/news/kerameikos.html.

Bao, Jessica. "Emily Wilson: Not the First Woman to Translate the *Odyssey*." *34th Street*, October 22, 2019. https://www.34st.com/article/2019/10/emily-wilson -penn-classical-studies-translation-the-odyssey-macarthur-foundation-genius -grant-fellowship.

Barchiesi, Alessandro. *Homeric Effects in Vergil's Narrative*. Oxford: Princeton University Press, 2015.

Bareis, J. Alexander, and Lene Nordrum. *How to Make Believe: The Fictional Truths of the Representational Arts*. Berlin: De Gruyter, 2015.

Barker, Sheila. "The First Biography of Artemisia Gentileschi: Self-Fashioning and Proto-Feminist Art History in Cristofano Bronzini's Notes on Women Artists." *Mitteilungen des Kunsthistorischen Institutes in Florenz* 60, no. 3 (2018): 404–35.

Barker, Sheila. "The Muse of History: Artemisia Gentileschi's First Four Centuries of Immortal Fame." In *Artemisia*, edited by Laetitia Treves and Sheila Barker, 62–73. London: National Gallery Company, 2020.

Bartsch, Shadi. "Introduction to the Poem." In Vergil, *Aeneid*, translated by Shadi Bartsch, xv–xlviii. New York: Random House, 2021.

Bartsch, Shadi. "Translator's Note." In Vergil, *Aeneid*, translated by Shadi Bartsch, xlix–lviii. New York: Random House, 2021.

Beard, Mary. *Women and Power: A Manifesto*. New York: W. W. Norton & Company, 2017.

Benjamin, Walter. "The Task of the Translator." In *Illuminations*, edited by Hannah Arendt, translated by Harry Zohn, 69–82. New York: Harcourt Brace Jovanovich, 1968.

Bennett, Jane. *Vibrant Matter: A Political Ecology of Things*. Durham, NC: Duke University Press, 2010.

Berger, Matt. "Why the Black Lives Matter Protests Didn't Contribute to the COVID-19 Surge." *Healthline*, July 8, 2020. https://www.healthline.com/health-news/black-lives-matter-protests-didnt-contribute-to-covid19-surge.

Berman, Antoine. *The Age of Translation: A Commentary on Walter Benjamin's "The Task of the Translator" = L'âge de la traduction: la tâche du traducteur de Walter Benjamin, un commentaire*. Translated and with an introduction by Chantal Wright. Abingdon: Routledge, 2018.

Biow, Douglas. *Vasari's Words: The Lives of the Artists as a History of Ideas in the Italian Renaissance*. Cambridge: Cambridge University Press, 2018.

Birchler Emery, Patrizia. "De la nourrice à la dame de compagnie: le cas de la *trophos* en Grèce antique." *Paedagogica Historica* 46, no. 6 (2010): 751–61.

Bissell, R. Ward. "Artemisia Gentileschi: A New Documented Chronology." *Art Bulletin* 50, no. 2 (1968): 153–68.

Blank, Hanne. *Unruly Appetites: Erotic Stories*. Berkeley: Seal Press, 2002.

Boccaccio, Giovanni. *Famous Women*. Edited and translated by Virginia Brown. Cambridge, MA: Harvard University Press, 2001.

Boland, Eavan. *Afterword to Alice Oswald, Memorial: A Version of Homer's Iliad*. New York: W. W. Norton & Company, 2013.

Bond, Sarah (@SarahEBond). "Not All of Sappho Comes to Us from Papyri." *Twitter*, August 28, 2021, 8:08 a.m. https://twitter.com/SarahEBond/status/1431589417194504193.

Bonfante, Larissa. "Nursing Mothers in Classical Art." In *Naked Truths: Women, Sexuality, and Gender in Classical Art and Archaeology*, edited by A. Koloski-Ostrow and C. Lyons, 174–7. London: Routledge, 2000.

Brahinsky, Rachel. "The Story of Property: Meditations on Gentrification, Renaming, and Possibility." *EPA: Economy and Space* 52, no. 5 (January 5, 2020). https://doi.org/10.1177/0308518X19895787.

Brahinsky, Rachel. "Tell Him I'm Gone: On the Margins in High-Tech City." In *A Political Companion to James Baldwin*, edited by Susan McWilliams, 373–98. Lexington: University Press of Kentucky, 2017.

Brara, Noor. "Author Roxane Gay, Who Loves Art but Dislikes the Art World, Has Some Advice for Galleries: 'Stop Being Terrible.'" *Art Net News*, April 12, 2021. https://news.artnet.com/art-world/roxane-gay-collecting-interview-1958221.

Breen, Margaret Sönser. *Gender, Sex, and Sexuality*. Ipswich, MA: Salem Press, 2014.

Brennan, Summer. *The Parisian Sphinx: A True Story of Art and Obsession*. Boston, MA: Mariner Books, 2022.

Brier, Bob. "Saga of Cleopatra's Needles." *Archaeology* 55, no. 6 (2002): 48–54.

Brine, Kevin. "The Judith Project." In *The Sword of Judith: Judith Studies across the Disciplines*, edited by Kevin R. Brine, Elena Ciletti, and Henrike Lähnemann, 3–21. Cambridge: OpenBook Publishers, 2010.

Brinkman, Bartholomew. "Making Modern 'Poetry': Format, Genre, and the Invention of Imagism(e)." *Journal of Modern Literature* 32, no. 2 (2009): 20–40.

Brinkmann, Vinzenz, Renée Dreyfus, and Ulrike Koch-Brinkmann, eds. *Gods in Color: Polychromy in the Ancient World*. San Francisco: Fine Arts Museums of San Francisco, Legion of Honor, 2017. https://buntegoetter.liebieghaus.de/en.

Broude, Norma, Mary D. Garrard, Thalia Gouma-Peterson, and Patricia Mathews. "An Exchange on the Feminist Critique of Art History." *Art Bulletin* 71, no. 1 (1989): 124–7.

Brown, Bill. "Thing Theory." *Critical Inquiry* 28, no. 1 (2001): 1–22.

Brown, Theresa. "An Unflinching Exploration of Trauma and Obesity." *American Journal of Nursing* 118, no. 6 (2018): 67.

Bryson, Valerie. *The Futures of Feminism*. Manchester: Manchester University Press, 2021.

Buchanan, Larry, Quoctrung Bui, and Jugal K. Patel. "Black Lives Matter May Be the Largest Movement in U.S. History." *New York Times*, July 3, 2020. https://www.nytimes.com/interactive/2020/07/03/us/george-floyd-protests-crowd-size.html.

Buncome, Andrew. "Trump Is the Biggest Threat to Press Freedom in U.S. in My Lifetime, Says Dan Rather." *The Independent*, October 6, 2020. https://www.independent.co.uk/news/world/americas/us-politics/dan-rather-interview-trump-press-freedom-fake-news-journalism-60-minutes-cbs-b811406.html.

Burchard, L., and Nationaal Centrum voor de Plastische Kunsten van de XVIde en XVII de Eeuw, eds. *Corpus Rubenianum Ludwig Burchard: An Illustrated Catalogue Raisonné of the Work of Peter Paul Rubens Based on the Material Assembled by the Late Dr. Ludwig Burchard in Twenty-Six Parts*. London: Phaidon, 1968.

Burke, Tarana. *Unbound: My Story of Liberation and the Birth of the Me Too Movement*. New York: Flatiron Books, 2021.

Butler, Judith. *Antigone's Claim: Kinship between Life and Death*. New York: Columbia University Press, 2000.

Butler, Judith. *Gender Trouble*. New York: Routledge, 1990.

Butterworth, Jo, and Liesbeth Wildschut, eds. *Contemporary Choreography: A Critical Reader*. 2nd ed. Milton Park: Routledge, 2018.

Calame, Claude. "Choral Polyphony and Ritual Functions of Tragic Songs." In *Choral Mediations in Greek Tragedy*, edited by Renaud Gagné and Marianne Govers Hopman, 35–57. New York: Cambridge University Press, 2013.

Calhoun, Adam J. "Punctuation in Novels." *Medium*, February 15, 2016. https://medium.com/@neuroecology/punctuation-in-novels-8f316d542ec4.

Canfora, Luciano. *Il papiro di Dongo*. Milan: Adelphi edizioni, 2005.

Caplan, Allison. Introduction to and translation of "Blowers of Sun-Excrement: Nahua Lost-Wax Gold Casting in the Florentine Codex Book 9, Chapter 16." *West 86th: A Journal of Decorative Arts, Design History, and Material Culture* 28, no. 2 (2022): 215–231.

Carson, Anne. *If Not, Winter: Fragments of Sappho*. New York: Alfred A. Knopf, 2002.

Carson, Tiffany L. "Heavy Hunger: Managing Weight and Obesity in Black American Communities." *JAMA: The Journal of the American Medical Association* 322, no. 16 (2019): 1534–6.

Cast, David, ed. *The Ashgate Research Companion to Giorgio Vasari*. Burlington, VT: Ashgate, 2014.

Castro, Olga, and Emek Ergun, eds. *Feminist Translation Studies: Local and Transnational Perspectives*. New York: Routledge, 2017.

Castronuovo, Celine. "Amanda Gorman Captures National Interest After Inauguration Performance." *The Hill*, January 21, 2021. https://thehill.com/homenews/news/535325-amanda-gorman-captures-national-interest-after-inauguration-performance.

Chae, Yung In. "Women Who Weave." *Eidolon*, November 16, 2017. https://eidolon.pub/women-who-weave-c3a8dd322447.

Chatelain, Marcia. "How to Teach Kids about What's Happening in Ferguson: A Crowdsourced Syllabus about Race, African American History, Civil Rights, and Policing." *The Atlantic*, August 25, 2014. https://www.theatlantic.com/education/archive/2014/08/how-to-teach-kids-about-whats-happening-in-ferguson/379049.

Chiasson, Dan. "The Classics Scholar Quietly Redefining What Twitter Can Do." *New Yorker*, March 19, 2018. https://www.newyorker.com/culture/rabbit-holes/the-classics-scholar-redefining-what-twitter-can-do.

Chilvers, Ian. "Venus of Willendorf." In *The Oxford Dictionary of Art*. 3rd ed. Oxford: Oxford University Press, 2004.

Cho, Sumi, Kimberlé Crenshaw, and Leslie McCall. "Toward a Field of Intersectionality Studies: Theory, Applications, and Praxis." *Signs* 38, no. 4 (2013): 785–810.

Choma, Russ. "Sunday's Heart-Wrenching New York Times Cover Marks Almost 100,000 Coronavirus Deaths in the U.S." *Mother Jones*, May 24, 2020. https://www.motherjones.com/politics/2020/05/new-york-times-cover-sunday-coronavirus-death-toll-memorial.

Chotiner, Isaac. "A Black Lives Matter Co-Founder Explains Why This Time Is Different." *New Yorker*, June 3, 2020. https://www.newyorker.com/news/q-and-a/a-black-lives-matter-co-founder-explains-why-this-time-is-different.

Christian, Barbara. "The Race for Theory." *Feminist Studies* 14, no. 1 (1988): 67–79.

Christiansen, Keith. "Becoming Artemisia: Afterthoughts on the Gentileschi Exhibition." *Metropolitan Museum Journal* 39 (2004): 101–26.

Christiansen, Keith, and Judith Walker Mann, eds. *Orazio and Artemisia Gentileschi*. New York: Metropolitan Museum of Art, 2001. Exhibition catalog.

Ciletti, Elena, and Henrike Lähnemann. "Judith in the Christian Tradition." In *The Sword of Judith: Judith Studies across the Disciplines*, edited by Kevin R. Brine, Elena Ciletti, and Henrike Lähnemann, 41–66. Cambridge: OpenBook Publishers, 2010.

"Cite Black Women." *Cite Black Women Collective*, April 12, 2021. https://www.citeblackwomencollective.org.

Cixous, Hélène. *Homère est morte*. Paris: Éditions Galilée, 2014.

Cixous, Hélène. "The Laugh of the Medusa." Translated by Keith Cohen and Paula Cohen. *Signs* 1, no. 4 (1976): 875–93.

Cixous, Hélène. *Mother Homer is Dead.* Translated by Peggy Kamuf. Edinburgh: Edinburgh University Press, 2018.

Clay, Meilani. "Response to Philip." Unpublished manuscript, last modified November 20, 2020. Typescript.

Coates, Ta-Nehisi. *Between the World and Me.* New York: Random House Publishing Group, 2015.

Coates, Ta-Nehisi. "The First White President: The Foundation of Donald Trump's Presidency Is the Negation of Barack Obama's Legacy." *The Atlantic,* October 2017. https://www.theatlantic.com/magazine/archive/2017/10/the-first-white -president-ta-nehisi-coates/537909.

Cohen, Elizabeth S. "The Trials of Artemisia Gentileschi: A Rape as History." *Sixteenth Century Journal* 31, no. 1 (2000): 47–75.

Cohen, Jeffrey Jerome, ed. *Monster Theory: Reading Culture.* Minneapolis: University of Minnesota Press, 1996.

Colburn, Cynthia S., and Ella Gonzalez. "The Complex Biographies of Ancient Political Sculptures and their Relevance Today." Paper presented at the annual meeting of the Archaeological Institute of America, online, January 2021.

Colburn, Cynthia S., Ellen C. Caldwell, and Ella J. Gonzalez, eds. *Gender Violence, Art, and the Viewer: An Intervention.* University Park: Pennsylvania State University Press, forthcoming.

Coleman, Nancy. "On the Front Page, a Wall of Grief." *Times Insider,* February 21, 2021. https://www.nytimes.com/2021/02/21/insider/covid-500k-front-page.html.

Collins, Patricia Hill. "The Social Construction of Black Feminist Thought." *Signs* 14, no. 4 (1989): 745–73.

"Commitment to Distributed Leadership." *Bridge Project,* April 13, 2021. https:// www.bridgeproject.art/distributed-leadership.

"Company." *Hope Mohr Dance.* https://www.hopemohr.org/company. Accessed May 1, 2021.

"Conversation with the Taxman about Poetry by Vladimir Mayakovsky, 1926, Translated from the Russian by James Womack." *Rakish Light,* July 2020. http:// rakishlight.com/projects.

Cook, Jill. *Ice Age Art: The Arrival of the Modern Mind.* London: British Museum Press, 2013.

Cooney, Kara. *The Woman Who Would Be King.* New York: Crown, 2014.

Cranston, Jodi. *The Muddied Mirror: Materiality and Figuration in Titian's Later Paintings.* University Park: Pennsylvania State University Press, 2010.

Craven, Christa. "Teaching Antiracist Citational Politics as a Project of Transformation: Lessons from the Cite Black Women Movement for White Feminist Anthropologists." *Feminist Anthropology* 2, no. 1 (2021): 120–9.

Crenshaw, Kimberlé. "Demarginalizing the Intersection of Race and Sex: A Black Feminist Critique of Antidiscrimination Doctrine, Feminist Theory, and Antiracist Politics." *University of Chicago Legal Forum* no. 1 (1989): 139–67.

Crenshaw, Kimberlé. "Mapping the Margins: Intersectionality, Identity Politics, and Violence against Women of Color." *Stanford Law Review* 43, no. 6 (1991): 1241–99.

Crenshaw, Kimberlé. "The Urgency of Intersectionality." *TEDWomen*, November 14, 2016. https://www.ted.com/talks/kimberle_crenshaw_the_urgency_of _intersectionality.

Cropper, Elizabeth. "New Documents for Artemisia Gentileschi's Life in Florence." *Burlington Magazine* 135, no. 1088 (1993): 760–1.

Crowley, Patrick R. "Crystalline Aesthetics and the Classical Concept of the Medium." *West 86th: A Journal of Decorative Arts, Design History, and Material Culture* 23, no. 2 (Fall–Winter 2016): 237–45.

Culler, Jonathan. *Theory of the Lyric*. Cambridge, MA: Harvard University Press, 2015.

"Cultural Studies: Here, Let Me Explain Mansplaining (and Rebecca Solnit) to You." *National Post*, May 10, 2014. https://nationalpost.com/life/cultural-studies-here-let -me-explain-mansplaining-and-rebecca-solnit-to-you.

Curto, Justin. "K-Pop Stans Continue to Run the Internet, Flood Racist Twitter Hashtags." *Vulture*, June 3, 2020. https://www.vulture.com/2020/06/kpop-stans -fancams-racist-hashtags-twitter.html.

Dacier, Anne Le Fèvre. *L'Illiade d'Homère*. Paris: Chez Rigaud, 1711.

Daly, Ian. "You Call That Poetry?! How Seven Letters Managed to Freak Out an Entire Nation." *Poetry Foundation*, August 25, 2007. https://www.poetryfoundation.org/ articles/68913/you-call-that-poetry.

Daniels, J. Yolande. "Exhibit A: Private Life without a Narrative." In *Black Venus 2010: They Called Her "Hottentot,"* edited by Deborah Willis, 62–7. Philadelphia: Temple University Press, 2010.

Dawson, Aimee. "Facebook Censors Famous 30,000-year-old Nude Statue as Pornographic." *Art Newspaper*, February 27, 2018. https://www.theartnewspaper .com/news/facebook-censors-famous-30-000-year-old-nude-statue-as -pornographic.

de León, Concepción. "'It Will Always Be a Part of My Life': Chanel Miller Is Ready to Talk." *New York Times*, September 22, 2019. https://www.nytimes.com/2019/09 /22/books/chanel-miller-know-my-name-emily-doe.html.

Derbew, Sarah. "(Re)membering Sara Baartman, Venus, and Aphrodite." *Classical Receptions Journal* 11, no. 3 (2019): 336–54.

Douglas, Kate. *Contesting Childhood: Autobiography, Trauma, and Memory*. New Brunswick, NJ: Rutgers University Press, 2010.

D'Oyen, Paula. "Response to Chanel Miller *Know My Name* Reading on March 16, 2021." Unpublished manuscript, last modified March 18, 2021. Typescript.

Dove, Rita. "The Venus of Willendorf." *Poetry* 161, no. 1 (October 1992): 25–7.

"Do Women Still Have to Be Naked to Get into the Met. Museum?" *Guerilla Girls*, February 1, 2021. https://www.guerrillagirls.com/naked-through-the-ages.

Drimmer, Sonja. "Seeing the Bigger Picture on Public Memorials to Women." *Hyperallergic*, November 27, 2020. https://hyperallergic.com/601877.

D'Souza, Aruna. "Biography Becomes Form: William Rubin, Pablo Picasso, and the Subject of Art History." *Word and Image* 18, no. 3 (2002): 126–36.

D'Souza, Aruna, with artwork by Parker Bright and Pastiche Lumumba. *Whitewalling: Art, Race, and Protest in 3 Acts*. New York: Badlands Unlimited, 2018.

Dugdale, Sasha (@SashaDugdale). "The Translator is Many Kilos of Flesh, Hair, Bones, Fingernails, Teeth. Wherever She Goes She Leaves Her Fingerprints, Dust, Oils and Smell." *Twitter*, June 23, 2021, 11:50 p.m. https://twitter.com/SashaDugdale/status/1407954237170937863.

Dumitrescu, Irina. "Dudes Without Heirs." *New York Review of Books*, December 3, 2020. https://www.nybooks.com/articles/2020/12/03/dudes-without-heirs.

Earle, Elizabeth R. "'The Consequences Will Be with Us for Decades': The Politicization and Polarization of the #MeToo and Time's Up Movements in the United States." *Interactions: Studies in Communication and Culture* 10, no. 3 (2019): 257–71.

Easa, Leila. "'Advice from My 80-Year-Old Self' by Susan O'Malley." *Art Practical*, February 9, 2016. https://www.artpractical.com/column/printed-matters-advice -from-my-80-year-old-self.

"Edinburgh Showcase 2019: 'It's True, It's True, It's True' by Breach Theatre." *British Arts Council*, July 16, 2019. https://www.youtube.com/watch?v=5H4yc4E1nRU.

Edney, Matthew H. "Academic Cartography, Internal Map History, and the Critical Study of Mapping Processes." *Imago Mundi* [Lympne] 66 [supplement 1] (2014): 83–106.

Eidinger, Andrea. "Cultivating a Conscientious Citation Practice." *Unwritten Histories*, May 7, 2019. https://www.unwrittenhistories.com/cultivating-a -conscientious-citation-practice.

Eliot, T. S. *The Three Voices of Poetry*. Cambridge: Cambridge University Press, 1954.

Embrick, David G., and Wendy Leo Moore. "White Space(s) and the Reproduction of White Supremacy." *American Behavioral Scientist (Beverly Hills)* 64, no. 14 (2020): 1935–45. https://doi.org/10.1177/0002764220975053.

"Emily Wilson on Translations and Language." *Conversations with Tyler*, March 27, 2019. https://conversationswithtyler.com/episodes/emily-wilson.

Estrin, Seth. "Memory Incarnate: Material Objects and Private Visions in Classical Athens, from Euripides' *Ion* to the Gravesite." In *The Materialities of Greek Tragedy: Object and Affect in Aeschylus, Sophocles, and Euripides*, edited by Mario Telò and Melissa Mueller, 111–32. London: Bloomsbury, 2018.

Evans, Whittney, and David Streever. "Virginia's Massive Robert E. Lee Statue Has Been Removed." *NPR*, September 8, 2021. https://www.npr.org/2021/09 /08/1035004639/virginia-ready-to-remove-massive-robert-e-lee-statue-following -a-year-of-lawsuit.

Fabre, G. "Medea Norsa ebrea?" *Analecta Papyrologica* 14–15 (2002–2003): 337–50.

Fairbank, Viviane. "Why I Don't Read Rebecca Solnit." *The Walrus*, April 23, 2020. https://thewalrus.ca/why-i-dont-read-rebecca-solnit.

Fanon, Frantz. *Black Skin, White Masks*. London: Pluto Press, 1986.

Farrow, Ronan. "From Aggressive Overtures to Sexual Assault: Harvey Weinstein's Accusers Tell Their Stories." *New Yorker*, October 10, 2017. https://www .newyorker.com/news/news-desk/from-aggressive-overtures-to-sexual-assault -harvey-weinsteins-accusers-tell-their-stories.

Farrow, Ronan. "Harvey Weinstein's Army of Spies." *New Yorker*, November 6, 2017. https://www.newyorker.com/news/news-desk/harvey-weinsteins-army-of-spies.

Farrow, Ronan. "Harvey Weinstein's Secret Settlements." *New Yorker*, November 21, 2017. https://www.newyorker.com/news/news-desk/harvey-weinsteins-secret-settlements.

Farrow, Ronan. "Weighing the Cost of Speaking Out against Harvey Weinstein." *New Yorker*, October 27, 2017. https://www.newyorker.com/news/news-desk/weighing-the-costs-of-speaking-out-about-harvey-weinstein.

Felman, Shoshana, and Doris Laub. *Testimony: Crises of Witnessing in Literature, Psychoanalysis, and History*. New York: Routledge, 1991.

Fennell, Emerald, dir. *Promising Young Woman*. Universal City, CA: Universal Pictures Home Entertainment, 2020.

Fields, Karen, and Barbara J. Fields. *Racecraft: The Soul of Inequality in American Life*. New York: Verso, 2012.

Figlerowicz, Marta, and Matylda Figlerowicz. "Multilingual Style." *Textual Practice* 35, no. 6 (2021): 1015–36.

Fischels, Josie. "Arkansas Governor Wants to Reverse a Law That Forbids Schools to Require Masks." *NPR*, August 4, 20218. https://www.npr.org/2021/08/04/1024939859/arkansas-governor-reverse-law-let-schools-require-masks.

Fish, Stanley Eugene. *Is There a Text in This Class? The Authority of Interpretive Communities*. Cambridge, MA: Harvard University Press, 1980.

Ford, Kianga. "Playing with Venus: Black Women Artists and the Venus Trope in Contemporary Visual Art." In *Black Venus 2010: They Called Her "Hottentot,"* edited by Deborah Willis, 96–106. Philadelphia: Temple University Press, 2010.

Foster, R. Daniel. "Silver Lake Expands Its 'Say Their Names' Project." *Cultural Daily*, June 24, 2020. https://www.culturaldaily.com/silver-lake-expands-its-say-their-names-project.

Foucault, Michel. *Discipline and Punish: The Birth of the Prison*. New York: Vintage Books, 1979.

Fowles, Severin. "The Perfect Subject (Postcolonial Object Studies)." *Journal of Material Culture* 21, no. 1 (2016): 9–27.

Frank, Priscilla. "What Happened When a White Male Poet Read Michael Brown's Autopsy as Poetry." *HuffPost*, March 17, 2015. https://www.huffpost.com/entry/kenneth-goldsmith-michael-brown_n_6880996.

Franklin, Ruth. "A 'Beowulf' for Our Moment: Maria Dahvana Headley's Revisionist Translation Infuses the Old English Poem with Feminist and Social Media Slang." *New Yorker*, August 24, 2020. https://www.newyorker.com/magazine/2020/08/31/a-beowulf-for-our-moment.

Franks, Hallie, and Matthew S. Santirocco. "Monuments and Memory." *Roundtable Presentation at Center for Ancient Studies*, New York University, October 29, 2020.

Frey, Angelica. "How Judith Beheading Holofernes Became Art History's Favorite Icon of Female Rage." *Artsy*, April 4, 2019. https://www.artsy.net/article/artsy-editorial-judith-beheading-holofernes-art-historys-favorite-icon-female-rage.

Frick, Carole Collier, Stefania Biancani, and Elizabeth S. G. Nicholson, eds. *Italian Women Artists: From Renaissance to Baroque*. Milano: Skira, 2007.

Gaifman, Milette, and Verity Platt. "Introduction: From Grecian Urn to Embodied Object." *Art History* 41, no. 3 (2018): 402–19.

Gaillot, Anne-Derrick. "When 'Stan' Became a Verb." *The Outline*, October 26, 2017. https://theoutline.com/post/2425/when-stan-became-a-verb.

Gainsford, Peter. "Not 'The Oldest Written Record of the Odyssey.'" *Kiwi Hellenist*, July 12, 2018. http://kiwihellenist.blogspot.com/2018/07/not-oldest-written-record-of-odyssey.html.

Garrard, Mary D. *Artemisia Gentileschi: The Image of the Female Hero in Italian Baroque Art*. Princeton, NJ: Princeton University Press, 1989.

Garrard, Mary D. "Artemisia Gentileschi's Self-Portrait as the Allegory of Painting." *Art Bulletin* 62, no. 1 (1980): 97–112.

Gay, Roxane. *Hunger: A Memoir of (My) Body*. New York: Harper, 2017.

Gay, Roxane, ed. *The Selected Works of Audre Lorde*. New York: W. W. Norton & Company, 2020.

Gay, Roxane. "When Twitter Does What Online Journalism Can't." *Salon*, June 27, 2013. https://www.salon.com/2013/06/26/when_twitter_does_what_journalism_cant.

Gera, Deborah Levine. "The Jewish Textual Traditions." In *The Sword of Judith: Judith Studies across the Disciplines*, edited by Kevin R. Brine, Elena Ciletti, and Henrike Lähnemann, 81–95. Cambridge: OpenBook Publishers, 2010.

Gerhart, Ann, and Lucio Villa. "Rose Garden Ceremony Attendees Who Tested Positive for Coronavirus." *Washington Post*, October 3, 2020. https://www.washingtonpost.com/graphics/2020/politics/coronavirus-attendees-barrett-nomination-ceremony.

Gerolemou, Maria, and Lilia Diamantopoulou, eds. *Mirrors and Mirroring: From Antiquity to the Early Modern Period*. London: Bloomsbury, 2020.

Gidrewicz, Dominica A., and Tanis R Fenton. "A Systematic Review and Meta-Analysis of the Nutrient Content of Preterm and Term Breast Milk." *BMC Pediatrics* 14, no. 1 (2014): 1–14.

Gilligan, Carol, and Naomi Snider. *Why Does Patriarchy Persist?* Cambridge: Polity Press, 2018.

Goldsmith, Nafeesah, and Emily Allen-Hornblower. "The Hurts of the Past, the Wounds of the Present: Reading the Classics to Elucidate Mass Incarceration." Talk at the Classics Department at Johns Hopkins University, Baltimore, MD, November 11, 2021.

Gonzalez, Ella, and Cynthia Colburn. "How to Teach Ancient Art in the Age of #MeToo." *Hyperallergic*, September 5, 2018. https://hyperallergic.com/456269/how-to-teach-ancient-art-in-the-age-of-metoo.

Gouma-Peterson, Thalia, and Patricia Mathews. "The Feminist Critique of Art History." *Art Bulletin* 69, no. 3 (1987): 326–57.

Graff, Amy. "17-Year-Old Mission District Teen Leads Protest of Thousands in San Francisco." *SF Gate*, June 3, 2020. https://www.sfgate.com/news/slideshow/Simone-Jacques-Mission-District-protest-203235.php.

Granacki, Alyssa. "Boccaccio's Sappho: Female auctoritas in 'De mulieribus claris' and 'Saphos.'" *Renaissance Society of America*, April 21, 2021. https://rsa.confex.com/rsa/21virtual/meetingapp.cgi.Paper/9754.

Gray-Hopkins, Marion. "Antigone in Ferguson: Online Premiere." August 9, 2020. 1:37–1:45. https://youtu.be/Z6v5KpKqv6I.

Green, Adrienne. "The Boldness of Roxane Gay's *Hunger*." *The Atlantic*, June 13, 2017. https://www.theatlantic.com/entertainment/archive/2017/06/the-boldness-of -roxane-gays-hunger/530067.

Greenidge, Kaitlyn. "My Mother's Garden." *New York Times*, March 26, 2016. https://www.nytimes.com/2016/03/27/opinion/sunday/my-mothers-garden.html.

Greenwood, Emily. "Review of *If Not, Winter: Fragments of Sappho*, by Anne Carson." *Journal of Hellenic Studies* 125 (2005): 158–9.

Greer, Chris. "News Media, Victims, and Crime." In *Victims, Crime, and Society: An Introduction*, 2nd ed., edited by Pamela Davies, Peter Francis, and Chris Greer, 20–49. London: Sage Publications, 2017.

Grisales, Claudia, and Audrey Carlson. "Congress and COVID-19: Members' Cases and Quarantines." *NPR*, February 8, 2021. https://www.npr.org/2020/04/15 /833692377/how-the-coronavirus-has-affected-individual-members-of-congress.

Grosz, Elizabeth. *Volatile Bodies: Toward a Corporeal Feminism*. Bloomington: Indiana University Press, 1994.

Guerilla Girls. https://www.guerrillagirls.com/projects. Accessed February 9, 2021.

Hahnemann, Carolin. "Book of Paper, Book of Stone: An Exploration of Alice Oswald's *Memorial*." *Arion* 22, no. 1 (2014): 1–32.

Hahnemann, Carolin. "Feminist at Second Glance? Alice Oswald's *Memorial* as a Response to Homer's *Iliad*." In *Homer's Daughters: Women's Responses to Homer in the Twentieth Century and Beyond*, edited by Fiona Cox and Elena Theodorakopoulos, 89–104. Oxford: Oxford University Press, 2019.

Hall, Harriet. "It's True, It's True, It's True: All-Female Play Based on Rape Trial of Artemisia Gentileschi Strikes Uncanny Chord a Year On from #MeToo." *Independent*, October 30, 2018. https://www.independent.co.uk/arts-entertainment /theatre-dance/features/its-true-its-true-its-true-play-metoo-artemisia-gentileschi -diorama-theatre-tickets-a8608486.html.

Hallett, Judith P. "Introduction: Looking at Ancient Women Writers through Male and Female Lenses." In *Ancient Women Writers*, edited by Bartolo Natoli, Angela Pitts, and Judith P. Hallett. London: Routledge, forthcoming.

Hanink, Johanna. "The Twists and Turns of Translation." *Eidolon*, February 4, 2019. https://eidolon.pub/the-twists-and-turns-of-translation-33f1272dffa8.

Hanisch, Carol. "The Personal Is Political." *Woman's World* 2, no. 1 (1972): 15 and 22.

Hanisch, Carol. "The Personal is Political." *Women of the World, Unite!* Writings by Carol Hanish. http://www.carolhanisch.org/CHwritings/PIP.html. Accessed February 13, 2021.

Hansel, Emily. "Cultivating Healthy, Equitable Workplaces for Dancers." *Life As a Modern Dancer*, April 4, 2021. https://blog.lifeasamoderndancer.com/2021/04/ cultivating-healthy-equitable-workplaces-for-dancers.html.

Hansel, Emily. "Relearning Agency: A Dancer's Call for Collective Action." *Life As a Modern Dancer*, January 1, 2021. https://blog.lifeasamoderndancer.com/2021/01 /relearning-agency-a-dancers-call-for-collective-action.html.

Hao, Karen. "We Read the Paper That Forced Timnit Gebru Out of Google. Here's What It Says." *MIT Technology Review*, December 4, 2020. https://www.tech-nologyreview.com/2020/12/04/1013294/google-ai-ethics-research-paper-forced-out-timnit-gebru.

Harris, Duchess. *Black Feminist Politics from Kennedy to Trump*. Cham, Switzerland: Springer International Publishing, 2018.

Hartman, Saidiya V. "Venus in Two Acts." *Small Axe: A Caribbean Journal of Criticism* 26, no. 1 (2008): 1–14.

Harvey, Dennis. "Review of *Promising Young Woman* (film)." *Variety*, January 26, 2020. https://variety.com/2020/film/reviews/promising-young-woman-review-1203480660.

Havelock, Christine Mitchell. *The Aphrodite of Knidos and Her Successors: A Historical Review of the Female Nude in Greek Art*. Ann Arbor: University of Michigan Press, 1995.

Haynes, Natalie. *The Children of Jocasta*. London: Mantle, 2017.

Haynes, Natalie. *Pandora's Jar: Women in the Greek Myths*. London: Picador, 2020.

Headley, Maria Dahvana. *Beowulf: A New Translation*. New York: Farrar, Straus and Giroux, 2020.

Headley, Maria Dahvana. *The Mere Wife*. London: Picador, 2018.

"Health Equity Considerations and Racial and Ethnic Minority Groups." Centers for Disease Control and Prevention (CDC), updated April 19, 2021. https://www.cdc.gov/coronavirus/2019-ncov/community/health-equity/race-ethnicity.html.

Heisler, Gregory. "2002: The Whistleblowers." *Time Magazine*, March 5, 2020. https://time.com/5793757/the-whistleblowers-100-women-of-the-year.

Heller-Nicholas, Alexandra. *Rape-Revenge Films: A Critical Study*. Jefferson, NC: McFarland, 2011.

Henderson, Jason. "INFINITE CITY: A San Francisco Atlas." *Geographical Review* 102, no. 2 (2012): 268–70.

Henwood, Daisy. "Ecofeminist 'Lines of Convergence': Remapping the American West in Rebecca Solnit's Savage Dreams." *European Journal of American Culture* 39, no. 1 (2020): 105–18.

Hewitt, Chris. "Jittery Comedy *Promising Young Woman* Has Serious Issues on Its Mind." *Star Tribune*, January 14, 2021. https://www.startribune.com/jittery-comedy-promising-young-woman-has-serious-issues-on-itsmind/600010537.

Hill, Evan, Ainara Tiefenthäler, Christiaan Triebert, Drew Jordan, Haley Willis, and Robin Stein. "How George Floyd Was Killed in Police Custody." *New York Times*, May 31, 2020, updated October 29, 2021. https://www.nytimes.com/2020/05/31/us/george-floyd-investigation.html.

Hill, Faith, and Karen Yuan. "How Instagram Saved Poetry." *The Atlantic*, October 15, 2018. https://www.theatlantic.com/technology/archive/2018/10/rupi-kaur-ins-tagram-poet-entrepreneur/572746.

Homer. *The Odyssey*. Translated by A. T. Murray. Loeb Classical Library 104. Cambridge, MA: Harvard University Press, 1919.

Homer. *The Odyssey*. Translated by Emily Wilson. New York: W. W. Norton, 2018.

Homer. *The Odyssey*. Translated by Richmond Lattimore. New York: Harper Perennial, 1967.

Homer. *The Odyssey*. Translated by Robert Fagles, with an introduction by Bernard Knox. New York: Viking, 1996.

Honig, Bonnie. *Antigone, Interrupted*. Cambridge: Cambridge University Press, 2013.

Honig, Bonnie. *A Feminist Theory of Refusal*. Cambridge, MA: Harvard University Press, 2021.

Honig, Bonnie. *Shell-Shocked: Feminist Criticism After Trump*. New York: Fordham University Press, 2021.

Hopman, Marianne Govers. "Chorus, Conflict, and Closure in Aeschylus' *Persians*." In *Choral Mediations in Greek Tragedy*, edited by Renaud Gagné and Marianne Govers Hopman, 58–77. Cambridge: Cambridge University Press, 2013.

Hunte, Tracie. "The Ashes on the Lawn." *Radiolab*, December 17, 2020. https://www.wnycstudios.org/podcasts/radiolab/articles/ashes-lawn.

Hunter, Kathryn M. "Silence in Noisy Archives: Reflections on Judith Allen's 'Evidence and Silence: Feminism and the Limits of History' (1986) in the Era of Mass Digitisation." *Australian Feminist Studies* 32, nos. 91–92 (2017): 202–12.

Hywel, Dix. *Autofiction in English*. Cham, Switzerland: Springer International Publishing, 2018.

"An Incalculable Loss." *New York Times*, last updated May 27, 2020. https://www.nytimes.com/interactive/2020/05/24/us/us-coronavirus-deaths-100000.html.

Innes, Lyn. "No Man Is an Island: National Literary Canons, Writers, and Readers." In *Islanded Identities: Constructions of Postcolonial Cultural Insularity*, edited by Maeve McCusker and Anthony Soares, 189–206. New York: Rodopi, 2011.

Irigaray, Luce, and Carolyn Burke. *This Sex Which is Not One*. Ithaca, NY: Cornell University Press, 1985.

"It's True, It's True, It's True." *Breach Theatre*, January 24, 2021. https://www.breachtheatre.com/shows/its-true-its-true-its-true.

Jackson, Virginia. "Lyric." In *The Princeton Encyclopedia of Poetry and Poetics*, 4th ed., edited by Stephen Cushman, Clare Cavanagh, Jahan Ramazani, and Paul Rouzer, 826–34. Princeton, NJ: Princeton University Press, 2012.

Jhally, Sut, and Jean Kilbourne. *Killing Us Softly 4: Advertising's Image of Women*. Northampton, MA: Media Education Foundation, 2010.

Johnson, Dennis Loy. "Make Big Money: Become a Canadian Poet." *MOBYlives*, June 18, 2001. http://www.mobylives.com/Griffin_Prize.html.

Johnson, Jessica Marie. *Wicked Flesh: Black Women, Intimacy, and Freedom in the Atlantic World*. Philadelphia: University of Pennsylvania Press, 2020.

Johnson, Richard Greggory, and Hugo Renderos. "Invisible Populations and the #MeToo Movement." *Public Administration Review* 80, no. 6 (2020): 1123–26.

Jones, Kellie. "A. K. A. Saartjie: The 'Hottentot Venus' in Context (Some Recollections and a Dialogue) 1998/2004." In *Black Venus 2010: They Called Her "Hottentot,"* edited by Deborah Willis, 126–43. Philadelphia: Temple University Press, 2010.

Jones, Martha S. *Vanguard: How Black Women Broke Barriers, Won the Vote, and Insisted on Equality for All*. New York: Basic Books, 2020.

Jong, Anneke. "You Can't Be What You Can't See: How to Get More Women in Tech." *The Muse*, March 06, 2021. https://www.themuse.com/advice/you-cant-be-what-you-cant-see-how-to-get-more-women-in-tech.

Joseph, Brandon W., ed. *Carolee Schneemann: Uncollected Texts*. New York: McNaughton & Gunn, 2018.

Julious, Britt. "Roxane Gay: New Memoir Is 'about My Body and the Things That Happened to My Body.'" *Rolling Stone*, June 19, 2017. https://www.rollingstone .com/culture/culture-features/roxane-gay-new-memoir-is-about-my-body-and-the -things-that-happened-to-my-body-204081.

Jurecic, Ann, and Daniel Marchalik. "On Obesity: Roxane Gay's *Hunger*." *The Lancet* (British Edition) 390, no. 10102 (2017): 1577.

Kantor, Jodi, and Megan Twohey. "Harvey Weinstein Paid Off Sexual Harassment Accusers for Decades." *New York Times*, October 5, 2017. https://www.nytimes .com/2017/10/05/us/harvey-weinstein-harassment-allegations.html.

Kaplan, Walker. "Jhumpa Lahiri Is Writing a New Translation of Ovid's *Metamorphoses*." *LitHub*, May 18, 2021. https://lithub.com/jhumpa-lahiri-is -working-on-a-new-translation-of-ovids-metamorphoses-for-the-modern-library.

Keenan, James. "The History of the Discipline." In *The Oxford Handbook of Papyrology*, edited by Roger S. Bagnall, 59–78. Oxford: Oxford University Press, 2011.

Keesling, C. M. "The Marathon Casualty List from Eua-Loukou and the Plinthedon Style in Attic Inscriptions." *Zeitschrift für Papyrologie und Epigraphik* 180 (2012): 139–49.

Keller, Jessalynn. "A Politics of Snap: Teen Vogue's Public Feminism." *Signs* 45, no. 4 (2020): 817–43.

Kelly, Mary Louise. "#PublishingPaidMe: Authors Share Their Advances to Expose Racial Disparity." *NPR*, June 8, 2020. https://www.npr.org/2020/06/08/872470156/ -publishingpaidme-authors-share-their-advances-to-expose-racial-disparities.

Kim, Annabel, ed. "Citation, Otherwise." *Diacritics* 48, no. 3 (2020).

Kim, David Young. *The Traveling Artist in the Italian Renaissance: Geography, Mobility, and Style*. New Haven, CT: Yale University Press, 2014.

Kim, Jihyun, and Hayeon Song. "Celebrity's Self-Disclosure on Twitter and Parasocial Relationships: A Mediating Role of Social Presence." *Computers in Human Behavior* 62 (2016): 570–77.

Kindelanvia, Katie. "Dr. Jill Biden Responds after Op-Ed Called for Her to Drop 'Doctor' from Name." *ABC News*, December 18, 2020. https://abcnews.go.com/ GMA/News/dr-jill-biden-responds-op-ed-called-drop/story?id=74797472.

Kirk, Athena. *Ancient Greek Lists: Catalogue and Inventory across Genres*. Cambridge: Cambridge University Press, 2021.

Knox, Bernard. "Introduction to Homer." In *The Odyssey*, translated by Robert Fagles, 3–64. New York: Viking, 1996.

Komunyakaa, Yusef. "Venus of Willendorf." With an introduction by Faith Hill. *The Atlantic*, August 9, 2020 [September 1998]. https://www.theatlantic.com/books/ archive/2020/08/poem-yusef-komunyakaa-venus-willendorf/615061.

Kott, Lidia Jean. "This Is the Official Poem of 2016." *The World*, December 31, 2016. https://www.pri.org/stories/2016-12-31/official-poem-2016.

Krauss, Rosalind. "In the Name of Picasso." *October* 16 (1981): 5–22.

Krug, Nora. "Maggie Smith and the Poem That Captured the Mood of a Tumultuous Year." *Washington Post*, December 23, 2016. https://www.washingtonpost.com

/entertainment/books/maggie-smith-and-the-poem-that-captured-the-mood-of-a
-tumultuous-year/2016/12/22/a652b43c-c3a6-11e6-9578-0054287507db_story.html.

Kurke, Leslie V. "Archaic Greek Poetry." In *The Cambridge Companion to Archaic Greece*, edited by H. A. Shapiro, 141–68. Cambridge: Cambridge University Press, 2007.

Labonte, Rachel. "Lin-Manuel Miranda Refused CG Removal of Hamilton's King George Lip Spit." *Screen Rant*, July 23, 2020. https://screenrant.com/hamilton -movie-king-george-spit-jonathan-groff-remove.

Lamberton, Robert, and John J. Keaney, eds. *Homer's Ancient Readers: The Hermeneutics of Greek Epic's Earliest Exegetes*. Princeton, NJ: Princeton University Press, 1992.

Lang, Cady. "Art History Experts Explain the Meaning of the Art in Beyoncé and Jay Z's 'Apesh-t' Video." *Time Magazine*, June 19, 2018. https://time.com/5315275/ art-references-meaning-beyonce-jay-z-apeshit-louvre-music-video.

Laskaris, Julie. "Nursing Mothers in Greek and Roman Medicine." *American Journal of Archaeology* 112, no. 3 (2008): 459–64.

Lazar, David. *Truth in Nonfiction: Essays*. Iowa City: University of Iowa Press, 2008.

Lebron, Christopher J. *The Making of Black Lives Matter: A Brief History of an Idea*. Oxford: Oxford University Press, 2017.

Leonard, Zoe. "I Want a President." *High Line*, October 11, 2016. https://www .thehighline.org/art/projects/zoeleonard.

Leong, Michael. *Contested Records: The Turn to Documents in Contemporary North American Poetry*. Iowa City: University of Iowa Press, 2020.

Leontis, Artemis. *Eva Palmer Sikelianos: A Life in Ruins*. Princeton, NJ: Princeton University Press, 2019.

Levine, Caroline. "Strategic Formalism: Toward a New Method in Cultural Studies." *Victorian Studies* 48, no. 4 (2006): 625–57.

Levine, Emily J. "PanDora, or Erwin and Dora Panofsky and the Private History of Ideas." *Journal of Modern History* 83, no. 4 (2011): 753–87.

Levitan, Rebecca. "A Rape by Any Other Name: Against Teaching Abductions in Greek Art." *Journal of the History of Ideas Blog*, June 6, 2019. https://jhiblog.org /2019/05/06/a-rape-by-any-other-name-against-teaching-abductions-in-greek-art-2.

Lewinsky, Monica. "Roxane Gay on How to Write Trauma." *Vanity Fair*, February 18, 2021. https://www.vanityfair.com/style/2021/02/roxane-gay-on-how-to-write -about-trauma.

Lezama Lima, José. "Julián del Casal." Translated by Robin Myers. *Small Axe: A Caribbean Journal of Criticism* 23, no. 3 (November 1, 2019): 131–54.

Lindwall, Courtney. "Black Walden Came First, Thoreau After." *Natural Resources Defense Council*, February 1, 2021. https://www.nrdc.org/stories/black-walden -came-first-thoreau-after.

Lipton, Eunice. "Representing Sexuality in Women Artists' Biographies: The Cases of Suzanne Valadon and Victorine Meurent." *Journal of Sex Research* 27, no. 1 (1990): 85–7.

Llewellyn, Kathleen M. *Representing Judith in Early Modern French Literature*. Farnham: Ashgate, 2014.

"Locking Up Women for Killing Their Rapists." *The Appeal*, January 30, 2020. https://theappeal.org/the-appeal-podcast-locking-up-women-for-killing-their-rapists.

Long Soldier, Layli. "38." *WHEREAS*. Minneapolis, MN: Graywolf Press, 2017.

Lorde, Audre. "Difference and Survival: An Address at Hunter College (undated)." In *The Selected Works of Audre Lorde*, edited by Roxane Gay, 173–82. New York: W. W. Norton & Company, 2021.

Luce, Edward. "Historian Heather Cox Richardson: 'Now People See What's Happening. Thank God!'" *Financial Times*, July 16, 2021. https://www.ft.com/content/08f3728c-bbff-493f-aa66-a1aa35dd3924.

Machado, Carmen Maria. "How *Promising Young Woman* Refigures the Rape-Revenge Movie." *New Yorker*, January 29, 2021. https://www.newyorker.com/culture/cultural-comment/how-promising-young-woman-refigures-the-rape-revenge-movie.

Machado, Maria Helena Pereira Toledo. "Between Two Beneditos: Enslaved Wet-Nurses amid Slavery's Decline in Southeast Brazil." *Slavery and Abolition* 38, no. 2 (2017): 320–36.

Mack, Rainer. "Reading the Archaeology of the Female Body." *Qui Parle* 4, no. 1 (1990): 79–97.

MacNeill, Kate. "Spilling Blood in Art: A Tale of Tampons, Trump, and Taboos." *The Conversation*, July 31, 2017. https://theconversation.com/spilling-blood-in-art-a-tale-of-tampons-trump-and-taboos-81455.

Maharawal, Manissa M., and Erin McElroy. "The Anti-Eviction Mapping Project: Counter Mapping and Oral History toward Bay Area Housing Justice." *Annals of the American Association of Geographers* 108, no. 2 (2018): 380–9.

Malech, Dora. *Stet: Poems*. Princeton, NJ: Princeton University Press, 2018.

Manoff, Marlene. "Theories of the Archive from across the Disciplines." *Portal: Libraries and the Academy* 4, no. 1 (2004): 9–25.

Marcus, Ezra. "Will the Last Confederate Statue Standing Turn Off the Lights?" *New York Times*, June 23, 2020. https://www.nytimes.com/2020/06/23/style/statue-richmond-lee.html.

Marshall, Alex. "Amanda Gorman's Poetry United Critics. It's Dividing Translators." *New York Times*, March 26, 2021. https://www.nytimes.com/2021/03/26/books/amanda-gorman-hill-we-climb-translation.html.

Marshall, C. W. "Breastfeeding in Greek Literature and Thought." *Illinois Classical Studies* 42, no. 1 (2017): 185–201.

Martin, Katherine Connor. "How Brothers Became Buddies and Bros." *Oxford University Press Blog*, April 30, 2016. https://blog.oup.com/2016/04/brothers-buddies-bros-oed-update.

Martinčič, Julia. "Let It Bleed: Art's Revival of Menstrual Blood." *The Guardian*, December 12, 2016. https://www.theguardian.com/lifeandstyle/2016/dec/12/let-it-bleed-arts-revival-of-menstrual-blood.

Mason, Wyatt. "The First Woman to Translate *The Odyssey* into English." *New York Times*, November 2, 2017. https://www.nytimes.com/2017/11/02/magazine/the-first-woman-to-translate-the-odyssey-into-english.html.

Mazza, Roberta. "Powerful Text-Things: Papyrology and the Material Turn." *Everyday Orientalism Online*, December 11, 2020. https://www.youtube.com/watch?v=RGoWbzdY7RA.

Mbembe, Achille. "The Power of the Archive and Its Limits." In *Refiguring the Archive*, edited by Carolyn Hamilton et al., 19–27. Boston, MA: Kluwer Academic Publishers, 2002.

McCoid, Catherine Hodge, and Leroy D. McDermott. "Toward Decolonizing Gender: Female Vision in the Upper Paleolithic." *American Anthropologist*, n.s. 98, no. 2 (1996): 319–26.

McDonald, Helen. *Erotic Ambiguities: The Female Nude in Art*. London: Routledge, 2001.

McGinley, Terence. "What the Cyan! How the *New York Times* Gets Inked." *New York Times*, May 23, 2017. https://www.nytimes.com/2017/05/23/insider/new-york-times-printing-plant-press.html.

McGregor, Hannah. "Citing Your Sources." *Secret Feminist Agenda*, March 15, 2019. https://secretfeministagenda.com/2019/03/15/episode-3-21-citing-your-sources.

McKittrick, Katherine. "Mathematics Black Life." *Black Scholar* 44, no. 2 (2014): 16–28.

Meimaris, Yiannis. "The Discovery of the Madaba Mosaic Map." In *The Madaba Map Centenary, 1897–1997: Travelling through the Byzantine Umayyad period=al-Dhikrá al-miʾawīyah li-khāriṭat Mādabā : Khilāla al-ʿaṣr al-Umawī al-Bīzanṭī : Proceedings of the International Conference Held in Amman, 7–9 April 1997*, edited by Michele Piccirillo and Eugenio Alliata, 35–44. Jerusalem: Studium Biblicum Franciscanum, 1999.

Melesio, Lucina. "Case of 43 Ayotzinapa Missing Students Unresolved Five Years On." *Al Jazeera*, September 26, 2019. https://www.aljazeera.com/features/2019/9/26/case-of-43-ayotzinapa-missing-students-unresolved-five-years-on.

Melius, Jeremy. "Connoisseurship, Painting, and Personhood." *Art History* 34, no. 2 (April 2011): 288–309.

Mendelsohn, Daniel. "In Search of Sappho." *New York Review*, August 14, 2003. https://www.nybooks.com/articles/2003/08/14/in-search-of-sappho.

Menzio, Eva, ed. *Artemisia Gentileschi/Agostino Tassi: atti di un processo per stupor*. Milan: Edizioni delle donne, 1981.

Meskell, Lynn. "Negative Heritage and Past Mastering in Archaeology." *Anthropological Quarterly* 75, no. 3 (2002): 557–74.

Messina, Chris. "Groups for Twitter; or A Proposal for Twitter Tag Channels." *Factory Joe*, August 25, 2007. https://factoryjoe.com/2007/08/25/groups-for-twitter-or-a-proposal-for-twitter-tag-channels.

"Me Too Rising: A Visualization of the Movement Using Google Trends." *Me Too Rising*, January 17, 2021. https://metoorising.withgoogle.com.

Milano, Alyssa (@Alyssa_Milano). "If You've Been Sexually Harassed or Assaulted Write 'Me Too' as a Reply to This Tweet." *Twitter*, October 15, 2017, 1:21 p.m. https://twitter.com/alyssa_milano/status/919659438700670976.

Miller, Chanel. *Know My Name: A Memoir*. New York: Viking, 2019.

Miller, Daniel. *Materiality*. Durham, NC: Duke University Press, 2005.

Miller, Madeline. *Circe*. New York: Little Brown, 2018.

Miller, Paul Allen. *Diotima at the Barricades: French Feminists Read Plato*. Oxford: Oxford University Press, 2016.

Mitchell, Robin. "Another Means of Understanding the Gaze: Sarah Bartmann in the Development of Nineteenth-Century French National Identity." In *Black Venus 2010: They Called Her "Hottentot,"* edited by Deborah Willis, 32–46. Philadelphia: Temple University Press, 2010.

Mitchell, Robin. "Bringing Ourselves Along with Us: The Realities of Historical Writing." *Women's History Network*, June 28, 2021. https://womenshisto rynetwork.org/bringing-ourselves-along-with-us-the-realities-of-historical -writing.

Mitchell, Robin. *Vénus Noire: Black Women and Colonial Fantasies in Nineteenth-Century France*. Athens, GA: University of Georgia Press, 2020.

Mittman, Asa Simon, and Marcus Hensel, eds. *Classic Readings on Monster Theory*. York: Arc Humanities Press, 2018.

Monteiro, Lyra. "How a Trump Executive Order Aims to Set White Supremacy in Stone." *Hyperallergic*, January 23, 2021. https://hyperallergic.com/614175/how-a -trump-executive-order-aims-to-set-white-supremacy-in-stone.

Morales, Helen. *Antigone Rising: The Subversive Power of the Ancient Myths*. New York: Bold Type Books, 2020.

Morineau, Camille, and Lucia Pesapane, eds. *Women House*. Washington, DC: National Museum of Women in the Arts, 2018.

Morrissey, T. *Between the Lines: Photographs from the National Vietnam Veterans Memorial*. Syracuse, NY: Syracuse University Press, 2000.

Most, Glenn, and Alice Schreyer, eds. *Homer in Print: A Catalogue of the Bibliotheca Homerica Langiana at the University of Chicago Library*. Chicago: University of Chicago Press, 2013.

Mott, Carrie, and Daniel Cockayne. "Citation Matters: Mobilizing the Politics of Citation toward a Practice of 'Conscientious Engagement.'" *Gender, Place, and Culture* 24, no. 7 (2017): 954–73.

Murnaghan, Orla. "Open-Access JSTOR Materials Accessible to the Public." *University Times*, March 19, 2020. https://universitytimes.ie/2020/03/jstor-makes -database-accessible-to-the-public.

Murrell, Denise. *Posing Modernity: The Black Model from Manet and Matisse to Today*. New Haven and London: Yale University Press, 2018.

Myers, Bess. "Women Who Translate." *Eidolon*, August 5, 2019. https://eidolon.pub /women-who-translate-7966e56b3df2.

Nagy, Gregory. "Genre, Occasion, and Choral Mimesis Revisited, with Special Reference to the 'Newest Sappho.'" In *Genre in Archaic and Classical Greek Poetry: Theories and Models; Studies in Archaic and Classical Greek Song,* vol. 4, edited by Margaret Foster, Leslie Kurke, and Naomi Weiss, 31–54. Leiden: Brill, 2020.

Nash, Jennifer C. "Citational Desires: On Black Feminism's Institutional Longings." *Diacritics* 48, no. 3 (2020): 76–91.

Nead, Lynda. "Framing the Female Body (1992)." In *Feminism—Art—Theory: An Anthology, 1968–2014*, 2nd ed., edited by Hilary Robinson, 322–8. London: Wiley-Blackwell, 2015.

Neer, Richard. "Connoisseurship and the Stakes of Style." *Critical Inquiry* 32, no. 1 (2005): 1–26.

Nelson, Charmaine. *The Color of Stone*. Minneapolis: University of Minnesota Press, 2007.

Nelson, Charmaine. *Representing the Black Female Subject in Western Art*. New York: Routledge, 2010.

Nguyen, Viet Thanh (@viet_t_nguyen). "In 1992, My English Department Chairman Told Me I Couldn't Write a Dissertation on Vietnamese American Literature. In 2020's Modern Language Association …." *Twitter*, January 3, 2020, 4:18 p.m. https://twitter.com/viet_t_nguyen/status/1213253385874395136.

Noble, Safiya Umoja, and Brendesha M. Tynes. "Introduction." In *The Intersectional Internet: Race, Sex, Class, and Culture Online*, edited by Safiya Umoja Noble and Brendesha M. Tynes, 1–20. New York: Peter Lang, 2016.

Nochlin, Linda. "Courbet's 'L'Origine du monde': The Origin without an Original." *October* 37 (1986): 77–86.

Nochlin, Linda. "Why Have There Been No Great Women Artists?" *Art News* (January 1971; republished May 2015).

Nooter, Sarah. "The Materialities of Greek Tragedy: Objects and Affect in Aeschylus, Sophocles, and Euripides." *Bryn Mawr Classical Review*, 2019.11.03. https://bmcr .brynmawr.edu/2019/2019.11.03.

Norsa, Medea. "Dai papiri della Società Italiana." *Annali della R. Scuola Normale Superiore di Pisa. Lettere, Storia e Filosofia* 6, no. 1/2 (1937): 1–15.

Noveck, Jocelyn. "For Top #MeToo Legal Duo, a Pandemic Year Brings No Pause." *Associated Press*, July 11, 2021. https://apnews.com/article/business-sports -football-health-government-and-politics-8446ed43b95ecd728a3ed662d8a3859c.

Oatman, Maddie. "Hollywood Loves Rape-Revenge Plots. But What Story Are They Really Telling?" *Mother Jones*, July 22, 2021. https://www.motherjones .com/media/2021/07/hollywood-loves-rape-revenge-plots-but-what-story-are-they -really-telling.

Okorafor, Nnedi. *Akata Witch*. New York: Viking Books, 2011.

Okwodu, Janelle. "In *Hunger*, Roxane Gay Says What No One Else Will about Being Fat in America." *Vogue*, June 18, 2017. https://www.vogue.com/article/roxane-gay -interview-hunger-memoir.

Oluo, Ijeoma. *Mediocre: The Dangerous Legacy of White Male America*. New York: Seal Press, 2020.

"One City One Book: *Know My Name*." *San Francisco Public Library*, March 18, 2021. https://sfpl.org/books-and-media/read/one-city-one-book-know-my-name.

O'Reilly, Meag-gan. "Systems Centered Language: Speaking Truth to Power during COVID-19 while Confronting Racism." *Medium*, June 5, 2020. https://medium .com/@meagoreillyphd/systems-centered-language-a3dc7951570e.

Oswald, Alice. *Memorial: A Version of Homer's Iliad*. With an afterword by Eavan Boland. New York: W. W. Norton & Company, 2013.

Pandey, Nandini B., *The Poetics of Power In Augustan Rome: Latin Poetic Responses to Early Imperial Iconography*. Cambridge: Cambridge University Press, 2018.

Pandian, Anand (@anandspandian). "There's a Precise Parallel Between the Conservative Clamor over Free Speech, and the Deep Opposition to Pandemic Masks. Both Positions Insist …" *Twitter*, January 1, 2021, 9:21 a.m. https://twitter.com/anandspandian/status/1348683516876386306.

Panofsky, Erwin. "On the Problem of Describing and Interpreting Works of the Visual Arts." Translated by Jaś Elsner and Katharina Lorenz. *Critical Inquiry* 38, no. 3 (2012): 467–82.

"Papyrus Making 101." *University of Michigan Papyrus Collection*, March 19, 2021. https://apps.lib.umich.edu/papyrus_making/slides.html.

Pebworth, Alison. "Atlas Series Drawings." *Alison Pebworth*, March 18, 2021. https://alisonpebworth.com/section/467496-Atlas-Series-Drawings.html.

Pebworth, Alison. "Third Street Phantom Coast Map." *Alison Pebworth*, March 18, 2021. https://alisonpebworth.com/artwork/4409679.html.

Pelley, Scott. "Whistleblower: Facebook Is Misleading the Public on Progress against Hate Speech, Violence, Misinformation." *CBS News*, October 4, 2021. https://www.cbsnews.com/news/facebook-whistleblower-frances-haugen-misinformation-public-60-minutes-2021-10-03.

Pells, Rachael. "Understanding the Extent of Gender Gap in Citations." *Inside Higher Ed*, August 16, 2018. https://www.insidehighered.com/news/2018/08/16/new-research-shows-extent-gender-gap-citations.

Penn, Irving, and Maria Morris Hambourg. *Earthly Bodies: Irving Penn's Nudes, 1949–50*. Boston: Metropolitan Museum of Art in association with Little, Brown and Co., 2002.

Perloff, Marjorie. "The 'I' of Lyric." *Boston Review*, December 6, 2012. http://bostonreview.net/forum/poetry-brink/i-lyric.

Perloff, Marjorie. "Language Poetry and the Lyric Subject: Ron Silliman's 'Albany,' Susan Howe's 'Buffalo.'" *Critical Inquiry* 25, no. 3 (Spring 1999): 405–34.

Perloff, Marjorie. "Review of *Theory of the Lyric*, by Jonathan Culler." *Nineteenth-Century Literature* 71, no. 2 (2016): 256–61.

Philip, M. NourbeSe. *Zong!* Middleton, CT: Wesleyan University Press, 2008.

Pieraccioni, Dino. "Ricordo di Medea Norsa (dieci anni dalla morte)." *Belfagor* 17, no. 4 (January 1, 1962): 482–5.

Pitz, Marylynne. "SLAY Shows Judith from Very Different Points of View at The Frick." *Pittsburgh Post-Gazette*, April 08, 2022. https://www.post-gazette.com/ae/art-architecture/2022/04/08/frick-pittsburgh-art-slay-judith-holofernes/stories/202204080048.

Platt, Verity. "Classicism and the Statue Crisis in the Age of Black Lives Matter." *Talk at the University of California–Los Angeles*, October 28, 2020.

Platt, Verity. "Why People Are Toppling Monuments to Racism." *Scientific American*, July 3, 2020. https://www.scientificamerican.com/article/why-people-are-toppling-monuments-to-racism.

Platt, Verity, and Michael Squire, eds. *The Frame in Classical Art: A Cultural History*. Cambridge: Cambridge University Press, 2017.

Pollock, Griselda. "Review of *Artemisia Gentileschi: The Image of the Female Hero in Italian Baroque Art*, by Mary D. Garrard." *Art Bulletin* 72, no. 3 (1990): 499–505.

Pomeroy, Jordana. "Italian Women Artists from Renaissance to Baroque." In *Italian Women Artists: From Renaissance to Baroque*, edited by Carole Collier Frick, Stefania Biancani, and Elizabeth S. G. Nicholson, 19–22. Milan: Skira, 2007.

Power, Timothy. "Sappho's Parachoral Monody." In *Genre in Archaic and Classical Greek Poetry: Theories and Models; Studies in Archaic and Classical Greek Song*, vol. 4, edited by Margaret Foster, Leslie Kurke, and Naomi Weiss, 82–108. Leiden: Brill, 2020.

Poxy: Oxyrhynchus Online. "Paper Wraps Stone?" http://www.papyrology.ox.ac.uk/POxy/oxyrhynchus/parsons4.html. Accessed January 9, 2021.

Prescod-Weinstein, Chanda (@IBJIYONGI). "I'm a Second Generation Track Athlete, and I Medaled at the National Championships as a Kid and Also Ran in the Regional Junior Olympics …" *Twitter*, July 2, 2021, 5:12 a.m. https://twitter.com/IBJIYONGI/status/1410934459914932225.

Prins, Yopie. *Ladies' Greek: Victorian Translations of Tragedy*. Princeton, NJ: Princeton University Press, 2017.

Prins, Yopie. "Sapphic Stanzas: How Can We Read the Rhythm?" In *Critical Rhythm: The Poetics of a Literary Life Form*, edited by Ben Glaser and Jonathan Culler, 247–73. New York: Fordham University Press, 2019.

Prins, Yopie. "Sappho's Afterlife in Translation." In *Re-Reading Sappho: Reception and Transmission*, edited by Ella Greene, 36–67. Berkeley: University of California Press, 1996.

"The Quarry: A Social Justice Poetry Database." *Split This Rock*, February 18, 2021. https://www.splitthisrock.org/poetry-database.

Quema, Anne. "M. NourbeSe Philip's *Zong!*: Metaphors, Laws, and Fugues of Justice." *Journal of Law and Society* 43, no. 1 (2016): 85–104.

Quin, Sally. "Describing the Female Sculptor in Early Modern Italy: An Analysis of the *Vita* of Properzia de' Rossi in Giorgio Vasari's *Lives*." *Gender and History* 24, no. 1 (2012): 134–49.

Quinault, Roland. "Gladstone and Slavery." *Historical Journal* 52, no. 2 (2009): 363–83.

Rasmussen, Tom. "Herakles' Apotheosis in Etruria and Greece." *Antike Kunst* 48 (2005): 30–9.

Raymond, Laurel (@RayOfLaurel). "Entrance to the Yale Law School this Morning." *Twitter*, October 22, 2018, 6:14 a.m. https://twitter.com/RayOfLaurel/status/1054360220971995137.

Read, Jacinda. *The New Avengers: Feminism, Femininity, and the Rape-Revenge Cycle*. Manchester: Manchester University Press, 2000.

"Rear Window: Maya Lin and the Vietnam Memorial." *teleSUR*, December 14, 2014. https://www.dailymotion.com/video/x2dt2wl.

Reckitt, Helena. "Generating Feminisms: Italian Feminisms and the 'Now You Can Go' Program." *Art Journal* 76, no. 3/4 (2017): 101–11.

"Red Feed, Blue Feed." Infographic. *Wall Street Journal*, archived 2019. https://graphics.wsj.com/blue-feed-red-feed.

Reed, Carey. "'There Still Is a Lot Stacked against Us': Ferguson Inspires Year of Art." *PBS Arts*, August 9, 2015. https://www.pbs.org/newshour/arts/still-lot-stacked-us-ferguson-inspires-year-art.

Rehak, Melanie. "Things Fall Together." *New York Times Magazine*, March 26, 2000. https://archive.nytimes.com/www.nytimes.com/library/magazine/home/20000326mag-annecarson.html.

Reynolds, Margaret, ed. *The Sappho Companion*. New York: Palgrave for St. Martin's Press, 2001.

Richardson, Heather Cox. "June 30, 2021." *Letters from an American*, June 30, 2021. https://heathercoxrichardson.substack.com/p/june-30-2021.

Richardson, Heather Cox. "September 15, 2021." *Letters from an American*, September 15, 2021. https://heathercoxrichardson.substack.com/p/september-15-2021.

Robinson, Elizabeth. "An Antipoem That Condenses Everything: Anne Carson's Translations of the Fragments of Sappho." In *Anne Carson: Ecstatic Lyre*, edited by Joshua Marie Wilkinson, 181–7. Ann Arbor: University of Michigan Press, 2015.

Robinson, Hilary. *Feminism—Art—Theory: An Anthology, 1968–2014*. 2nd ed. London: Wiley-Blackwell, 2015.

Roche, Jenny. "Dancing Strategies and Moving Identities: The Contributions Independent Contemporary Dancers Make to the Choreographic Process." In *Contemporary Choreography: A Critical Reader*, 2nd ed., edited by Jo Butterworth and Liesbeth Wildschut, 150–64. Milton Park: Routledge, 2018.

Rodriguez, Nathian Shae, and Jennifer Huemmer. "Pedagogy of the Depressed: An Examination of Critical Pedagogy in Higher Ed's Diversity-Centered Classrooms Post-Trump." *Pedagogy, Culture, and Society* 27, no. 1 (March 2019): 133–49.

Roth, Cassia. "Black Nurse, White Milk: Breastfeeding, Slavery, and Abolition in 19th-Century Brazil." *Journal of Human Lactation* 34, no. 4 (2018): 804–9.

Roth, Cassia. "Disembodied Reproduction: Enslaved Wet Nurses, Stratified Reproduction, and Commercial Advertisements in Nineteenth-Century Rio de Janeiro." Talk at *Critical Conversations on Reproductive Health/Care: Past, Present, and Future*, Johns Hopkins University, February 3, 2021. https://hopkinshistoryofmedicine.org/events/reproconvo2021.

Roth, Cassia. *A Miscarriage of Justice: Women's Reproductive Lives and the Law in Early Twentieth-Century Brazil*. Stanford, CA: Stanford University Press, 2020.

Rowe, Aimee Carrillo, and Sheena Malhotra. *Silence, Feminism, Power: Reflections at the Edges of Sound*. New York: Palgrave Macmillan, 2013.

Rutgers, A. J. "Hera and Herakles." *Numen* 17, no. 3 (1970): 245–7.

Saenger, P. "Physiologie de la lecture et séparation des mots." *Annales* 44, no. 4 (1989): 943–50.

Saenger, P. *Space between Words: The Origins of Silent Reading*. Redwood City, CA: Stanford University Press, 1997.

Saint-Exupéry, Antoine de. *Le petit prince*. Paris: Gallimard, 1999 [1945].

Saint-Exupéry, Antoine de. *The Little Prince*. Translated by Katherine Woods. New York: Reynal & Hitchcock, 1943.

Sánchez, Lola. "Translations That Matter: About a Foundational Text in Feminist Studies in Spain." Special issue, *Signs* 39, no. 3 (Spring 2014), 570–6.

Santaemilia, José, ed. *Gender, Sex and Translation*. New York: Routledge, 2005.

Sappho. *If Not, Winter: Fragments of Sappho*. Translated by Anne Carson. London: Virago, 2003.

Saunders, Patricia. "Defending the Dead, Confronting the Archive: A Conversation with M. NourbeSe Philip." *Small Axe: A Caribbean Journal of Criticism* 12, no. 2 (2008): 63–79.

Schafer, Paul, ed. *The First Writings of Karl Marx*. Brooklyn, NY: Ig Publishing, 2006.

Schaffer, Talia. "Feminism and the Canon." In *The Routledge Companion to Victorian Literature*, edited by Dennis Denisoff and Talia Schaffer, 273–83. New York: Routledge, 2020.

Schaffer, Talia. "Victorian Feminist Criticism: Recovery Work and the Care Community." *Victorian Literature and Culture* 47, no. 1 (2019): 63–91.

Schiebinger, Londa L. *Feminism and the Body*. Oxford: Oxford University Press, 2000.

Schultz, Gretchen, and A. Atik. "Introduction." In *An Anthology of Nineteenth-Century Women's Poetry from France: In English Translation, with French Text*, edited by Gretchen Schultz, xi–xxvii. New York: Modern Language Association of America, 2008.

Seaman, Kris. "Retrieving the Original Aphrodite of Knidos." *Atti della Accademia Nazionale dei Lincei. Rendiconti: classe di scienze morali, storiche e filologiche* 9, no. 15 (2004): 531–94.

Serrano, C. Montes. "La contribución de Ernst H. Gombrich a la *Revista EGA*." *Expresión Gráfica Arquitectónica* 23, no. 34 (2018): 48–55.

Shahani, Aarti. "Zuckerberg Denies Fake News on Facebook Had Impact on the Election." *NPR*, November 11, 2016. https://www.npr.org/sections/alltechconsidered/2016/11/11/501743684/zuckerberg-denies-fake-news-on-facebook-had-impact-on-the-election.

Sharpe, Christina. *In the Wake: On Blackness and Being*. Durham, NC: Duke University Press, 2018.

"She Knew Where She Was Going: Gee's Bend Quilts and Civil Rights." *Baltimore Museum of Art*, March 10, 2021–September 12, 2021. https://artbma.org/exhibition/she-knew-where-she-was-going-gees-bend-quilts-and-civil-rights. Accessed March 7, 2021.

Shildrick, Margrit. *Leaky Bodies and Boundaries: Feminism, Postmodernism, and (Bio)ethics*. London: Routledge, 1997.

Siklosi, Kate. "'The Absolute/of Water': The Submarine Poetic of M. NourbeSe Philip's *Zong!*" *Canadian Literature* no. 228/229 (Spring/Summer 2016): 111–30.

Skloot, Rebecca. *The Immortal Life of Henrietta Lacks*. New York: Crown Publishing, 2010.

Small, Zachary. "Trump Makes Classical Style the Default for Federal Buildings." *New York Times*, December 21, 2020. https://www.nytimes.com/2020/12/21/arts/design/trump-executive-order-federal-buildings-architecture.html.

Smith, Danez. *Don't Call Us Dead: Poems*. Minnesota: Graywolf Press, 2017.

Smith, Danez. "Not an Elegy for Mike Brown." *Poets*, 2014. https://poets.org/poem/not-elegy-mike-brown.

Smith, Maggie. *Good Bones*. North Adams, MA: Tupelo Press, 2014.

Smith, Zadie. "Speaking in Tongues." *New York Review of Books*, February 26, 2009. https://nybooks.com/articles/2009/02/26/speaking-in-tongues-2.

Smith-Doerr, Laurel. "Universities Should Look in the Mirror." *Inside Higher Ed*, September 15, 2021. https://www.insidehighered.com/views/2021/09/15/colleges-should-research-dei-their-own-campuses-opinion.

Snow, Philippa. "In *Promising Young Woman* Revenge Is a Dish Served Lukewarm." *Frieze*, January 19, 2121. https://www.frieze.com/article/promising-young-woman-revenge-dish-served-lukewarm.

Söderbäck, Fanny. *Feminist Readings of Antigone*. Albany: State University of New York Press, 2010.

Soffer, O., J. M. Adovasio, and D. C. Hyland. "The 'Venus' Figurines: Textiles, Basketry, Gender, and Status in the Upper Paleolithic." *Current Anthropology* 41, no. 4 (2000): 511–37.

Solnit, Rebecca. *Infinite City: A San Francisco Atlas*. Berkeley: University of California Press, 2010.

Solnit, Rebecca. "Men Explain Things to Me." *Guernica*, August 20, 2012. https://www.guernicamag.com/rebecca-solnit-men-explain-things-to-me.

Solnit, Rebecca. *Men Explain Things to Me*. London: Haymarket Books, 2015.

Sorek, Susan. *The Emperors' Needles: Egyptian Obelisks and Rome*. Exeter: Bristol Phoenix Press, 2010.

Spivak, Gayatri Chakravorty. "Translating in a World of Languages." In *Profession*, edited by Rosemary G. Feal, 35–43. New York: Modern Language Association, 2010.

Spreiregan, Paul. "The Vietnam Veterans Memorial Design Competition." In *Architectural Competition: Research Inquiries and Experiences*, edited by Magnus Rönn, Reza Kazemian, and Jonas E. Andersson, 578–600. Stockholm: Axl Books, 2010.

Stager, Jennifer. "The Materiality of Color in Ancient Mediterranean Art." In *Essays in Global Color History*, edited by Rachael Goldman, 97–120. Piscataway: Gorgias Press, 2016.

Stager, Jennifer. "A Mother's Odyssey: The Journey to Integrating the Roles of Scholar and Mother." *Eidolon*, August 31, 2018. https://eidolon.pub/a-mothers-odyssey-9c1c6ea218b9.

Stager, Jennifer M.S. *Seeing Color in Classical Art: Theory, Practice, and Reception from Antiquity to the Present*. Cambridge: Cambridge University Press, 2022.

Stager, Jennifer. "Space as Form: Sappho Now." *Open Space*, April 9, 2020. https://openspace.sfmoma.org/2020/04/space-as-form-sappho-now.

Stager, Jennifer. "The Unbearable Whiteness of Whiteness." *Art Practical*, January 16, 2018. https://www.artpractical.com/column/feature-the-unbearable-whiteness-of-whiteness.

Stamberg, Susan. "'Rumors of War' in Richmond Marks a Monumentally Unequal America." *NPR*, June 25, 2020. https://www.npr.org/2020/06/25/878822835/rumors-of-war-in-richmond-marks-a-monumentally-unequal-america.

Steinhauer, Jillian. "Old Women." *Believer Magazine*, June 1, 2021. https://believermag.com/old-women.

Stewart, Andrew. *Classical Greece and the Birth of Western Art*. Cambridge: Cambridge University Press, 2009.

Stewart, Andrew. *Greek Sculpture: An Exploration*. Cambridge: Cambridge University Press, 1990.

St. Felix, Doreen. "What It Means When Beyoncé and Jay-Z Take Over the Louvre." *New Yorker*, June 19, 2019. https://www.newyorker.com/culture/culture-desk/what-it-means-when-beyonce-and-jay-z-take-over-the-louvre.

Straussman-Pflanzer, Eve. *Violence and Virtue: Artemisia Gentileschi's Judith Slaying Holofernes*. Chicago, IL: Art Institute of Chicago, 2013.

Stubblefield, Thomas. "Do Disappearing Monuments Simply Disappear?: The Counter-Monument in Revision." *Future Anterior* 8, no. 2 (2011): xii–11.

Sturken, Marita. "The Wall, the Screen, and the Image: The Vietnam Veterans Memorial." *Representations* 35 (1991): 118–42.

Suleiman, Susan, ed. *The Female Body in Western Culture: Contemporary Perspectives*. Cambridge, MA: Harvard University Press, 1986.

Swetnam-Burland, Molly. "'Aegyptus Redacta': The Egyptian Obelisk in the Augustan Campus Martius." *Art Bulletin* 92, no. 3 (2010): 135–53.

Taylor, Brandon. "The Tiny White People in Our Heads: Black Subjectivity, Elaine de Kooning, Autofiction." May 11, 2021. https://blgtylr.substack.com/p/the-tiny-white-people-in-our-heads.

Taylor, Keeanga-Yamahtta. *From #BlackLivesMatter to Black Liberation*. Chicago, IL: Haymarket Books, 2016.

Taylor, Keeanga-Yamahtta, ed. *How We Get Free: Black Feminism and the Combahee River Collective*. Chicago, IL: Haymarket Books, 2017.

Taylor, Sonya Renee. *The Body Is Not an Apology*. Oakland, CA: Berrett-Koehler Publishers, 2018.

Theater of War Productions. "Antigone in Ferguson: Online Premiere." August 9, 2020, https://youtu.be/Z6v5KpKqv6I.

Theater of War Productions. "Theater of War." https://theaterofwar.com/projects/theater-of-war. Accessed January 24, 2021.

Theisen, Tiffini. "People Who Claim to Have Coronavirus and Spit, Cough on Victims Face Variety of Charges." *Orlando Sentinel*, April 9, 2020. https://www.orlandosentinel.com/coronavirus/os-ne-coronavirus-people-charged-with-spitting-coughing-in-faces-20200409-ps5dgw64pfeobhthwvr6mhbuuy-story.html.

Thompson, Anne. "Response: Thompson on Goldhill on Stray, Clarke and Katz, Liddell and Scott: The History, Methodology, and Languages of the World's Leading Lexicon of Ancient Greek." *Bryn Mawr Classical Review*, 2021.06.35. https://bmcr.brynmawr.edu/2021/2021.06.35.

Thompson, Nicholas, and Fred Vogelstein. "15 Months of Fresh Hell Inside Facebook." *Wired*, April 16, 2019. https://www.wired.com/story/facebook-mark -zuckerberg-15-months-of-fresh-hell.

Tjandra, Lia, and Dore Brown. "Behind-the-Scenes at UC Press: The Making of Rebecca Solnit's Atlas Series." *UC Press Blog*, April 3, 2021. https://www .ucpress.edu/blog/22817/behind-the-scenes-at-uc-press-the-making-of-rebecca -solnits-atlas-series.

Tomášková, Silvia. "Nationalism, Local Histories, and the Making of Data in Archaeology." *Journal of the Royal Anthropological Institute* 9, no. 3 (2003): 485–507.

"Tracking the #MeToo Movement across Social Media on a Map." *esri*, June 22, 2021. https://storymaps.arcgis.com/stories/f302610237df41cbbf9276c03c17ac45.

Translation Talk (@translationtalk). "Writer Nikolai Gogol on Translation: 'The Translator Should be Like Glass: So Transparent that You Can't See Him.'" *Twitter*, June 23, 2021, 6:36 a.m. https://twitter.com/translationtalk/status /1407693949234450437.

Treves, Letizia. "Artemisia in Her Own Words." *National Gallery of Art Online*, February 1, 2021. https://www.nationalgallery.org.uk/exhibitions/past/artemisia/ artemisia-in-her-own-words.

Treves, Letizia. "Artemisia's Rape Trial." *National Gallery of Art Online*, February 1, 2021. https://www.nationalgallery.org.uk/exhibitions/past/artemisia/artemisias -rape-trial.

Treves, Laetitia, and Sheila Barker, eds. *Artemisia*. London: National Gallery Company, 2020. Exhibition catalog.

Trimble, Jennifer. "Modern Statue Destructions and Ancient Roman Damnatio Memoriae." *Talk at Johns Hopkins University*, September 29, 2020.

Tripodi, Francesca. "Ms. Categorized: Gender, Notability, and Inequality on Wikipedia." *New Media and Society*, June 27, 2021. https://doi.org/10.1177 /14614448211023772.

Tsotsis, Alexia. "Entenmann's Hashtag Surfing Fails Hard With #NotGuiltyTweet." *Tech Crunch*, July 5, 2011. https://techcrunch.com/2011/07/05/entenmanns -hashtag-surfing-fails-hard-with-notguilty-tweet.

Tuck, Eve, and K. Wayne Yang. "Decolonization Is Not a Metaphor." *Decolonization: Indigeneity, Education, and Society* 1, no. 1 (2012): 1–40.

"Unsettled: Mapping #MeToo." *NPR and Iowa Public Radio*, January 16, 2021. https://www.npr.org/podcasts/666302911/unsettled-mapping-me-too.

"Unsettling Knowledge #9: Decolonizing the Archive; Sites of Memory or Manipulation?" *Utrecht University*, January 29, 2021. https://soundcloud.com /utrechtuniversity/unsettling-knowledge-9-decolonising-the-archive-sites-of -memory-or-manipulation.

Uppenkamp, B. *Judith und Holofernes in der italienischen Malerei des Barock*. Berlin: Reimer, 2004.

Usher, Craigan. "The Body and the Traumatic Real." *Journal of the American Academy of Child and Adolescent Psychiatry* 57, no. 9 (2018): 703.

Van der Kolk, Bessel. *The Body Keeps the Score: Brain, Mind, and Body in the Healing of Trauma*. New York: Penguin Books, 2015.

Van Dijck, José. *The Culture of Connectivity: A Critical History of Social Media*. Oxford: Oxford University Press, 2013.

Vankin, Deborah. "A 2.2 Mile L. A. Memorial Says Their Names: George, Breonna, Corey …." *Los Angeles Times*, June 8, 2020. https://www.yahoo.com/news/2-2 -mile-l-memorial-223946602.html.

Vasari, Giorgio. *Lives of the Artists: Biographies of the Most Eminent Architects, Painters, and Sculptors of Italy*. Translated by Betty Burroughs and Jonathan Foster. New York: Simon and Schuster, 1946.

"Venus Cabinet." *Naturhistorisches Museum Wien*, September 12, 2020. https:// www.nhm-wien.ac.at/en/exhibitions/permanent_exhibitions/mezzanine_level/hall _11-13_prehistory.

Vergil. *Aeneid*. Translated by Shadi Bartsch. New York: Random House, 2021.

Veterans Attend Dedication of the Vietnam War Memorial Ca. 1982. Part 1. WPA Film Library.

Vietnam Veterans Memorial, Directory of Names. Washington, DC: Vietnam Veterans Memorial Fund, 1991.

Virginia Museum of Fine Arts. "Rumors of War." https://www.vmfa.museum/about/ rumors-of-war. Accessed April 04, 2021.

Vitali, Ali, Kasie Hunt, and Frank Thorp. "Trump Referred to Haiti and African Nations as 'Shithole' Countries." *NBC News*, January 11, 2018. https://www .nbcnews.com/politics/white-house/trump-referred-haiti-african-countries-shithole -nations-n836946.

Vivien, Renée. "Sur le rythme sapphique." In *An Anthology of Nineteenth-Century Women's Poetry from France: In English Translation, with French Text*, edited by Gretchen Schultz, 354–5. New York: Modern Language Association of America, 2008.

von Flotow, Luise. *Translation and Gender: Translating in the "Era of Feminism."* Manchester: St. Jerome Publishing, 1997.

Wagner, Anne M. "Once Upon a Time: The Vietnam Memorial at Age Twenty-Five." *Threepenny Review* 112 (Winter 2008): 19–20.

Wagner-Pacifici, Robin, and Barry Schwartz. "The Vietnam Veterans Memorial: Commemorating a Difficult Past." *American Journal of Sociology* 97, no. 2 (1991): 376–420.

Waldstreicher, David. "Ancients, Moderns, and Africans: Phillis Wheatley and the Politics of Empire and Slavery in the American Revolution." *Journal of the Early Republic* 37, no. 4 (2017): 701–33.

Walker, Alice. *In Search of Our Mothers' Gardens: Womanist Prose*. San Diego: Harcourt Brace Jovanovich, 1983.

Warburg, Aby. *The Renewal of Pagan Antiquity*. Los Angeles: Getty Research Institute, 1999.

Waters, Terri. "Roxane Gay's Latest Project Talks Unruly Bodies and Redefining Body Image." *The Unedit*, April 10, 2018. https://www.the-unedit.com/posts/2018 /4/10/roxane-gays-latest-project-talks-unruly-bodies-and-redefining-body-image.

Watkins, Paul. "We Can Never Tell the Entire Story of Slavery: In Conversation with M. NourbeSe Philip." *Toronto Review of Books*, April 30, 2014. https://torontorevi ewofbooks.com/2014/04/in-conversation-with-m-nourbese-philip.

Watts, Marina. "Poet Amanda Gorman Gains 300K Twitter Followers After Inauguration Recitation." *Newsweek*, January 20, 2021. https://www.newsweek .com/poet-amanda-gorman-gains-300k-twitter-followers-after-inauguration -recitation-1563135.

Webber, Jasmine. "A Tribute to Christine Blasey Ford Appears at the Entrance to Yale Law School." *Hyperallergic*, October 22, 2018. https://hyperallergic.com /466934/a-tribute-to-christine-blasey-ford-appears-at-the-entrance-of-yale-law -school.

Weinstock, Jeffrey, ed. *The Monster Theory Reader*. Minneapolis: University of Minnesota Press, 2020.

Weise, Elizabeth. "Trending Hashtags Co-Opted by Pro-Terrorist Accounts." *USA Today*, September 11, 2015. https://www.usatoday.com/story/tech/2015/09/11/pro -isis-twitter-commandeering-hijack-hashtags/72078270.

West, M. L. "The Invention of Homer." *Classical Quarterly* 49, no. 2 (1999): 364–82.

Wilkinson, Alissa, and Emily Stewart. "*Time*'s 2017 Person of the Year is the 'Silence Breakers.'" *Vox*, December 6, 2017. https://www.vox.com/identities/2017 /12/6/16741324/times-person-of-the-year-silence-breakers.

Williams, Caroline Randall. "Opinion: You Want a Confederate Monument? My Body Is a Confederate Monument." *The New York Times*, June 26, 2020. https:// www.nytimes.com/2020/06/26/opinion/confederate-monuments-racism.html.

Willis, Deborah. "Introduction." In *Black Venus 2010: They Called Her "Hottentot,"* edited by Deborah Willis, 3–14. Philadelphia: Temple University Press, 2010.

Wilmer, S. E., and Audrone Zukauskaite, eds. *Interrogating Antigone in Postmodern Philosophy and Criticism*. Oxford: Oxford University Press, 2010.

Wilson, Emily. "Ah, How Miserable!" *London Review of Books* 42, no. 19 (October 8, 2020). https://www.lrb.co.uk/the-paper/v42/n19/emily-wilson/ah-how-miserable.

Wilson, Emily. "Found in Translation: How Women Are Making the Classics Their Own." *The Guardian*, July 7, 2017. https://www.theguardian.com/books/2017/jul /07/women-classics-translation-female-scholars-translators.

Wilson, Emily. "Introduction." In Homer, *The Odyssey*, translated by Emily Wilson, 1–80. New York: W. W. Norton, 2018.

Wilson, Emily. "Scholia Tweets." *Emily RC Wilson*, January 12, 2021. https://www .emilyrcwilson.com/emilyrcwilson-scholia.

Wilson, Emily. "Tongue Breaks." *London Review of Books* 26, no. 1 (January 8, 2004). https://www.lrb.co.uk/the-paper/v26/n01/emily-wilson/tongue-breaks.

Wilson, Emily. "Translator's Note." In *The Odyssey*, translated by Emily Wilson, 81–91. New York: W. W. Norton, 2018.

Wilson, Emily. "A Translator's Reckoning with the Women of the *Odyssey*." *New Yorker*, December 8, 2017. https://www.newyorker.com/books/page-turner/a -translators-reckoning-with-the-women-of-the-odyssey.

Wilson, Emily (@EmilyRCWilson). "I put 'NOT the First Woman to Publish a Translation of the Odyssey' on My Twitter-Bio, after Seeing It Asserted for the

Gazillionth Time. Here is Why." *Twitter*, October 2, 2019, 9:03 a.m. https://twitter
.com/EmilyRCWilson/status/1179426687047614464.

Wilson, Emily (@EmilyRCWilson). "I've Been Asked/Praised/Scolded/Mansplained/
Ad Norovirus Nauseam My Rendition of the First Line of the Odyssey...."
Twitter, March 19, 2019, 1:27 p.m. https://twitter.com/EmilyRCWilson/status
/1108057446180945923.

Wilson, Emily (@EmilyRCWilson). "Many Translations Import Misogynistic
Language When It Isn't There in the Greek." *Twitter*, March 8, 2018. https://twitter
.com/emilyrcwilson/status/971823043512360960.

Wilson, Jennifer. "No One Disagrees with Rebecca Solnit." *New Republic*, April
2, 2020. https://newrepublic.com/article/157136/no-one-disagrees-rebecca-solnit
-memoir-feminism.

Winkler, John J. *The Constraints of Desire: The Anthropology of Sex and Gender in
Ancient Greece*. New York: Routledge, 1990.

Wisner, Geoff. "Fragments of Sappho." *Words without Borders*, March 30, 2011.
https://www.wordswithoutborders.org/dispatches/article/fragments-of-sappho.

Wolfe, Tom. "Art Disputes War: The Battle of the Vietnam Memorial." *Washington
Post*, October 13, 1982. https://www.washingtonpost.com/archive/lifestyle/1982
/10/13/art-disputes-war-the-battle-of-the-vietnam-memorial/89ef84dc-00d8-42ce
-bfa8-318f51ea15c5.

Wolfson, Elizabeth. "The 'Black Gash of Shame': Revisiting the Vietnam Veterans
Memorial Controversy." *Art* 21, March 15, 2017. https://art21.org/read/the-black
-gash-of-shame-revisiting-the-vietnam-veterans-memorial-controversy.

Wood, Christopher S. *A History of Art History*. Princeton, NJ: Princeton University
Press, 2019.

"Word of the Year 2018: Shortlist." *Oxford Languages*, December 17, 2020. https://
languages.oup.com/word-of-the-year/2018-shortlist.

Worman, Nancy. *Tragic Bodies: Edges of the Human in Greek Drama*. London:
Bloomsbury, 2020.

Wright, Lawrence. "The Plague Year: The Mistakes and the Struggles behind
America's Coronavirus Tragedy." *New Yorker*, December 28, 2020. https://www
.newyorker.com/magazine/2021/01/04/the-plague-year.

Yatromanolakis, Dimitrios. "Fragments, Brackets, and Poetics: On Anne Carson's
If Not, Winter." *International Journal of the Classical Tradition* 11, no. 2 (2004):
266–72.

Yong, Ed. "Where Year Two of the Pandemic Will Take Us." *The Atlantic*, December
29, 2020. https://www.theatlantic.com/health/archive/2020/12/pandemic-year-two
/617528.

Young, James E. "The Counter-Monument: Memory against Itself in Germany
Today." *Critical Inquiry* 18, no. 2 (1992): 267–96.

Zacharek, Stephanie, Eliana Dockterman, and Haley Sweetland Edwards. "The
Silence Breakers." *Time Magazine*, December 18, 2017. https://time.com/time
-person-of-the-year-2017-silence-breakers.

Zakarinjan, Jordan. "How Patrisse Cullors, Alicia Garza, and Opal Tometi Created
the Black Lives Matter Movement." *Biography*, January 27, 2021. https://www

.biography.com/news/patrisse-cullors-alicia-garza-opal-tometi-black-lives-matters
-origins.

Zimmer, Carl. "The Coronavirus Unveiled." *New York Times*, October 9, 2020.
https://www.nytimes.com/interactive/2020/health/coronavirus-unveiled.html.

Ziyad, Hari. "Tarana Burke Was Omitted from the Time Magazine Cover, so Let's
Celebrate the Shit out of Her Today." *AfroPunk*, December 7, 2017. https://
afropunk.com/2017/12/tarana-burke-omitted-time-magazine-cover-lets-celebrate
-sht-today.

Index

Page references for figures are italicized.

141, 227; and feminist translations, 15–16, 127, 128; feminization of, 132; individuals within, 190; and metatranslation, 16, 127–28; and paradigm of lone genius, 12, 128; and "plural lyric I," 15–16, 96, 127–29, 132, 134, 138, 143, 146–47, 147n2; and public feminism, 16, 127–28, 147n2, 158; of Sappho, 134, 138, 144–46, 152n42; and women translators, 127, 128, 149n13

Collins, Patricia Hill, 175

colonialism: and archives, 27; colonial violence, 33, 49–50n33, 166, 206; and modern nation-state, 7; structural systems of, 12

Combahee River Collective, 8

communities of care, 5, 159

Confederate monuments: Caroline Randall Williams on, 214n12; Congressional vote for removal of, 213n10; and counter monuments, 193–94; equestrian monument tradition, 193, 215n20; and fallism, 192, 193; projection of Harriet Tubman portrait and quotation and "BLM" on Robert E. Lee statue, *xiv*, 17, 18n3, 212; removal of, 193–94, 215n20; and Roman ruler-portrait tradition, 191

contamination: and interconnection, 161, 162; and patriarchal society, 16

Cooper, Anna Julia, 138

Corinna, 151n37

corporations, hashtags used by, 11

counter monuments, 12, 192–94

Courbet, Gustave, 32

COVID-19 pandemic: in Black communities, 174–75; and bodily fluids mingling in air, 157, 158, 160, 161; and collapse of time, 225; as collective public experience, 180n31; communities of care during, 159; HIV/AIDS epidemic compared to, 166, 180n31, 216n36;

inequalities widened during, 4, 6, 157, 198; interconnectedness of, 157–58; and interdependence, 160; and mask wearing, 158–60, 166, 177–78; material connectedness of bodies revealed by, 16; and memorialization, 189; *New York Times* printed list of deaths, 17, 196–99, 205, 207–9, 216n33, 216n37, 216n39, 216–17n41, 217n42, 217n45; and public feminism, 13; restrictions for collective protection and care, 160; sheltering in place due to, 5–6, 155n89, 166, 175, 221; and social conflict, 158; and spitting as form of assault, 178n6; spread of, 159, 178; testing for, 159–60; virus as transborder and transnational, 217n42; virus in pursuit of survival, 166; and vital materialism, 166; and women translators, 15

craft, feminized history of term, 128

Crandall, Maxe, 16, 142–46

Craven, Christa, 150n24

Crenshaw, Kimberlé, 8–9, 189–90

crises, public feminism as force during, 3, 13

critical fabulation, 32–33, 50n43, 207–8, 220n83

Cukor, George, 74

Culler, Jonathan, 147–48n4

Cullors, Patrisse, 176

Cuvier, Georges, 50n49

Dacier, Anne Le Fèvre, 94

dance, Hope Mohr and Maxe Crandall's metatranslation of Anne Carson's Sappho translation, 16, 127–28, 141–47

Daschle, Tom, 201

David Parrish Photography and Dustin Klein Projection, Portrait and quotation of Harriet Tubman "Slavery is the next thing to hell" and "BLM" projected onto the

About the Authors

Jennifer Stager is assistant professor of history of art at Johns Hopkins University, where she teaches and researches the art and architecture of the ancient Mediterranean and its afterlives. Her research has been supported by the Center for Advanced Study in the Visual Arts, National Gallery of Art, Washington, DC; the Getty Research Institute; and the Harvard Center for Hellenic Studies. Her areas of focus include theories of color and materiality, feminisms, ancient Greek medicine, and classical receptions, on which she has published essays and a book, *Seeing Color in Classical Art: Theory, Practice, and Reception, from Antiquity to the Present* (2022).

Leila Easa is a professor of English at City College of San Francisco, where she teaches and researches in the areas of composition, contemporary American literature, creative writing, and women's and gender studies. Her research has been supported by the Mellon Foundation/American Council of Learned Societies (for her project "Palestinian American Women's Poetry: Contesting and Constructing Home through Articulation and Embodiment") and the University of California, Davis (with a Provost's Fellowship in the Arts, Humanities, and Social Sciences). Her areas of focus include gender and ethnicity studies, silence and disclosure, elegy, and protest in the context of contemporary American literature.

In addition to this cowritten book, the authors have together published "Overwriting the monument tradition: Lists, loss, and scale" *(Res: Anthropology and Aesthetics* 75/76 2021).